Engaging. Trackable. Affordable.

CourseMate brings course concepts to life with interactive learning, study, and exam preparation tools that support Cultural ANTHRO.

INCLUDES:
Integrated eBook, **Interactive teaching and learning tools,** and **Engagement Tracker**, a first-of-its-kind tool that monitors student engagement in the course.

ONLINE RESOURCES INCLUDED!

FOR INSTRUCTORS:
- First Day of Class Instructions
- Custom Options through 4LTR+ Program
- Instructor's Manual
- Test Bank
- PowerPoint® Slides
- Instructor Prep Cards
- Engagement Tracker

FOR STUDENTS:
- Interactive eBook
- Student Review Cards
- Auto-Graded Quizzes
- Flashcards
- Games: Crossword Puzzle and more
- PowerPoint® Slides
- Videos
- Discussion Questions
- Web links

Students sign in at **login.cengagebrain.com**

WADSWORTH
CENGAGE Learning™

***ANTHRO* 2011-2012 Edition**
Richard H. Robbins

Senior Publisher: Linda Schreiber-Ganster
Acquisitions Editor: Erin Mitchell
Developmental Editors: Lin Gaylord; John Choi, B-books, Ltd.
Assistant Editor: Linda Stewart
Editorial Assistant: Mallory Ortberg
Product Development Manager, 4LTR Press: Steven E. Joos
Executive Brand Marketing Manager, 4LTR Press: Robin Lucas
Marketing Manager: Andrew Keay
Marketing Coordinator: Dimitri Hagnéré
Sr. Marketing Communications Manager: Tami Strang
Production Director: Amy McGuire, B-books, Ltd.
Sr. Content Project Manager: Christy A. Frame
Media Editor: Melanie Cregger
Print Buyer: Linda Hsu
Production Service: B-books, Ltd.
Sr. Art Director: Caryl Gorska
Internal Designer: Ke Design
Cover Designer: Riezebos Holzbaur Design Group
Cover Image: Frans Lemmens/Getty Images
Photo Researcher: Charlotte Goldman

Library of Congress Control Number: 2010934262

ISBN-13: 978-1-111-30089-0
ISBN-10: 1-111-30089-5

Wadsworth
20 Davis Drive
Belmont, CA 94002-3098
USA

Cengage Learning is a leading provider of customized learning solutions with office locations around the globe, including Singapore, the United Kingdom, Australia, Mexico, Brazil, and Japan. Locate your local office at **www.cengage.com/global**.

Cengage Learning products are represented in Canada by Nelson Education, Ltd.

To learn more about Wadsworth visit **www.cengage.com/wadsworth**
Purchase any of our products at your local college store or at our preferred online store **www.CengageBrain.com**.

Printed in the United States of America
1 2 3 4 5 6 7 13 12 11 10

Brief Contents

87% of students surveyed feel that 4LTR Press Solutions are a better value than other textbooks.

Cultural ANTHRO was built on a simple principle: to create a new teaching and learning solution that reflects the way today's faculty teach and the way you learn.

Through conversations, focus groups, surveys, and interviews, we collected data that drove the creation of the current version of Cultural ANTHRO that you are using today. But it doesn't stop there—in order to make Cultural ANTHRO an even better learning experience, we'd like you to SPEAK UP and tell us how Cultural ANTHRO worked for you.

What did you like about it? What would you change? Are there additional ideas you have that would help us build a better product for next semester's students?

At **www.cengagebrain.com** you'll find all of the resources you need to succeed—**videos, flash cards, interactive quizzes,** and more!

Speak Up! Go to **www.cengagebrain.com.**

Contents

CHAPTER 2 THE MEANING OF PROGRESS AND DEVELOPMENT 28

CHAPTER 3 GLOBALIZATION, NEOLIBERALISM, AND THE NATION-STATE 56

CHAPTER 4 THE SOCIAL AND CULTURAL CONSTRUCTION OF REALITY 82

CHAPTER 5 PATTERNS OF FAMILY RELATIONS 108

CHAPTER 6 THE CULTURAL CONSTRUCTION OF IDENTITY 132

CHAPTER 7 CULTURAL CONSTRUCTION OF SOCIAL HIERARCHY 152

CHAPTER 8 THE CULTURAL CONSTRUCTION OF VIOLENT CONFLICT 178

PROBLEM 1

HOW CAN PEOPLE BEGIN TO UNDERSTAND BELIEFS AND BEHAVIORS THAT ARE DIFFERENT FROM THEIR OWN?

Chapter 1 Culture and Meaning

We have come to think of our social and cultural world as a series of sign systems, comparable to languages. What we live among and relate to are not physical objects and events; they are objects and events with meaning; not just complicated wooden constructions but chairs and tables; not just physical gestures but acts of courtesy or hostility. If we are able to understand our social and cultural world, we must think not of independent objects but of symbolic structures, systems of relations which by enabling objects and actions to have meaning, create a human universe.

Jonathan Culler

* * *

QUESTIONS

In examining this problem, we will consider the following questions:

1.1 Why do human beings differ in their beliefs and behaviors?

1.2 Why do people judge the beliefs and behaviors of others?

1.3 Is it possible to see the world through the eyes of others?

1.4 How can the meanings that others find in experience be interpreted and described?

1.5 What can learning about other people tell Americans about themselves?

INTRODUCTION

The World behind Everyday Appearances

"For the cultural anthropologist, the classroom chair tells some interesting tales and poses some interesting questions."

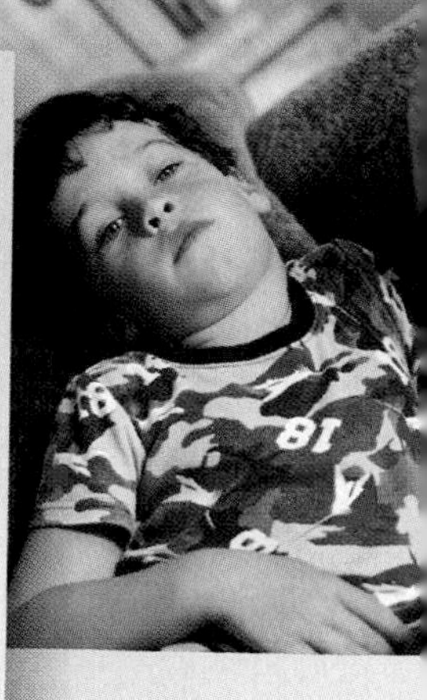

cultural anthropology an examination of the world of everyday experiences to discover the patterns and meanings that lie behind that world

In **cultural anthropology**, as in every science, we strive to look beyond the world of everyday experiences to discover the patterns and meanings that lie behind that world. Take, for example, the typical classroom chair with attached desk.

In our taken-for-granted, everyday world, this piece of furniture is a utilitarian object—something to sit on, write on, or even put our feet on. But for the cultural anthropologist, the classroom chair tells some interesting tales and poses some interesting questions. For example, why do we have chairs at all? Many societies don't; people sit or squat on the ground or sit on stools or benches. Historically, the chair probably first appeared in Europe or the Near East, but it wasn't even common in Europe until the eighteenth century. Why does the classroom chair take the form it does? Why don't we sit on stools? One feature of the classroom chair and desk that anthropologists might explore as they try to decipher its meaning is the erect position into which it forces the body, compelling it, in effect, to "pay attention." We might take a clue from the French philosopher Michel Foucault, who refers to the shaping of the human body as "political anatomy," a way that people's bodies are controlled by others to operate with the necessary speed and efficiency.

An anthropologist might suggest that the classroom chair and desk are part of the political anatomy of educational settings, part of the system of relations that gives meaning to the classroom. This piece of furniture forms the body into a shape that prepares it (or forces it) to attend to a teacher and not to others in the same room. Moreover, it is appropriate to its unique setting in the classroom, as are other objects of furniture. Imagine, for example, replacing classroom chairs with bar stools, whose main purpose is to promote mobility and conversation with others.

Once alert to the idea that the classroom chair might serve as an instrument of control, we might notice other ways in which classroom design serves as a mode of discipline. The distribution of people in space, with each person in a particular "spot" in neat, ordered rows, serves to discipline people to "pay attention" to the classroom center and not to others around them. We might also notice the distinctive ordering of time and the use of clocks, bells, and whistles to control the movement and activities of people in school settings. We can take our analysis a step further and examine the

discipline of the school setting sequentially, from kindergarten through high school. Contrast, for example, the wide-open space of the kindergarten classroom with its open, movable chairs and tables and teacher's desk set off to the side with the enclosed, partitioned space of a second- or third-grade classroom with its neatly arranged desks facing the centered desk of the teacher. This is the evolution of classroom discipline.

Students, of course, do not always obey the subtle commands that direct their bodies to do certain things at certain times. Simply examine the strange bodily contortions of students as they resist the form into which the classroom chair tries to force them. They also try, occasionally, to resist the isolation imposed by the arrangement of classroom furniture or the timetables set by clocks, bells, and whistles.

The way that specific societies order behavior through the arrangement of space and time is just one area examined by cultural anthropology, but it serves as an example of how, from an anthropological perspective, we cannot take anything about our beliefs and behavior for granted, let alone the behavior and beliefs of those whose backgrounds and histories differ from our own. This book is about how cultural anthropology can help us see beyond our taken-for-granted world. We will examine how cultural anthropology helps us to understand others and, in the process, to better understand ourselves. In addition, each chapter contains case studies that illustrate how the concepts and perspectives discussed in the chapter can be applied in various career paths to solve real-life problems, such as preventing HIV/AIDS, designing public policy, designing shopping environments, and helping adolescent girls deal with negative body images.

Because any area of inquiry always begins with certain basic issues or questions, this book is organized around eight general problems that arise from the human condition, problems such as how to understand people with different beliefs and behaviors, reasons why ways of life change, how people justify violence, and whether there is any solution to problems of social inequality. These are problems that concern everyone, not just cultural anthropologists. None of these problems has a definitive answer. The best we can do is reach a greater understanding of why the problem exists and what we might do about it. There are some specific questions, however, that we can ask concerning these problems for which anthropologists have sought answers. We will focus on these questions. At various points we will ask you to supply your own answers to questions and, perhaps, to discuss your solutions to these questions with others. Understanding others requires you to recognize that your behaviors and beliefs, as well as those of people in other societies, are socially patterned and constructed. For that reason, you will find many comparisons between American life and life in other societies.

In considering the principal problem of how we can begin to understand beliefs and behaviors that are different from our own, in this first chapter we explore five questions.

The first and most basic question is why human beings differ in their beliefs and behaviors; that is, what is it about human nature that produces such a variety of ways of believing and behaving? The second question involves values. More often than not, people react to different ways of life with shock, scorn, or disapproval. Are such reactions warranted, and if they aren't, how

QUESTIONS

1.1 Why do human beings differ in their beliefs and behaviors?

1.2 Why do people judge the beliefs and behaviors of others?

1.3 Is it possible to see the world through the eyes of others?

1.4 How can the meanings that others find in experience be interpreted and described?

1.5 What can learning about other people tell Americans about themselves?

do we judge the beliefs and behaviors of others? The third question is critical to anthropological inquiry: Is it possible to set aside the meanings that we ascribe to experience and see the world through the eyes of others? Fourth, assuming that it is possible to come to some understanding of how others see the world, how can the meanings that others find in experience be interpreted and described? The fifth question concerns what learning about other people can tell us about ourselves.

QUESTION 1.1

Why do human beings differ in their beliefs and behaviors?

Differences in Beliefs and Behaviors

From an anthropological perspective, members of a society view the world in a similar way because they share the same **culture**; people differ in how they view the world because their cultures differ. A good place to start to understand the concept of culture is with the fact that members of all human societies experience specific life events, such as birth, death, and the quest for food, water, and shelter. But from society to society, the meanings people give to such events differ.

Attitudes toward death provide one example. For some people, death marks the passage of a person from one world to another. For others, death is an ending, the final event of a life span, whereas still others consider death a part of a never-ending cycle of birth, death, and rebirth. Members of some societies accept death as a natural and inevitable occurrence, whereas others always attribute death to the malevolent act of some person, often through sorcery. In these societies, every death elicits suspicion and a demand for vengeance. Along with differing views on why people die, different cultures have different ways of grieving for the dead.

The Kwakiutl of British Columbia, for example, believe that when a person dies the soul leaves the body and enters the body of a salmon. When a salmon is caught and eaten, a soul is released and is free to enter the body of another person. In traditional China, the dead were to be revered. Each household contained a shrine to family ancestors, and before any major family decision could be made, the head of the household addressed the shrine to ask the ancestors' advice, thus making the dead a part of the world of the living. In southern Italy, funeral customs are designed to discourage the dead from returning to the world of the living. Relatives place useful objects such as matches and small change near the body of the deceased in order to placate the soul and ensure that it does not disturb the living.

The Dani of New Guinea require a close female relative of a recently deceased person to sacrifice a part of a finger. It was the practice of the Wari of western Brazil, when they still lived independent of Western civilization, to dispose of the bodies of their dead by eating the roasted flesh, certain internal organs, and sometimes the ground bones. They ate the dead out of respect and compassion for the dead person and the dead person's family, not because they needed the meat or because they liked the taste of human flesh. In southern Europe, widows were required to shave their heads, whereas in traditional India, widows threw themselves on top of their deceased husband's funeral pyre. In the United States, survivors of the deceased are expected to restrain their grief almost as if it were a contagious disease. To Americans, the sight of Indian women throwing themselves on a fire, or the Wari eating their deceased is just as bewildering as their own restraint of grief would be to Indians or the Wari.

Food is one of the best illustrations of the differences between cultures. No society accepts all items in their edible universe as "good to eat." Insects such as grubs, beetles, and ants are acceptable fare in some societies, whereas others regard eating insects with horror. Americans generally do not define insects as food (although federal regulations do allow a certain percentage of insect matter to be included in processed food). Most Americans like and are encouraged to drink milk, although some people in China consider milk undrinkable. On the other hand, the Chinese practice of raising dogs for meat is repulsive to most Americans. Many American tastes in food originate in biblical definitions of what is considered edible and

culture the meaning that people give to things, events, activities, and people

inedible. Thus, of edible land animals, the book of Leviticus says that they must chew their cud and have split hoofs, consequently eliminating not only the pig but camel and rock badger as well. Of animals of the water, edible things must have scales and fins, removing clams, lobster, and sea urchins. And of animals of the air, only things that have wings and fly are legitimate dining fare, eliminating the penguin, ostrich, and cassowary. Thus, human beings create and define for themselves what they may eat and what they may not eat independent of what is or is not truly edible.

Of all the nearly two million species of living organisms that inhabit the earth, only humans dwell in worlds that they themselves create by giving meanings to things, events, activities and people. This creation is what anthropologists mean by the term *culture*. Human beings are cultural animals; they ascribe meanings of their own creation to objects, persons, behaviors, emo-

WOULD YOU EAT?

Food is a cultural creation—people define what is and what is not food. Consider the items listed below, all of which serve as food for one group of people or another. Which of these would you eat, and which would you not eat? If there are any you would not eat, explain why.

Yes, please!		No way!
☐	eel	☐
☐	kangaroo tail	☐
☐	dog	☐
☐	guinea pig	☐
☐	raw squid	☐
☐	sea urchin	☐
☐	ants	☐
☐	monkey brains	☐
☐	grubs	☐
☐	opossum	☐
☐	rattlesnake	☐
☐	iguana	☐
☐	horse	☐
☐	dolphin	☐
☐	pickled pig's feet	☐
☐	haggis (stuffed intestines)	☐
☐	cow brains	☐
☐	blood sausage	☐
☐	raw steak	☐
☐	rotten meat	☐
☐	armadillo	☐

tions, and events and then act as though those meanings are real. All facets of their lives—death, birth, courtship, mating, food acquisition and consumption—are suffused with meaning.

Clifford Geertz suggests that human beings are compelled to impose meaning on their experiences because without these meanings to help them comprehend experience and impose order on the universe, the world would seem a jumble, "a chaos of pointless acts and exploding emotions." Geertz says that human beings are "incomplete or unfinished animals who complete themselves through culture—not culture in general, but specific forms of it: Balinese, Italian, Ilongot, Chinese, Kwakiutl, American, and so on." (1973, 49) When people share the meanings they give to experiences, they share and participate in the same culture.

Differences in culture arise in part from the fact that different groups of human beings, for various reasons, create, share, and participate in different realities, assigning different meanings to death, birth, marriage, and food. Objects, persons, behaviors, emotions, and events in a human world have meanings ascribed to them by those who share, use, or experience them. The clothes people wear, the way they wear them, the food they eat (or refuse to eat), and even their gender are defined through the meanings that different groups of people give them.

One of the problems that cultural anthropologists address is understanding why different groups of human beings have different cultures. Why does one group assign one set of meanings to what they experience, whereas another group assigns it another set of meanings? Many of the questions to be addressed in later chapters concern how these differences can be explained. We may be able to overcome our initial shock or bewilderment upon confronting different cultures if we understand something of why cultural differences exist. But how should we react if the meanings that others ascribe to experiences differ from our own? It is difficult enough to look beyond everyday appearances at our own beliefs and behaviors, but it is far more difficult when we confront beliefs and behaviors of others that we initially consider wrong, horrible, or bizarre.

QUESTION 1.2

Why do people judge the beliefs and behaviors of others?

Judging Others' Beliefs and Behaviors

Richard Scaglion is fond of telling the story of his friend, a member of the Abelam tribe of Papua New Guinea, who was looking through an issue of *Sports Illustrated* magazine. The friend, dressed in full ceremonial regalia with a feather through his nose, was laughing uncontrollably at a woman shown in a liquor advertisement. When he managed to stop laughing long enough to explain what he thought was so funny, he said, "This white woman has made holes in her ears and stuck things in them." When Scaglion pointed out that his friend had an ornament in his nose, the reply was, "That's different. That's for beauty and has ceremonial significance. But I didn't know that white people mutilated themselves."

© RITA WILLAERT/HTTP://WWW.FLICKR.COM/PHOTOS/RIETJE / © STEFAN KLEIN/ISTOCKPHOTO.COM

An Abelam tribesmen, in full ceremonial regalia, was laughing uncontrollably at a woman shown in an American liquor advertisement.

Scaglion's friend confronted a problem that many people have when they encounter behavior or beliefs that seem to differ from their own, and his response was not unusual. He was both shocked and mystified at the strange behavior. And this poses a dilemma: Because there are so many versions of what the world is like, how do we try to understand each of them without making positive or negative judgments? Which version is correct? Are there any we can reject or condemn? Can we say, as so many have, that one culture is superior to another?

In the catalog of human behaviors and beliefs, it is not difficult to find practices or ideas that may seem bizarre or shocking, even to trained anthropologists. Cultural anthropologists have described the beliefs of the Ilongots of the Philippines, who must kill an enemy to obtain a head they can throw away in order to diminish the grief and rage they feel at the death of a kinsman or kinswoman. They have studied the historical records of the Aztecs of Mexico, who, when contacted by Cortes in 1519, believed that the universe underwent periodic destruction and that the only way to ward off disaster was to pluck hearts from live sacrificial victims to offer to the gods. They have reported on the circumcision practices of the people in the Nile Valley of the Sudan, who, in order to ensure a young girl's chastity and virginity, mutilate her genitalia to close the vaginal opening so completely that additional surgery is often required to allow intercourse and childbirth later in life. They have also studied modern states that routinely engage in or sanction torture, terror, and genocide. The question is, how should we react to practices and beliefs such as these?

The Aztecs believed that the universe underwent period destruction and that the only way to ward off disaster was to pluck the hearts from live sacrificial victims to offer to the gods.

The Ethnocentric Fallacy and the Relativist Fallacy

If we condemn or reject the beliefs or behaviors of others, we may be committing the **ethnocentric fallacy**—the idea that our beliefs and behaviors are right and true, whereas those of other peoples are wrong or misguided. Cultural anthropologists have long fought against ethnocentrism. They try to show that what often appears on the surface to be an odd belief or a bizarre bit of behavior is functional and logical in the context of a particular culture. They find the ethnocentric fallacy *intellectually* intolerable; if all people everywhere think that they are right and others must be wrong, they can only reach an intellectual and social dead end. Furthermore, if we assume that we have all the right answers, our study of other cultures becomes simply the study of other people's mistakes.

ethnocentric fallacy a group's belief that their beliefs and behavior are right and true, whereas those of other groups are wrong

relativism the thought that no behavior or belief can be judged to be odd or wrong because it is different

Because of the intellectual implications of ethnocentrism, cultural anthropologists emphatically reject this position. But the alternative to ethnocentrism, **relativism**, is equally problematic. Relativism, simply stated, holds that no behavior or belief can be judged to be odd or wrong simply because it is different from our own. Instead, we must try to understand a culture in its own terms and to understand behaviors or beliefs in terms of the purpose, function, or meaning they have for people in the societies in which we find them. In other words, relativism holds that a specific belief or behavior can be understood only in relation to the culture—the system of meanings—in which it is embedded.

For example, according to Renato Rosaldo, the ceremonies and rituals accompanying a successful headhunting expedition psychologically help the Ilongot manage their grief over the death of a kinsperson. Rose Oldfield-Hayes explains that the genital mutilation of young girls makes perfect sense to the women of the northern Sudan. Because family honor is determined in part by the sexual modesty of female family members, the operation, by preventing intercourse, protects the honor of the family, protects girls from sexual assault, and protects the honor and reputation of the girl herself.

However, relativism poses a *moral* predicament. We may concede that it is permissible to rip hearts out of living human beings, provided you believe this is necessary in order to save the world, or that it is permissible to subject young girls to painful mutilation to protect family reputations or control population growth. But this quickly leads us into the **relativistic fallacy**—the idea that it is impossible to make moral judgments about the beliefs and behaviors of others. This, of course, seems morally intolerable because it implies that there is no belief or behavior that can be condemned as wrong. So we are left with two untenable positions: the ethnocentric alternative, which is intellectually unsatisfactory, and the relativist alternative, which is morally unsatisfactory. How do we solve this problem?

The Wari and Cannibalism

To illustrate the dilemma of relativism and the difficulty of appreciating the cultures of others without making moral judgments, let's consider the Wari practice of eating the dead. As Beth Conklin points out in *Consuming Grief*, cannibalism pushes the limits of cultural relativism, guaranteeing reactions of revulsion and fascination. But in addition to the emotional reactions, it has political implications as well. For centuries, cannibalism was the ultimate smear tactic; the accusation of cannibalism was the ultimate justification for conquest, domination, and exploitation. In 1503, Queen Isabella of Spain decreed that Spaniards could legally enslave Native Americans who were cannibals. Pope Innocent IV, in 1510, ruled that Christians could punish, by force of arms, the sin of cannibalism. By claiming moral superiority, they were claiming the right to decide ultimately what is right and what is wrong. Armed with that kind of power, they felt justified in imposing their own views and way of life. What Queen Isabella and Pope Innocent the IV conveniently overlooked, however, was the fact that Europeans themselves practiced cannibalism. As Conklin notes, medicinal cannibalism, the consumption of human body parts for curing purposes, had a long tradition in Europe. Up until two centuries ago, European physicians prescribed the consumption of human flesh, heart, bones and other body parts as cures for such afflictions as arthritis, reproductive disorders, sciatica, warts, and skin blemishes. Human blood was thought to be a cure for epilepsy; physicians recommending that it be drunk immediately after the supplier died. Physicians also thought that the blood of someone who died violently was particularly effective. Thus in Denmark epileptics would stand around the scaffolds, cups in hand, waiting to catch the blood of executed criminals.

relativistic fallacy the idea that it is impossible to make moral judgments about the beliefs and behaviors of others

In their ethnocentric justifications for conquest and racism, people of medieval Europe managed to accept in their own lives the same types of practices they condemned in others. Furthermore, they failed to understand those practices from the point of view of the others. The Wari ate their dead because they believed it was the compassionate thing to do. As Conklin puts it, "More painful than having the corpse eaten would have been to have it *not* eaten." For the Wari, a corpse left intact was a painful reminder of the deceased; people unrelated to the deceased ate the corpse, in spite of the fact that sometimes the smell or taste repulsed them, because it was believed it would help family members come to terms with their loss. Furthermore, the Western

"It was better in the old days, when the others ate the body. Then we did not think about our child's body much. We did not remember our child as much, and we were not so sad."

—bereaved Wari father

practice of burying the dead (which missionaries and government officials forced the Wari to do after contact) was almost as horrific to the Wari as their cannibalism might have been for us. "It's cold in the earth," a father who had recently lost a 2-year-old son explained to Conklin. "We keep remembering our child, lying there, cold. We remember and we are sad. It was better in the old days, when the others ate the body. Then we did not think about our child's body much. We did not remember our child as much, and we were not so sad."

By consuming the dead, the Wari are trying to obliterate the painful memories of their loss. But equally painful as the memory of the body are the material objects associated with the deceased and even the mention of the deceased's name. Thus, they not only consume the body, they also burn the house and personal possessions of the deceased. For months, they also make trips into the forest to find places associated with the person, such as a place where a hunter made a kill or a woman felled a fruit tree, cut the vegetation around it, and after it has dried, burn the spot, changing the appearance of the last earthly places to which memories of the deceased might

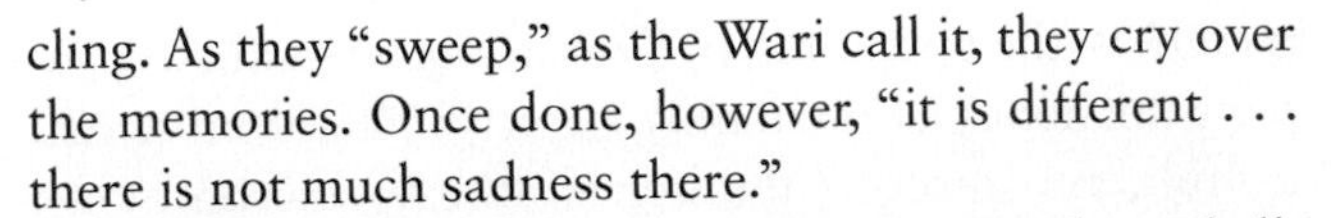

cling. As they "sweep," as the Wari call it, they cry over the memories. Once done, however, "it is different . . . there is not much sadness there."

In American culture, a dead body is only a shell, missing its soul or spiritual essence. Thus we often prepare the dead to look as they did in life and think of them buried that way with comfort. In contrast, the Wari, as well as other groups, want to separate the dead from the living, and cannibalism is an important way in which they obliterate the painful memories of the deceased. If we did not have a deeper understanding of Wari culture, we would not know how consuming the dead fits in with dealing with their emotions and with the meaning that they impose on their world. By imposing the meanings we have adopted for something such as cannibalism and failing to see it as others may, we miss the point. But does this mean that any practice or belief, once we understand it from "the native's point of view," is acceptable? Does understanding the cultures of others require that we accept and justify all beliefs and practices?

The Taj Mahal, a monument built to honor a 17th-century Mughal emperor's wife, who died in childbirth.

Remembering the Departed

The Wari attempt to obliterate the memory of the dead in their funeral practices, as do many other societies. Others, however, such as ours, memorialize the dead; forgetting them would be an act of disrespect. Try to list the ways that we try to keep the memory of deceased persons alive, and speculate why we emphasize remembering them, rather than trying to forget them.

Objectivity and Morality

The conflict between ethnocentrism and relativism is not just a theoretical one for anthropologists. In their choice of research subject, anthropologists may face the dilemma of either maintaining a "moral distance" from the objects of their studies and remaining "objective" or becoming actively involved in criticizing behavior or beliefs they encounter (such as genital mutilation).

The contradiction between "objective" anthropology and a politically committed anthropology became apparent to Nancy Scheper-Hughes when she returned as an anthropologist to a shantytown in Brazil where she had previously worked as a community organizer. The women with whom she worked became angry, asking why, when as a community organizer she had helped them fight for clean

VIRGINITY TESTING IN TURKEY

Traditionally, young women in Turkey, as in some other cultures, are expected to avoid sexual relations prior to marriage, although the same rule does not apply to men. The morning after the wedding, the bride's virginity is revealed by displaying the sheet that was spread on the couple's wedding bed with the telltale hymeneal blood stain. An American human rights group condemned this practice, as well as reports of forced virginity tests on hospital patients, students and applicants for government jobs. Here is the question: Is the human rights group being ethnocentric in judging Turkish customs by American cultural norms, or is it correctly identifying abuses of women that must be corrected? And does it help if we further understand the so-called logic behind the belief?

Anthropologist Carol Delaney, in her book on Turkish village society, *The Seed and the Soil*, describes how virginity testing is related to the way that Turkish villagers conceptualize and explain the reproductive process. They see reproduction as analogous to the planting and growing of crops; the man provides the "seed" with his semen, and the woman serves as the "soil" in which the seed germinates and grows. As a metaphor for reproduction, the idea of the seed and the soil provides villagers with a way of thinking about and understanding reproduction. However the metaphor of seed and soil has at least one very important implication. Because seeds do not have a limited life span, villagers believe that once planted, the seed (semen) may grow at any time. Consequently, if a woman has had sexual relations with a man other than her husband at any time prior to her marriage, the paternity of the child will be in doubt. And because descent in traditional Turkish villages is closely tied to many things, including property rights, uncertainty about the identity of the true father can have major implications. Thus, in the context of Turkish beliefs about procreation, virginity testing may make sense. Furthermore, Turkish beliefs about conception are not that far removed from our own, since our language draws from the same agricultural metaphors as that of Turkish villagers to explain reproduction. We talk about women being "fertile" or "barren" and semen "fertilizing" "eggs." "Sowing one's oats" as an expression of sexual activity is still heard in parts of the United States and Canada. Furthermore, these views are reinforced by religious proscription, legitimized in the Koran and the Old Testament. Thus, before we either condemn or accept the Turkish villagers for their treatment of women, we need to examine what their beliefs tell us about our own, which may be equally problematic.

water, decent wages, and protection from police brutality, was she now, as an anthropologist, so passive, so indifferent to the destruction around her? She tried to explain that as an anthropologist her work was different, that she was now there to observe, document, and write about their lives as truthfully as she could. The women refused to accept that and insisted that if they were to work with her, she had to also work with them to fight for better lives. "What," they said, "is anthropology to us?"

As a consequence of her experience, Scheper-Hughes argues for a politically committed, morally engaged, and ethically grounded anthropology. "Those of us who make our living observing and recording the misery of the world," she says, "have a particular obligation to reflect critically on the impact of the harsh images of human suffering that we foist upon the public." (1995, 416)

Scheper-Hughes proposes a more humanitarian anthropology, one that is concerned with how people treat one another. Moral relativism, she says, is no longer appropriate to the world in which we live, and anthropology, if it is to be worth anything at all, must be, as she puts it, "critically grounded." Anthropologists cannot ignore the massacres and disappearances of vulnerable people that often occur in communities in which anthropologists work. Anthropologists must, she insists, serve as witnesses and reporters of human rights abuses and the suffering of the poor and the oppressed.

But even serving as a witness for the poor and oppressed can lead to still other moral dilemmas for the anthropologist when the people with whom the anthropologist works engage in behavior that may appear morally questionable. Scheper-Hughes confronted this question when she discovered and reported that impoverished women in the Brazilian shantytowns would sometimes allow their starving infants to die in the belief that they were doomed anyway. When Philippe Bourgois studied the world of crack dealers on the upper east side of New York City, he worried about the negative images he would convey if he reported the personal violence, sexual abuse, addiction, and alienation he witnessed. He recalled the advice of anthropologist Laura Nader, who advised others not to study the poor and powerless, because whatever one says will be used against them.

The Indian practice of sati, the burning of a widow on her husband's funeral pyre, has been formally outlawed, but many Hindus still revere the custom.

Human rights activists, particularly, are skeptical about the idea of cultural relativity. If, they say, we must tolerate the beliefs and practices of other cultures because to do otherwise would be ethnocentric, how can we ever criticize what seem to be violations of basic human rights, such as the right to bodily integrity or the right to be free from torture, arbitrary imprisonment, slavery, or genocide? Cultural relativism, say human rights advocates, makes arguments about human rights meaningless by legitimizing almost any behavior.

Consider the Indian practice of *sati*, the burning of a widow on her deceased husband's funeral pyre. Though it has been formally outlawed, and criticized by numerous women's rights groups, many are still in favor of the practice, describing it as a revered Hindu custom. Further, they accuse protestors of being Western imperialists imposing their own cultural standards. Does it matter if the widows committed *sati* voluntarily? What would happen if she objected? Does it matter that it is only women who are burned? Is *sati* a practice to deny a widow the inheritance of her husband's family's land?

WHAT WOULD YOU DO?

You have been doing anthropological research in the United States with a group of people who believe they must live life as described in the Bible, particularly the book of Acts. They live communally, sharing all property; they believe that women should be subservient to their husbands; they enforce rules against drinking alcoholic beverages and smoking. The group has lately come under attack in the local community as being a "dangerous cult." Although their beliefs and practices differ from those of the larger society around them, you know that they are not dangerous and in fact lead lives of harmony. They have asked you to speak in their defense. Can you do this without sacrificing your objectivity?

Elizabeth Zechenter, who makes the argument for the establishment of some universal principles for human rights, says that cultural relativists are right to claim that the endorsement or rejection of some foreign custom risks imposing one's own cultural prejudices on others. But the idea that we can make no judgments without being ethnocentric is illusory:

> One simply cannot avoid making judgments when faced with oppression and brutality masquerading under the guise of cultural tradition. Such a nonjudgmental tolerance of brutality is actually an ultimate form of ethnocentrism, if not an outright ethical surrender. (Zechenter 1997, 336)

There is obviously no easy answer to the question of when or if it is proper to judge the beliefs and practices of others to be right or wrong or when to actively work to change behaviors or beliefs judged to be wrong. Ideally, our attempts to understand what at first seems puzzling in some cultures and our arrival at some solution to that puzzle should result in questioning what it was about us that made the behavior or belief seem puzzling in the first place. In addition, we need to understand that if each culture orders the world in a certain way for its members, it also blocks off or masks other ways of viewing things. We need to appreciate that there are perspectives different from our own and that our ethnocentric biases may blind us to those alternatives. In other words, although culture provides us with certain meanings to give to objects, persons, behaviors, emotions, and events, it also shields us from alternative meanings. What our culture hides from us may be more important than what it reveals.

QUESTION 1.3

Is it possible to see the world through the eyes of others?

Translating Cultural Meaning

This question lies at the heart of the anthropological enterprise. The anthropologist must be able to look beyond everyday appearances to decipher the often hidden meanings of beliefs, objects, and behaviors, while at the same time setting aside preconceptions of what is normal or proper. The anthropologist must also learn one culture and then relate that learning to members of another culture by translating the meanings of one world into the meanings of another.

Anthropologists, as other social scientists, use surveys, written documents, historical accounts, and questionnaires as part of their research toolbox. But the unique feature of cultural anthropology is the application of the **ethnographic method**—the immersion of investigators into the lives of the people they are trying to understand and, through that experience, the attainment of some level of understanding of the meanings those people ascribe to their existence. This immersion process utilizes the techniques of **anthropological fieldwork** which requires **participant observation**—the active participation of observers in the lives of their subjects.

ethnographic method the immersion of investigators in the lives of the people they are trying to understand, and through that experience, the attainment of some level of understanding of the meanings those people ascribe to their experience

anthropological fieldwork firsthand or direct immersion and observation of the people or culture a researcher is trying to understand

participant observation the active participation of observers in the lives of their subjects

The ethnographic method is only part of the anthropological enterprise. The anthropologist also seeks to explain why people view the world as they do and to contribute to the understanding of human behavior in general. But fieldwork is the beginning of the enterprise. Fieldwork involves the meeting of at least two cultures: that of the researcher and that of the culture the researcher is trying to understand. Anthropological researchers must set aside their own views of things and attempt to see the world in a new way. In many respects they must assume the demeanor and status of children who must be taught by their elders the proper view of the world. And like children making their way in a world they do not fully comprehend, anthropologists often find themselves in awkward, embarrassing, or dangerous situations and must be prepared to learn from these moments.

The Embarrassed Anthropologist

Awkwardness and embarrassment are a part of fieldwork, as well as a part of the process through which the fieldworker learns about another culture. Richard Scaglion spent more than a year with the Abelam of Papua New Guinea. Shortly after he arrived in the field, he observed and photographed an Abelam pig hunt in which the men set out nets and waited while the women and children made lots of noise to drive the pigs into the nets. Soon after, he was invited by the Abelam to participate in a pig hunt, and he took this as a sign of acceptance, that the people "liked him." He started to go with the men, but they told him they wanted him to go with the women and children to beat the bush, explaining "We've never seen anyone who makes as much noise in the jungle as you." Later, wanting to redeem himself, Scaglion offered to help an Abelam who was planting crops with a digging stick. A crowd gathered to watch as Scaglion used a shovel to try to dig a demonstration hole. After he had struggled for several minutes to get the shovel into the hard-packed soil, someone handed him a digging stick, and he was amazed at how easy it was to use. Later he found out that several Abelam had shovels but rarely used them because they didn't work well.

After months of answering Scaglion's questions about their view of the natural world, such as the moon, sun, and stars, an Abelam man asked him about his views of the universe. Feeling on safe ground, he gave the usual grade-school lecture about the shape of the earth, its daily rotation, and its travels around the sun. Using a coconut, he showed them the relative positions on the Earth of New Guinea, Australia, Europe, and the United States. Everyone listened intently, and Scaglion thought it went well until about a week later, when he overheard some elders wondering how it was that Americans walked upside down!

Beginning again, Scaglion used the coconut to explain how, as the earth rotates, sometimes the United States would be upright and New Guinea would be on the bottom. The Abelam rejected this because they could see that they were *not* upside down, and no one, not even some of the old people in the community, remembered ever having walked upside down. Scaglion began to draw on the physics he had in college, and as he tried to explain Newton's law of gravity (or "grabity," as his friends pronounced it), he suddenly realized that he didn't understand "grabity" either. It was something he had accepted since third grade, a concept that even physicists simply take for granted as a convenient theoretical concept.

"Using a coconut, he showed them the relative positions on the Earth of New Guinea, Australia, Europe, and the United States."

Confronting Witchcraft in Mexico

When Michael Kearney began his work in Santa Catarina Ixtepeji in the valley of Oaxaca, Mexico, he was secure in the scientific view of the world in which he was raised. He was, though, fascinated with the worldview of the locals, who saw mystic notions of fate, malevolent witches and spiritual forces as controlling the world. But instead of just studying this worldview, Kearney experienced it firsthand.

While walking to an appointment, he came upon Doña Delfina, a witch that he had been trying to interview for some time. She explained that her sister-in-law had a "very bad disease in her arms," and she asked for help. At Doña Delfina's house, he found the sister-in-law's arms covered with deep, oozing lesions. They rejected his offer to take the sick woman to a doctor, but allowed him to apply some ointment. Much to Delfina's amazement, her sister-in-law felt better immediately, and was completely healed after two days.

Later that day, a Ixtepejanos friend asked Kearney what he had done, and he proudly explained. The friend replied that it was not a good thing to do, since the sister-in-law was the victim of black magic. A woman named Gregoria was attacking her with black magic to steal her husband, while Deflina was using her own magic to defend her brother. By intervening, the friend explained, Kearney tipped the balance of power towards Delfina, and made an enemy in Gregoria. "Maybe you should leave town for a while until Gregoria calms down," the friend suggested.

At first, Kearney did not take the danger seriously, but he soon would. About a week later, Kearney was lying in bed and felt an itch on his arm. He rolled up his sleeves and saw several angry welts that seemed to be growing before his eyes. Immediately his mind turned to the chancrous arms of Delfina's sister-in-law, and the fact that Gregoria lived only 50 yards away, and he thought "**She got me**." Though this initial terror may have only lasted a few minutes, Kearney came to realize that systems of belief which at first seem so alien are eminently reasonable when we participate in the lives of the people who hold those beliefs.

The Endangered Anthropologist

The risk of injury, disease, or hostile reactions has always been a feature of anthropological fieldwork. But as anthropologists increasingly work in areas where human rights violations are common, these risks are intensified. When the work of anthropologists threatens the power, authority, or prerogatives of powerful groups, these anthropologists often expose themselves to violent retaliation. The dangers that anthropologists face may serve to provide insights into how the people with whom they are working live with the daily threat of violence.

In 1989 and 1990, Linda Green was doing fieldwork in the Guatemalan community of Xe'caj. As with many similar communities, Xe'caj was only beginning to recover from some 35 years of violence. Beginning with a military coup orchestrated by the CIA in 1954, Guatemala experienced regular violence as the military regime tried to suppress revolutionary movements. The government killed hundreds of thousands of Guatemalans. The late 1970s and early 1980s were a particularly brutal time as the government embarked on a campaign to destroy peasant villages and relocate people to government-controlled towns. In addition, paramilitary groups, largely supplied and supported by the regular military, embarked on campaigns of terror and torture in an attempt to control the peasant population.

The people of Xe'caj lived in a state of constant surveillance from the military encampment located above the town. Many of the residents had husbands, fathers, or sons taken away by the military. There were rumors of death lists. They had difficulty sleeping and reported nightmares of recurring death and violence. Soon, said Green, "I, too, started to experience nighttime hysteria, dreams of death, disappearances, and torture."

Green interviewed women who were widowed by the conflict. Without prompting, the women recounted in vivid detail their stories of horror, the deaths and disappearances of husbands, fathers, sons, and brothers as if they had happened last week or month, not many years ago. Then one day when Green arrived to continue the interviews, the women were anxious and agitated. When she asked what had happened, they told her that the military commissioner was looking for her and that people were saying that she was helping the widows and

A DANGEROUS PROFESSION

Ruth First--killed in 1982 by a mail bomb sent to her office.

Arnold Ap--tortured and killed by Indonesian army in 1984.

David Webster--shot and killed by a pro-apartheid death squad in 1989.

Myrna Mack--killed in 1990 by Guatemalan soldier.

George Aditjondro--expelled from his native Indonesia in 1995 for criticizing the government.

talking against other people in the community. When Green told the women that she was going to go see the commissioner, they pleaded with her not to go, explaining that they knew of people who had gone to the military garrison and never returned. Her visit would provide a vivid experience of the kinds of fears confronted by the villagers. She describes her feelings as she approached the garrison:

> I saw several soldiers sitting in a small guardhouse with a machine gun perched on a three-foot stanchion pointed downward and directly at me. The plight of Joseph K. in Kafka's *Trial* flashed through my mind, accused of a crime for which he must defend himself but about which he could get no information. I didn't do anything wrong, I must not look guilty, I repeated to myself like a mantra. I must calm myself, as my stomach churned, my nerves frayed. I arrived breathless and terrified. Immediately I knew I was guilty because I was against the system of violence and terror that surrounded me. (1995, 116)

Fortunately the Commandante said he knew nothing about why she was being harassed and assured her that she could continue with her work. Everything went smoothly from there, but Green gained a fuller understanding of the experiences of people who live under the constant threat of violence.

The experiences of Scaglion, Kearney and Green highlight certain features of the ethnographic method. They especially illustrate the attempt of anthropologists to appreciate the views of others while at the same time questioning their own views of the world. They also illustrate what makes the ethnographic method unique. By participating in the lives of others and in their cultural practices, the anthropologist can take himself or herself as a subject of investigation. If one can succeed in seeing the world as others do, even for a brief moment, then it becomes far easier to understand and describe that world. It also helps the anthropologist to understand how others can believe what they do. Tanya M. Luhrmann learned this when she studied contemporary witchcraft in England. After reading materials surrounding the practice of contemporary witchcraft and attending ceremonies, she found herself interpreting events in the world in much the same way as the people she was working with. We return to her experiences in a later chapter.

Claude Levi-Strauss, one of the leading anthropologists of the twentieth century, says that fieldwork and the attempts of anthropologists to immerse themselves in the world of others makes them "marginal" men or women. They are never completely native because they cannot totally shed their own cultural perceptions, but they are never the same again after having glimpsed alternative visions of the world. Anthropologists are, as Roger Keesing put it, outsiders who know something of what it is to be insiders.

"Immediately I knew I was guilty because I was against the system of violence and terror that surrounded me."

QUESTION 1.4

How can the meanings that others find in experience be interpreted and described?

Cultural Texts

Sir Arthur Conan Doyle first introduced his now famous detective hero, Sherlock Holmes, in 1887. In his adventures, Holmes had the unique ability to apply deductive reasoning to solve the most baffling of mysteries. In one story, Dr. Watson, Holmes's assistant, decides to teach the great detective a lesson in humility. He hands Holmes a pocket watch once owned by Watson's late brother and challenges Holmes to infer from it the character of its owner.

What if Sherlock Holmes had been an anthropologist?

CASE: Anthropology at the Mall

© PAUL PIEBINGA/ISTOCKPHOTO.COM

An anthropological perspective can be invaluable in all sorts of career areas.

Whether it's management, public policy or medicine, various fields involve ways that people give meaning to their experiences, and so, can benefit from anthropological insights. Paco Underhill is a retail anthropologist who studies the way people shop. More specifically, he examines the interaction between people and products and people and spaces. Through his work, he helps businesses identify how people experience the act of shopping.

Underhill's work on retail anthropology is based on William H. Whyte's work on public spaces. Observing people in streets, parks and buildings, Whyte measured nearly everything about how people use space: the ideal width for a ledge for sitting, how weather affected park use, and how a public place's surroundings determined quality of life. By adapting Whyte's methods, Underhill watches people shop, traces the paths they take in stores, and observe how they react to merchandise. This information then helps retailers design a shopping experience that will cater to customers and increase sales.

According to Underhill, store organization is critical to the shopping experience. He found that when people enter a store, they need a period to adjust. Almost anything near the entrance will go unnoticed, but move them ten feet in, and they catch the shopper's eye. Retailers can also encourage shoppers to traverse the store by putting commonly purchased items in the back.

Underhill also shows patterns of behavior that differentiate male and female shoppers. In a study that Underhill did for Dockers apparel, he found that men generally look for a pair of trousers in their size and head directly for the checkout without looking at anything else. "The time spent in the section," says Underhill, "was roughly identical to what men devote to shopping for beer in convenience stores." Men are much less likely to ask for help from employees, and if they can't find what they want, they will just leave. They are also less likely to look at price tags (72% of men compared to 86% of women). But, for that reason, men will also spend more. According to Underhill, men act as providers; although shopping is not their thing, paying is. When men and women are together in the supermarket checkout line, the men almost always pay.

As for women, Underhill found that they generally coolly weigh their purchases, consider the pros and cons, and carefully examine the price. He suggests that women demand more of shopping environments: Men want to find what they want and get out fast; women are more patient and inquisitive. He also found that women like space. In what he calls the "butt-brush effect," Underhill found that when women are touched from behind while shopping, they will immediately move away from the merchandise and try to leave the store. The narrower the quarters, the less time a woman is likely to spend there. This is the reason why many cosmetics counters have small recesses which allow shoppers to stand clear.

Today, children are a major segment of the consumer market, with some estimating that children 2–14 directly influence $188 billion of parental spending. Underhill has a number of suggestions for making stores more kid-friendly. Aisles, especially in the children's department, need to be wide enough to accommodate baby strollers and wandering toddlers. Items geared for kids need to be placed where children can see and reach them. In one study, Underhill found that kids and the elderly most frequently purchased dog snacks, yet these were placed on high, difficult to reach shelves. When they were moved to lower shelves, sales immediately increased.

Underhill notes that retailers must become adept at controlling the experience of time. In study after study, Underhill discovered that the single most important determinant of shoppers' opinions of a shopping experience is waiting time. If they think the wait wasn't too bad, they'll have positive feedback; if they wait too long, they will think that the service was inept. In his work, Underhill discovered that it is possible to make time appear to go faster for customers. Perceived waiting time goes faster after interaction with an employee, or even other customers. At Disney World, engineers organized lines to wind back and forth, making lines appear shorter, and encouraging people to talk to one another as they wait. Diversions also help time go faster. Almost anything will do—short videos, stacks of stuff, even the sleazy tabloids at supermarket checkout counters.

So where is anthropology at the mall? It's just about everywhere, from the location of the checkout counter, to the selection of inventory, to the employee who greets you as walk in. By looking at how culture influences the meaning people give to things and how they experience events, anthropology helps retailers design an ideal shopping experience.

© NENAD AKSIC/ISTOCKPHOTO.COM / © DAN BAYLEY/ISTOCKPHOTO.COM / © ROBERT CHURCHILL/ISTOCKPHOTO.COM / © GERARD FRITZ/PHOTOGRAPHER'S CHOICE/GETTY IMAGES

Researching a Store

Paco Underhill leads CEOs through a self-exam—for 30 minutes, they observe the store together. Inevitably they see things they never even thought about. In this exercise, you are going to play CEO a retail chain. Pick a local store, and do the following:

1. As you approach the store, what do you see? Do you know from a distance what is sold there?
2. Stand right outside the store. What do you see in the windows?
3. Go into the store. Are there baskets to put things in? Where are they located?
4. What strikes you as you transition into the store? What attracts your attention?
5 What is the register setup? Do people have to wait, and if so, are there any distractions to help time go faster?
6. Are there any opportunities to touch, feel, or try the merchandise?
7. How is the merchandise grouped? Are things arranged so that the sale of one might prompt the sale of the other? Are they arranged in ways that would appeal to women, men, kids, the elderly?
8. How are nonpublic spaces designed? What are the restrooms like? If there are dressing rooms, are they likely to encourage or discourage sales?

© JOSELITO BRIONES/ISTOCKPHOTO.COM / © DNY59/ISTOCKPHOTO.COM

cultural text a way of thinking about culture as a text of significant symbols—words, gestures, drawings, natural objects—that carries meaning

Holmes's interpretation: "[Your brother] was a man of untidy habits—very untidy and careless. He was left with good prospects, but he threw away his chances and finally, taking to drink, he died."

Watson, astounded at the accuracy of Holmes's description of his late brother, asks if it was guesswork. "I never guess," replies Holmes:

> I began by stating that your brother was careless. When you observe the lower part of the watch case, you notice that it is not only dented in two places, but it is cut and marked all over from the habit of keeping other hard objects, such as coins or keys, in the same pocket. Surely it is no great feat to assume that a man who treats [an expensive] watch so cavalierly must be a careless man. Neither is it a very far-fetched inference that a man who inherits one article of such value is pretty well provided for in other respects.

"But what about his drinking habits?" asks Watson. Holmes responds:

> Look at the innerplate which contains the keyhole [where the watch is wound]. Look at the thousands of scratches all around the hole-marks where the key has slipped. What sober man's key could have scored those grooves? But you will never see a drunkard's watch without them. He winds it at night, and he leaves these traces of his unsteady hand. Where is the mystery in all this? (Doyle 1930, 93)

Had Sherlock Holmes been an anthropologist, he might have been tempted also to draw some inferences about the society in which the watch was manufactured, particularly about their conceptions of time. For example, in some societies, time is task oriented, not clock oriented; time might be measured by how long it takes to cook rice, as in Madagascar. In other societies, time patterns depend on natural events, such as the rising of the sun or the ebb and flow of tides. British anthropologist E. E. Evans-Pritchard, in his classic account of the life of the Nuer of the Sudan, noted:

> The Nuer have no expression equivalent to "time" in our language, and they cannot, therefore, as we can, speak of time as though it were something actual, which passes, can be wasted, can be saved, and so forth. I don't think they ever experience the same feeling of fighting against time because their points of reference are mainly the activities themselves, which are generally of a leisurely character. Events follow a logical order, but they are not controlled by an abstract system, there being no autonomous points of reference to which activities have to conform with precision. Nuer are fortunate. (1940, 103)

An anthropologist might also infer that clocks are instruments of discipline; they tell us when to get up, when to go to bed, when to eat, when to start work, when to stop work. Clocks define our work patterns and our wages may depend on the constant repetition over time of a particular task. Historian E. P. Thompson notes that until the institution of modern notions of time and the need to measure it with clocks, work patterns were characterized by alternating bouts of intense labor and idleness, at least whenever people were in control of their own working lives. He even suggests that this pattern persists today, but only among a few self-employed professionals such as artists, writers, small farmers, and, he suggests, college students.

Watson's brother's watch was a product of Western society, part of its culture. Holmes "read" the watch as if it were a collection of symbols or words, a **cultural text** that revealed the character of its owner. He could just as easily have viewed it as a text inscribed with the symbols that revealed the ideas about time and work that characterized the civilization that produced it.

One way to think about culture is as a text of significant symbols: words, gestures, drawings, natural objects—anything, in fact, that carries meaning. To understand another culture, we must be able, as Holmes was with the pocket watch, to decipher the meaning of the symbols that comprise a cultural text. We must be able to interpret the meaning embedded in the language, objects, gestures, and activities that are shared by members of a society. Fortunately, the ability to decipher a cultural text is part of being human; in our everyday lives, we both read and maintain the text that makes up our own culture. We have learned the

Rarely is a cockfight without social significance, and rarely do cocks owned by members of the same family or village fight each other.

© AP IMAGES/CHARLES DHARAPAK

meanings behind the symbols that frame our lives, and we share those meanings with others. Our task in understanding another culture is to take the abilities that have enabled us to dwell in our own culture and use them to understand the cultures of others.

Deciphering the Balinese Cockfight

To illustrate how an anthropologist might decipher a cultural text, imagine yourself coming upon a cockfight on the island of Bali, which Clifford Geertz studied in great detail (1972). You see a ring in which two roosters with sharpened metal spurs attached to their legs are set at each other until one kills the other. Surrounding the fighting cocks are men shouting encouragement to their favorites, each having placed a wager that his favorite will kill its opponent.

What do you make of this? Your first reaction might be shock or disgust at the spectacle of the crowd urging the cocks to bloody combat. After a while you might begin to find similarities to events that are meaningful to you, such as some American sports. But what if, like Sherlock Holmes, you want to understand the meaning of what is happening and what that meaning tells you about how Balinese view their world? If you assume that the cockfight is a feature of Balinese culture, a Balinese text filled with symbols that carry meaning about what it is to be Balinese, how might you read this text?

You might begin by finding out the language the Balinese use to talk about the cockfight. You would no doubt discover that the double entendre of "cock" both as a synonym for rooster and as a euphemism for penis is the same for the Balinese as it is for Americans. The double entendre even produces the same jokes, puns, and obscenities in Bali as it does in the United States. You would discover that *sabung*, the Balinese word for cock, has numerous other meanings and is used metaphorically to mean hero, warrior, champion, political candidate, bachelor, dandy, lady-killer, or tough guy. Court trials, wars, political contests, inheritance disputes, and street arguments are compared with cockfights. Even the island of Bali is thought of as being cock shaped. You would also find that men give their fowls inordinate attention, spending most of their time grooming them and feeding them a special diet. As one of Clifford Geertz's Balinese informants put it, "We're all cock crazy."

Having discovered the importance of cockfights to the Balinese and the connection they make between cocks and men, you next examine the cockfight itself. You learn that cockfights are public events held in arenas from late afternoon until after sundown. Handlers, expert in the task, attach sharp spurs to the cock's legs; for a cock thought to be superior to an opponent, the spurs are adjusted in a slightly disadvantageous position. The cocks are released in the center of the ring and fly at each other, fighting until one kills the other. The owner of the winning cock takes the carcass of the loser home to eat, and the losing owner is sometimes driven in despair to wreck family shrines. You discover that the Balinese contrast heaven and hell by comparing them to the mood of a man whose cock has just won and the mood of a man whose cock has just lost.

You find out that although the Balinese place odds on cockfights, there are strict social conventions that dictate the wagering. For example, a man will never bet against a cock that is owned by someone of his family group or village or a friend's family group or village, but he will place large bets against a cock owned by an enemy or the friend of an enemy. Rarely is a cockfight without social significance, and rarely do cocks owned by members of the same family or village fight each other. Moreover, the owners of the cocks, especially in important matches, are usually among the leaders of their communities. You might learn that cockfights come close to encouraging an open expression of aggression between village and kin group rivals—but not quite, because the cockfight is, as the Balinese put it, "only a cockfight."

Given the social rules for betting and the ways odds are set, you might reason, as Geertz did, that the Balinese rarely make a profit betting on cockfights. Geertz says, in fact, that most bettors just want to break even. Consequently, the meaning of the cockfight for a Balinese has little to do with economics. The question is, what meaning does the cockfight have for the Balinese? What is the cockfight really about, if it is not about money?

Geertz concludes that the Balinese cockfight is above all about status, about the ranking of people *vis-à-vis* one another. The Balinese cockfight is a text filled with meaning about status as the Balinese see it. Cocks represent men, or, more specifically, their owners. The fate of the cock in the ring is linked, if only temporarily, to the social fate of its owner. Each cock has a following consisting of the owner, the owner's family, and members of the owner's village, and these followers "risk" their status by betting on the cockfight. Furthermore, Geertz maintains, the more a match is between near equals, personal enemies, or high-status individuals, the more the match is about status. And the more the match is about status, the closer the identification of cock and man, the finer the cocks, and the more exactly they will be matched. The match will inspire greater emotion and absorption, and the gambling will be more about status and less about economic gain.

For Geertz, the cockfight is like any art form; it takes a highly abstract and difficult concept—status—and depicts it in a way that makes it comprehensible to the participants. The cockfight is meaningful to the Balinese because it tells them something real about their own lives in a way that does not directly affect their lives. They see the struggle for status that is part of everyday life vividly portrayed, even though, in the cockfight itself, no one really gains or loses status in any permanent sense.

A few words of caution are necessary concerning what you might learn about the Balinese from this particular cultural text. First, it would probably be a mistake to assume that the people gain status by being on the winning side or lose it by being on the side of the loser. The status outcomes of the cockfight do not translate into real life any more than the victory of your favorite sports team increases your status. Instead, says Geertz, the cockfight illustrates what status is about for the Balinese. The cockfight is a story the Balinese tell themselves about themselves. It would also be a mistake to assume that the character of the Balinese could be read directly from the cockfight; a conclusion that the cockfight is indicative of an aggressive, competitive, violent national character would quickly be dispelled. The Balinese are shy about competition and avoid open conflict. The slaughter in the cockfight is not how things are literally, but how they could be. Finally, the cockfight reveals only a segment of the Balinese character, as Watson's brother's watch revealed only a segment of its owner's character. The culture of a people, like the possessions of a person, is an ensemble of texts—collections of symbols and meanings—that must be viewed together to provide a full understanding.

QUESTION 1.5

What can learning about other people tell Americans about themselves?

Studying Your Own Culture

Anthropologists do not limit themselves to the study of cultures that are different from their own. They often apply concepts and techniques that are useful in understanding and interpreting other cultures to understand and interpret their own. One of the objectives of studying other cultures is to help us recognize the meanings we impose on our experiences. Whether we approach other cultures as anthropologists, as travelers, or as professionals who need to communicate with people of other cultures, the confrontation with other ways of believing and behaving should cause us to reflect on our own way of viewing the world. To illustrate, let us try to step outside ourselves and objectify an experience whose meaning we take for granted. Pretend you are a Balinese anthropologist who suddenly comes upon a spectacle as important to Americans as the cockfight is to the Balinese: a football game.

As a Balinese, your first reaction to this American text might be one of horror and revulsion, as you see men violently attacking one other while thousands

cheer them on to even more violent conflict. As you settle in, however, you soon find some obvious similarities between the football game and the more familiar cockfight. Both are competitions in which the spectators sort themselves into supporters of one side or the other. In fact, in football, the sorting is even more carefully arranged, because supporters of one team are seated on one side of the arena and fans of the other team are seated opposite them.

Your next step (as in interpreting the cockfight) is to examine the language Americans use to refer to the football game. You discover that they use similar expressions in talking about football and war: *defensive line*, *blitz*, *bomb*. Coaches talk about getting "revenge" for defeats, as generals might talk about getting revenge on the battlefield. You conclude that Americans seem to feel the same way about football as they do about war.

One of the words Americans use to refer to players is *jock*, a term also applied to an athletic support garment worn by men. Because you see only men attacking one another, you might assume that the gender meanings of cockfights and football games are also similar. *Cocks* stand for men; football players are men. Moreover, football players dress to emphasize their maleness: large shoulders, narrow hips, big heads, and pronounced genitals. You might test your interpretation with an American spectator, who would argue that football gear is simply protective but, if pressed, would have to admit that it is used offensively as much as defensively. Furthermore, you see young women participating in the spectacle as cheerleaders, dressed to highlight their femininity in the same way the players dress to accent their masculinity. This contrast between male and female in American society leads you to conclude that football is also a story about the meanings that Americans ascribe to gender differences.

You soon discover that winning and losing football games is as important to Americans as winning and losing cockfights is to Balinese. Winners engage in frenzied celebrations called *victory parties*, and losers are often despondent in defeat. As anthropologists know, this is not always the case in other societies. When the Gahuku-Gama of the Highlands of New Guinea started playing soccer, they always played until a committee of elders decided that the score was tied, and then the match was considered completed. So you speculate that football is also about the meanings that Americans give to the idea of success. You learn that success in America (like status in Bali) is a highly abstract idea; because it is abstract, its meaning is embedded in activities whose meanings are shared by members of the society. You need to find answers to certain questions about the meaning of success in American society: How is success defined? How is it obtained? Why doesn't everyone who follows all the rules for gaining success attain it?

Through your fieldwork, you find that Americans believe that "all men are created equal" and every person has (or at least should have) an equal opportunity to succeed. People compete for success, and they ought to compete on an equal footing, on a "level playing field," as some put it. Success, Americans believe, comes from hard work, sacrifice, and self-denial. But you wonder how Americans know that hard work, sacrifice, and denial bring success. Aren't there instances where they do not? How do Americans explain why women and minorities succeed less often than white males do? And why do some people achieve more success than others? You conclude that it is, in fact, impossible to prove directly in real life the correctness of this American success model, which maintains that hard work and sacrifice lead to success. Faith in the value of work and self-denial must be generated in other ways. As a Balinese anthropologist studying the American custom of football, you conclude, then, that in addition to its meanings relative to war and gender, the meaning of American football also lies in its demonstration of the American success model as it is supposed to work.

Anthropologists have found that football, like the Balinese cockfight, is carefully controlled by fixed rules so there is only one outcome: almost always there is a winner and a loser. As a text that carries meaning about success, *who* wins is unimportant; it is only important that *someone* wins. ("A tie," it has been said, "is like kissing your sister.") But more than that, football tells Americans what it takes to win or lose. Success in football not only takes hard work and sacrifice, but, as William Arens points out, specialization, mechanization, and submission to a dominant authority—the coach. Two other anthropologists, Susan P. Montague and Robert Morais, note that the football team looks very much like one of the most important settings in which Americans seek success—business corporations. Both football teams and corporations are compartmentalized, hierarchical, and highly sophisticated in the coordinated application of a differentiated, specialized technology, and they both try to turn out a winning product in a competitive market. Football coaches are sometimes hired to deliver inspirational lectures to corporate groups on "winning"; they may draw analogies between football and corporate life or portray sport as a means of preparing for life in the business world.

Anthropologists therefore can conclude (as did Montague and Morais) that football provides for Americans, as the cockfight does for the Balinese, a small-scale rendering of a concept that is too complex to be directly comprehended. In the case of the Balinese, it's status; in the case of Americans, it's success. Football is compelling because it is a vivid demonstration of the validity of the value of success, as well as a dramatic set of instructions on how to attain it. Consequently, the audience for a football game is led to believe that if the rules that govern the world of football are equated with those of the business world, then the principles that govern success on the football field must also apply in the world of work. That is, if hard work, dedication, submission to authority, and teamwork lead to success in a game, they will lead to success in real life. The rules by which success is won in football can also be applied to win success in the real world.

Of course, football is also a game that people enjoy. Analyz-

Both football teams and corporations try to turn out a winning product in a competitive market.

© MIKE KEMP/RUBBERBALL/GETTY IMAGES

ing it should not reduce our enjoyment of it but rather heighten our fascination with it. By looking at football from the same perspective as Geertz viewed the cockfight, we should gain an understanding of why the meaning carried by the game is important. Although understanding the cockfight heightens our appreciation of the football game, it also helps us to see similarities between Americans and Balinese. If you were shocked by the cockfight, seeing the similarities to football should lessen that shock, while at the same time making football seem just a bit more exotic.

An Anthropologist Looks at a "Happy Meal"

© JOHN PEACOCK/ISTOCKPHOTO.COM

Nothing is too mundane to provide insights into the culture of which it is a part. Take the kids' combo meal, variations of which are offered by many fast-food establishments in the United States. It usually consists of a hamburger, French fries, a cola drink, and a plastic toy, often a Barbie doll, a Hot Wheels car, or something related to a popular film. What can we learn about the culture of the United States by looking beyond the "taken-for-granted" quality of this meal? Among other things, we can get some idea of American demographic and ecological patterns, agricultural and industrial history, and gender roles.

Why, for example, is meat the center of the meal? Most cultures have diets centered on some complex carbohydrate—rice, wheat, manioc, yams, taro—or something made from these—bread, pasta, tortillas, and so on. Meat and fish are generally at the edge of the meal. Why is beef the main ingredient, rather than some other meat, such as pork?

Anthropologists Marvin Harris and Eric Ross note that one advantage of beef is its suitability for the outdoor grill, which became more popular as people moved from cities into suburbs. Suburban cooks soon discovered that pork patties crumbled and fell through the grill, whereas beef patties held together better. In addition, to reduce the risk of trichinosis, pork had to be cooked until it was gray, which makes it very tough.

Beef farmers, as well as the farmers who grew the corn fed to cows to achieve a desirable fat content, benefited from the definition of a hamburger set by the United States Department of Agriculture:

> "Hamburger" shall consist of chopped fresh and/or frozen beef with or without the addition of beef fat as such and/or seasonings, shall not contain more than 30 percent fat, and shall not contain added water, phosphates, binders, or extenders. Beef cheek (trimmed Beef cheeks) may be used in the preparation of hamburgers only in accordance with the conditions prescribed in paragraph (a) of this section. (quoted in Harris 1987, 125)

As Marvin Harris notes, we can eat ground pork and ground beef, but we can't combine them and still call it a hamburger. Even when lean, grass-fed beef is used for hamburger and fat must be added as a binder, the fat must come from beef scraps, not from vegetables or a different animal. This definition of the hamburger protects both the beef industry and the corn farmer, whose income is linked to cattle production. Moreover, it helps the fast-food industry, because the definition of hamburger permits the use of inexpensive scraps of fat. Thus an international beef patty was created that overcame what Harris calls the "pig's natural superiority as a converter of grain to flesh."

The cola drink that accompanies our hamburger is the second part of the fat- and sugar-centered diet that has come to characterize our culture. People in the United States consume, on average, about 60 pounds of sugar a year. Why so much? Sugar, as anthropologist

Sidney Mintz suggests, has no nutritional properties, but does provide a quick and inexpensive energy boost for hardworking laborers with little time for a more nutritious meal. Sugar also serves as an excellent complement to the fat in hamburgers, because it has what nutritionists call "go-away" qualities that remove the fat coating and the beef aftertaste from the mouth.

We can also learn from the the kids' meal that the fat and sugar diet is highly environmentally destructive. Raising beef is among the most environmentally inefficient and destructive form of raising food. For example, half the water consumed in the United States is used to grow grain to feed cattle, and the amount of water used to produce ten pounds of steak equals the household consumption of a family for an entire year. Fifteen times more water is needed to produce a pound of beef protein than an equivalent amount of plant protein. Cattle raising plays a major role in the destruction of tropical forests in Brazil, Guatemala, Costa Rica, and Honduras, where forests have been leveled to create pasture for cattle. Because burning is used to clear most of the forest, the creation of cattle pasture also creates carbon dioxide and, according to some environmentalists, contributes significantly to global warming.

People in the United States consume, on average, about 60 pounds of sugar a year.

Sugar is no less destructive a crop. Forests must be cleared to plant sugar; wood or fossil fuel must be burned in the evaporation process; wastewater is produced in extracting sucrose from the sugarcane; and more fuel is burned in the refining process. Contemporary sugar production in Hawaii not only has destroyed forests, but waste products from processing have severely damaged marine environments. "Big sugar," as the sugar industry is called in Florida, is largely responsible for the pollution, degradation, and virtual destruction of the Everglades.

© JORDAN MCCULLOUGH/ISTOCKPHOTO.COM

Thus one of "texts" anthropologists can read from a Happy Meal relates to the extent to which consumption patterns associated with our culture create waste and environmental damage. Because of these consumption patterns, the average child born in the United States will, in the course of his or her lifetime, do twice the environmental damage of a Swedish child, 3 times that of an Italian child, 13 times that of a Brazilian child, 35 times that of an Indian child, and 280 times that of a Chadian or Haitian child.

And what of Barbie dolls and Hot Wheels? Clearly there is a message about the definition of gender roles, because girls are expected to choose dolls and boys, cars. But one can deduce, if one looks closely enough, even more about our culture from this meal.

WE'VE EXAMINED SOME OF THE LESSONS WE CAN LEARN ABOUT OUR CULTURE FROM FAST FOOD MEALS.

But there are obviously others. See what you might deduce about the following dimensions of life in the United States from the fast food meals.

1. What can you say about gender roles in the United States?
2. What can you deduce about race relations?
3. What can you say about the physical attributes of people favored in the United States?

© JOAO VIRISSIMO/ISTOCKPHOTO.COM / © DMITRIY TERESCHENKO/ISTOCKPHOTO.COM

PROBLEM 2 HOW DO WE EXPLAIN THE TRANSFORMATION OF HUMAN SOCIETIES OVER THE PAST 10,000 YEARS FROM SMALL-SCALE, NOMADIC BANDS OF HUNTERS AND GATHERERS TO LARGE-SCALE, URBAN-INDUSTRIAL STATES?

Chapter 2
The Meaning of Progress and Development

Development fostered a way of conceiving of social life as a technical problem, as a matter of rational decision and management to be entrusted to that group of people—the development professionals—whose specialized knowledge allegedly qualified them for the task. Instead of seeing change as a process rooted in the interpretation of each society's history and cultural tradition . . . these professionals sought to devise mechanisms and procedures to make societies fit a preexisting model that embodied the structures and functions of modernity. Like sorcerers' apprentices, the development professionals awakened once again the dream of reason that, in their hands, as in earlier instances, produced a troubling reality.

Arturo Escobar

* * *

QUESTIONS

In examining this problem, we will consider the following questions:

2.1 Why did hunter-gatherer societies switch to sedentary agriculture?

2.2 Why are some societies more industrially advanced than others?

2.3 Why don't poor countries modernize and develop in the same way as wealthier countries?

2.4 How do modern standards of health and medical treatment compare with those of traditional societies?

2.5 Why are simpler societies disappearing?

The Death of a Way of Life

Over the past 10,000 years, human society has transformed from hunting and gathering to sedentary dwelling.

We live in an era in which we will witness (if we have not already) the extinction of a way of life that is more than 100,000 years old. Up to 10,000 years ago, virtually all human beings lived in small-scale, nomadic groups of 30 to 100 people, gathering wild vegetables and hunting game as they had for thousands of years. Today virtually no human beings anywhere in the world live by hunting and gathering, although every society in existence is descended from such people.

We have also witnessed the creation of a world with radical differences between the wealthy and poor. Although some enjoy a standard of living that gives them abundant food, comfortable shelters, and a plethora of consumer goods, more than a billion people worldwide suffer from hunger and poverty, live in urban and rural slums, and lack even basic health care.

The gradual extinction of a way of life that flourished for nearly 100,000 years and the creation of a world with considerable income gaps poses both a riddle and a moral predicament. The riddle is why, approximately 10,000 years ago, after thousands of years of living as hunters and gatherers, some of these societies began to abandon their way of life. Why did they begin to domesticate plants and animals and exchange their nomadic existence for **sedentary** dwelling? And how, over the next 10,000 years, did these villages and towns come to be divided into rich and poor nations? The moral predicament involves our perceptions of the few small-scale, tribal societies that exist in the world today and the millions of poor who go hungry each day. Do we assume, as many have and still do, that human beings chose to abandon a nomadic hunting and gathering life because they discovered better ways of living? Do we assume that small-scale tribal societies are remnants of an inferior way of life and that, given the opportunity, they will choose to adopt modern life? Do we assume that the division of wealth is due to **progress**—the idea that human history is the story of a steady advance from a life dependent on the whims of nature to a life of control and domination over natural forces? Or is that concept a fabrication of contemporary societies based on ethnocentric notions of technological superiority?

A thumbnail sketch of what we know about the course of cultural history and evolution will be useful before we examine these

sedentary
a style of living characterized by permanent or semipermanent settlements

progress
the idea that human history is the story of a steady advance from a life dependent on the whims of nature to a life of control and domination over natural forces

culture change the change in meanings that a people ascribe to experience and changes in their way of life

slash-and-burn (swidden) agriculture a form of agriculture in which forests are cleared by burning trees and brush, and crops are planted among the ashes of the cleared ground

state a form of society characterized by a hierarchical ranking of people and centralized political control

irrigation agriculture a form of cultivation in which water is used to deliver nutrients to growing plants

problems. Combining what we have learned about human history from the work of archaeologists and historians with information provided by cultural anthropologists who have worked among hunting-gathering and tribal societies gives us a relatively clear picture of **culture change**. As stated previously, until approximately 10,000 years ago Earth's inhabitants were scattered in small, nomadic bands who lived by gathering wild plants and hunting game. Because the search for food required mobility, it was not unusual for them to move every few days. With groups that were small and mobile, simple economic, social, and political arrangements sufficed; there were no formal leaders and little occupational specialization. If there was a specialist, it was likely to be a person who was believed to have special spiritual powers that could be used to cure or cause illness. Kinship served as the main organizing principle of these societies, and social differences among people were based largely on age and gender. Because there was little occupational specialization and little difference in individual wealth or possessions, relations among people likely were of an egalitarian nature.

At some point in history, some hunter-gatherers began to plant crops and domesticate wild animals. These groups became sedentary, living in permanent or semipermanent settlements of 200 to 2,000 people. They practiced **slash-and-burn**, or **swidden, agriculture**; they cleared forests by burning the trees and brush and planted crops among the ashes of the cleared ground. They would cultivate this land from one to three years, then move on to another plot of land. As the groups became larger, they began to form villages consisting of extended family groups and organized themselves into clans—groups of 200 to 500 people who claimed descent from common ancestors. Because larger groups required more formal leadership, certain members assumed the roles of chief or elder, with the authority to make decisions or resolve disputes. Simple occupational roles also developed. As a result, members of some groups were ranked in importance.

Later in history, perhaps because of a need for defense against other groups, settlements combined under common leaders to form **states** consisting of many thousands of people. The development of agriculture intensified, and plow or **irrigation agriculture** replaced slash-and-burn techniques. Leaders organized labor for the purpose of constructing public works—roads, defensive fortifications, irrigation networks, or religious structures. Competition between groups over available resources contributed to the development of standing armies, hereditary leaders emerged, and settlements grew into cities. As technological complexity increased, people

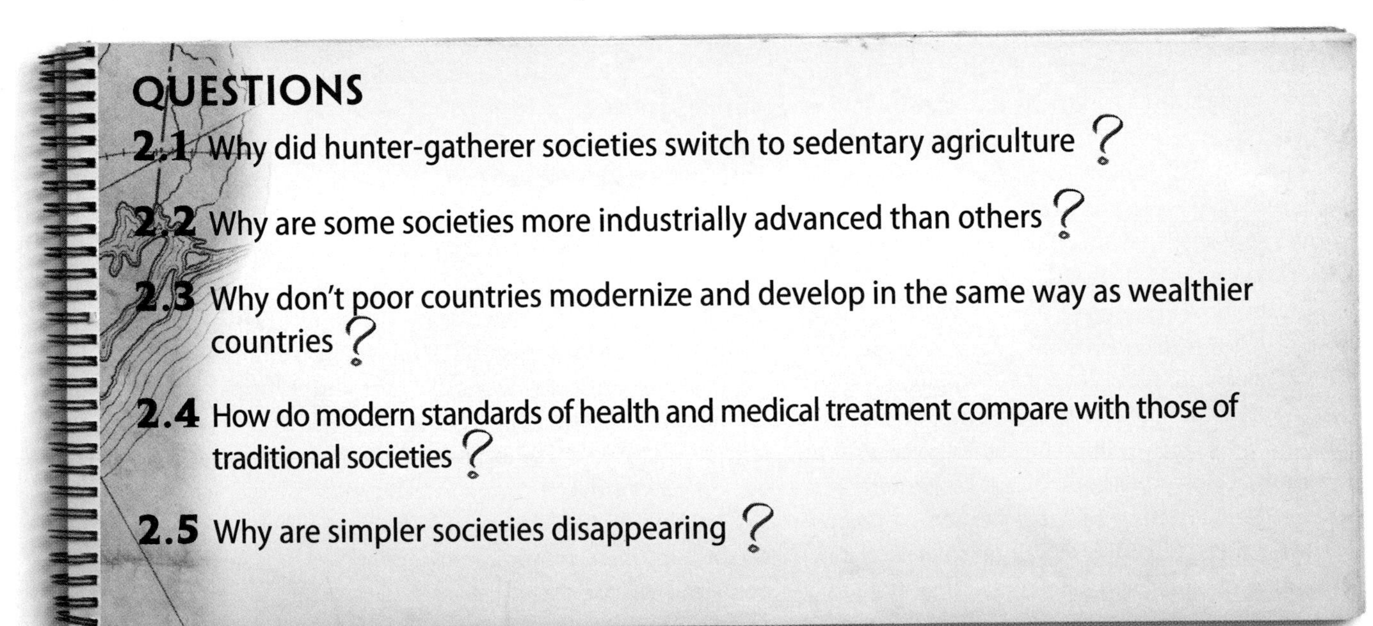

TABLE 2.1

A BRIEF HISTORY OF SOCIETAL DEVELOPMENT

	Hunters and Gatherers	Horticulturalists	State Societies
Population Density	Approximately 1 person per square mile.	Approximately 10 to 15 people per square mile.	Approximately 300 people per square mile.
Subsistence	Hunting, gathering, and fishing.	Slash-and-burn agriculture with mixed livestock herding.	Plow or irrigation agriculture.
Work, Labor, and Production	Very high yield relative to labor expended.	High yield relative to labor expended.	High labor needs relative to yield. High degree of occupational specialization.
Political Organization	Informal political organization. Few, if any, formal leaders. Conflict controlled by limiting group size, mobility, and flexibility of group membership. Little intergroup conflict.	More formalized political organization, often with well-established leaders or chiefs. Increased population density and wealth result in increased potential for conflict. Intergroup warfare, motivated by desire for wealth, prestige, or women, is common.	Highly developed state organization, with a clear hierarchy of authority. Often a two-class society with rulers (landowners) and peasants. Authority of the elite backed by organized use of force (police or army). Warfare for purpose of conquest is common. Well-established mechanisms for resolving conflict (e.g., courts) exist side by side with informal mechanisms.

began to specialize in occupational tasks (such as herders, bakers, butchers, warriors, or potters). Occupational specialization, meanwhile, led to increased trade and the rise of merchants. Some 300 years ago, some of these ranked, state societies began to develop into large-scale, industrialized states, which are now found all over the world. Table 2.1 provides a summary of this brief sketch of human social and cultural history.

One simple explanation for the transformation of societies from nomadic bands to industrial states is that human inventions created better ways of doing things; in other words, human culture progressed. In the past forty years, however, anthropologists have begun to question the idea that the life of hunters and gatherers was harsh and difficult. They propose instead that in many ways this way of life was superior to that of groups maintained by sedentary agriculture.

Some have proposed further that slash-and-burn agriculture was actually more efficient and less wasteful than modern methods of food production. If that is true, what other explanations are there for why groups abandoned hunting and gathering for sedentary agriculture? Moreover, if life in small-scale, tribal societies is not inferior to modern life, why are people in societies without advanced agriculture and industry starving and dying of disease? And why are small-scale, tribal societies disappearing?

QUESTION 2.1

Why did hunter-gatherer societies switch to sedentary agriculture?

Changes in Society

A common explanation of why hunter-gatherers chose at some point to settle down and domesticate plants and animals is that sedentary agriculture was an easier and more productive way to get food. People who discovered they could plant and harvest crops and domesticate animals rather than having to search for their food began to do so. They had progressed.

The idea that change occurs because of a desire to progress is well entrenched in Western society, and, beginning in the nineteenth century, anthropologists contributed significantly to this view. Lewis Henry Morgan, a Rochester, New York attorney who took great interest in the evolution of culture, offered his own idea of how humankind had progressed. In his book *Ancient Society*, first published in 1877, Morgan postulated a theory of human development in which human societies evolved through three stages: savagery, barbarism, and civilization. He further divided savagery and barbarism into early, middle, and late stages. He noted that some societies, such as the United States, had evolved completely to civilization while others had yet to complete their transformation and remained in the stages of savagery or barbarism. The passage of societies from one stage to the next, Morgan reasoned, required some major technological invention. Thus, the advance from early to middle savagery was marked by the invention of fire; from middle to late savagery by the invention of the bow and arrow; from late savagery to late barbarism by the invention of pottery, agriculture, and animal domestication, and so on, until certain societies had progressed to civilization. Other writers (including many anthropologists) have elaborated on the scheme developed by Morgan, sharing the assumption that humankind was progressing and would continue to do so.

Technology is the driving force of cultural evolution.

In the mid-twentieth century, Leslie White formulated what was then one of the more influential evolutionary schemes to explain the historical development of culture. Like Morgan, White saw technology as the driving force of cultural evolution. From White's perspective, human beings seek to harness energy through technology and to transform that energy into things that are required for survival, such as food, clothing, and shelter. Through technology, energy is put to work. The more efficient a technology is, the more food, clothing or other goods will be produced. Because hunter-gatherers had only their own muscle power to work with, the amount of energy that could be applied to production was limited. Technological advances such as the plow, the waterwheel, and the windmll enabled people to transform more and more energy to their use, enabling them go grow more crops and domesticate more animals. Later, when new forms of energy in the form of coal, oil, and gas were discovered, the amount of energy human beings could harness again increased.

Cultural development, from White's perspective, varies directly with the efficiency of technology. More efficient technology allows human societies to transform more energy to fulfill their needs, and these societies then can produce more food and support larger populations. At some point the increased efficiency in food production allowed a few people to produce enough food for everyone, freeing others to develop other skills, thereby promoting occupational specialization. Specialization then led to the development of commerce. The increase in population, along with the increase in contact between groups, required the development of the state to coordinate group activities and organize armies to protect the growing wealth of its members from other groups.

White's view of technology as the driving force in cultural evolution was highly influential in the development of anthropological theory in the twentieth century. His theory represents the coalescence of a point of view that is prevalent among many people today: that technology is the true measure of progress and the more energy human societies can harness through the development of new power sources, the more social, economic, and political problems they will solve.

The benefits of technological progress remain a popular explanation for the transformation of societies, and many people view the application of technology as the solution to continuing world problems. Nevertheless, the progress theory of cultural transformation began to be seriously questioned by anthropologists during the twentieth century. These questions were raised in part by

studies of hunting and gathering societies that suggested that life as a nomadic hunter and gatherer was not nearly as harsh and dangerous as had been supposed. In fact, some anthropologists suggested that hunting and gathering represented something of a lost paradise.

Life among Hunter-Gatherers: The Hadza and the Ju/wasi

In the 1960s, James Woodburn studied the Hadza, a small group of nomadic hunters and gatherers in Tanzania, eastern Africa. Hunters and gatherers are often depicted as living on the verge of starvation, but Woodburn found the Hadza area rich in food and resources. Wild game such as elephant, giraffe, zebra, and gazelle was plentiful. Plant foods—roots, berries, and fruit—were also abundant for those who knew where to look and constituted about 80 percent of the Hadza diet. The Hadza spent about two hours a day obtaining food.

Hadza women were responsible for almost all the plant food gathered, whereas hunting was exclusively a male activity. The men hunted with bows and poisoned arrows, and, when Woodburn lived among them, used no guns, spears, or traps. Although the Hadza considered only meat as proper food and may have said they were hungry when there was no meat, there was, in fact, plenty of food available. According to Woodburn, it was almost inconceivable for the Hadza to go hungry. Plant food was so plentiful that the Hadza made no attempt to preserve it. Physicians who examined Hadza children found them in good health by tropical standards, and Woodburn says that from a nutritional point of view, the Hadza were better off than their agricultural neighbors.

The Ju/wasi* (pronounced zhut-wasi) of the Kalahari Desert, in Namibia in southwest Africa, are another hunting and gathering society that has contributed extensively to what anthropologists have learned about small-scale societies. Lorna Marshall, assisted by her children Elizabeth and John, began research among the Ju/wasi in the 1950s. Their work, along with later studies by Richard Lee and others, has provided us with a good description of Ju/wasi hunting and gathering activities.

Ju/wasi groups lived around waterholes, from which they would wander as far as six miles in search of plant and animal foods. Their groups numbered from 30 to 40 people during the rainy season when waterholes were full and plentiful and increased to 100 to 200 during the dry season when only larger holes retained water. Richard Lee found that the food quest was constant among the Ju/wasi. They did little food processing, so they had to get food supplies every third or fourth day. Vegetable foods constituted 60 to 80 percent of the diet, and women gathered most of it, producing two to three times as much as men.Though they had to get food every few days, it did not take the Ju/wasi much time. In a careful study of Ju/wasi work habits, Lee found that they spent less than 20 hours per week gathering food.

*The terms that people use to refer to themselves are often different from those assigned by others. Unfortunately, the latter sometimes becomes more widely accepted than the former. The Ju/wasi (also spelled JU/'hoansi), for example, were referred to as Bushmen by early Europeans and as !Kung by anthropologists.

The Mongongo Nut—Nutrition Facts

Serving Size 100 g

Total Fat	57g		
Saturated fat	10g		
Polyunsaturated	14g		
Monounsaturated	10g		
Protein	24g		
Calcium	193mg	Magnesium	527mg
Iron	3.7mg	Copper	2.8mg
Zinc	4mg	Vitamin B1 (Thiamine)	0.3mg
Vitamin B2 (Riboflavin)	0.2mg	Vitamin B3 (Nicotinic Acid)	0.3mg
Vitamin E	565mg		

Ju/wasi women gathering food.

Lee reports that the Ju/wasi never exhausted their food supply. The major food source was the mongongo nut, which is far more nourishing than our own breakfast cereals and which provided more than 50 percent of the Ju/wasi caloric intake. Their territory also contained more than 80 other species of edible plants, of which about 20 was regularly consumed. In addition, an occasional giraffe, antelope, or other large game, and the more usual porcupine, hare, or other small game provided meat. Their meat intake was between 175 and 200 pounds per person per year, an amount comparable to the meat consumption in developed countries.

In sum, Lee found that the environment of the Ju/wasi provided ample readily accessible food. Their diet consisted of some 2,300 calories a day, with a proper balance of protein, vitamins, and minerals. If the Ju/wasi diet was deficient in anything, it was in carbohydrates, because they ate no white bread, pasta, rice, or equivalents.

Contrary to the stereotype that hunters and gatherers struggle to obtain food, Lee shows that they in fact do not have to work very hard to make a living. Lee argues that the supposed struggle of hunter/gatherers is only an ethnocentric bias based on the assumption that our own

WHAT WOULD YOU DO?

You are the elder of a group of around 80 people. For as long as you can remember, you have lived by gathering plants and hunting game. Your territory, though small, has always been adequate to supply food for your people. But recently, there have been reports that people have had to travel farther and farther to find food. What's worse, your territory now overlaps with other nomadic groups.

Some of the younger members of the group, tired of traveling great distances and fearful of conflict with others, argue for settling down in one spot and taking advantage of wild crops. As with other hunting and gathering groups, yours knows how to plant and harvest, and there is an abundance of wild vegetables and grains that can be easily cultivated.

What will you decide to do? Will you take the advice of the younger generation and settle down? If you say yes, you need to give reasons why this is necessary in order to convince others in the group who are against the move. If you say no, you need to be able to defend your decision to the younger members of the group and explain to them the consequences of settling down.

technologically oriented society represents the pinnacle of development. But if Lee and others are correct about the ease of survival of hunter-gatherers, why did ancient groups abandon hunting and gathering for sedentary life?

The Transition to Agriculture

There is a perspective on cultural evolution that views the change from hunting and gathering to modern industrial society as a necessary evil, rather than progress. This perspective emphasizes **population density**, the number of people living in a given area. To understand this point of view, we need to examine the transition from hunting and gathering to agriculture and also explore the reasons for the change from relatively simple slash-and-burn agriculture to more complex labor-intensive irrigation agriculture.

Anthropologist Mark Cohen set out to explain why individuals or groups abandoned hunting and gathering for agriculture and why so many did so in a relatively short period of time. First, he examined the food-gathering strategies of hunting and gathering societies. Hunters and gatherers settle in a given area to collect food, and as food resources decline in one spot, they enlarge the area within which they gather. Imagine this area as a series of concentric circles. Cohen suggests that when population density in a given geographical area reached a point at which different groups began to bump into each other, or when groups found they had to travel farther and farther to get enough food to feed a growing population, they began to cultivate their own crops. According to Cohen, anthropological and archaeological evidence suggests they knew how to farm all along, but chose instead to gather crops until the labor involved in traveling to new food sources surpassed the labor involved in growing their own crops. In other words, the historical transition from hunting and gathering to simple agriculture was a consequence of population growth rather than

population density the number of people in a given geographic area

an invention that made life better. Cohen and others argue, in fact, that agriculture didn't make life better at all, but made it worse.

In most parts of the world, when societies abandoned gathering and hunting, they likely began to utilize slash-and-burn techniques. As a form of growing crops, it is highly efficient and productive. The Kuikuru, who inhabit the tropical rainforest of central Brazil, produce about two million calories per acre of land farmed per year, enough to feed two million people. Moreover, the Kuikuru work only about two hours a day.

However, swidden agriculture requires large tracts of land because after a plot is farmed for a couple of years, it must lie fallow for 20 to 30 years to allow the brush and trees to grow back so it can be used again. If the population and the amount of land needed to feed it both increase, plots must be used more frequently, perhaps every five or ten years. But when land is cultivated more frequently, the yield per acre declines. Thus, swidden agriculture is efficient only if the population and the amount of land available remain constant.

Farmland may become scarce not only because of increasing population, but also because of environmental changes or the encroachment of other groups. New agricultural techniques must then be developed to increase the yield of available land. The digging stick may be replaced with the plow, or irrigation systems may be devised, and each of these developments requires a great deal of labor. In other words, the more food the group needs to produce, the more complex is the technology needed to produce it; and the more complex the technology, the greater is the amount of work involved.

Relationships among land, labor, population, and methods of agriculture are shown in Tables 2.2 and 2.3. Table 2.2 indicates that the amount of labor required to produce a harvest increases with the complexity of agricultural techniques. For example, it requires up to ten times more labor to produce a harvest with irrigation agriculture than it does to produce one with swidden agriculture.

Then why abandon swidden agriculture? Because there is not enough land to support the population. Table 2.3 lists the amount of land needed to feed 100 families using different agricultural methods. For example, as little as 90 acres of land are required to feed 100 families with irrigation, whereas 3,000 acres are needed with swidden agriculture. If a group has enough land, it might as well keep its farming methods simple. The history of humankind, however, has in fact been marked by an increase in population and an increase in the ratio of people to land.

Hunter-gatherers settle in one area to collect food. As resources decline, or as population increases, they enlarge the area in which they search for food.

According to Robert L. Carneiro, an increase in the number of people relative to available land creates two problems. First, if there are more people than there is available land, conflict may arise between people vying for the available resources. Second, if a growing population decides to intensify farming methods, there is a need for greater societal organization. Irrigation agriculture, for example, requires the digging of ditches, the building of water pumps, and the coordination of harvests. Thus, whether a society deals with an increasing ratio between land and people by intensifying efforts to produce more food or it addresses the problem by denying some people access to the necessary resources, the groundwork is laid for the emergence of a stratified society and the need for a state organization.

The views of anthropologists such as Cohen and Carneiro suggest that the evolution of societies from hunting and gathering to more labor-intensive methods of agriculture was not a matter of choice. Slash-and-burn agriculture wasn't easier than hunting and gathering, and plow-and-irrigation agriculture wasn't more efficient than slash-and-burn agriculture. Instead, the changes in farming method represented necessities brought about by an increase in population density. This in turn created the need for more formal and elaborate political and social institutions, both to organize labor and to maintain order among more and more people.

If we conclude (and not all anthropologists do) that the transition from hunting and gathering to complex agriculture does not represent progress, isn't it at least safe to say that modern agricultural techniques are vastly superior to those of small-scale, tribal societies? Those who defend this view point out that in the United States, only 1 calorie of human energy is needed to produce 210 calories of food, whereas hunter-gatherers produce fewer than 10 calories of food for every calorie they expend.

Others argue that these figures are deceptive. While modern farming vastly decreases the amount of human labor required to produce food, it dramatically increases the amount of nonhuman energy needed. From that perspective, we expend 1 calorie of nonhuman energy in the form of nonrenewable fossil fuels (e.g., oil and coal) for every 8 calories of food.

Producing Potato Calories

To illustrate this point, John H. Bodley compares the production of sweet potatoes in New Guinea with potato production in the United States. In New Guinea, people cultivate sweet potatoes by slash-and-burn agriculture; plots of land are burned, cleared, and planted with digging sticks. The people use only 10 percent of the arable land, and there is no danger of resource depletion. With their agricultural techniques, New Guinea farmers can produce about 5 million calories per acre.

American potato farms produce more than twice as many calories, about 12 million, per acre. However, as Bodley points out, in addition to human energy, vast amounts of nonhuman energy are expended. Chemicals must be applied to maintain soil conditions and to control insects and fungus. For example, in the state of Washington in the 1960s, 60 percent of potato acreage was airplane-sprayed five to nine times each season to control insects; another 40 percent was treated for weeds. In 1969, 36,000 tons of fertilizer were applied to 62,500 acres—more than 1,000 pounds per acre. These farms also need energy in the form of fuel for specialized machines.

Americans must also deal with distribution costs, which are minimal in traditional cultures, where most households consume what they produce. In modern industrial socie-ties, where 95 percent of the population is concentrated in or around urban centers, the energy expended in distributing the food now exceeds the energy expended in producing it. Taking the food-producing process as a whole—the manufacture and distribution of farm machinery, trucks, and fertilizer; irrigation projects; food processing; packaging; transportation; manufacturing of trucks;

TABLE 2.2

DAYS OF LABOR PER ACRE PER HARVEST BY TYPE OF AGRICULTURE

Type of Agriculture	Days of Labor per Acre
Advanced swidden	18–25
Plow cultivation	20
Hoe cultivation	58
Irrigation agriculture	90–178

Source: Data from Eric R. Wolf, *Peasants* (Englewood Cliffs, NJ: Prentice Hall, 1966).

TABLE 2.3

LAND NEEDED TO FEED 100 FAMILIES USING DIFFERENT AGRICULTURAL METHODS

Agricultural Method	Number of Acres Needed to Feed 100 Families
Swidden agriculture	3,000*
Swidden with garden plots	1,600*
Irrigation agriculture	90–200

*Includes unworked land that must be allowed to lie fallow to regain fertility.

Source: Data from Eric R. Wolf, *Peasants* (Englewood Cliffs, NJ: Prentice Hall, 1966).

MORE THAN 99 CENTS

John Bodley illustrates the wastefulness and inefficiency of modern agricultural practice by examining the production of potato chips, which the average American eats 4.6 pounds of per year. Roughly half of the potatoes grown in the United States are sold raw; the rest are processed into products such as instant mashed potatoes, frozen french fries, and, of course, potato chips. All potatoes undergo significant processing after harvest. They are mechanically washed, chemically sprayed to inhibit sprouting, colored and waxed to increase consumer appeal, and transported and stored under controlled conditions. Potatoes destined to become chips, meanwhile, are sprayed weeks before harvest in order to kill their stems. Otherwise, the starch buildup would produce unappealing (but perfectly edible) dark chips. These are also chemically treated to prevent darkening after being peeled and sliced, salts and preservatives are added in the cooking process, and, finally, the end product is packaged in special containers and shipped. Manufacturers also incur additional marketing costs to convince consumers to buy the chips. In short, the sum of the human and nonhuman energy required to convert a potato into a potato chip is far greater than the energy expended in New Guinea to produce a more nutritious sweet potato.

industrial and domestic food preparation; and refrigeration—Americans expend 8 to 12 calories of energy to produce a single calorie of food!

QUESTION 2.2

Why are some societies more industrially advanced than others?

The Rich and the Poor

Even if we agree that hunters and gatherers don't struggle for food and that simpler forms of agriculture are more efficient than modern techniques, we still have not explained the vast divisions in the modern world between rich and poor. The economic disparities in the world economy can be illustrated through a pyramid (see Figure 2.1). The top level consists of roughly 1 billion people who live in developed nations and make more than $20,000 annually. The bottom tier, meanwhile, consists of roughly 4 billion people who make less than $2,000 per year.

If progress is not the reason, why do most people in the industrial world enjoy a standard of living superior to those in underdeveloped countries? Trying to answer

FIGURE 2.1

THE GLOBAL ECONOMIC PYRAMID

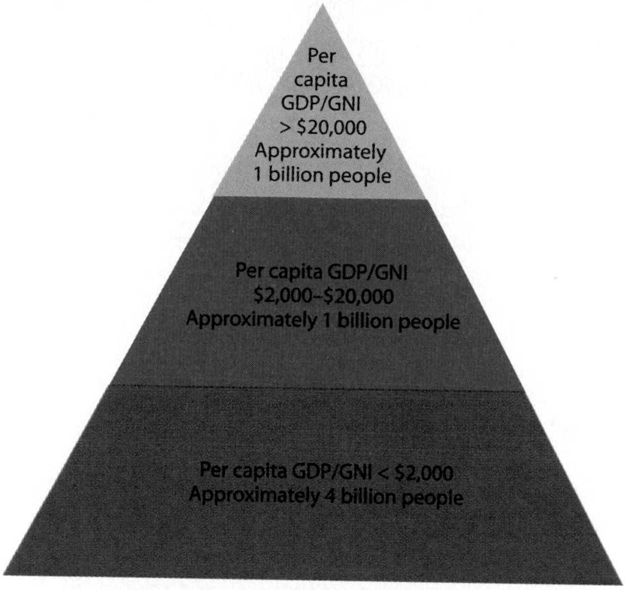

Per capita GDP/GNI > $20,000
Approximately 1 billion people

Per capita GDP/GNI $2,000–$20,000
Approximately 1 billion people

Per capita GDP/GNI < $2,000
Approximately 4 billion people

Source: C. K. Prahalad and S. Hart, "The fortune at the bottom of the pyramid," *Strategy + Business 26* (2002): 54–67; and S. Hart, *Capitalism at the Crossroads* (Philadelphia: Wharton School Publishing, 2005), 111.

these questions requires a complex discussion of world history during the past 300 years. But we can learn a lot from the story of the expansion of one industry, in one country, during one phase of its development—the textile industry in England in the last half of the eighteenth and first half of the nineteenth century.

Prior to the **Industrial Revolution** in Europe, China was arguably the richest country in the world, as gold and silver taken from the mines of South America by the Spanish and Portuguese were funneled into China to pay for silks, spices, teas, and luxury goods. India was developing a thriving cotton textile industry by selling calicoes in Europe. Wealthy states had developed in western Africa, and Islamic traders thrived from Africa into Southeast Asia. On the other hand, seventeenth-century England was a largely rural and agricultural country. Even by 1700, only 13 percent of the population lived in towns of 5,000 or more people. England, however, had long enjoyed a thriving trade in textile goods, most notably raw wool and inexpensive wool textiles.

Early on, textile production was largely a handicraft industry, and most steps in the production of wool cloth, from cutting and degreasing the wool to dyeing and spinning the thread to weaving the cloth, were in the hands of rural families or small cooperatives. The finished product would be sold at a local market or fair or, more often, sold to urban-based merchants or traders for resale.

Though the trade in home-produced textiles was profitable for all, traders and merchants discovered that they needed more control over the type, quantity, and quality of cloth produced by spinners and weavers. The merchants' first solution to this problem was the **"putting out" system**, in which merchants supplied weavers with materials and required them to produce cloth of the desired type. The merchants delivered the supplies and tools and picked up the finished products, generally paying the producers for each piece.

Beginning in the eighteenth century, English merchants began to transform the putting-out system into a **factory system** by bringing spinners, weavers, and others together into one production facility. For many reasons, merchants were not particularly anxious about investing in factories. Profits from manufacture were not nearly as great as profits from trade, especially long-distance exchange. Moreover, removing people from the home-based family to urban-based factories required new mechanisms of discipline and control, a fact that explains why early factories were modeled on penal workhouses and prisons. Finally, the entrepreneur, who previously could halt putting out when demand slackened, now had to keep the factories busy to pay for the investment in buildings and technology and, consequently, had to create demands for products.

In spite of these problems, investing in manufacturing was attractive because subsidies and laws ensured cheap labor. Peasant farmers, who were forced off their land by laws supporting large farms, represented an accessible labor force. In addition, because there were no laws on minimum wage or child labor, factory owners could make use of the cheap labor of women and children. By 1834 children under 13 represented 13 percent of the British cotton industry, and by 1838 only 23 percent of textile

Industrial Revolution a period of European history, generally identified as occurring in the late eighteenth century, marked by a shift in production from agriculture to industrial goods, urbanization, and the factory system

"putting out" system a means of production, common in the sixteenth and seventeenth centuries and surviving today, in which a manufacturer or merchant supplies the materials and sometimes the tools to workers, who produce the goods in their own homes

factory system a system of production associated with the Industrial Revolution and characterized by the concentration of labor and machines in specific places

factory workers in England were adult men. In addition, government also played a major role in creating and defending overseas markets, as well as sources of raw materials such as cotton.

The growth of the textile industry had numerous effects. For example, it fueled the growth of cities—by 1800 a quarter of the English population lived in towns of 5,000 or more, and Manchester, a center of textile manufacture, grew from 24,000 inhabitants in 1773 to more than 250,000 by 1851. Moreover, factories spurred the development of technology. Mechanization of the textile industry began in earnest in 1733 with John Kay's flying shuttle, which doubled the weavers' output. But because spinners could not keep up with the need for thread for the new looms, bottlenecks developed. To meet this need, James Hargreaves introduced the spinning jenny in 1765. In 1769 Richard Arkwright invented the water frame, and then in 1779 Samuel Crompton developed the spinning mule, which combined features of the water frame and the jenny. Finally, in 1790, steam power was added to the production process. These inventions produced a staggering increase in textile production. A hand spinner in eighteenth century India took more than 50,000 hours to process 100 pounds of cotton into thread; in England, Crompton's mule reduced that to 2,000 hours, and by 1795, power-assisted mules reduced this time still further to 300 hours. By 1825 it took only 135 hours to process 100 pounds of cotton.

The growth of the textile industry obviously produced great wealth and employed millions of workers. It helped transform England into the wealthiest country in the world. But the increase in technology and production created two problems: Where was the market for all these textile products to be found, and where were the raw materials—notably the cotton—to come from?

Some historians point to the large domestic market available to English textile producers in the wake of the growth of the English population from 6 million in 1700 to 9 million in 1800. Moreover, English textile manufacturers were able to sell much of their product in Europe and the growing markets of the Americas. But the competition was fierce, as the Netherlands, France and Spain were also striving for overseas markets. This competition, along with the growing military superiority of Western Europe, often had dire consequences for once prosperous industries in other parts of the world. The story of textiles in India is instructive.

The British in India

During the 15th and 16th centuries, India was a major trading country that had extensive trade networks reaching Europe, the Islamic world and China. In 1690, the British government granted a monopoly in East Asian trade to the British East India Company. A relative latecomer to trade in India, it established a trade center in Bengal, in the city of Calcutta. The British East India Company soon had some 150 posts trading in India for fine silks, cotton, sugar, rice, saltpeter, indigo, and opium.

In the 1750s the British provoked the rulers of Bengal to war, defeating them conclusively in 1757. In the aftermath, the English plundered the state treasury for nearly 5 million pounds and gained control of 10,000 Bengali weavers. By 1765, the British East India Company had become the civil administrator of Bengal. It promptly increased the tax burden on peasants and artisans, leading to major famines in 1770 and 1783. From its base in Bengal, moreover, the company gradually began to extend its control over much of the Indian subcontinent.

Prior to the British military takeover, India produced cloth that was cheaper and better than English textiles. In fact, Indian cotton and calicoes were the craze of Europe. To meet this competitive challenge, the British government prohibited the British East India Company from importing Indian calicoes into England. English manufacturers took advantage by producing copies of popular Indian textiles for sale both in England and abroad. In addition, India was required to admit English manufacturers free of tariffs. These actions effectively destroyed what had been a thriving Indian textile industry.

The British East India Company also had considerable impact on China. The British, and Western European

A Chinese opium den.

nations in general, had a problem with trade into China. Chinese products, notably tea, were in high demand in Europe, but the Chinese demand for European products was quite low. There was demand in China for opium, however, and by 1773 the British East India Company had a monopoly over opium sales. Though illegal, the Chinese government was incapable of stopping smuggling, an activity that was hugely profitable for British, American, and French merchants. When the Chinese government tried to enforce the ban on opium by seizing British warehouses in Canton, the British responded with military force and effectively coerced the Chinese government into not enforcing the opium laws. Moreover, the British demanded and received additional trading rights into China, further opening a market not only for opium but for textiles as well.

British trade activity in India and China had three results. First, it reversed the flow of money between China and the rest of the world. During the first decade of the nineteenth century, China had a trade surplus of 26 million silver dollars. By the third decade, it had a trade deficit of 34 million dollars. Second, it is estimated that by the end of the nineteenth century one out of every ten people in China was addicted to opium. Finally, exports of cotton textiles from England to India and China increased from 6 percent of total British exports in 1815 to 22 percent in 1840, 31 percent in 1850, and more than 50 percent after 1873.

Cotton, Slavery, and the Cherokee Removal

Cotton and the growth of the textile industry in England figure not only in the story India and China, but also in the story of slavery and the removal of thousands of Native Americans from their homeland. The British were able to sell raw Indian cotton to China, but Indian cotton was not acceptable to European and American markets. Indian cotton produced a shorter fiber, whereas cotton produced elsewhere, notably in Egypt and the American South, produced a longer, more desirable fiber. But cotton production in the Americas was labor intensive and, to be profitable, required slave labor.

Slavery was not created solely by the need for cotton, but rather by the economic expansion and demands of European trade from the 15th to 19th centuries. Spanish silver mines, French sugar mills, and American cotton plantations all had great demand for labor, and this demand was met largely by the slave trade. From 1451 to 1600, some 275,000 slaves were sent from Africa to Europe and America. During the seventeenth century, nearly 1,341,000 slaves were sent, and from 1701 to 1810 more than 6 million people were forcibly exported from Africa.

The production of cotton with slave labor might be said to have fueled the Industrial Revolution in the United States. Between 1815 and 1860, raw cotton constituted half the value of domestic exports from the United States.

Part of the reason for the growth of the American cotton industry was Eli Whitney's cotton gin, an invention that easily separated the seeds from raw cotton fiber. It allowed a person to clean 50 pounds of cotton in the time it had previously taken to clean 1 pound. As a consequence, American cotton production increased enormously, from 3,000 bales in 1790 to 178,000 bales in 1810, 732,000 in 1830, and 4.5 million in 1860. But to be competitive, American cotton production required cheap labor, and slave labor cost half the price of wage labor.

By 1807, half of England's cotton imports came from the United States. While the British demand for American cotton was not the cause of slavery, it ensured

© BETTMANN/CORBIS / © AMANDA ROHDE/ISTOCKPHOTO.COM

its persistence in the United States into the second half of the nineteenth century. Between 1790 and 1860, some 835,000 slaves were moved from Maryland, Virginia, and the Carolinas to Alabama, Louisiana, Mississippi, and Texas in one of the largest forced migrations of all time. But it was not the only forced migration instigated by the world demand for cotton. It was also a driving force behind the forced removal of Native American groups.

The growth of the textile industry in England produced great wealth for some people but, in the process, destroyed textile manufacturing in India, led to the colonization of India and China, extended slavery in the United States, drained Africa of labor, and led to the forced removal of Native American tribes.

We must also consider that England was not the only producer of textiles or the only country seeking to open and control overseas markets. We must remember, too, that textiles represented only one of many industries of Western Europe that required raw materials and new markets. New demands for sugar, cocoa, palm oil, tobacco, and coffee also led to the conversion of millions of acres of land around the world from subsistence farms to cash crops, turning self-sufficient peasant farmers into dependent wage laborers. And, finally, we must remember that we have examined only a brief period of time. Looking at the bigger picture, we begin to understand why the problems of the so-called nonindustrial nations are due less to their own shortcomings than to the exploitative activities of others.

Why are some cultures wealthier than others? Consider the example of the Cherokees. The first threat to their territory, which stretched from North Carolina to Georgia, came in 1802, when Thomas Jefferson enacted the Georgia Compact. In order to persuade southeastern states to give up claims to western territory, the compact granted them land held by southeastern Native American tribes, including the Cherokees. But the tribes fought removal by embarking on a modernization plan. Within decades, the Cherokees had constructed plantations and had their own newspaper, schools, and alphabet.

The Cherokee lobbied Congress extensively to repeal the Georgia Compact, but to no avail. Andrew Jackson, who had made Indian removal one of the cornerstones of his presidential campaign of 1828, signed the final order, and the army was sent in to evict the population. White farmers using black slaves took over thousands of acres of what had been Cherokee land and converted much of them to cotton production. Thus, white farmers using Native American land and African labor to produce cotton for the English and American textile industries created much of the future wealth of the young American republic.

© UYEN LE/ISTOCKPHOTO.COM

QUESTION 2.3

Why don't poor countries modernize and develop in the same way as wealthier countries?

Economic Development

The Industrial Revolution radically transformed the lives of people in Western Europe and the United States, as the vast majority of the population went from being farmers to laborers. In most cases this was not a matter of choice; people began to sell their labor, not because wage labor offered a better life, but because they no longer possessed land on which to secure a livelihood.

Though there have been some notable periods of downturn, overall, the rate of economic growth and technological advancement has been astounding, resulting in a dramatic improvement in the standard of living of most people in Western countries. People in developing nations, meanwhile, saw their standard of living decline as their countries fell under the influence of Western powers. As these countries gained independence, they tried to emulate the standard of living of the industrial powers. This led to the push for what became known as **economic development**.

President Harry S. Truman first developed the idea of economic development in his inaugural address in 1949. The assumption was that nonindustrial countries of the world were backward and needed to develop, *development* being largely a code word for "westernized." This was going to be done to improve people's lives. As one United Nations report put it,

> There is a sense in which rapid economic progress is impossible without painful adjustments. Ancient philosophies have to be scrapped; old social institutions have to disintegrate; bonds of caste, creed and race have to burst; and large numbers of persons who cannot keep up with progress have to have their expectations of comfortable life frustrated. (1951, 15)

An unprecedented will to know everything about developing nations flourished, and these countries witnessed a massive landing of experts, each in charge of investigating, measuring, and theorizing about this or that aspect of society. Arturo Escobar suggests that these experts conceived of social life as a technical problem that could be entrusted to development professionals, consisting largely of economists and agricultural experts allegedly qualified for the task.

The idea of economic development was based on three key assumptions: (1) economic growth and development are the solution to national as well as global problems; (2) global economic integration will contribute to solving global ecological and social problems; and (3) foreign assistance to undeveloped countries will make things better. Countries that wanted to develop looked for loans and investments from other countries to create an industrial infrastructure and train workers. The loans would allow underdeveloped countries to produce things that people in developed countries didn't produce themselves—cash crops such as cotton, sugar, palm oil, tobacco, coffee, and cocoa, and natural resources such as oil, metal ores, and lumber. While this theory of economic development was not new, what was different during the last half of the 20th century was the degree of apparent support offered by wealthy nations. One major Western institution that promoted economic development was the **World Bank**.

economic development the term used to identify an increase in the level of technology and, by some, the standard of living of a population. Others view it as an ideology based on three key assumptions: (1) that economic growth and development are the solution to national as well as global problems; (2) that global economic integration will contribute to solving global ecological and social problems; and (3) that foreign assistance to undeveloped countries will make things better

World Bank originally called the Bank for Reconstruction and Development, one of the institutions created at the Bretton Woods, New Hampshire, meeting in 1944 of Allied nations; functions as a lending institution to nations largely for projects related to economic development

CASE: Doing It Better

When development professionals fail to understand the culture and values of the people they are trying to help, the consequences are disastrous.

© STAFFAN WIDSTRAND/CORBIS

The Mackenzie Delta, an area in the western Canadian Arctic, has been the home of Inuit, Metis, and Dene peoples for centuries. After World War II, the Canadian government wanted to develop the area in order to extract oil, gas, and mineral reserves. The government also wanted to prepare indigenous peoples for "modern" life through schooling and wage labor. Planning, however, was top down, with little or no participation from the people themselves.

The centerpiece of the modernization plan was the construction of a large-scale "science-town" called Inuvik that was to house a school, a commercial and service center, and a hospital. The government planners encouraged the establishment of various businesses in the town, including oil companies, hotels, and restaurants.

As Alexander M. Ervin describes it, the town had a profoundly negative impact on the people of the Mackenzie Delta. Of 5,000 inhabitants, only 150 lived off the land. Half the population were "southerners," transient workers from southern Canada who were paid generous salaries and allowances to encourage them to resettle, if only for a short time, in the Arctic. Few of the indigenous people were employed after the initial building phase, and they were overwhelmed by the social and economic advantages of the southerners. Southerners rarely interacted with the natives, and relations became hostile. School curricula, rather than being designed for northern youth, were modeled after programs in southern urban schools. This caused high dropout rates, and the alienation of young people was marked by a dramatic increase in petty crimes and assaults. Native women who had children with transient whites were stigmatized, and conflict arose between families that had a steady income and those dependent on government subsidies. The stress was evident also in high rates of alcohol consumption and crimes such as assault, theft, and wife battering, all associated with alcohol. Clearly the optimism of the government that the new town would better the lives of the native peoples was misplaced.

So what went wrong? There was no consultation with the indigenous people regarding the changes. Everything was planned and implemented by outsiders who had preexisting notions about what would be good for indigenous people. Nobody considered the complex interactions among family structure, cultural values, economics, education, and new residents. No one attempted to integrate local knowledge into the planning process. And no one considered the unintended consequences of the changes.

Contrast this with an agricultural project designed by anthropologist Ronald Nigh in Mexico. Like other Central American nations, Mexico

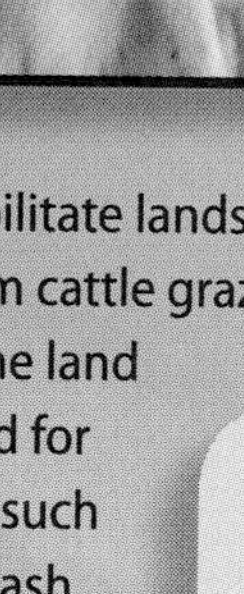

has lost vast amounts of its rainforest—more than 40,000 square miles since the beginning of the twentieth century. Though much of the deforested land was devoted to animal pastures, more than 50 percent of the population never consumes animal products.

According to Nigh, the destruction of the rainforest is the result of a **factory model** of agriculture, the production of a single product in as short a time as possible. It is technologically intensive and environmentally damaging. In Central America, the factory model of cattle raising has required clearing large tracts of land with fire and herbicides and reseeding with grasses that are not well suited to the environment. The result is degradation of the land by uncontrolled grazing and its eventual abandonment and return to secondary vegetation.

In his work, Nigh uses an **agroecological approach** that incorporates indigenous farming techniques, which are far more productive and less damaging to the environment than factory farming. An agroecological approach produces multiple crops and animals, rather than a single crop as in the factory model. This approach to production creates a system that enhances regeneration of land, flora, and fauna.

As an example, consider how the Maya grow corn in the rainforest. The farmers practice swidden agriculture, clearing a site, growing corn there for five to eight years, and then moving onto another site. At first glance, these sites may look identical to land devastated and abandoned by cattle ranchers, but Mayan farmers do not abandon the sites. They continue to work the land so that native plant and animal life will return, eventually creating a highly productive space. The agroecological model, drawing as it does on indigenous systems developed over centuries, creates an ecologically sustainable system of production modeled after natural systems.

Nigh says that a similar model, emphasizing diversity, should be used to rehabilitate lands damaged from cattle grazing. One area of the land would be used for annual crops, such as corn or squash. Another area can be used for fruit trees and forage. And another can be devoted to intensive grazing using selected animal breeds and grasses. Intensive grazing, according to Nigh, frees up rainforest land that should never have been converted to pasture to begin with. He also maintains that by using organic fertilizers and controlled grazing, it is possible to recover aquatic areas and take advantage of water resources such as fish, mollusks, turtles, and birds.

Development projects might begin with good intentions, but they can quickly devolve into ethnocentric, socially-damaging institutions. How, then, can development projects provide benefits to everyone involved? As the examples show, an anthropological perspective that carefully considers the cultures and values of indigenous people will go a long way to ease the potential pains of development.

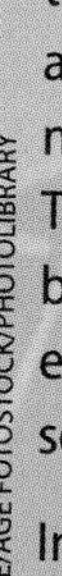

factory model an energy-intensive, ecologically damaging form of agriculture intended to grow or raise as many crops or livestock as possible in the shortest amount of time

agroecological approach agricultural methods that incorporate indigenous practices of food production that preserve the environment along with contemporary agricultural research

The World Bank was created in 1944 in Bretton Woods, New Hampshire, at a meeting of the nations allied against the Germans, Japanese, and Italians. Their task was to plan the economic reconstruction of countries devastated by World War II and develop a postwar plan for worldwide economic and monetary stability. Originally known as the International Bank for Reconstruction and Development, the World Bank was to be funded by donations from member nations, largely in the form of loan guarantees. The bank would then lend money to governments for specific projects—highways, dams, power plants, factories, and the like—with requirements for repayment over a set period of time. The bank's charter also specified that loans must be made without any regard for political or noneconomic factors, and that the bank must not interfere in the political affairs of any member or debtor nation.

The World Bank made its first loans in 1946 to European countries rebuilding after World War II. Soon after, the World Bank began making huge loans to countries such as Brazil, India, and Indonesia that were intended to transform their economies, bring wealth, and alleviate poverty. Moreover, once the World Bank approved loans, private banks would often follow. While these loans were intended to bring economic development, many argue that they in fact increased poverty and led to rampant environmental devastation in developing nations. How, in spite of apparently good intentions, could this happen?

The Case of Brazil

Brazil has been a major recipient of World Bank loans. In the 1960s, the government of Brazil made a conscious decision to industrialize. With loans from the World Bank, other lending institutions, and private investors, Brazil built dams, roads, factories, and modernized agriculture, becoming a world leader in the

© DIGITAL VISION/GETTY IMAGES / © MIKE BENTLEY/ISTOCKPHOTO.COM

export of crops such as soybeans. The economy surged ahead, and Brazil became a model of modern industrialization. Factories created jobs, and people flocked to the cities for employment as Brazil's cities began to rival those in the West.

But there was a downside: to repay the loans, Brazil needed to earn foreign income. Consequently, landowners were encouraged to expand the production of cash crops that could be sold in the United States and Europe. Because these areas already produced more than enough food, Brazilian farmers turned to soybeans, sisal, sugar, cocoa, and coffee. These products required modern farming techniques and lots of land, forcing small farmers off their land in search for jobs that, for the most part, did not exist. Those who found jobs on large farms were paid so little that they were not able to purchase the food that they had previously grown themselves on their small plots. And while the production of some food items, such as beef, did increase, most of it was exported, since poor Brazilians could not pay as much as relatively wealthy Americans and Europeans could.

To make matters worse, in the mid-1980s Brazil and other debtor countries discovered that they could not keep up their payments and threatened to default on their loans. To help avoid default, the World Bank allowed these countries to renegotiate their loans, but with the condition that they had to make drastic cuts in government spending on public education, welfare, housing, and health. These cutbacks resulted in still greater hardships for the poorest portion of the population.

Through its economic development program, Brazil has increased its total wealth, and some people have become very rich. But it is estimated that more than 40 percent of Brazil's population is living in poverty. And Brazil is not unique, as most of Central and South America, Africa, and Southeast Asia followed the same formula for development and experienced similar increases in poverty and hunger for a majority of their people.

Are the people of the world better off now than they were before the industrial revolution? The answer depends on who you are. If you are fortunate enough to live and work in one of the wealthy countries of the world, you are likely to be materially better off than your counterpart of five centuries ago. If you are a laborer or small farmer in one of the poorer countries, or one of the millions of landless and unemployed, it is hard to see how you are better off than your counterpart of centuries past.

Illness and Inequality

Even if the economic changes of the past two centuries have not improved the lives of many people, can't we at least assume that some technologies, notably medical technologies, have improved the lives of virtually everyone? To answer this question, we need to examine two things. First we have to ask whether or not we have progressed in our ability to treat disease. Second, we have to ask whether or not we fully understand the traditional medical techniques that modern medicine has sought to replace.

One of the supposed triumphs of modern society is the treatment and cure of disease. Life expectancy has more than doubled in the twentieth century—in 1900, world life expectancy was approximately 30 years; in 2000, it was 63 years. Antibiotics save millions each year from death, and modern diagnostic methods and equipment allow medical practitioners to identify the onset of disease more easily. Yet the progress that we often take for granted is not available to all. In fact, the single most important determinant of a country's ability to protect its citizens from disease is the degree of economic equality.

In developing countries, infectious disease is responsible for 42 percent of all deaths, compared to just 1.2 percent in industrial countries. Around the world, 40 percent of all deaths are caused by environmental factors, particularly organic and chemical pollutants. These pollutants are far more deadly in poorer countries where, for example, 1.2 billion people lack clean, safe water. Your income determines your chances of coming into contact with a deadly pollutant. This is true even in the United States, where three out of four hazardous landfills in southern states were located primarily in African American communities, though African Americans represent only 20 percent of the population.

pathogen an infectious agent such as a bacterium or a virus that can cause disease

vector when referring to disease, an organism, such as a mosquito, tick, flea, or snail, that can transmit disease to another animal

We can perhaps better judge the extent to which we have "progressed" by examining what it takes for us to die of an infectious disease. At least four things have to happen: first, we have to come into contact with some **pathogen** or **vector** that carries a disease. Second, the pathogen must be virulent—that is, it must be able to kill us. Third, if we come into contact with a deadly pathogen, it must evade our body's immune system. Finally, the pathogen must be able to circumvent whatever measures our society has developed to prevent it from doing harm. As we will see, our chances of dying are affected at every step by social and cultural patterns, particularly by the degree of economic and social inequality.

First, cultural complexity has served to increase our exposure to infectious agents. Large, permanent settlements attract and sustain vermin such as rats and fleas, which serve as hosts to microorganisms and ensure their survival and spread. Permanent settlements also result in the buildup of human wastes. Sedentary agriculture requires altering the landscape in ways that can increase the incidence of disease. Schistosomiasis, for example, is a disease caused by worms or snails that thrive in irrigation ditches. The domestication of animals such as dogs, cats, cattle, and pigs increases contact between people and disease-causing microorganisms. The requirements of large populations for the storage and processing of food also increases the likelihood of the survival and spread of disease-causing agents. Coming into contact with an infectious pathogen need not be enough to kill; the pathogen must be deadly. But this also depends on your social and cultural situation and your income. Generally it is not to the advantage of pathogens—viruses, bacteria, parasites—to kill their hosts; it is better for the pathogen to allow its host to live and supply nutrients. However, if the pathogen does not need its host in order to survive, it can evolve into a more deadly form. This is the case with waterborne infections. Pathogens that spread by contaminated water can survive regardless of how sick their host becomes, and by reproducing extensively in their host, they make it more likely that they can contaminate water supplies through the laundry or bodily wastes. Thus, you are far more likely to contact a deadly disease if you do not have access to clean and treated water.

Even if you come into contact with a deadly pathogen, your immune system is designed to prevent it from killing you. However, the potency of your immune system is clearly a function of diet, and diet is largely determined by income level. In this respect, we have not progressed. In 1950, 20 percent of the world's population (500 million people) was malnourished. Today some 50 percent (3 billion) is malnourished. Insufficient food is one of the main factors that increase the likelihood of immune system failure.

Finally, even if our immune system fails to repel an infectious pathogen, societies do develop methods to cure illnesses. And there is little doubt that the discovery of cures to infectious disease marks one of the great success stories of modern culture. Unfortunately, access to these cures is determined largely by the degree of economic inequality in a country, not by its absolute wealth. For example, the United States, the wealthiest country in the world, ranks 38th in the world in life expectancy. Not coincidentally, the United States has the largest income gap of any industrialized country. Japan, which has the lowest gap between rich and poor, also has the highest life expectancy, in spite of having triple the cigarette usage of the United States.

In sum, although we have indeed made dramatic progress in understanding and curing infectious disease, we have made no progress and, in fact, have regressed in our ability to provide access to these cures. At the same time, we have increased global exposure to environmental pollutants and infectious pathogens.

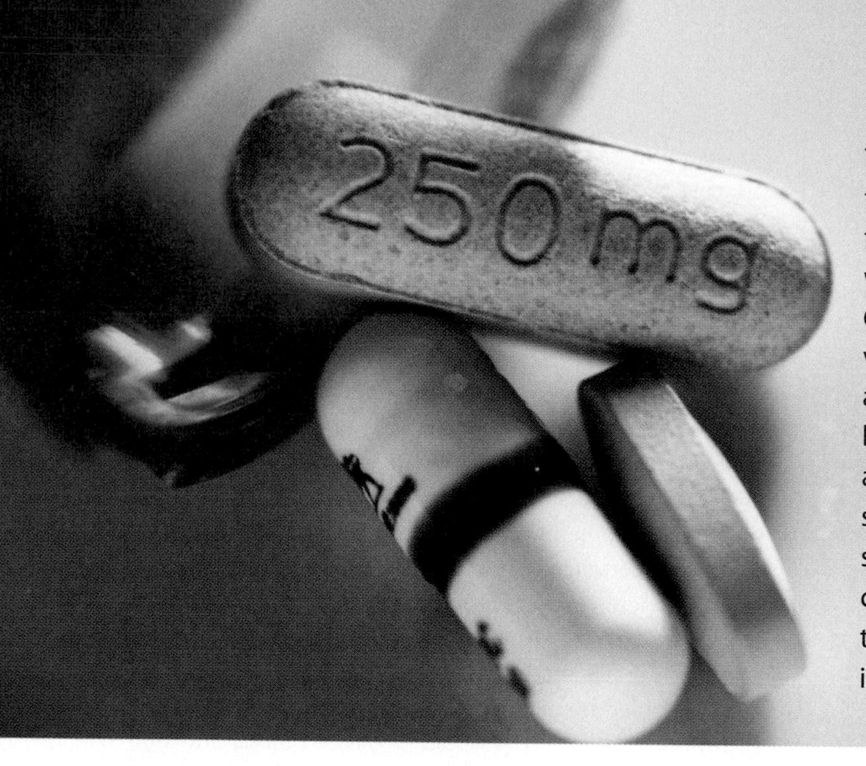

The relationship between economics and access to cures is most evident with HIV/AIDS. According to the United Nations, about 33.4 million people were infected with HIV as of 2009. Of those, nearly 67% live in sub-Saharan Africa. Though there is no vaccine, treatment with a cocktail of drugs, known as Highly Active Antiretroviral Therapy (HAART) has dramatically reduced HIV-related illnesses and death. HAART therapy, however, is expensive—$10,000 to $15,000 per year. When we consider that only three countries in Africa have a per capita GDP higher than $10,000, it is obvious that this potentially life-saving treatment is completely inaccessible to those who need it most.

The Meaning of Illness

Even if we conclude that modern societies are more susceptible to contagious disease, have they not at least improved the techniques for curing illness? To answer this question, it is important to realize that the meanings members of different societies give to illness vary as much as the meanings they give to other aspects of their lives. In American society, illness is viewed as an intrusion by bacteria or viruses. Our curing techniques emphasize the elimination of these agents. Death can occur, we believe, when we have failed to eliminate them.

In many other societies, the interpretation of illness is completely different. It may be attributed to witchcraft, the belief that a witch or sorcerer can use magical power to inflict illness on another person. It may be attributed to soul loss, the belief that that the soul leaves the body. Or it may be attributed to spirit possession, the idea that a foreign spirit enters the patient and causes illness. These explanations are not mutually exclusive; the soul, for example, may flee the body as the result of witchcraft or sorcery.

Those who believe in spiritual or magical causes for illness do not believe that a witch or sorcerer strikes at random, that the soul leaves the body without cause, or that a spirit possesses just anyone. They believe that there must be a social reason for these things to occur. Witchcraft involves relationships between people; the witch voluntarily or involuntarily afflicts someone who has caused offense or breached a rule of conduct. Likewise, the soul leaves the body of a person who is having difficulty with others, or a spirit possesses a person who has not honored social obligations.

The Chewa of Malawi in southeast Africa claim that illness and death are induced by witchcraft when someone fails to observe some social norm. Whereas Americans react to illness or death by seeking the disease or accident responsible, the Chewa ask what wrong the victim has committed, with whom the victim has quarreled, or who is jealous of the victim. The Chewa explicitly recognize the connection between sorcery and social tension.

A Chewa who becomes ill consults a diviner to discover the cause of the illness. During the consultation, the patient and the diviner discuss the social roots of the illness. The diviner needs to know about the patient's relationships with kin and, if ancestral spirits may be responsible, the genealogy of the patient. Thus, Chewa medical theory, although couched in the idiom of sorcery, is a social theory of illness, not simply a supernatural one.

There is a condition in Latin America called *susto* (also known as *pasmo*, *espanto*, *perdida de la somba*) that is believed to occur when the soul has detached itself from the body. Symptoms of *susto* include restlessness, listlessness, loss of appetite, disinterest in dress or bodily appearance, loss of strength, and introversion. The onset of the illness is said to follow a fright brought on by a sudden encounter or accident, and the cure begins with a diagnostic session between the patient and a healer. After deciding what brought on the disorder, the healer coaxes the soul back into the body. The patient is then sweated, massaged, and rubbed with some object to remove the illness.

Anthropologist Arthur Rubel analyzed specific cases of *susto* and found that all cases share two characteristics. *Susto* occurs only when the patient perceives some situation as stressful, and the stress results from difficulties in social relations with specific people. In one case, a father was afflicted when he discovered he could no longer provide for his family. In another, a mother was stricken when she was not able to take proper care of her child. In every case, according to Rubel, *susto* resulted when a person did not or could not fulfill an expected social obligation.

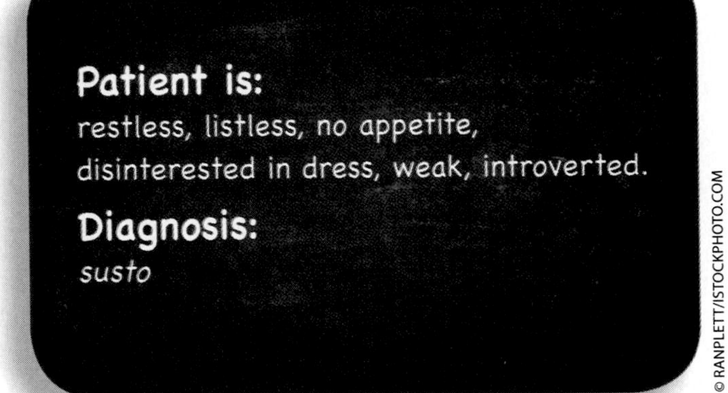

© RANPLETT/ISTOCKPHOTO.COM

These theories of illness—soul loss, spirit possession, sorcery, and witchcraft—all have one thing in common. They are all expressions of the **interpersonal theory of disease**. Simply stated, in the interpersonal theory of disease it is assumed that illness is caused not by microorganisms but by tensions or conflicts in social relations. In this view, witches, spirits, and souls are mediating agents that link a social cause—tension and conflict—to a physical result—illness or death.

If an illness is thought to occur because of social causes, then it follows that the cure must also be, at least in part, social. Therefore, a curer attempts not only to remove a spell, return the soul to the body, or remove a spiritual object that is causing illness, but also to repair the social problem. To illustrate, Victor Turner provides a look at one society, the Ndembu, an agricultural society in northwestern Zambia.

interpersonal theory of disease a view of disease in which it is assumed that illness is caused by tensions or conflicts in social relations

The Ndembu believe that a persistent or severe illness is caused either by the punitive action of some ancestral ghost or the secret malevolence of a sorcerer or witch. The ghosts punish people when they forget to make a ritual offering to their ancestors or when, as the Ndembu put it, "kin are not living well together."

To effect a cure, the Ndembu patient consults a native doctor. The doctor first inquires about the patient's social relations: Has he or she quarreled with anyone? What is the state of the patient's marital relations? Is anyone jealous of the patient? The doctor asks those with whom the patient has quarreled to participate in the ceremony, a dramatic affair with chanting and drumming, sometimes lasting for hours. People who have complaints about the patient's social behavior may come forward, and the patient may report grudges against neighbors. At the climax, the doctor may dramatically extract from the patient's body some object that could have been causing the illness.

The Ndembu recognize, at least implicitly, that social strain and stress may produce physical illness, and one way to treat illness is to treat the sources of social strain. Western medicine also recognizes the negative health effects that stress can have. Events such as the death of a spouse, the loss of a job, relocation to a new home, even holidays such as Christmas, can increase the chances of illness. These are the same kinds of events that can trigger the need for ceremonial cures in some societies. Thus, rather than viewing the healing practices of traditional societies as inferior, it makes far more sense to recognize that they focus on social stress as a cause of illness.

Furthermore, traditional cures not only can be beneficial, they are also affordable. One of the consequences of medical advances is our increasing dependence on expensive technology. Consequently, although significant advances have been made in medicine, the cost to the patient of many such advances has made them unavailable to all but a small percentage of the world's population. Indeed, they are unavailable to many Americans. But in traditional societies, when healing arts are lost or discouraged by people who consider them backward, members are left with no other form of medical treatment.

QUESTION 2.5

Why are simpler societies disappearing?

Extinct People

Modern societies have not been kind to groups that have retained or tried to retain a way of life that is thousands of years old. Societies such as the Ju/wasi, the Inuit (the proper term for the people we call eskimos), and the people of the New Guinea highlands have not fared well after contact with modern cultures. Living in small, scattered groups with little need for complex political structures or technology, they were no match for well-armed, organized, acquisitive people who coveted their land or labor. Even hunting and gathering peoples in isolated, seemingly inhospitable locations have proven susceptible to cultural extermination.

The Ona (also known as the Selk'nam) inhabited the island of Tierra del Fuego just off the southern tip of South America. After their first encounters with Europeans in the 1870s and 1880s, the Ona were exposed to deadly diseases such as syphilis, measles, and tuberculosis, to which they had no resistance. They were systematically hunted and killed by European sheepherders and miners, and were later captured by

Angela Luij, one of the last Ona, died in 1974.

WHAT WOULD YOU DO?

You are a member of a task force that has been asked to evaluate the living conditions of the Ju/wasi. Some government officials have recommended that the Ju/wasi be resettled in permanent villages, given domesticated animals to ensure a steady food supply, and introduced to modern health services.

Your job is to evaluate these recommendations and then make your own as to how the lives of the Ju/wasi could be improved. Should the Ju/wasi be allowed to live in their "primitive" state? Should the government take active steps to lead the Ju/wasi into civilization? What are the benefits and drawbacks of either approach?

Argentine soldiers and sent to mission stations or kept as servants. Those who survived on the island were pushed farther inland, and European hunters systematically depleted the animals on which they depended for food. Having little to eat, they resorted to raiding sheep ranches and were shot by hunters or ranchers who were paid a bounty for every Ona killed. At the turn of the twentieth century, Europeans built lumber camps in the last forests in which the Ona could live without being in contact with Europeans. Finally, in 1974, 100 years after the first European settlement was built on Tierra del Fuego, the last full-blooded Ona died. The extermination of the Ona is not an isolated event, as societies all over the world have systematically exterminated native groups. In areas of Brazil that are now being entered by Europeans, members of the native population, many of whom still live by gathering and hunting or small-scale agriculture, are being hunted and killed much as the Ona were some 100 years ago.

Cultural Devastation and Radical Hope

The experiences of peoples such as the Ona raise an important question: What does it mean to experience cultural devastation? This question is important not only for what it tells us of the experiences of other people, but for how we understand what culture is and what culture change can mean. Clearly all cultures are vulnerable. The way that people view the world, what counts as important, what is valued, and what the good life means are all subject to sudden upheaval.

One of the best examples is what happened to indigenous peoples of the United States. When Columbus arrived in the "New World," there were hundreds of thriving societies. These were quickly devastated by European diseases that wiped out nearly 90 percent of the population. The devastation continued well into the nineteenth century as the remnants of these people struggled to adapt to the westward expansion of settlers.

The indigenous peoples of the Plains, such as the Lakota, Blackfeet, Cheyenne, Kiowa, and Crow, had adapted by organizing their societies around the horse and the buffalo, often competing against each other for control of hunting territory. But from roughly 1850 to 1880, these cultures were forced by the United States government onto reservations and became dependent on government rations—which were often undelivered—to replace the buffalo that had been virtually exterminated to make way for cattle ranchers. But what did it mean to go from a culture built on buffalo hunting and horse raiding to one on a government reservation?

In 1930, Plenty Coups, the chief of the Crow, dictated his life story to rancher Frank B. Linderman. Linderman's book, *Plenty-Coup: Chief of the Crows* became an anthropological classic. In the book, Plenty Coups told of his life as a Crow hunter and warrior, but he refused to talk about his life after the buffalo were killed and the Crow were restricted to their reservation. "I have not told you half of what happened when I was young," he told Linderman. "I can think back and tell you much more of war and horse stealing. But when the buffalo went away," he said, "the hearts of my people fell to the ground and they could not lift them up again. *After this, nothing happened.*" (italics added)

Philosopher Jonathan Lear devotes his book on Plenty Coups, *Radical Hope: Ethics in the Face of Cultural Devastation*, to trying to explain what it means to say "After this, nothing happened." In so doing, he

Plenty Coup: Chief of the Crows

helps us to understand what it means to experience cultural devastation and live through it.

. . . *when the buffalo went away, the hearts of my people fell to the ground and they could not lift them up again. After this, nothing happened.*

In the early nineteenth century, the Crow lived by hunting buffalo, raising horses, and raiding rival groups, particularly the Lakota, Blackfeet, and Cheyenne. War and raiding were central to the entire tribe. Girls and boys derived their names from the exploits of warriors. Wives publicly displayed their husbands' war trophies, and a woman grieving the loss of a husband or son was cause for retaliatory raids. Religion was suffused with the symbolism and rituals of war, and visions, dreams, and prayers inspired military undertakings.

Counting coup was the ultimate sign of courage. In battle, counting coup involved planting one's coup stick in the ground and defending it against an enemy until death. As Lear put it, it "marked a boundary across which a non-Crow enemy must not pass" (2006, 13). Plenty Coups described it as follows:

> To count coup a warrior had to strike an armed and fighting enemy with his coup stick, quirt, or bow before otherwise harming him, or take his weapons while he was yet alive, or strike the first enemy falling in battle, no matter who killed him, or strike the enemy's breastworks while under fire, or steal a horse tied to a lodge in an enemy's camp. (Linderman 1962, 55–56)

The value of courage in war was such that a common adage held "old age is a thing of evil, it is well for a young man to die in battle" (Lowie 1983, 218).

The Crow concern for war was built on the need to defend the territory on which they depended for sustenance. The westward advance of Europeans had forced groups such as the Lakota and Crow to struggle for what land remained. These struggles ended only with the cultural devastation that accompanied U.S. military action against indigenous groups and the virtual extermination of the buffalo.

For the Crow, the end began when they signed the Fort Laramie Treaty in 1851, giving the tribe rights to some 33 million acres and $50,000 worth of supplies a year—although these supplies were only delivered once. In 1867 the treaty was renegotiated, giving the Crow 25 percent of the land recognized in the first treaty, and in 1882 the land was further reduced to about 2 million acres. Then disease struck as they moved to a reservation in 1882–1884. In this life imposed on them by the United States, nothing that had meaning to them existed any longer. If things that counted as events, such as planting a coup stick, counting coup, going on a raid, or hunting buffalo, were no longer possible, it would make sense to say that "after that, nothing happened." Their context for living was destroyed. According to Lear, the problem for the Crow "was not simply that they could not pursue happiness in the traditional ways. Rather, their conception of *what happiness is* could no longer be lived" (2006, 56).

How can one survive such devastation? While some tribes fought and others fled, the Crow chose an option that was revealed to Plenty Coups in a dream vision.

When he was 9 years old, Plenty Coups went on a vision quest, a spiritual journey in which young Crow men sought a vision that would reveal their destiny. He went to a mountaintop, cut off one of his fingers to elicit pity from the spirits, and, on the second night, had his dream. He saw a buffalo bull, which turned into a man-person wearing a buffalo robe. He was led to a hole in the ground. Man-person shook his red rattle, and Plenty Coups saw endless numbers of buffalo emerging from the hole and covering the plains. But then they disappeared, and strange spotted animals emerged from the hole to replace them. "Do you understand what I have shown you?" asked Man-person. "No," Plenty Coups replied, "I [am] only 9 years old."

Then Man-person showed Plenty Coups an old man sitting under a tree and asked, "Do you know him, Plenty Coups?" "No," he said. "This old man is yourself," said Man-person. At this point a tremendous storm arose and, as Plenty Coups related it, the Four Winds began a war against the forest, knocking down all the trees but one. Man-person said that that the only tree left standing was the lodge of the chickadee. The chickadee, for the Crow, represented a good listener; nothing escaped his ears, he never missed a chance to learn from others, and he gained success from learning how others succeeded.

When he returned from his vision quest, Plenty Coups related the story to Yellow Bear, a tribal elder considered to be the wisest. He gave this interpretation of the dream: In

Plenty Coups' lifetime, the buffalo would go away forever and in their place would come the bulls and calves of the white man. "I have myself seen these Spotted-Buffalo drawing loads of the white man's goods," said Yellow Bear.

> The dream of Plenty Coups means that the white man will take and hold this country and that their Spotted-buffalo will cover the plains. He was told to think for himself, to listen, to learn to avoid disaster by the experience of others. He was advised to develop his body but not to forget his mind. The meaning of this dream is plain to me. I see its warning. The tribes who have fought the white man have all been beaten, wiped out. By listening as the Chickadee listens we may escape this and keep our lands. (Lear 2006, 72)

Lear imagines Plenty Coups reasoning as follows:

- Traditional life will end.
- The conception of the good intrinsic in a hunting life must end.
- Things will change in unexpected ways.
- There is more to hope for than mere physical survival—a dignified passage "across the abyss."
- My commitment to God and goodness is involved in the idea that something good will emerge, even if I don't know what it could be.
- I am thus committed to the idea that since we Crow must abandon the goods associated with our way of life, we must abandon the conception of the good life that our tribe has worked out over the centuries.
- We shall get the good back, though at the moment we can have no more than a glimmer of what that might mean.

We do not, of course, know the depth of Plenty Coups's thoughts, whether he was simply being practical in the face of overwhelming power, whether he may have had profound insights into history, or whether he was expressing some religious conviction. We may even be disappointed that he didn't face up to the evil inflicted on his people. But, as Lear emphasizes, Plenty Coups responded to the devastation of his culture with *radical hope*. It was radical because there was no understanding of what one is hoping for, only a conviction that some other good will emerge. And it was radical because it avoided despair.

On the basis of his dream, the tribe elected to ally itself with the United States, joining with them to fight the tribe's traditional enemies, the Sioux, Blackfoot, and Cheyenne. Although the United States kept revising its treaties with the Crow, the Crow were never displaced from their land, and they could say that they had never been defeated. They listened, as the chickadee listens. They sent their children to school, built a college, and adopted many traits of white culture. In his old age, Plenty Coups could feel that the dream had been confirmed by his experiences. In fact, he related his story to Linderman sitting under the same tree revealed to him in his dream: "And here I am, an old man, sitting under this tree just where that old man sat 70 years ago when it was a different world." He had, says Lear,

> brought himself to the spot where the dream told him he would be. And the recitation of the dream to Linderman was in its own way the triumphal counting of coup: he was telling the story of how he successfully went to "battle" to protect his land. He was now sitting under the tree that the dream told him he would if he adopted the virtue of the chickadee. (2006, 143)

Chapter 3

Globalization, Neoliberalism, and the Nation-State

The incredible concentration of wealth and power that now exists in the upper echelons of capitalism has not been seen since the 1920s. The flows of tribute into the world's major financial centres have been astonishing. What, however, is even more astonishing is the habit of treating all of this as a mere and in some instances even unfortunate byproduct of neoliberalization. The very idea that this might be—just might be—the fundamental core of what neoliberalism has been about all along appears unthinkable.

David Harvey

The History of Neoliberalism, 2005

© BLACKRED/ISTOCKPHOTO.COM

* * *

QUESTIONS

In examining this problem, we will consider the following questions:

3.1 How do we define happiness and well-being?

3.2 Where does the wealth needed to sustain growth come from?

3.3 What kind of economic system is necessary to sustain growth?

3.4 What is the role of the nation-state in sustaining growth?

3.5 Why do economies collapse?

INTRODUCTION

My T-Shirt

What is the biography of a commodity?

In 2006 economist Pietra Rivoli walked into a Walgreen's drugstore in Fort Lauderdale, Florida, and bought a T-shirt. Earlier that year she had attended a demonstration at Georgetown University, where she taught. Students had occupied administrative offices to protest what they thought were unfair policies of multilateral institutions such as the World Trade Organization (WTO), the International Monetary Fund (IMF), and the World Bank and their impact on the environment and workers all over the world. They were protesting what is commonly termed globalization.

As an economist, Rivoli assumed that globalization was a good thing, that the increased production and sale of commodities such as T-shirts were helping create jobs in poor countries as well as supplying inexpensive goods to consumers. To convince herself of the benefits of trade, she wanted to trace the chain of production and distribution of her T-shirt, from the growing of the cotton to the delivery of the final product to Walgreen's. In other words, she wanted to examine what Igor Kopytoff calls the biography of a commodity.

She began by locating the company that printed and distributed the T-shirt, Sherry Manufacturing of Fort Lauderdale. Sherry Manufacturing purchased the shirt from China, one of about 25 million cotton T-shirts shipped from China that year. Rivoli then traveled to China to visit the factory

What can a cotton T-shirt purchased in a **FORT LAUDERDALE** *drugstore, printed and distributed by a* **FLORIDA** *textile manufacturer, assembled, sewn, and spun in* **CHINESE** *factories out of cotton grown in* **TEXAS** *tell us about globalization and our role in it?*

that assembled the T-shirt, the place where the fabric was knit, and finally the factory where the yarn was spun out of raw cotton. The cotton, she was surprised to discover, was grown in Lubbock County, Texas. This led Rivoli to ask what a cotton T-shirt purchased in a Fort Lauderdale drugstore, printed and distributed by a Florida textile manufacturer, assembled, sewn, and spun in Chinese factories out of cotton grown in Texas can tell us about globalization and our role in it?

The T-shirt purchased by Rivoli is an infinitesimal fraction of what people all over the world consume every day. Each year people spend more than $20 trillion on goods and services. Almost a billion and a half households in the world have a TV, and each year some 41 million passenger vehicles roll off the assembly lines, adding to the 531 million vehicles already on the road. Of course, this consumption is highly skewed toward the well-off. Some 20 percent of the world's population, living in the richest countries, account for 86 percent of total private consumption while the poorest 20 percent account for only 1.3 percent.

Why do we spend so much and what impact does this have on our lives? While many people enjoy shopping, and even see it as a form of therapy, there is much evidence that buying more stuff does not make people happy. Surveys show that people in the U.S. were happier in the 1950s consuming about one-quarter of what they consume today. The question of why we spend so much is also important because, as research suggests, we are literally consuming our planet and ourselves to death. Global warming, industrial pollution, the rapid decrease of clean water, and the piling up of waste are clearly major problems linked to our consumption habits.

To understand how and why human beings have reached levels of consumption that threaten their existence, we need to ask five questions.

First, how do we define happiness and well-being? All societies have conceptions of the good life. For some it's success in growing crops, for others it's the ability to give gifts to others. In many contemporary societies, it is the ability to make and spend money. How did this happen, and what are its consequences?

Second, attaining this good life means that the amount of goods and services into which we convert our money must continually grow. Where does this growth come from?

Third, few societies in the history of the world have been as successful at economic growth as contemporary market economies. What sort of policies and philosophies have made them so successful at maintaining perpetual economic growth?

Fourth, the modern nation-state is instrumental in the workings of the modern economy. What is the role of the nation-state, and how does it assist the growth of the economy?

Finally, we need to ask why economies occasionally collapse.

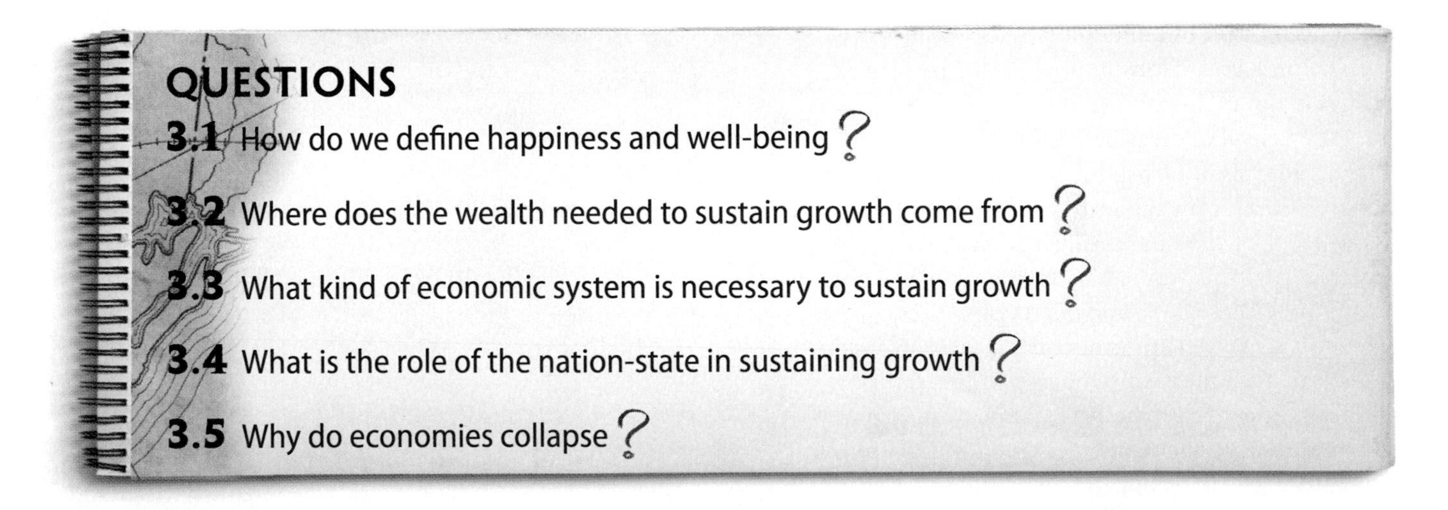

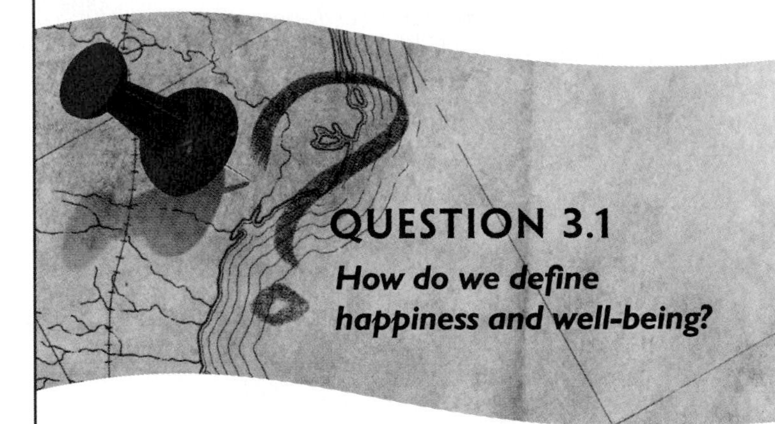

Money, Wealth, and Well-Being

Every culture has a distinct material symbol or activity that defines for its members what is most important in life, what is needed for well-being and happiness. The Trobriand Islanders engaged in the accumulation of yams and the ritual exchange of shell necklaces and bracelets. For the indigenous peoples of the American Plains, the key to life was the buffalo and, after European contact, the horse, warfare, and raiding. For contemporary society, the key is money. As anthropologist Jack Weatherford notes, money defines relationships not only in the marketplace and workplace, but also between parent and child, among neighbors, and even between friends. "Other than love and fear," writes economist Robert Guttmann (1994, xvii), "there is probably no more powerful motivating force in our lives than money."

But in other times and places, not everyone wanted money. Instead, people desired salvation, strength, adventure, or power. Even in some societies that use money, it is often viewed with suspicion and as a threat to the social order. In coastal Malay fishing villages, men and women occupy different spheres of the economy. Men work on fishing boats for wages while women maintain communal households. Fishing crews are composed of people unrelated by kinship and tied together by commercial relations. Members of fishing crews are not related by kinship, largely because of a fear that, if they were related, any conflict among crew members would spread to kin. Household work groups are composed of relatives who work together and share what they produce, and rarely is money exchanged. Since money is associated with the commercial sphere of fishing, its presence in the household could threaten the social bonds of kinship, and is consequently dangerous. Thus when men earn money, they immediately give it to their wives to absorb into the household where everything is shared. The money is, in effect, cleansed of its association with the world of impersonal commercial relations. As anthropologist Janet E. Carsten notes, it is in effect "cooked" in the household and made acceptable.

Anthropological accounts are filled with similar accounts of how money is viewed as dangerous and threatening and has to be somehow cleansed of its association with the world of the impersonal market exchange. Even in advanced market economies such as ours, we make a distinction between relations characterized by monetary exchanges and those defined by kinship or friendship. When we buy something at a store, our relationship to the person or persons we are buying from begins and ends with the transaction. This contrasts with kin relations, which are permanent and enduring. Thus, all societies seem to make a distinction between spheres of exchange that involve long-standing intimate relations and spheres of exchange that are short-term, based on commercial relations, and defined by the use of money.

One reason that money is so important to us is that it is often the only thing we can use to get what we want or need. In Malay villages you could depend on kin or friends to provide you with what you needed. And of course, some things in our society are available without money. But, as we shall see, for our economy to function, things provided to us by family and friends are constantly diminishing as more and more of our needs are met by the market.

As societies have become more complex and as economic activities have become more central to our lives, more and more of life's necessities, as well as luxuries, are available only through the market. Few of us grow our own food, build our own houses or make our own clothes. We have to buy these things. Without money we could barely survive. And of course, we must work to obtain money. But what exactly is money, and where does it come from?

© ZORAN SINKO/ISTOCKPHOTO.COM

Types of money used throughout history. A silver ingot, silver coins, and paper notes.

A Brief History of Money

Money is, among other things, a medium of exchange; that is, it is recognized by people as something to give or accept in exchange for other things. Societies throughout the world have made use of various objects such as shells or furs as a medium of exchange. Precious metals were used as objects of exchange in Mesopotamia about 5,000 years ago, and the use of coins dates back to the seventh century BCE. This was called **commodity money** because the substance had some value in itself and could be used for some practical purpose, such as manufacturing jewelry.

Paper money, also known as "exchange" or "demand" notes, were first used in China in the twelfth century and its use spread to Europe some two to three hundred years later. This allowed a trader in Venice to buy textiles from someone in Bruges and pay with a paper note backed by gold that the seller could retrieve from a bank in Paris. The issuing of paper money was a major step, because it meant that the amount of money that could be created was theoretically unlimited; you just needed more paper. In practice, however, the printing of paper money was in fact limited since people would not accept it unless it was backed by some precious metal, usually gold or silver, that people could retrieve with the paper.

commodity money money that is backed by something of worth, such as gold or silver

fiat money money that is backed by nothing other than a government decree that it be accepted for the sale of goods or services or the settlement of debt

credit money money that is created by loans

However, there were some problems with commodity-based paper money. For example, the commodity being used might be worth more in one area than another. Also, anyone could produce paper currency. In the nineteenth century, there were some 30,000 different currencies in circulation in the United States, and banks or other institutions often lent out far more money than they had gold or silver on hand. That worked fine as long as everyone didn't demand their gold or silver at once. But if they did, banks failed, and people lost faith in paper money.

The U.S. government addressed some of these problems in 1913 by creating the Federal Reserve Bank to control and stabilize the money supply and regulate the amount of gold banks were required to keep on hand. This amount was generally equal to 10 percent of the deposits they held. That allowed banks and other lending institutions to lend out and, in effect, create $9 of new money for every $1 deposited. But the Federal Reserve still could not address the limitations imposed on economic growth by tying money to a fixed commodity. Solving that problem required two government decrees.

First, in 1931, the United States government announced that it would no longer allow citizens to convert their paper money into gold, although the value of money was still tied to the value of gold, and exchanges with foreign governments still occurred in gold. Then, in 1971, the United States government declared that its currency would no longer be backed by gold, or anything else for that matter. This marked the final shift from commodity money to **fiat money** or **credit money**—paper that was used as evidence of a claim to economic value but that, legally, was not redeemable for anything.

As might be expected, with dollars backed by nothing, the money supply could grow rapidly as banks and other financial institutions lent out more and more. The only thing that limited the supply of money was the amount that governments and financial institutions were willing to lend.

When we think of money, we think of bills and coins. But that is only a small part of the money supply—only 5 to 10 percent. The rest exists only as figures on paper or

TABLE 3.1

U.S. MONEY SUPPLY BY TYPE IN 1959, 1971, 1987, 2007 (IN BILLIONS)

Year	M1	M2	M3
1959	138.9	286.6	288.8
1971	215.4	632.8	685.4
1985	619.1	2,494.9	3,207.6
2007	1,368.9	7,093.0	10,221.9

M1 = most liquid forms of money, including currency and bank account deposits.

M2 = in addition to M1, includes savings deposits, small time deposits, and retail money market mutual funds.

M3 = in addition to M1 and M2, includes institutional money funds and certain managed liabilities of depositories, namely large time deposits, repurchase agreements, and Eurodollars.

Source: http://www.federalreserve.gov/releases/h6/hist

in computers in banks and in the records of other financial institutions. Credit money, for example, is a promise by the borrower of money to repay it at some future date. Table 3.1 shows how the U.S. money supply has changed during the past 50 years.

As you can see, the money supply in 2007 was 35 times larger than it was in 1959. This points to a key consequence of debt money—since money is created as debt and since debt requires repayment with interest, every dollar created through debt must generate itself plus an additional amount to account for interest. Thus, if the lenders of money are to collect their interest, the money supply must grow. Put another way, once an economy allows people or institutions to make money with money through loans at interest, perpetual economic growth becomes a necessity. If economic growth falls below a critical level (generally less than 3%) or, worse yet, declines, borrowers are unable to repay their debts, lenders can't collect on their loans, banks and businesses fail, people lose their jobs, government revenue collections decline, and ultimately, if the decline continues, the economy, and the society built upon it, collapses. A worldwide recession that began in late 2007 paralyzed most economies, especially those of the richest nations, and led to historic levels of unemployment, numerous bank closures, the failure of many corporations, and even caused a catastrophic banking and political crisis in Iceland.

The Society of Perpetual Growth

Although it is necessary, perpetual economic growth is not an easy thing to achieve. China's economy, for example, has been growing at rates of 9–10 percent a year, largely thanks to exports. In 2007, China earned some $1.2 trillion from exporting goods, an increase of 25 percent from the previous year. Still, China must continue to increase its exports and ship even more T-shirts, along

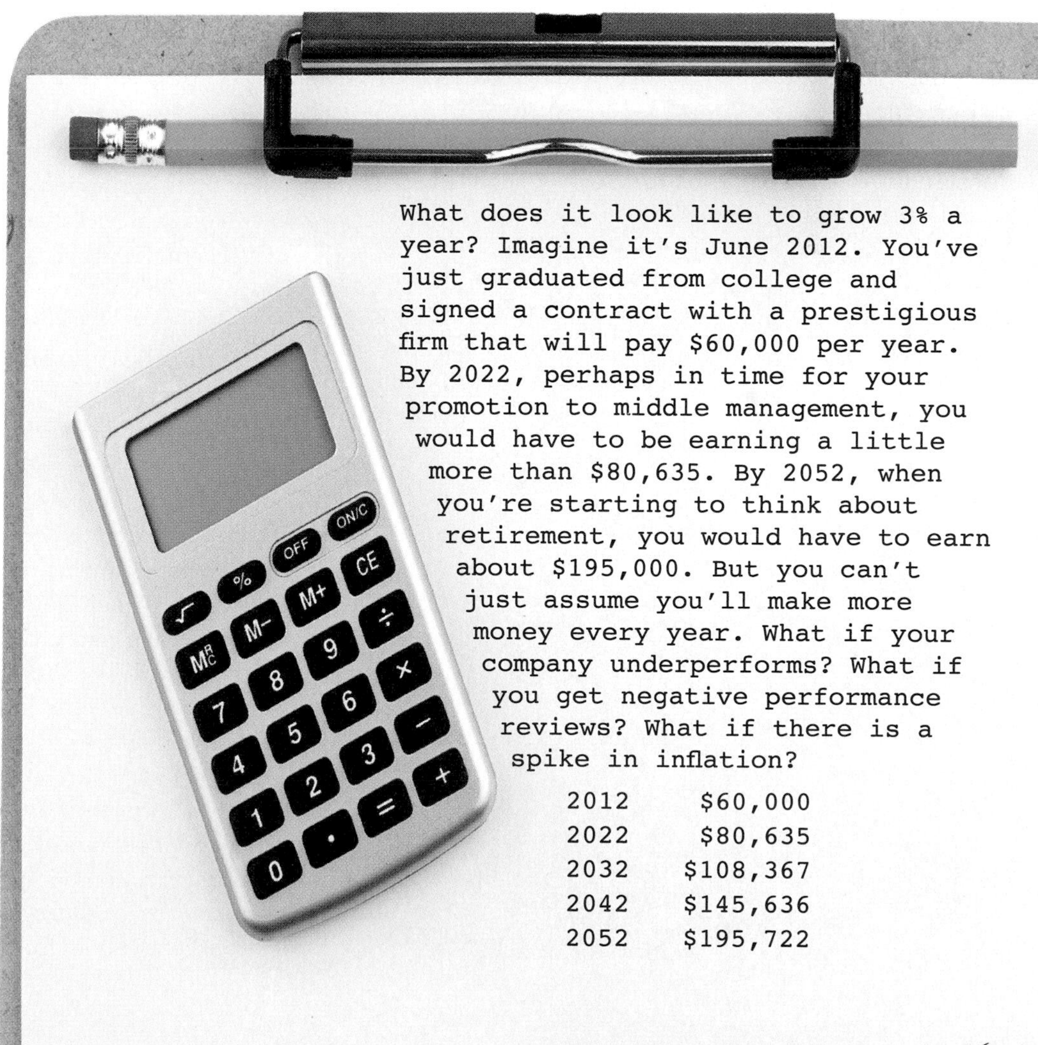
What does it look like to grow 3% a year? Imagine it's June 2012. You've just graduated from college and signed a contract with a prestigious firm that will pay $60,000 per year. By 2022, perhaps in time for your promotion to middle management, you would have to be earning a little more than $80,635. By 2052, when you're starting to think about retirement, you would have to earn about $195,000. But you can't just assume you'll make more money every year. What if your company underperforms? What if you get negative performance reviews? What if there is a spike in inflation?

2012	$60,000
2022	$80,635
2032	$108,367
2042	$145,636
2052	$195,722

capital conversion the transformation of something that has no monetary value into something that can be bought and sold in the market

with other commodities, in order to maintain this level of growth.

It would be easy, of course, to keep creating more and more money by giving more and more loans. The problem is that money itself is "worthless" since it is backed by nothing but the government's decree that it be accepted in payment for goods, services, and debt. In order for money to have worth, it must be converted into something of value—a house, a car, a pair of shoes, and so on. In other words, to keep the money supply growing, there has to be more and more stuff to buy. Furthermore, if the amount of money increases faster than the increase in stuff, people will pay more and more for whatever is available, creating inflation where the value of money decreases.

This brief introduction to the origins and use of money and its growth should begin to give you a basic idea of the nature of the modern economy. But a problem remains. We mentioned that the economy must grow at a rate of at least 3 percent a year, that this requires steady growth in the money supply, and that money itself is worthless until it can be turned into some commodity such as T-shirts, shoes, or medical service. Thus, not only must the money supply increase, but so must the stuff that money can buy. The question, then, is where does all this perpetually growing stuff come from?

QUESTION 3.2

Where does the wealth needed to sustain growth come from?

Capital Conversion

Producing the goods and services that we acquire with money is a complex undertaking. It requires mines, forests, factories, roads, financial institutions, legal institutions, educational centers, retail outlets, and much more that make up a productive economy. At another level, however, the process of producing stuff is a relatively simple one. We convert some nonmonetary resource—forests, music, family functions, collectively held land—directly or indirectly into money. That is, people find ways to make some good or service available on the market, and it is this process of **capital conversion** that keeps the economy going.

There is a basic rule involved in maintaining economic growth: The more things people must pay for, the more the economy grows. For example, if you do your friend a favor by driving her to the store, you may have advanced your friendship, but you've done little for the economy (other than using gasoline). If, on the other hand, you charge her (and report the charge on your taxes), you have added to the nation's GDP. In a similar sense, the greater the number of goods and services that can be obtained only by purchase, the better it is for economic growth. This means that some things that we would not considerable desirable—a divorce, an oil spill, an illness or natural disaster—are economically positive events because they result in more money being spent. Other things that we might think are desirable, such as sharing your car or your lawnmower, are negative because, by allowing someone to use something without paying for it, you hinder economic growth.

Societies vary considerably in terms of what can be obtained from the market—that is, what can be bought and sold—and what is available outside the market. We can imagine two extremes: a "perfectly commoditized world" in which you have to buy everything and a world in which nothing is commoditized. In small-scale societies, particularly those without money, most needs are met by sharing. Food is hunted, gathered, or grown and shared within small or large family groups. Natural resources are owned collectively by the group. Medicinal plants are available to all. Even when money enters the economy of these societies, most goods and services remain outside the market.

But for an economy to grow, there has to be a constant transfer of things and activities into the monetary sphere. Think about things we can get without money—

FIGURE 3.1
CAPITAL CONVERSION

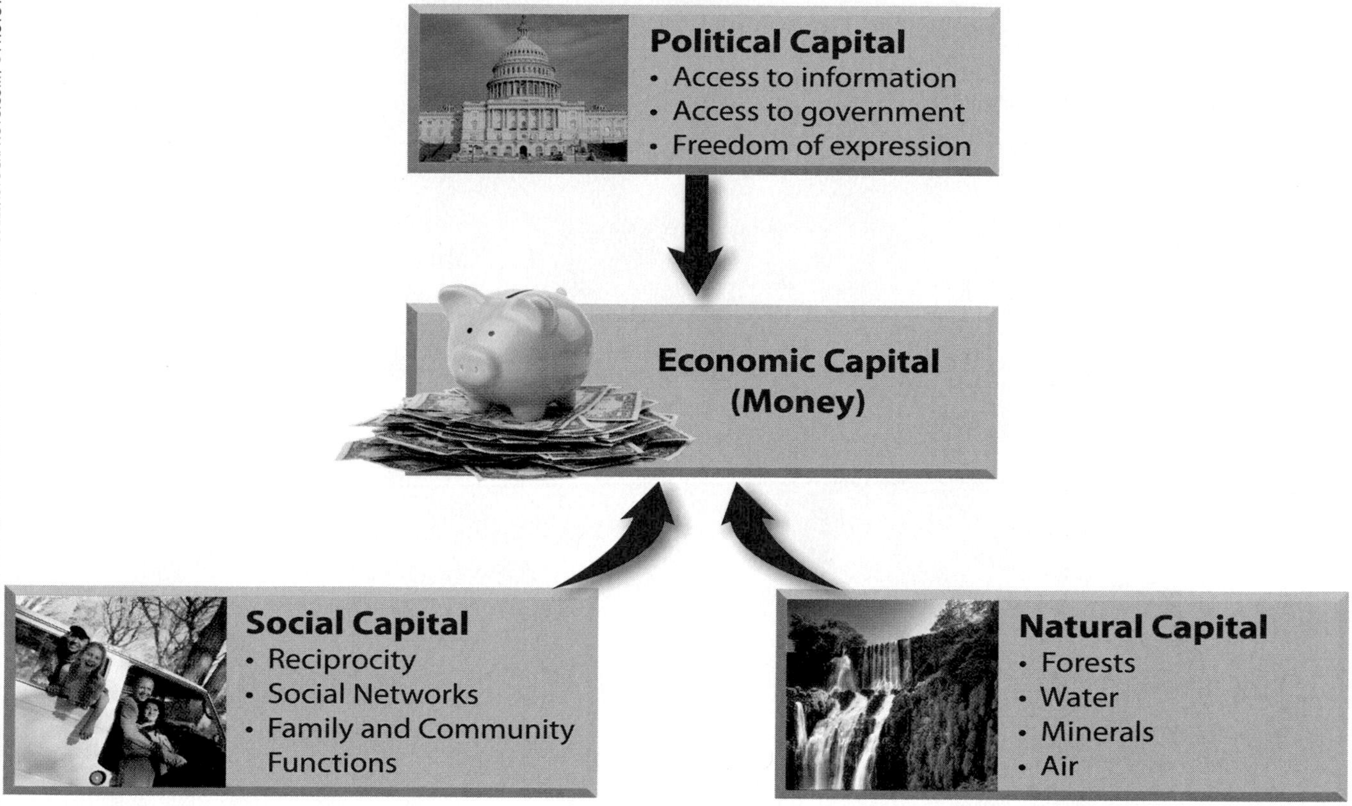

Political Capital
- Access to information
- Access to government
- Freedom of expression

Economic Capital (Money)

Social Capital
- Reciprocity
- Social Networks
- Family and Community Functions

Natural Capital
- Forests
- Water
- Minerals
- Air

parental love, a companion's devotion, a sunset. There is a constant attempt to commodify these things. Advertising agencies employ some of the most creative minds in the world to entice people to equate friendship with beer or love with diamonds. The travel industry would like you to believe that a sunset can only be enjoyed from the bow of a cruise ship or from some far-off beach. In Japan, lonely businessmen or elderly people can hire actors, including children, to come for a family meal complete with conversation. The music industry has constantly appropriated and exploited grassroots culture and creativity by converting music forms from folk culture into forms that are sold to the public.

In the process of capital conversion lies the genius of the modern market economy. Through the operation of a myriad of rules, regulations, values, and laws, the modern economy encourages the conversion of items and activities that have no intrinsic monetary worth into items and activities that can only be bought and sold in the marketplace.

Water is something we think of as a necessity available to everyone. But today more and more of our water supply is being commodified. Globally, only 10 percent of water usage goes to households; the other 90 percent is used by industry, 65 percent of that for agriculture and meat production. The industrial usage is good for the GDP, but not for the billion or more people who lack access to fresh drinking water.

We also convert our **political capital**, the freedom we have to regulate our own lives and the access we have to societal leaders and decision makers, into money. For example, the need to maintain economic growth has resulted in the formation of powerful entities such as multinational corporations with enormous economic and political power. CEOs can assign or withdraw resources at will, open and close plants, change product lines, or lay off workers with little recourse. The modern economy, in the interests of increasing GNP, has transferred planning functions from governments accountable to their citizens to corporations accountable only to their shareholders.

In 2008, 43 of the 100 richest institutional entities in the world were transnational corporations (see Table 3.2 on the following page). One consequence of this development is that corporate interests, as opposed to human interests, dominate the policy agendas of nation-states

political capital the freedom we have to regulate our own lives and the access we have to societal leaders and decision makers

TABLE 3.2

TOP 100 GLOBAL FINANCIAL ENTITIES OF 2008

Rank	Country or Company	GDP/Revenue in Billions	Rank	Country or Company	GDP/Revenue in Billions
1	United States	13,820	26	Pakistan	392.5
2	China	6,473	27	Egypt	386.5
3	Japan	4,262	28	Wal-Mart Stores	378.7
4	India	2,816	29	Exxon Mobil	372.8
5	Germany	2,816	30	Belgium	375.6
6	United Kingdom	2,154	31	Colombia	358.9
7	France	2,074	32	Royal Dutch Shell	355.7
8	Russia	1,985	33	Malaysia	345.9
9	Italy	1,814	34	Sweden	336.6
10	Brazil	1,794	35	Greece	320.5
11	Mexico	1,494	36	Venezuela	314.6
12	Spain	1,337	37	Austria	313.9
13	Canada	1,263	38	Ukraine	306.6
14	South Korea	1,243	39	Switzerland	300.9
15	Turkey	853.6	40	Nigeria	299.4
16	Indonesia	810.9	41	BP	291.4
17	Australia	752.2	42	Philippines	285.6
18	Iran	733	43	Hong Kong	281.4
19	Taiwan	672.9	44	Norway	253.2
20	Netherlands	635.9	45	Czech Republic	242.6
21	Poland	596.7	46	Romania	238.6
22	Saudi Arabia	535.1	47	Portugal	232.3
23	Thailand	508.6	48	ConocoPhillips	230.7
24	Argentina	494.3	49	Toyota Motor	230.2
25	South Africa	453.1	50	Chile	226.3

and the international agencies that they create, support, and control.

Finally, economic growth and development also require the expenditure of social capital. **Social capital** refers to connections among individuals—social networks and the norms of reciprocity and trustworthiness that arise from them. Social capital can improve our lives by making people aware of how our fates are linked while building networks that help people fulfill individual goals.

social capital relations of reciprocity and trust that enable people collectively to solve their problems

In his book *Bowling Alone*, Robert Putnam traces the history of social capital in the United States and concludes that, "By virtually every conceivable measure, social capital has eroded steadily and sometimes dramatically over the past two generations." Putnam attributes the decline of social capital to four factors. About half of the decline, he says, is a result of the slow, steady replacement of a long "civic generation" by a generation that is less involved. He attributes another quarter to the advent of electronic entertainment, particularly television. The rest of the decline he attributes to time and money pressures on two-career families and the increase of suburban sprawl that creates communities with no centers.

Rank	Country or Company	GDP/Revenue in Billions	Rank	Country or Company	GDP/Revenue in Billions
51	Algeria	218.3	76	Dexia Group	147.6
52	Singapore	217.8	77	HSBC Holdings	146.5
53	Chevron	210.7	78	BNP Paribas	140.7
54	ING Group	201.5	79	Allianz	140.6
55	Vietnam	209.8	80	Credit Agricole	138.1
56	Peru	206.8	81	State Grid	132.8
57	Denmark	202.8	82	Kuwait	131.3
58	Bangladesh	201	83	China National Petroleum	129.7
59	Hungary	193.1	84	Morocco	125.6
60	Total	187.2	85	Deutsche Bank	122.6
61	Finland	184.1	86	ENI	120.5
62	Israel	183.4	87	Bank of America	119.1
63	Ireland	183.3	88	AT&T	118.9
64	General Motors	182.3	89	Berkshire Hathaway	118.2
65	ConocoPhillips	178.5	90	UBS	117.2
66	Daimler	177.1	91	J.P. Morgan Chase and Co.	116.3
67	General Electric	176.6	92	Carrefour	115.5
68	Ford Motor	172.4	93	Assicurazioni Generali	113.8
69	Fortis	164.8	94	New Zealand	112.9
70	AXA	162.7	95	American International Group	110
71	United Arab Emirates	159.3	96	Royal Bank of Scotland	108.3
72	Sinopec	159.26	97	Siemens	106.4
73	Citigroup	159.22	98	Samsung	106
74	Kazakhstan	158.2	99	ArcelorMittal	105.2
75	Volkswagen	149	100	Honda Motor	105.1

Sources: Data compiled from http://money.cnn.com/magazines/fortune/global500/2008/full_list/ and http://www.indexmundi.com/g/r.aspx?t=100&v=65&l=en

It is significant, of course, that most of the factors Putnam identifies as contributing to the decline of social capital also contribute to economic growth. That is, we have converted social capital into economic capital by enacting rules and regulations that encourage suburban sprawl, which reduces contact among people while creating larger homes, more expenditures on household items, more road and bridge construction, and more dependence on automobiles and all the expenses they involve. Two-income families exchange time that might be spent in family activities for increased income, while television, which further reduces family interaction, exposes people to thousands of hours of advertisements that create new consumer desires and offer happiness through goods.

To a great extent, the economic growth in core countries of the past 50 years has been produced by transferring social capital–rich functions, such as child care, food preparation, health care, and entertainment from households, where they did not count in GDP figures, to the market, where they do count. The acceleration of the conversion of social capital into money over the past few centuries has completely transformed our social environments. When families gathered to collect food or slaughter game, multiple social interactions ensued. In the modern economy, those interactions are replaced by a simple exchange of money at the grocery checkout counter.

Converting nonmonetary capital into money, then, is essential for maintaining our economic system. But, as economists have noted, the wealthier a country becomes, the harder it is to maintain growth. Consequently, economic policy makers must come up with more and more ways to enhance capital conversion. Next, then, let's examine how that has been done historically.

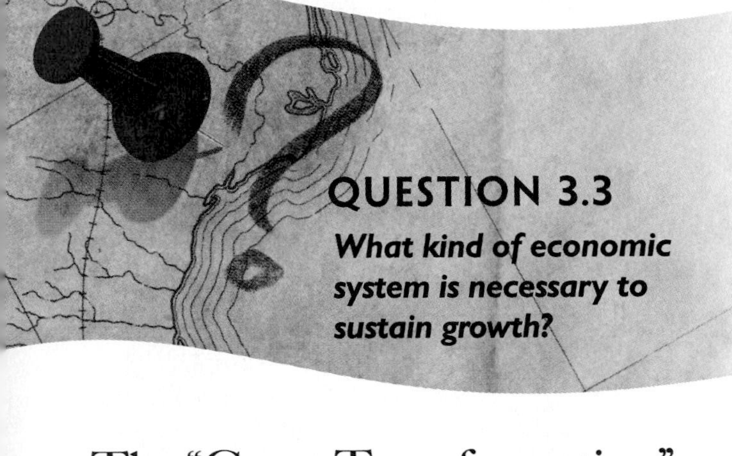

The "Great Transformation"

Economic systems are about the distribution of goods and services—that is, the rules, mechanisms, institutions, and systems of relations through which people get what they want. This process can be as simple as the borrowing of a cup of sugar or a pair of shoes, or as complex as the production, distribution, consumption, and disposal of automobiles, houses, or military weapons.

Markets, as we mentioned, go back thousands of years. Communities would set up areas where merchants, farmers, and artisans could bring their goods or services for sale or barter. But as new modes of transportation and manufacture developed, markets were no longer only places to trade, but whole networks whereby silk manufactured in China could be sold in Paris. At some point about 200 to 300 years ago, technological changes instigated what economist Karl Polanyi termed "the great transformation," or the industrial revolution.

One of the major questions regarding the maintenance of economic growth is the role of government. States have always played a major role in the economy. But some eighteenth-century economists argued that the state should play as small a role as possible. Ideally, they argued, people will supply only those goods and services for which there are demands and, generally, a balance will be established between what is demanded and what is supplied. In his classic work, *The Wealth of Nations* (1776), Adam Smith saw the workings of the market as an "invisible hand" by which a benevolent God administered a universe in which human happiness was maximized, an ideal system whereby each person, seeking his or her own ends, would contribute to the betterment of society as a whole. Thus, by seeking money and wealth, each person would work toward supplying what others needed or demanded. For Smith, the market represented a utopian vision in which wealth was perpetually created for the benefit of all.

The problem was that an unregulated market, in which the generation of wealth is the only goal, resulted in abysmal working conditions, environmental degradation, and wild economic fluctuations that saw people suddenly plunged into poverty. In his book *The Great Transformation*, Polanyi addressed the tension between the need to allow the market—that is, the mechanisms for buying and selling—to operate freely without government interference and the need to somehow minimize the social and natural damages inflicted by the market. Allowed to operate unhindered, Polanyi suggested, the market would soon destroy the very foundations of society. It would disrupt social relations though

Adam Smith (1723–1790) believed that by seeking money and wealth, each person would work toward supplying what others needed or demanded.

Though economic systems are generally categorized as market or state-run (also known as command) economies, in reality, almost all represent some mix between the two principles. North Korea is one of the last remnants of a state-run economy, in which the government controls virtually every economic activity. And yet, the North Korean government also sponsors the Kaesong Industrial Region, a development zone that welcomes foreign investment and encourages market principles. The United States, on the other hand, is a hallmark example of a market economy. But during the recent global recession, there was significant government intervention in the form of corporate bailouts and promises of stricter financial regulations.

the operation of the labor market; it would destroy the environment; it would reduce freedom. Regulating the market, on the other hand, with laws on pollution, working conditions, and land use, could destroy the market. It is the working out of this dilemma that Polanyi saw as one of the major driving forces of history since the early nineteenth century.

Governments have tried to maintain a balance, then, between regulation and noninterference in the workings of the market. At one extreme is the almost completely state-run economies of Cuba and North Korea. At the other extreme are capitalist economies such as that of the United States. But rarely are even the most capitalist economies free of significant state involvement, and the tension between the state and the market that Polanyi wrote of results in ebbs and flows of regulation.

The British economist John Maynard Keynes advocated a policy of using government to regulate the economy through spending, tax policies, interest rates, and so on. Government involvement in the economy, support of labor unions, and a progressive tax system in which marginal tax rates ranged as high as 90 percent resulted in rapid economic growth in the United States and Canada through the 1960s.

Then, in the 1970s, there was a period of slow economic growth and resulting pressure to change economic policies. Economists began to abandon Keynesian economic philosophy, arguing for the withdrawal of the state from any involvement in regulating the economy. This economic philosophy, known as **neoliberalism**, is often synonymous with globalization. Since the application of neoliberal principles may determine your career path and what goods and services you can acquire for what price, not to mention the natural, political, and social environment in which you live, it is useful to understand where it came from and what it is trying to accomplish.

The Emergence of Neoliberalism

Neoliberalism emerged with a group of economists, historians, and philosophers, who gathered around political philosopher Friedrich von Hayek to create the Mont Pelerin Society (named after the Swiss spa at which they first met in 1947). Prompted by a concern about the spread of totalitarian societies and religious and racial intolerance, they argued that totalitarian philosophies not only endangered freedom but also threatened the belief in private property and the free market, without which, they argued, freedom cannot be preserved. They called themselves "liberals" because they adhered to ideals of freedom, and "neo" because they adhered to neoclassical economic theory that was opposed to the Keynesian idea of state involvement in the economy.

Well-being, neoliberals argued, is best served by liberating individual entrepreneurs to operate in a framework of strong property rights, free markets, and free trade. The role of the state should be limited to safeguarding the integrity of money and maintaining military, police, and legal structures to secure property rights and protect markets. The state should also open markets in areas such as education, water, land, health care, and social security. Other than that, state intervention should be kept to a minimum because states can never have enough information to second-guess markets on matters such as prices, and because their involvement allows special interest groups such as unions, environmentalists, and trade groups to distort the operation of the market.

Through the 1960s, few people were interested in neoliberalism

neoliberalism an economic philosophy that argues for minimal government involvement in the economy and greatly accelerated economic growth. Well-being, neoliberals argued, is best served by liberating individual entrepreneurs to operate in a framework of strong property rights, free markets, and free trade

Over the past decade, there has been a significant growth in the United States of large-scale, factory pig farms, or "hog hotels."

© RAIMUND KOCH/PHOTONICA/GETTY IMAGES

Small-scale family farms are being replaced by corporate-owned facilities designed to minimize cost and maximize profit.Thousands of pigs are raised in long, low-lying metal buildings set on concrete foundations. Elevated bulk-feeding tanks complete the factory appearance of the facilities, where every stage of the production process is monitored. Animal waste is deposited on cement floors, where it runs off into open waste pits called "lagoons." Large transport trucks pick up the pigs, which never see the light of day.

For more than half a century, anthropologists have been warning that the industrialization of agriculture is a threat to family farms and communities, and can have severe negative impacts on health and the environment. These problems are clearly revealed Laura B. Delind's study of Parma, Michigan.

In 1983, the Michigan Department of Commerce sponsored a feasibility study to build 10 500-sow hog production facilities in Parma. The study projected that the new factory farms would increase hog production by 8 percent and realize a 24 to 27 percent profit. Although the feasibility study closely examined the economic benefits of the project, it paid no attention to its environmental, social, or health effects. In fact, residents of Parma were not even consulted, and they only found out about the project when construction began.

As soon as building started, residents had lots of questions: What was being built? Why had the public not been consulted? How large a facility would it be? How would the pig waste be managed? What would it do to the creek, which passed only 200 feet from the 20-acre site? What would happen to the groundwater, the air, property values? What environmental safeguards existed? These questions drew only vague assurances from government and corporate officials that there would be no problems.

By the time the residents had firsthand experience with their new neighbor and its 42-million-gallon open-air anaerobic manure lagoons, their worst fears were realized. Many reported a "horrific stench" that could be detected up to five miles away, which caused nausea, headaches, respiratory ailments, irritated eyes, noses, and throats, and prevented sleep. Pig carcasses were found piled along the road, airborne particles were contaminating swimming pools, and fish disappeared from the creek. In response to residents' complaints, the state reported that the operation did not violate any state codes.

However, when Parma residents were told that the facility was going to be expanded, they decided to fight. They searched state regulations and laws and hired legal representation, finally forcing the hog facility to install new equipment and to regulate the pollution. They also succeeded in getting restrictions placed on any new hog farms. Then, in 1992, the company declared bankruptcy and, citing the cost of litigation and low hog prices, closed the facility, leaving behind 30 steel buildings and 3 empty lagoons on 20 denuded acres. The company has since gone on to construct and operate new hog confinement facilities in Wyoming, China, and Korea. In spite of the promises made by government and corporate representatives, the town of Parma realized few, if any, economic benefits. Project planners promised to buy local corn as hog feed, but DeLind found that the factory farm purchased most of its corn from outside suppliers. Project planners also promised to create local jobs. However, the company bypassed local contractors and brought in its own construction crew, filled all senior-level positions with outsiders, and only hired 10 local people to fill a staff of 27. What's worse, a locally-owned apple orchard and historical museum, which had 4 full-time and 28 part-time employees, was forced to close because of the farm. All the investors, some with ties to the governor's office, were from outside the area, and local property values collapsed because people were hesitant to purchase property.

But the damage to Parma was more than just financial. There were great human costs, as residents of Parma lost confidence in the democratic process after years of being ignored by government officials. The experience with the hog hotel convinced them that authorities were reluctant to embrace their interests over those of power and profit. As one resident told DeLind, "For a long time we were laboring under the illusion that if we got to the right person, he would say: 'Wait a minute! You can't do this to the people of Parma.' That person does not exist." Though the community ultimately forced the company to leave, its social fabric was destroyed by years of tension and conflict.

Corporate-owned and-run hog production facilities are realities of the current agricultural economy and are likely to become more common, in spite of evidence that successful, modest-sized, family-operated hog farms contribute more to the economic and social well-being of rural communities. But anthropologists are among those who are striving for a greater input into agricultural policy. By taking a critical perspective on public policy and by carefully examining how different groups of people are affected by policy decisions, anthropologists often serve as advocates for those whose interests are being ignored by government, corporate, or nongovernmental policy makers.

since the state-assisted economies of the major industrial nations were growing rapidly. But in the 1970s, for various reasons, global economies began to stagnate, and in some countries, such as the United States, inflation became a major problem—so much so that in 1979 President Jimmy Carter went on television to appeal to Americans to stop driving up prices by spending so much!

One of the first applications of neoliberalism was in New York City in the 1970s. By the start of the decade, industry was fleeing New York and people who could afford new housing were moving to the suburbs. This left the city with a diminished tax base and an impoverished and socially restive inner city—what became known as the "urban crisis." The initial solution was typical Keynesian economics: expand public employment and public assistance. But when President Richard Nixon declared the urban crisis over in the early 1970s, he also reduced federal aid to the city. The economic slowdown of the 1970s that hit the city, combined with a reduced tax base and reduced federal aid, led New York City to the brink of bankruptcy. Financial institutions were unwilling to nenegotiate the city's debts unless it met strict conditions that included severe budget cuts. They also required unions to put their pension funds in city bonds, which meant that if the city went bankrupt, workers would lose their pensions. The overall result was a diminished standard of living for New Yorkers, particularly the poor. But ultimately, the city became financially solvent and represented to neoliberals what could be done through free market principles.

This soon became the pattern with countries in trouble. The economic stagnation of the 1970s impacted developing countries that, with the encouragement of banks, had borrowed heavily but could no longer repay their debts. As a condition for restructuring their loans, multilateral institutions such as the World Bank and the International Monetary Fund (IMF) imposed neoliberal economic policies on these countries. These included privatizing state-run enterprises, reducing the value of their currency, making goods produced in the country cheaper for foreign buyers (thus encouraging exports), and making foreign goods more expensive for citizens (thus discouraging imports). These conditions also included reducing state funding for education, welfare, and health, and imposing user fees for school attendance. These neoliberal policies had few positive results. Only a small number of countries were able to escape debt, and the total amount of money sent to wealthy countries was over $4.6 trillion. According to financier George Stiglitz, the poor countries subsidized the richest.

market externalities
costs or benefits of economic transactions that are not included in prices; may include the environmental, social, or political consequences of market transactions

Market Externalization

Removing government involvement in the economy is central to neoliberal economic philosophy; without such involvement, so the thought goes, business can be more profitable, create more jobs, and so on. One way that less government involvement can help economic growth is by allowing costs that are involved in the production, distribution, consumption, and disposal of goods and services to be externalized. All along the commodity chain, from the production of goods to their transport to their sale and disposal, there are **market externalities**, costs that are not included in the price that people pay.

Take an item such as a Twinkie. Twinkies are described by their producer, the Hostess Corporation, as "golden sponge cake filled with creamy filling." More exactly, the Twinkie consists of some 26 ingredients.

Many consider the revival of New York City from its urban crisis of the 1970s as a fruit of neoliberalism.

TWINKIES

Enriched Wheat Flour—enriched with ferrous sulphate (iron), B vitamins [niacin, thiamine mononitrate (B1), ribofavin (B12) and folic acid], sugar, corn syrup, water, high fructose corn syrup, vegetable and/or animal shortening—containing one or more of partially hydrogenated soybean, cottonseed, or canola oil, and beef fat, dextrose, whole eggs, modified corn starch, cellulose gum, whey, leavenings (sodium acid pyrophosphate, baking soda, monocalcium phosphate), salt, cornstarch, corn syrup solids, mono- and diglycerides, soy lecithin, polysorbate 60, dextrin, calcium caseinate, sodium stearol lactylate, wheat gluten, calcium sulphate, natural and artificial flavors, caramel color, sorbic acid, color added (yellow 5, red 40).

In the United States and in Canada, a package of two Twinkies sells for approximately $1. But that is only the retail price. To arrive at the real price, we would need to examine the hidden costs of each ingredient; in other words, we need to calculate the additional monetary and nonmonetary expenses involved in producing and distributing each ingredient in a Twinkie—expenses that, for some reason, are not reflected in the store price, and hence are externalized.

Let us examine just one ingredient—cane sugar. Environmentally, sugar is not a benign crop. Its production is responsible for damage to coral reefs in Hawaii, water pollution in Buenos Aries, and damage to river estuaries in Brazil. Florida's sugarcane industry dumps phosphorus-laden agricultural runoff that destroys native species. As a result, almost $8 billion will be spent over the next two years to help restore the Everglades. Although sugar producers will pay some of that cost, most of it will be passed on to taxpayers and never be reflected in the price people pay for products containing sugar, such as a Twinkie.

Then there are the hidden health costs. For example, 17 percent of the calories consumed by North Americans are from sugar and other sweeteners. Among other things, that means that our basic nutrition must come from the other 83 percent. Although there are no specific data on the direct contribution of sugar to excess weight and obesity (fat is obviously another major culprit), 65 percent of Americans are overweight. One estimate of the direct and indirect cost of obesity in the United States puts the cost at $118 billion annually, or 12 percent of the nation's healthcare costs. The amount spent on diet drugs and weight-loss programs adds another $33 billion.

Part of the cost of producing, distributing, and consuming sugar is borne by the state, which provides the infrastructure necessary for doing business, including road, power, water, and sanitation systems. The entire water management infrastructure that supports the Florida sugarcane industry, for example, was built with federal tax dollars.

HOW MUCH DOES IT (REALLY) COST?

Each morning, we begin our day by brushing our teeth, washing our face, and using the toilet facilities. Then maybe it's a glass of orange juice or a cup of coffee. What are the hidden environmental, health, and economic costs of these routine activities?

Activity or Product	Hidden Cost
Brushing teeth	
Flushing the toilet	
Orange juice	
Coffee	

These are only some of the hidden costs of one ingredient in a Twinkie. To arrive at the total real cost, we would need to examine each of the other ingredients and then add the hidden costs of processing, packaging, delivery, marketing and waste disposal. We might also have to include the military expenses necessary to keep markets open and to keep in power national leaders who are receptive to neoliberal economic policies.

Rarely do consumers pay the real costs of production and consumption. These costs are passed on to future generations or to people in other countries in the form of low wages, polluted environments, health risks, and the like. None of this would be possible without nation-states that allow its citizens to pass on the real cost of things in the form of environmental damage, health risks, and poverty to others. Therefore, we need to examine the role of the nation-state in sustaining growth.

QUESTION 3.4

What is the role of the nation-state in sustaining growth?

T-Shirt Travels

While neoliberal philosophy is the driving force behind what we call globalization, there is a basic contradiction in how it is applied. The central idea behind neoliberalism is to keep governments from interfering in the functioning of the market; yet the nation-state still plays a vital role in how the economy functions.

For the sake of illustrating how nation-states assist economic growth, let's focus on the cotton in the T-shirt that Pietra Rivoli bought in Fort Lauderdale. Cotton is a major global commodity. Millions of 500-pound bales travel the world's shipping lanes to be converted into cotton goods. Much of that cotton, including that in Pietra Rivoli's T-shirt, is grown in Texas.

However, cotton is a labor-intensive product. Why, then, do T-shirt makers in China, where labor costs are lower, use Texas cotton and not, say, Chinese cotton? Part of the answer to that question is that Texas cotton is embedded in a web of policies enacted by the nation-state to ensure profit. For example, the U.S. government has long paid various kinds of subsidies to cotton farmers, amounting to billions of dollars a year. Without these payments, Texas cotton farmers could not make a profit. In 2002, for example, it cost a U.S. farmer 86 cents to produce a pound of cotton, which then sold for 37 cents a pound. Texas cotton farmers were able to make a profit, however, because the difference between the actual cost to produce the cotton and the price that farmers sold it for was made up by U.S. taxpayers. From 1995 to 2003, Lubbock county, where the cotton for Rivoli's T-shirt was grown, received $86 million in subsidies. Of course, by allowing cotton producers to sell their cotton for less, the taxpayer subsidy also reduced the price that Pietra Rivoli paid for her T-shirt.

The government also helps cotton farmers by regulating the labor market, more specifically, the price that farmers pay for workers. The regulation of the labor market for cotton workers began with the slave trade. By permitting the import and ownership of human beings, the nation-state permitted Southern cotton planters to keep their labor costs artificially low. When slavery ended, Southern cotton planters introduced a system of tenant farming, made possible by laws that changed the status of the sharecropper to a laborer whose wages were paid in crops.

When labor was scarce during World War II, Congress responded by authorizing the *bracero* program, which allowed Mexican nationals to enter the United States for short periods of time to work in agriculture. This policy is part of a general trend in which immigration restrictions are relaxed during periods of labor shortages. The government also assists cotton farmers, and all agribusiness, by refusing to set a minimum wage for farm workers.

Buoyed by nearly $3.5 billion in subsidies, U.S. cotton growers were able to weather a 66% decline in worldwide cotton prices from 1995–2002. Such programs, however, had tremendous negative impact on farmers in developing nations. Without the support of subsidies, the typical cotton grower in West Africa could expect to take home less than $2,000 per year. By some estimates, if U.S. cotton subsidies were removed, revenues for West African countries would increase by $250 million or more.

U.S. cotton subsidies were ruled illegal by the World Trade Organization in 2006 and have now ceased, at a great financial cost to American cotton growers. But why would the United States allow a nonelected, nonrepresentative body such as the WTO to override the policy of protecting Texas cotton growers? To understand that, we need to know something about free trade, its role in globalization, and how it affects us.

Free Trade

Free trade is another term commonly associated with globalization. To promote free trade means to remove barriers to the free flow of goods and capital between nations. Traditionally these barriers consisted of tariffs or quotas on goods from other countries that might compete with domestic industries. They might also include subsidies of the sort that the U.S. government paid to cotton producers. Today the major watchdog of free trade is the World Trade Organization (WTO).

The WTO emerged, as did the World Bank and the International Monetary Fund (IMF), from the Bretton Woods conference of 1944. It began as the Global Agreement on Tariffs and Trade (GATT), and became formalized as the WTO in 1994. The job of the WTO is to obtain agreements from countries to remove restrictions to free trade.

Neoliberals argue that free trade stimulates economic growth and helps alleviate poverty and environmental degradation. Since economic prosperity provides people with more money, they argue, citizens can use that money however they want to. The problem is that not everyone gains from free trade. For example, neoliberals argue that the government should play no role in regulating the environmental damage that our lifestyle creates. Instead, they say, a clean environment should be viewed as another commodity that, if people wish, they can purchase. For that reason, when there is a choice between economic growth and a clean environment, growth should be the first priority. And this is basically how the WTO rules. When researchers discovered that dolphin populations were being endangered by tuna fishing, the U.S. government reacted by banning importation of tuna from countries whose fishing fleets did not follow rules to protect dolphins. Mexico claimed that this law violated articles of the WTO and appealed to the WTO to have the United States rescind the rules or permit retaliatory tariffs to be applied to U.S. exports. The WTO ruled that the laws protecting dolphins were unnecessary barriers to trade.

And yet free trade undoubtedly has advantages. Young women working in the Chinese factories visited by Rivoli, for example, were happy for the work. For all the terrible working conditions in the factories, the workers say, "It sure beats work on the farm." And while millions of textile jobs in the United States have been lost to cheaper foreign labor, Rivoli says that those jobs would have been lost anyway to mechanization and technology.

Her point is that those who argue for tariffs on foreign cotton, yarn, and cloth create higher prices all along the line and reduce competitiveness. The cost of trying to protect U.S. textile manufacturers from foreign competition is estimated in the range of $7 to $11 billion a year, or more than $80,000 a year for each job preserved. Import tariffs are said to represent a tax on clothing of 48 percent. When the United States places restrictions on the quantity of textiles that can be imported, says Rivoli, this encourages foreign countries to maximize their incomes by producing more expensive products rather than lower-priced items.

Avoiding Democratic Decision Making

For neoliberals, the only significant function of government is to advance trade and do whatever it takes to maintain economic growth. The problem they face, however, is that in countries with democratically elected governments, citizens may demand more than that. They may want the government to pass environmental laws, enact higher minimum wage standards, or provide more funds for education—all things that neoliberals say are economically harmful. Governments all over the world face a dilemma: How do they respond to public demands for the government to protect workers, children, consumers, and the environment while, at the same time, responding to pressure from corporate interests not to pass legislation that might affect corporate profits and economic growth?

free trade the removal of barriers to the free flow of goods and capital between nations by eliminating import or export taxes or subsidies paid to farmers and businessmen; it may also mean reducing environmental or social laws when they restrict the flow of goods and capital

Generally speaking, governments have adopted three strategies to address this dilemma. The first is to pay lip service to social, political, and environmental concerns by emphasizing such values as democracy, freedom, social justice, and environmental sustainability while, in effect, doing little about them. The idea of environmentally sustainable growth is a good example. The idea gained popularity as a result of a report issued in 1987 by a commission headed by Norwegian Prime Minister Gro Harlem Brundtland (World Commission on Environmental Development 1987). The report, *Our Common Future*, defined sustainable development as that which "meets the needs of the present without compromising the ability of future generations to meet their own needs." The problem is that whenever economic growth clashes with environmental concerns, economic growth almost always wins. Sustainability seems to mean the greatest amount of environmental damage the public will accept as the price for economic growth.

A second strategy that governments can adopt is to displace regulatory power onto unelected and largely remote global governance institutions such as the WTO. In other words, by giving the WTO the right to decide cases in which environmental protection conflicts with economic growth, governments can absolve themselves of failing to respond to citizens' environmental demands.

The third strategy governments can adopt to avoid taking significant action on social or environmental problems is to free corporations and the mass media to spin events and news to allay public fears and interests. For example, neoliberals in the United States have proposed privatizing Social Security, which would release billions of dollars now collected by the state for investment in the stock market. Regardless of the pros and cons of the argument, the Social Security fund is fully solvent into the 2040s, and if the retirement of the large cohort of people born after World War II burdens the fund, a small rise in Social Security taxes would fix it. Yet for years, media reports have dwelled on the coming demise of the Social Security fund and the potential that millions of Americans would lose their pensions. Obviously if the story of the coming demise of Social Security gains credibility, the chances of the public's approving privatization increases.

Three strategies for balancing public demand and corporate interests:

1. *Pay lip service to social, political, and environmental concerns by emphasizing values such as democracy and freedom, but take little action.*
2. *Displace regulatory power onto unelected and largely remote global governance institutions.*
3. *Free corporations and the mass media to spin events and news to allay public fears and interests.*

The Use of Force

The manufacturing of consent through the media or other public outlets is an example of "soft" power. When that fails, however, the state can always turn to "hard" power—the use of force. As many scholars have pointed out, one key trait of the nation-state is that it is the only entity granted the legitimate use of force.

- "Stateness" can be identified by locating "the power of force in addition to the power of authority."
  –Elman Service (1975, 15)
- If anyone other than a representative of the state kills someone, it will result in retribution by state authorities.
  –Morton Fried
- The state is a form of social contract in which the public has ostensibly consented to assign to the state a monopoly on force to constrain and coerce people.
  –Carol Nagengast

The application of force is essential to protect an economy's access to critical resources, to open countries to the sale of products, and to repress protests against policies that may be harmful to people. The U.S. invasion of Iraq is an example of the attempted use of force to impose a neoliberal regime. In 2003, the United States established the Coalition Provisional Authority (CPA) to govern Iraq prior to democratic elections. However, before elections could be held, the director of the CPA, L. Paul Bremer, imposed a set of orders that were intended to turn Iraq into a model of "free trade" and neoliberal economic theory. These orders included suspending all tariffs, customs duties, import taxes, and licensing fees on goods and services entering or leaving Iraq; giving security firms brought in to work in Iraq full immunity from Iraqi law; privatizing some 200 state-owned enterprises; permitting 100 percent foreign ownership of Iraqi businesses; allowing investors

In 2003–2004, Paul Bremer and the Coalition Provisional Authority issued the 100 Orders, which fundamentally changed Iraq's political and economic policies.

to take 100 percent of the profits they made in Iraq out of the country, with no requirement that the profits be reinvested; and prohibiting any requirement that foreign companies hire local workers, recognize unions, or reinvest any profits back into the country. In addition, CPA orders allowed foreign banks to open in Iraq and to take a 50 percent interest in Iraqi banks and lowered the corporate tax rate from 40 percent to a flat 15 percent.

These orders constituted a corporate wish list of rules and regulations that virtually no democratic legislature would openly support, let alone implement. Furthermore, the CPA planned to build these rules into the Iraqi constitution so that they would have to be acknowledged by any subsequent government. This was particularly important because without guarantees that these economic policies would be retained in the future, no corporation or bank would risk investing money in the Iraq economy. The results of these orders included the firing of 500,000 state workers and allowing unrestricted imports, much to the dismay of Iraqi businesspeople. "Getting inefficient state enterprises into private hands," Bremer said, "is essential for Iraq's economic recovery." It is noteworthy that in the beginning of 2007, with the rising possibility of a United States defeat in Iraq, the Pentagon began a program to reopen state-run factories in order to provide jobs for the mass of Iraqi people put out of work by the CPA.

The imposition of neoliberal policies on Iraq, a country in which the state had played a major role in the economy, may have been a main reason for the Iraqi insurgency. Neoliberalism, with its emphasis on dismantling government programs to help the poor, public subsidies, funds for education, and privatizing virtually everything, generates protest at various levels. By prompting manufacturers to move factories to countries where labor is cheaper (and thus putting thousands out of work), by limiting the power of the government to limit the environmental damage done by corporations (thereby polluting the environments of those with little political power to prevent it), and by supporting tyrannical governments for the sake of economic "stability" (leaving millions in poverty), neoliberalism fuels dissent. To control and react to protest, the state relies upon a growing arsenal of surveillance and deadly weapons. The increasing militarization of the world is illustrated first by the enormous expenditures on weapons systems, even in countries that can't yet afford to ensure that its citizens have enough food. In 2008, worldwide military expenses passed the $1 trillion mark, while sub-Saharan countries, which have an average per capita GDP of roughly $1,300, spent $12.6 billion on arms.

The importance of force is also evident in what some call the United States Empire. Chalmers Johnson suggests

The increasing militarization of the world is illustrated first by the enormous expenditures on weapons systems, even in countries that can't yet afford to ensure that its citizens have enough food.

that the battery of military bases required to ensure U.S. access to energy resources and markets carries with it what he calls the "sorrows of empire," which will ultimately change the nature of the nation-state. These "sorrows" include a state of perpetual war that will lead to more violent attacks against U.S. citizens and an increase in reliance by smaller states on weapons of mass destruction; a loss of democracy and constitutional rights to an increasingly imperial presidency; a "shredded principle of truthfulness," as propaganda and spin are used to glorify war, power, and the military itself; and, finally, economic decline and neglect of education, health, and individual well-being as more and more economic resources are spent to maintain a military empire. The current need of the United States to staff more than 750 bases around the world requires the "professionalism" of the armed forces, producing people who will fight because they are told to, because it is their job, regardless of the political goals of military operations.

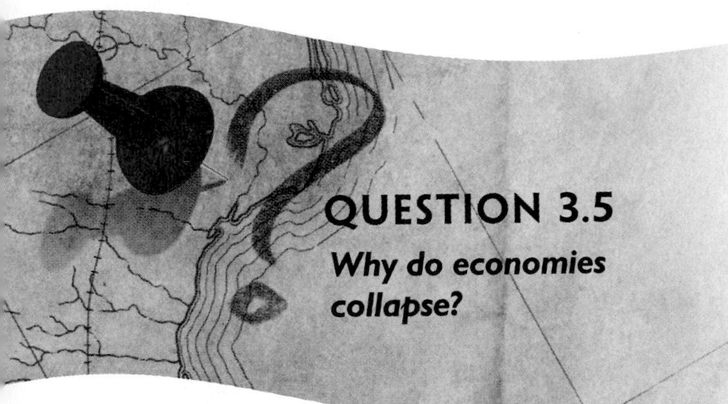

QUESTION 3.5

Why do economies collapse?

Recessions

In spite of the best efforts of governments, economies do occasionally collapse. In 2007, the world experienced the beginning of the worst economic decline since the Great Depression of the 1930s. At least 30 million people, and possibly as many as 50 million, lost their jobs. Losses to the financial sector, corporations, homeowners, and unincorporated businesses were more than $40 trillion, or two-thirds of the world's GDP (Blankenberg and Palma 2009).

The common explanation for this latest global recession is that it resulted from the collapse of a housing bubble in the United States. The story is that low interest rates in the United States along with high cash inflows from overseas, particularly China, sent Americans on a house-buying spree that sent home prices soaring at an unprecedented rate. The bubble was further fueled by "subprime" mortgages, loans to people with few financial resources. When people began to default and banks stopped lending, the housing market collapsed, resulting in the crash of home values and the wiping out of trillions of dollars of wealth. However, as we will see, it was a little more complex than that.

To examine why this recent crisis occured, it may first be useful to examine what may have been the first major economic collapse, and use that to better understand what happened in 2007. It occurred in 1636 and involved tulips.

Tulip Bulbs and Bubbles

The Dutch were inveterate investors, seeking to make money with money. From 1610 to 1640, for example, when the average annual income was 200–400 guilders, Dutch citizens invested at least 10 million guilders in new capital intensive technologies such as windmills and canals (deVries 1997, 29).

Dutch citizens also made money by financing public debt. In 1600, the state owed some 5 million guilders and the public could buy state bonds paying 8 to 16 percent interest (DeVries 1997, 114). By 1660 more than 65,000 people had invested money in and received interest on state bonds; they made money with money.

The tulip, a beloved symbol of the Netherlands, was one of the most popular investments of the time. The price of tulip bulbs varied immensely, as some patterns were more desired than others. Particularly treasured were bulbs that had been invaded by a mosaic virus, which produce multicolored patterns. Bulbs of this type were sometimes worth modest fortunes; a single Semper Augustus bulb sold for 5,500 guilders, almost 20 times the average annual income.

In the fall of 1637, Dutch citizens began to purchase tulip futures, specifying the kind of tulip they wished to purchase in their contracts with sellers. Most of the buyers had no intention of taking possession of the bulbs, betting that the prices would rise and that they could sell the rights to people who wanted the bulbs. Often the sellers did not have any bulbs, but were betting that they could get them at a price less than they were offered from the buyers. Thus, as DeVries and van der Woude (1997, 150) put it, "citizens crowded into taverns to buy and sell bulbs they could not deliver and did not want to receive."

Since there was no bank credit, payment was often promised in kind. A buyer of a single viceroy bulb, valued at 2,500 guilders, gave as collateral "two lasts (a unit of measure for grain) of wheat, four of rye, eight pigs, a dozen sheep, two oxheads of wine, four tons of butter, a thousand pounds of cheese, a bed, some clothing and a silver beaker" (Kindelberger 2000, 109).

Then in February of 1638, for reasons that are unclear, tulip prices began to collapse, and investors faced economic ruin. Since they had only given the sellers a portion of the agreed upon price, they had to somehow come up with the rest. And most did not have this since they depended completely on bulb prices to continue rising. Furthermore, the sellers, using the contracts as collateral for loans, were faced with coming up with additional collateral which they didn't have. There was a further complication—since futures contracts were, at the time, unenforceable in court, there was no incentive to honor them. Thus investors lost large sums of money or the goods that they had used as down payment on their bulb purchases.

TULIP, C.1675 (GOUACHE ON VELLUM), ROBERT, NICOLAS (1614–85)/BURGHLEY HOUSE COLLECTION, LINCOLNSHIRE, UK/THE BRIDGEMAN ART LIBRARY

The Housing Bubble of 2007

What happened with tulips in 1636 is basically what happened with houses in 2007. To understand the most recent recession, we begin with another market externality—the *Exxon Valdez* disaster. On March 24, 1989, the oil tanker *Valdez*, owned by Exxon Oil Company, ran aground in Prince William Sound, Alaska, and spilled 10.8 million gallons of crude oil into the sea.

In order to cover possible penalties, Exxon approached its bank, J. P. Morgan, for a $5 billion loan (Tett 2009). The bank had no problem with the loan itself, since Exxon was one of its best customers and one of the most profitable companies in the world. But it was concerned about the reserve requirement, a rule imposed by international regulatory agencies. In essence, the rule orders banks to keep a percentage of the money they lend in reserve so that they are protected against default.

Though the reserve requirement is designed to protect against nonpayment of loans, banks have a problem with it because money that is held in reserve is money that is not bringing in interest or fees. Thus the issue for banks is how they can put the money they hold in reserve to work. Banks sometimes deal with that problem by "offloading" a debt—selling it to another bank—but in this case, J. P. Morgan was concerned that it would violate client loyalty.

A group in the derivatives department of J. P. Morgan thought they had a perfect solution. They approached the European Bank for Reconstruction and Finance (EBRF), which had lots of money at its disposal, and asked whether, for a fee, they would insure the Exxon loan. In the unlikely event that Exxon defaulted on its obligation, EBRF was asked to make good. They called this a "credit-default swap" or CDS. When EBRF agreed to do this, the derivatives team at J. P. Morgan asked bank regulators to reduce the reserve requirement on the Exxon loan. They argued that since the loan was insured, even if Exxon defaulted, they would still collect. The regulators agreed. The result was that, whereas originally J. P. Morgan would have had to keep about $700,000 in reserve, it now only had to keep about $180,000.

This may seem like a fairly esoteric banking deal, but it set the stage for the economic disaster to follow. The team at J. P. Morgan reasoned that it could use the same financial strategy on other loans that it held. It could, in effect, industrialize the process, thus making it as easy for investors to buy credit derivatives as it was to buy stocks and bonds. J. P. Morgan thus offered securities called Broad Index Securities Trust Offerings (or BISTROS), which were securities derived from the roughly $10 billion in loans that J. P. Morgan had made. They also convinced insurance giant AIG to insure the securities issued on the corporate loans. This convinced regulatory agents to reduce the bank's reserve requirement, freeing up millions of dollars that could be invested elsewhere.

When other banks heard about the innovations of the derivatives team at J. P. Morgan, they enthusiastically followed suit, packaging loans or debt that they held into securities to sell to investors. These securities were also insured by AIG and other companies and seemed to have so little risk that investment rating services gave them double- and triple-A ratings, the same given to government-issued securities.

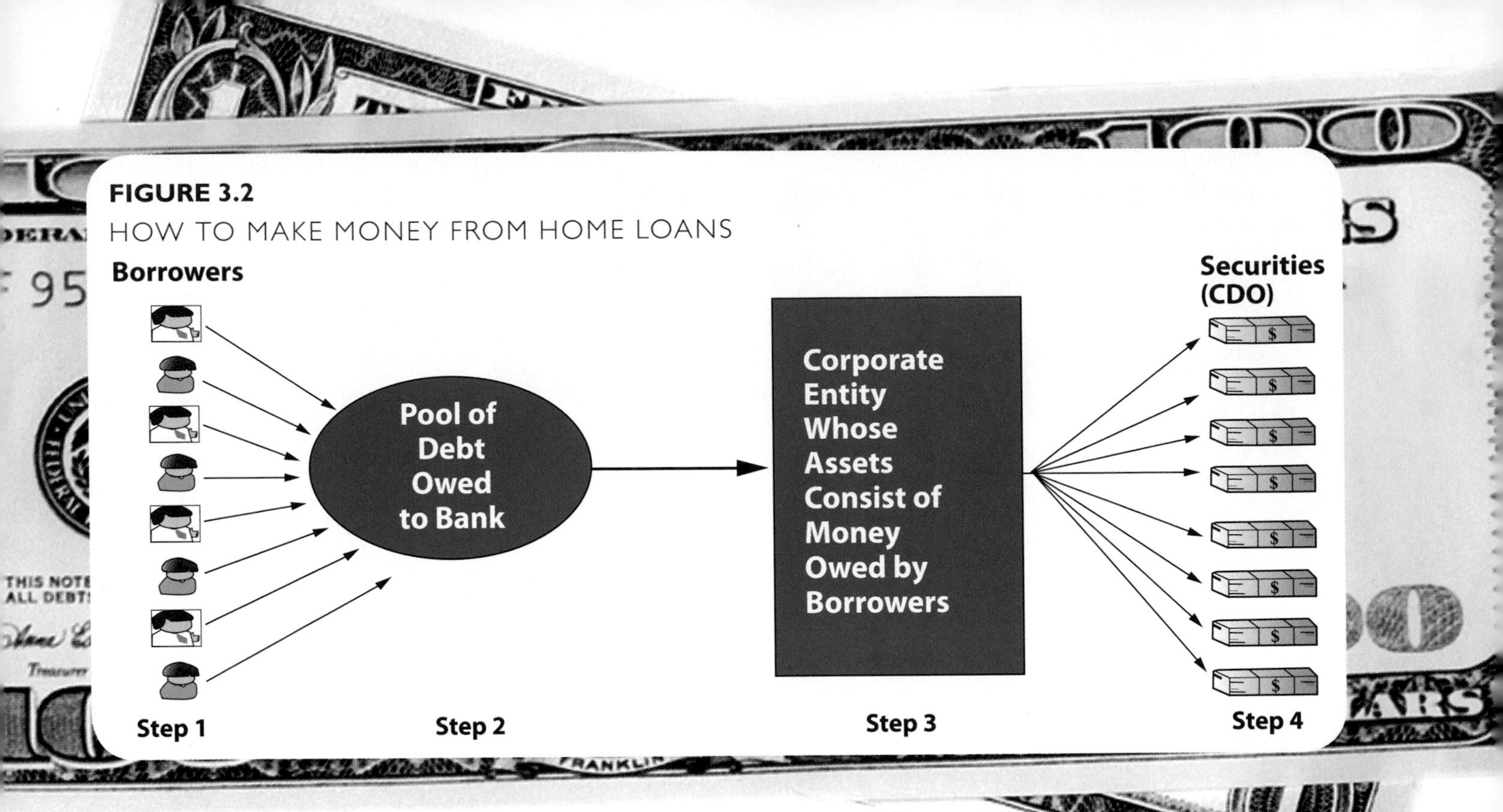

FIGURE 3.2
HOW TO MAKE MONEY FROM HOME LOANS

Then Bayerische Landesbank, a large German bank, approached the derivatives team at J. P. Morgan and asked them to package some $14 billion of U.S. home mortgages into securities to sell (see Figure 3.2). That, however, posed a problem. Unlike corporate loans, which had a long history that enabled banks to estimate the probability of default, there was no corresponding information for housing mortgages. Thus it was difficult to assess the risk of these securities. J. P. Morgan went ahead with the Bayerische Landesbank, but only after building in additional safeguards against default.

J. P. Morgan discontinued this practice after its deal with Bayerische Landesbank, but other banks continued to bundle trillions of dollars of home mortgages and other forms of debt (such as credit card loans, auto loans, and commercial loans) into credit derive options (CDOs), and sold them to eager investors. A key turning point may have come when large banks entered into agreements with mortgage companies to buy any mortgage they sold to homebuyers in order to meet the demand from investors for more debt to package into securities. This allowed mortgage companies to make millions of dollars in fees by making a loan and then selling it to larger investment banks as a part of CDOs. Consequently, the mortgage companies had little interest in whether or not a borrower had the means to repay the loan, since they were quickly passing on the risk to the larger banks. These companies were so anxious to give mortgages that they offered them with no down payment, background check, or verification of income. If the homebuyer expressed concern about repaying the mortgage, they were offered mortgages with low initial payments and told that if they had a problem once payments increased, they could, with home prices rapidly rising, sell the home at a profit or refinance the loan. In short, trillions of dollars were bet on the premise that the value of houses would continue to increase, but, in fact, they fell (see Figure 3.3).

As buyers defaulted on their loans, the value of the securities based on those loans greatly declined, making them impossible to sell. Furthermore, derivatives based on commercial loans, credit card debt, and automobile loans were threatened by defaults. With banks losing money, holding assets of unknown worth, not knowing the financial state of other institutions and borrowers, and insurance companies unable to compensate investors for their losses, banks stopped lending and the whole financial system threatened to freeze. The insurance companies that had guaranteed the securities were forced to pay out billions of dollars they didn't have and were on the verge of collapse until the U.S. government came to the rescue with a trillion-dollar bailout. The resultant banking crisis stopped the flow of money and credit and forced the massive selling of assets by people who needed to meet debt obligations, which further decreased asset value, affecting millions of business and putting millions of people all over the world out of work.

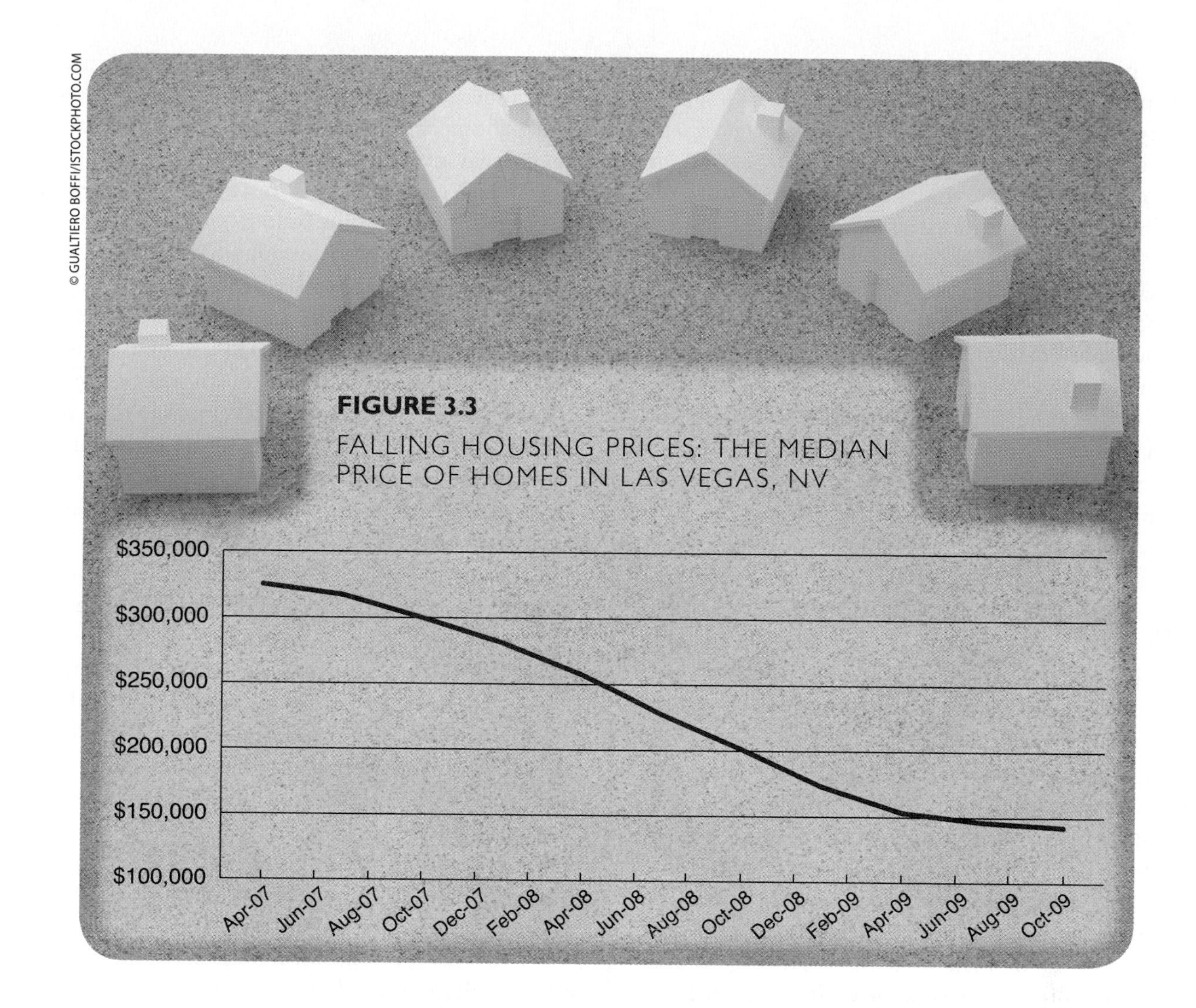

FIGURE 3.3
FALLING HOUSING PRICES: THE MEDIAN PRICE OF HOMES IN LAS VEGAS, NV

Institutional Factors Contributing to the Collapse

As we try to understand the factors that contributed to the economic crisis, we can identity certain ways that financial institutions work that contributed to the crash. For example, there were the perverse incentives whereby rating agencies were paid by the same companies whose securities they were evaluating. Others point to the complexities of the derivatives, such that it took a computer a day and a half to price a CDO. Still others point to the extent to which leverage or borrowing was used to purchase pricey CDOs. And finally there was the competition among investment houses. The people at J. P. Morgan and other firms had little choice but to jump on the derivative bandwagon as they would have failed to produce the profits their competitors were realizing.

Consequently there is much talk about changing the way that financial institutions work to ensure that a crisis doesn't happen again. Suggestions include changing the incentive structure and making bonuses contingent on success, regulating derivatives more closely and ensuring that investors know more about the instruments they are buying, and increasing the reserve requirement. The problem with each or all of these institutional measures is that they run smack dab up against the prime directive—perpetual economic growth.

Quite simply, our economy requires that we spend or produce more this year than last and more next year than this. As mentioned earlier, the minimum rate of growth is around 3 percent. If the economy grows at a lesser rate, it is considered "sluggish," or "stagnant," and often leads to high unemployment, more business failures, and low profits. Another factor receiving little attention contributes to our understanding of economic growth and financial crises—the wealthier a country becomes, the more difficult it is to maintain economic growth. That is why emerging economies such as China, India, and Brazil can grow 6–10 percent a year, while wealthy economies struggle to attain the necessary 3–5 percent.

The problem then is that any attempt to rein in the financial practices of investment bankers may significantly affect the rate of economic growth. The financial sector, which 30 years ago comprised only about 5 percent of the GDP, now makes up 17 percent. With the decline of the U.S. industrial sector over the last 30 years, it is conceivable that had not investment banks generated the growth they did, our economy might be in even worse shape. Wall Street as well as every other sector of the economy was compelled to find new ways to make money to generate the necessary overall growth of the economy. That is why the derivatives team at J. P. Morgan was told that "You will have to make at least half your revenues each year from a product that did not exist before" (Tett 2009, 7–8).

This gets to the central question, rarely, if ever, asked by economists: Why does the economy have to perpetually grow? The simple answer is that once a segment of an economy depends on making money with money, perpetual growth must ensue. That is, once money is lent or invested, it must work to produce more money to account for both the original amount lent (the principal) plus interest. The amount of growth required depends, obviously, on the interest, dividend, or profit required. If there is insufficient growth to generate the additional money, loans go unpaid, and/or dividends or profits unrealized. Thus, going back to the present crisis, as long as house prices continued to grow, the system worked well. But once they ceased growing and in fact collapsed, the entire economic system was threatened.

TABLE 3.3
DEBT OBLIGATIONS IN THE U.S. ECONOMY

Debt Type	Debt Amount	Debt per Person
Federal Government Sector	$10.6 Trillion	$ 34,868
State and Local Government Sector	$ 2.2 Trillion	$ 7,368
Household Sector	$13.8 Trillion	$ 45,395
Business Sector	$11.1 Trillion	$ 36,513
Financial Sector	$17.2 Trillion	$ 56,579
Other	$ 1.9 Trillion	$ 6,250
Sum of All Government and Private Sector Debt	$56.9 Trillion	$186,717

Source: Grandfather Economic Report: http://grandfather-economic-report.com/debt-summary-table.htm

The next question is how much growth is necessary given a specific level of debt? This is important because of the significant increase in debt obligations, both nationally and globally, over the last few decades (see Table 3.3).

We can understand the relationship between debt and growth with a household example. Let's assume I have a household that is earning $150,000 a year and I get a loan from the bank for $600,000 at 7 percent interest over 10 years. The $600,000 represents money that didn't exist before the bank issued it, but will continue to exist in the form of an asset—the house. Over the course of the loan (10 years) the total interest that I will pay is $235,981. That represents completely new money that I have to create. Given my income of $150,000 I must produce, on average, and additional $23,598 a year.

The numbers chosen to represent our hypothetical household were selected to reflect the U.S. economy on a smaller scale. The housing loan roughly corresponds to the total debt obligations of all sectors of the U.S. economy—some $57 trillion and growing, while the income corresponds to the total U.S. GDP of $14 trillion. If we assume that the average interest rate on all of the debts is 7 percent and that the repayment term is approximately 10 years, then the interest would total $235,596 trillion. Repaying this interest would require a growth rate of 15.7 percent a year, which is well above the average U.S. growth rate of 3–4 percent a year.

Thus the current economic crisis has more to do with the internal logic of our economic system—particularly the need for perpetual growth—than it does anything else. Institutional factors, as anthropologists such as Gillian Tett (2009) and Karen Ho (2009) illustrate, certain play a major role in contributing to the boom and bust nature of our economic system. But even those institutions must function in an environment that demands perpetual growth, and placing restrictions on how they operate may significantly hamper that goal.

Are There Solutions?

We have indices with which to measure our quality of life in terms other than economic. For example, the Human Development Index (HDI), published annually by the United Nations, ranks nations according to their citizens' quality of life (see Table 3.4). It considers factors such as life expectancy, adult literacy, school enrollment, gender equality, food, and income security, as well as GDP.

Redefining Progress, a nonprofit public policy institute, proposes that we assess the state of a society through the Genuine Progress Indicator (GPI). The GPI takes household consumption as a base figure and then adjusts it by adding factors such as the value of housework, parenting, and volunteer work and subtracting factors such as environmental pollution, crime, noise, family breakdown, and loss of leisure time. By subtracting items that diminish our quality of life, rather than adding them as does the GDP, we find that as GDP has risen over the last few decades, the GPI has declined (see Figure 3.4).

The difficulty is that any attempt to address the problems created by growth means reducing it, which can have dire immediate consequences. The change would have to be as great as that of the industrial revolution. And, since it is debt that requires perpetual growth, it would have to begin by wiping out all debt, a measure that creditors would forcibly resist. Furthermore, if all debt was forgiven, who would ever again want to lend or invest money in needed businesses or projects?

TABLE 3.4

TOP 25 NATIONS ON HUMAN DEVELOPMENT INDEX

Rank	Country
1	Norway
2	Australia
3	Iceland
4	Canada
5	Ireland
6	Netherlands
7	Sweden
8	France
9	Switzerland
10	Japan
11	Luxembourg
12	Finland
13	United States
14	Austria
15	Spain
16	Denmark
17	Belgium
18	Italy
19	Liechtenstein
20	New Zealand
21	United Kingdom
22	Germany
23	Singapore
24	Hong Kong
25	Greece

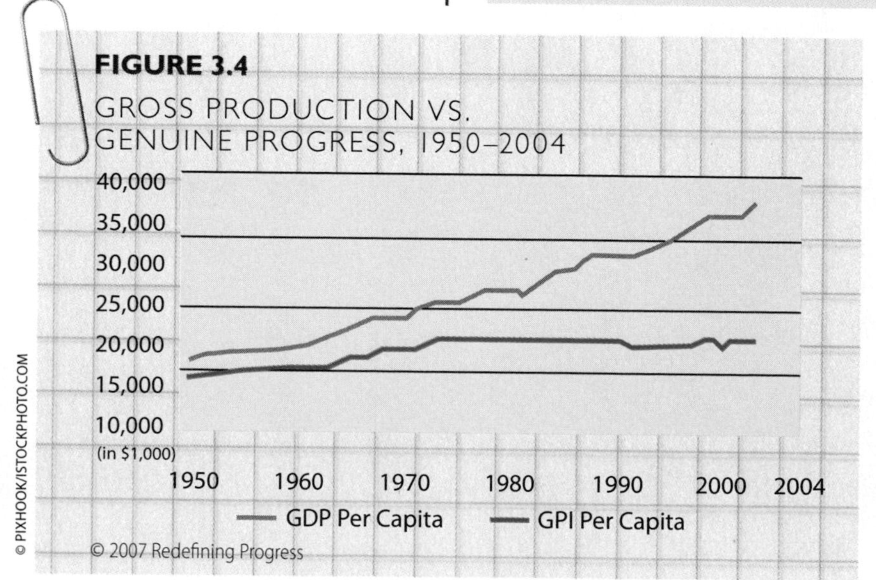

FIGURE 3.4

GROSS PRODUCTION VS. GENUINE PROGRESS, 1950–2004

WHY DO PEOPLE BELIEVE DIFFERENT THINGS, AND WHY ARE THEY SO CERTAIN THAT THEIR VIEW OF THE WORLD IS CORRECT AND OTHER VIEWS ARE WRONG?

Chapter 4 THE SOCIAL AND CULTURAL CONSTRUCTION OF REALITY

There is an obvious rightness about our own world view. It seems, in some way, to mirror reality so straightforwardly that it must be a consequence of direct apprehension rather than effort and imagination. Conversely, alternative beliefs possess an obvious wrongness. The more natural our own perspective becomes, the more puzzling become the strange propositions of ancestors, aliens and eccentrics. How did such mistaken ideas come to be held? However have they remained uncorrected for so long?

Barry Barnes

* * *

QUESTIONS

In examining this problem, we will consider the following questions:

4.1 How does language affect the meanings people assign to experience?

4.2 How does symbolic action reinforce a particular view of the world?

4.3 How do people come to believe what they do, and how do they continue to hold their beliefs even if they seem contradictory or ambiguous?

4.4 Can humor be used to resolve the contradictions inherent in language and metaphor?

4.5 How can people reorder their view of the world if it becomes unsatisfactory?

INTRODUCTION

The Central Question

"Symbolic actions, such as rituals, myths, arts, literature, and music, play a role in organizing and making concrete a particular view of the world."

How is it that people can believe in God or devils? How can they believe in the existence of ancestor spirits or the power to call forth spirits of the dead? Though there is no material proof, people do believe in these things and even take these beliefs for granted.

How to deal with the problem of belief has long been a concern of anthropologists. Early anthropological studies of religion sought to explain how people could believe in things that seemed illogical, such as witchcraft. Edward Tylor, considered by some to be the founder of modern anthropology, wrote in 1871 that religion and belief in the supernatural developed from attempts to explain basic phenomena such as death and dreaming. What is the difference, Tylor imagined early human beings thinking, between a live person and a dead one, between a sleeping person and someone who is awake? They must have reasoned, Tylor argued, that there was some thing, some essence, that traveled to distant places during dreams, or left the body permanently in death. According to Tylor, this reasoning produced the idea of a soul that animated the body but that departed in sleep and death. In his view, this is the reason why the word for "breath" and the word for "soul" are the same or similar in so many languages.

Once people arrived at a belief in souls, it was a small step to reason that there were places in which departed souls resided and an even smaller step to believe that souls became gods. The next step was when the living appealed to these departed spirits for help in controlling life's uncertainties. For Tylor, then, beliefs in gods and spirits developed through the attempts of human beings to explain certain events, to understand why things happened as they did.

In his classic work *The Elementary Forms of the Religious Life* (1912), French sociologist Émile Durkheim also asked what led to the concept of God. Durkheim speculated, as did Tylor, that the secret must lie in the beliefs of early human beings. Thinking that the lives of early human beings could best be studied by looking at societies that were relatively underdeveloped, Durkheim read about the religious beliefs of the indigenous people of Australia, particularly their beliefs about **totemism**. The totem, said Durkheim, was some element of nature—an animal, a plant, or

totemism the use of a symbol, generally an animal or a plant, as a physical representation for a group, generally a clan

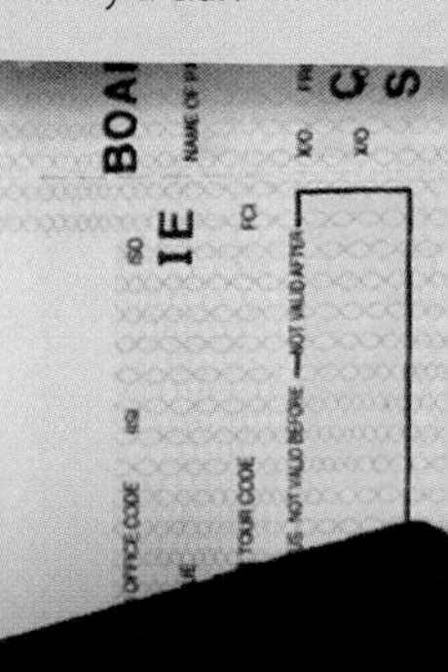

ritual a dramatic rendering or social portrayal of meanings shared by a specific body of people in a way that makes them seem correct and proper (*see also* symbolic actions)

symbolic actions the activities—including ritual, myth, art, dance, and music—that dramatically depict the meanings shared by a specific body of people

a celestial phenomenon—that served as a symbol for a group or clan. The totem was worshipped and was considered sacred and holy by the members of the group. It also served as a representation of the group. If members of the group worshipped the totem and if the totem was a symbol of the group, was it unreasonable to suppose, asked Durkheim, that the group itself was the object of worship?

But what would suggest to people that the totem had sacred power? The answer, said Durkheim, lies in the constraints that people feel are imposed on them by the special power that they feel when groups come together in celebration and **ritual**. And if in small-scale societies people worship the group through their symbolic representations, is it not reasonable to suppose that in large-scale societies people worship society through their god or gods? That God is society?

Early writers approached the question of God in particular, and religion in general, with the assumption that the beliefs were essentially in error. Nevertheless, they believed that religious beliefs served some purpose, increasing group cohesion or providing sanctions for the violation of group norms. More recent anthropological attempts to understand belief try to understand how it is that people are persuaded that their view of the world is correct. Some researchers have even extended their studies to include so-called scientific beliefs, reasoning that the processes that result in people taking the existence of God for granted must apply as well to belief in a naturally ordered universe of atoms, molecules, and magnetic forces.

To answer the question of how it is that people can so easily believe that their view of the world is correct, we need to examine a number of concepts. Because language is one of the mediums we use to make our knowledge concrete and to communicate with others, it plays a major role in giving us a sense of the universe and ourselves. **Symbolic actions**—the rituals, myths, arts, literature, and music that we enjoy or participate in—all play a role, as we shall see, in organizing and making concrete a particular view of the world. Also, we need to explore how people learn to view the world as they do and how they defend their beliefs against skeptics. Certainly the fact that others agree or disagree with us about the nature of the world will influence what we believe is true or not true and determine how we react to experiences that challenge a particular view of the world. What we believe must also be, in some way, a product of our social, economic, and political life. Then we need to ask why people sometimes radically change what they believe.

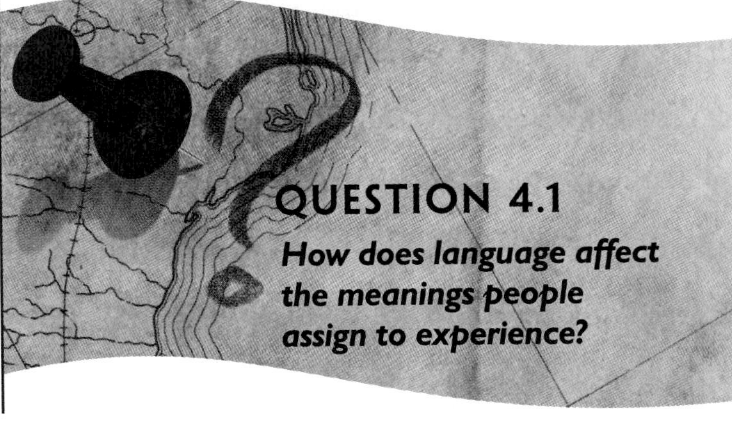

QUESTIONS

4.1 How does language affect the meanings people assign to experience?

4.2 How does symbolic action reinforce a particular view of the world?

4.3 How do people come to believe what they do, and how do they continue to hold their beliefs even if they seem contradictory or ambiguous?

4.4 Can humor be used to resolve the contradictions inherent in language and metaphor?

4.5 How can people reorder their view of the world if it becomes unsatisfactory?

Language and Thought

Language is one medium through which we make contact with the world. We tend to assume that it is a transparent medium for the transmission of thought. Anthropologist Edward Sapir challenged this view, suggesting that specific languages not only provide a medium of communication, but also define and guide our perception of experience. That is, specific languages, be it French, Tupi, or Chinese, order the experiences of the speakers. Benjamin Lee Whorf later elaborated on Sapir's ideas by suggesting that each language constitutes a frame of reference that orders a particular view of the world.

The relationship between language and thought can exist at various levels. The most obvious is at the level of vocabulary. According to Sapir and Whorf, vocabulary reflects a person's social and physical environment. Whorf noticed, for example, that the Inuit have a variety of words for kinds of snow, whereas the Aztecs of Mexico used the same word for "cold," "ice," and "snow." Sapir noted how the vocabulary of the Paiute, living in the desert regions of southern Utah and northern Arizona, where complex directions were needed for finding water, contained detailed descriptions of features of the landscape. He suggested that the vocabulary of a language not only reveals what is important to the speakers but also cues the speakers to be more sensitive to the named features of their environment.

Sapir and Whorf also explored the relationship between the grammar of a language and the modes of thought characteristic of its speakers. In English, Whorf points out, there are two dominant types of sentences: the subject–predicate type, such as "The book is green," and the actor–action type, such as "Sally runs." In both cases, the subject of the sentence is spoken of as if it were an enduring object, something stable through time that acts or is acted on by something else. Whorf maintains that this indicates a pervasive tendency in English to view the world as being made up of objects, so that experiences described in English lose the fluidity of passing experience. This is evident in the way we speak of time as if it were an object or a thing, as if we could isolate a piece of it ("I'll study for three hours"), the same way we select food ("I'll take three hamburgers"). In this sense our grammar reflects, reinforces, and perhaps determines our general view of the world as consisting of objects or substances, with everything perceived as an attribute of some object.

The ideas of Edward Sapir and Benjamin Lee Whorf, generally referred to as the **Sapir-Whorf hypothesis**, are suggestive, and both were very careful to avoid claiming that there is a causal link between language and thought.

© BIFFSPANDEX/ISTOCKPHOTO.COM / © MARIA TOUTOUDAKI/ISTOCKPHOTO.COM

Borrowing Meaning with Metaphors

Not all anthropologists are convinced that there is an explicit link between the grammar of a language and the culture of the people who speak the language. There is another sense in which language serves to give meaning to different events, and it has to do with the idea of **metaphor**.

One major characteristic of language is its economy; the same words we use to describe one area of experience can also be used to describe another. This occurs primarily through metaphor. Metaphors take language from one **domain of experience**, such as the domain of the body or the domain of

Sapir-Whorf hypothesis the idea that there is an explicit link between the grammar of a language and the culture of the people who speak the language

metaphor a figure of speech in which linguistic expressions are taken from one area of experience and applied to another

domain of experience an area of human experience (e.g., business, war, science, family life) from which people borrow meaning to apply to other areas

animals, and apply it to another domain, such as landscape features or persons. For example, "the shoulder of the road" is a metaphoric extension of a body part used to refer to landscape, while "Jeff is a dog" represents an extension from the animal world to the human world.

Consider how Americans borrow from the domain of economic exchange to talk about time: Time is money, I don't have the time to give you, that flat tire cost me an hour, you need to budget your time, etc. Sports is another domain from which Americans heavily borrow. A young male might describe a romantic encounter thusly: I met a girl, I thought she'd play ball and that I'd not only get to first base, but score, but I struck out.

Consider, further, the way our conception of illness is embedded in the language we use to describe it. We take language from the domain of war and use it to talk about health. We fight a cold, destroy germs, and wage war on cancer. Recent research reports describe how the AIDS virus weakens the "immune system attack force," or the "killer cells" that are meant to "destroy virus-stricken cells." Does our speaking of illness in terms of war and battle encourage us to take for granted that it *is* some kind of war? If so, how does that view determine the kinds of treatment that we seek? Doesn't the language that we use to describe illness predispose us to cures that destroy the agent of disease rather than return the patient to health?

It is important to note that when language is extended from one domain to another, meaning is also extended. Metaphor involves not only speaking of one experience in terms of another but also understanding one experience in terms of another. Our young male paramour, using a metaphor common to American youth, sees his romantic encounter as a contest to be won or lost. Metaphors, then, are not simply verbal devices that we use to make our language colorful and economical. Instead, they are like lenses that help us understand our experiences. By using language from one domain of experience to describe another, we transfer whole domains of meaning—arguments become wars, time becomes a commodity, and romantic encounters become contests. Moreover, the metaphors we use to describe experiences may predispose us to seek certain solutions to problems associated with those experiences.

key metaphors a term to identify metaphors that dominate the meanings that people in a specific culture attribute to their experience

myth a story or narrative that portrays the meanings people give to their experience

The fact that Americans borrow so heavily from the domains of war, sports, and economic exchange suggests another way to understand how language influences people's views of the world. Most societies seem to have a few domains from which they borrow extensively for metaphors. These domains become **key metaphors** that give each culture a distinctive style. Thinking and speaking of many domains of experience in terms of a particular domain is a way to achieve cohesive meaning in a culture.

Kwakwaka'wakw Metaphors of Hunger

Perhaps one of the most spectacular expressions of the elaboration of both a key metaphor and the human imagination is found among the Kwakwaka'wakw of British Columbia.* We owe much of our knowledge of the traditional life of the Kwakwaka'wakw to Franz Boas, one of the founders of American anthropology, his Kwakwaka'wakw assistant, George Hunt, and filmmaker and photographer Edward Curtis.

Stanley Walens suggests that the act of eating is a key metaphor for the Kwakwaka'wakw. A fundamental meaning the Kwakwaka'wakw find in their experience is that the universe is a place in which some beings must die so that other beings may eat them and live. Eating gives life in at least two ways: it provides nutrition and it frees souls. The Kwakwaka'wakw believe that when a person dies, the soul leaves the body and enters the body of a salmon. But the soul cannot be freed until the physical body is destroyed. For this reason the Kwakwaka'wakw place their dead on scaffolds where the body can be devoured by ravens and other birds. Once the soul enters the body of a salmon, it remains there, living in a salmon world that socially resembles the human world. However, when the salmon is caught and eaten by human beings, the soul is once again freed and enters the body of a newborn child. Thus, for the Kwakwaka'wakw, the act of eating becomes a metaphor through which much of their life is understood and described.

The importance of eating as a metaphor that orders experience is evident in the dominance of mouths in Kwakwaka'wakw art, ritual, and **myth**.

*In most ethnographic studies, particularly the work of Franz Boas, the Kwakwaka'wakw are known as the Kwakiutl. Technically, however, this term only applies to a single tribe within the group, who refer to themselves as Kwakwaka'wakw, "those who speak Kwak'wala."

A member of the Kwakwaka'wakw of British Columbia.

Their world, says Walens, is replete with the mouths of animals killing to satisfy their hunger. Their art is filled with gaping jaws of killer whales, fangs of wolves and bears, and tearing beaks of hawks, eagles, and ravens. Dancers wear masks of cannibal birds with nine-foot-long beaks that shatter human skulls to suck out the brains. In their myths, wild women with protruding lips inhabit the woods, waiting to rip apart travelers and misbehaving children. It is a world where suckling infants turn into monsters and devour their mothers.

The Kwakwaka'wakw use the eating metaphor to give meaning to a wide range of their experiences. Hunger is associated with greed, for, like unrestrained hunger, greed causes people to accumulate wealth far beyond what they need. Hunger is also associated with immorality, as the Kwakwaka'wakw believe that human desires create conflict and destruction that can quickly get out of hand, so that people must work together to prevent and control conflict before it threatens to destroy the group. People who hoard food are, in effect, hoarding souls, preventing the return of a soul from the spirit world. Consequently, the Kwakwaka'wakw place great emphasis on gift giving and generosity. Hunger is also associated with children, who constantly demand to be fed, and who will, if allowed, devour all the family's food.

The full impact of a metaphor lies in the fact that people are trying to impose order on their lives by describing the world according to a particular domain of experience. The Kwakwaka'wakw believe that greed, conflict, and child rearing can be solved by controlling hunger. Eating is thus highly ritualized and controlled. Food must be carefully handled and generously given to others to avoid accusations of greed. In fact, wealthy persons are said to vomit forth goods, vomit being for the Kwakwaka'wakw a life-giving substance. Animals that regurgitate their food, such as wolves and owls, occupy a special place in the Kwakwaka'wakw world. The socialization techniques of the Kwakwaka'wakw are geared to teaching children to control their hunger. In sum, a single domain of experience—eating—has been elaborated by the Kwakwaka'wakw to give to their world meaning.

The Metaphors of Contemporary Witchcraft and Magic

In addition to everyday experience, such as eating, metaphors may also be imbedded in myth and history. A good example is modern witchcraft and magic.

Anthropologist Tanya M. Luhrmann details some of these practices in her book *Persuasions of the Witch's Craft: Ritual Magic in Contemporary England* (1989). Luhrmann joined various covens and groups in England that consisted mostly of middle-class urbanites who

SEXUAL METAPHORS IN THE UNITED STATES

There are some interesting parallels between the metaphors of eating and hunger among the Kwakwaka'wakw and the metaphors of sexual intercourse and desire in the United States. Kwakwaka'wakw art, myth, and stories are filled with mouths and images of eating and hunger. What are some of the images that fill American expressive culture (advertising, for example)? Vomit is a life-giving substance for the Kwakwaka'wakw; what symbolizes life giving in the United States? Are there other ways Americans use sexual symbolism that are similar to the ways the Kwakwaka'wakw use hunger and food?

situate their magic in "New Age" ideology. They emphasize natural foods, good health, and personal stability, and their magical practices consist largely of conjuring spirits, reading the tarot, and magical healing.

Modern magic is based on the assumption that the mind and thought can affect matter without the thinker's actions. It assumes that thought and matter are one. Magicians believe, says Luhrmann, that it is a distortion to treat objects as isolated and unique. One manual describes a worldview that sees things as swirls of energy, rather than as objects. The physical world, it says, is formed by energy in a way that is similar to how stalactites are created by dripping water. Human beings can cause a change in the physical world by altering these energy patterns, as we might change the form of a stalactite by changing the flow of water.

A key metaphor imbedded in modern witchcraft and magic is that of stratification, of "planes" and "levels." For the follower of white (good) witchcraft, the universe is divided into a complex collection of entities and beings that exist on different planes, of which the everyday plane of material life is the lowest. After death, for example, souls do not die but exist on another plane, with some remaining in contact with the material world. Other magical forces exist on other levels, but they can be harnessed by human beings to influence events on the everyday plane of existence. Moreover, with proper training, the human mind can create forms on the astral plane that may in turn affect things in the material world.

Becoming a magician, Luhrmann says, requires the acquisition of specialized and esoteric knowledge. Consequently, magicians read books, attend rituals, go to meetings, and learn the tarot, astrology, mythology, and seventeenth-century Gaelic cures.

The tarot deck has 78 cards that comprise an elaborate and complex system of metaphoric associations linking various domains of experience, ranging from planets and other celestial objects to colors, material elements, emotions, personal qualities, and mythological beings. Each tarot card is said to have some meaning that is determined by its association with a specific planet, an element, an emotion or human quality, and so forth. Aleister Crowley, a well known practitioner of modern magic and witchcraft and tarot-deck designer, described each card as, in a sense, a living being.

The magician uses the tarot cards to divine the future, but the cards also provide ways for people to interpret their own lives. The cards, says Luhrmann, provide people with a symbolic map with which to interpret and understand themselves as they transfer the meaning of the cards to their own lives and experiences. Thus, some may associate themselves with the Empress, calm and fecund. They may say that someone has the temperament of Hermes, mercurial and unpredictable. In a sense, one can define the self in terms of the tarot and actually become the person that the cards delineate. The transfer of meaning creates meaning.

With metaphors, we must remember that there is no necessary connection between the domains from which people draw metaphors and the domains to which they apply them. There is no natural connection between commodities and time, war and health, or eating and immortality. These connections are the products of the human imagination. No man is really a tiger and no woman really a fox. On some level, then, metaphoric borrowings are intrinsically absurd. Yet we constantly seem to confuse one domain with another—we really do fight disease; we really win arguments. And so we need to explore by what means people are convinced that by controlling one domain of experience (e.g., eating), they can control another (e.g., greed).

QUESTION 4.2

How does symbolic action reinforce a particular view of the world?

A Game of Chess

Language represents one way that our experience of the world is socially filtered. By sharing a language, we also share a view of the world expressed in the vocabulary, grammar, and metaphors of the language. But language is not the only way that our social life mediates between our senses and the meanings that we assign to experience. We also participate in activities that express a particular view of the world. These include symbolic actions such as ritual, myth, literature, art, games, and music. Symbolic actions carry bundles of meanings that represent public displays of a culture. They are dramatic renderings and social portrayals of the meanings shared by a specific group. More importantly, symbolic actions render particular views of the world in a way that makes them seem correct and proper.

This idea can be illustrated with the game of chess. Chess originated in India or China as a favorite pastime of the aristocracy. Its original meanings are unknown, but the game is often considered to be a representation of war.

But chess is more than a game. It is a statement, a story about hierarchy and the social order. Pieces (pawns, rooks, knights, bishops, kings, and queens) are ranked in terms of importance and are given freedom of movement corresponding to their ranking. Consequently, each game of chess is a story that reinforces the validity of

a social system based on rank. Each time the game is played, the authenticity of this social system is proven true; the side with the highest-ranking pieces remaining is almost always the winner. The game also validates the importance of the generals (the two players), who control the movement of their pieces on the board. It is the strategist, the thinker, who wins the war (game), not the soldiers; even the king is dependent on the general. Since in every game each side starts out with the same number and kinds of pieces, it must be the strategist, the head of the hierarchy, who determines the outcome of the game, and by extension, the well-being of society. Chess reinforces the axiom that rank is power, and power is achieved by outwitting an opponent. A pawn, in itself, can never defeat a queen, any more than a peasant can threaten a king. There are winners and losers, but regardless of which side wins, the match represents the superiority of the aristocracy over the peasants.

Even with these embedded meanings, a single game of chess is not likely to convince anyone that the world works in the way it is portrayed in the game. Instead, the meanings that characterize a culture are repeated again and again in other symbolic actions, the most important of which may be ritual.

The Kwakwaka'wakw and the witchcraft and Western mystery groups described by Tanya Luhrmann provide good examples of how ritual portrays, reinforces, and provides evidence for a particular view of the world.

The Kwakwaka'wakw Cannibal Dance

The Kwakwaka'wakw view of the world, as we noted previously, rests on the metaphor of hunger and is graphically displayed in their language, myth, art, and ritual. One of the most important Kwakwaka'wakw rituals is the Cannibal Dance.

The Cannibal Dance is a four-day spectacle that serves as the highlight of the Kwakwaka'wakw Winter Ceremonial, a period of celebration and ritual observance in which all worldly activities cease. It is a time when the spiritual world of the Kwakwaka'wakw, filled with powerful beings and animal spirits, intersects with the real world. The dance varies in some detail from group to group, but in all it is the focal point of a youth's initiation into the Cannibal Society, a group responsible for performing certain rituals. In the ceremony, the initiate plays the role of the cannibal dancer, or *hamatsa*. Members of the Cannibal Society and others gather in a ceremonial house to call back the cannibal to the human world from his sojourn in the realm of Man Eater, one of the most important of the supernatural beings in the Kwakwaka'wakw pantheon of spirits.

At the beginning of the ceremony, the *hamatsa* is believed to be in the woods frantically searching for human flesh to devour. Some early ethnographic accounts of the dance report that he would actually eat human mummified remains. Meanwhile, members of the Cannibal Society gather around a fire in the ceremonial house to sing and recite prayers to entice the *hamatsa* into the house, periodically sending men out to see if he is approaching the village. Finally, the prayers and calls of the Cannibal Society attract the *hamatsa*, who arrives, dressed in branches of the hemlock tree, pushing aside roof boards and jumping down among the celebrants. Jumping through the roof is supposed to symbolize descent from the spirit world above to the world of the living below. In a seeming frenzy, the *hamatsa* runs around the fire and then into an adjacent room, leaving behind only the sacred hemlock branches he had worn. During the four days of the ceremony, the celebrants try by various means to entice him back into the house and, in effect, tame and socialize him, convincing him to forsake his craving for human flesh and accept normal food. In one part of the ceremony the *hamatsa* flees the house and a member of the Cannibal Society is sent as the bait to attract him. The *hamatsa*

> **The *hamatsa's* hunger is fearsome; but it is the same hunger felt by every human, and thus every human has the power to control it. Ultimately the *hamatsa* and the bestial ferocity he embodies can be conquered. Morally, the force of controlled social action—the strength of ritual—can conquer even a Cannibal's hunger. In fact, ritual can totally alter the impetus of the Cannibal's hunger, changing it from a destructive act to an affirmation of self control, an act of creative power. The winter ceremonials prove that no matter how terrible the power of hunger, no matter how many fearsome guises it assumes, no matter how many masks it wears, and no matter how many voices it speaks with, morality will be the ultimate victor. So long as humans have the knowledge to use food correctly, they need never fear hunger nor its awful accompaniment, death. (Walens 1981, 162)**

rushes upon him, seizes his arm, and bites it. Each time he bites someone, he dashes into a secret room and vomits, an act that is repeated various times during the ceremony.

During pauses, members of the audience exchange gifts. Later the *hamatsa* appears naked and is given clothes, but he flees again. At another point a woman who serves as a co-initiate appears naked, carrying mummified remains. She dances backward trying to entice the *hamatsa* to enter the house, but she fails. Finally the group succeeds in subduing the *hamatsa* by bathing him in the smoke of cedar bark that has been soaked in menstrual blood. After the conclusion of the public part of the Cannibal Dance, the initiate and a few members of the Cannibal Society go to another house and eat a normal meal, the final symbol that the *hamatsa* has been tamed.

Ritual can be viewed as a symbolic representation of reality. In another sense, ritual presents participants with solutions to real problems, in the same way as symbolic representations suggest real solutions. For the Kwakwaka'wakw, the *hamatsa* is the ultimate projection of the power of hunger, and his desire for human flesh is a manifestation of the forces that can destroy society. The participants in the ritual, by symbolically taming the hunger of the *hamatsa*, are asserting their moral responsibility to control greed and conflict. The ritual is the acting out of the successful efforts of the group to overcome forces that threaten their society.

The Cannibal Dance also contains a powerful message about socialization. Children, like the *hamatsa*, come from the spirit world and enter the physical world naked. Like the *hamatsa*, children have a female assistant, their mother, who must feed and socialize them. Children come into the world hungry, threatening to devour their parents' wealth. Thus, in the Kwakwaka'wakw view of things, all humans are cannibals who must be socialized and tamed. Through swaddling, ritual fasting, denial of food, and other actions, parents transform their children from cannibals into moral human beings. Through ritual enactment, the Kwakwaka'wakw have made their symbols real.

The Ritual of Contemporary Witchcraft and Magic

> In a witches' coven in northeast London, members have gathered from as far away as Bath, Leicester, and Scotland to attend the meeting at the full moon. . . . The sitting room has been transformed. The furniture has been removed, and a twelve-foot circle drawn on the carpet. . . . Four candlesticks stake out the corners of the room, casting shadows from stag antlers on the wall. The antlers sit next to a sheaf of wheat, subtle sexual symbolism. In spring and summer there are flowers everywhere. The altar in the centre of the circle is a chest which seems ancient. On top an equally ancient box holds incense in different drawers. On it, flowers and herbs surround a carved wooden Pan; a Minoan goddess figure sits on the latter itself amid a litter of ritual knives and tools. (Luhrmann 1989, 42)

This is the setting for one of the rituals that Tanya Luhrmann attended in the course of her fieldwork on contemporary witchcraft and magic. These rituals, she says, are particularly important because they comprise one of the ways that people become convinced of the validity of their beliefs. Going on to describe the ritual in this setting, Luhrmann writes:

> The high priestess begins by drawing the magic circle in the air above the chalk, which she does with piety, saying "let this be the boundary between the worlds of gods and that of men". . . . On this evening a coven member wanted us to "do" something for a friend's sick baby. Someone made a model of the baby and put it on the altar, at the Minoan goddess's feet. We held hands in a circle around the altar and then began to run, chanting a set phrase. When the circle was running at its peak the high priestess suddenly stopped. Everyone shut their eyes, raised their hands, and visualized the prearranged image: in this case it was Mary, the woman who wanted the spell, the "link" between us and the unknown child. . . . By springtime, Mary reported, the child had recovered, and she thanked us for the help. (1989, 42)

Rituals like this one, the Cannibal Dance of the Kwakwaka'wakw, or those enacted in thousands of mosques, churches, and synagogues, are special occasions that not only involve the enactment of key metaphors, but also serve as special events set aside from everyday existence, drawing participants into an emotional involvement with the metaphors. Rituals produce special feelings; people are carried away with symbolism, music, and social communion with others.

In this charged atmosphere, it is easy to believe that it is not the ritual itself that produces these feelings, but the forces or powers that the ritual is believed to summon or embrace. As Luhrmann puts it,

> Just because you have a profound experience during prayer, it does not mean that God exists. But people often find the distinction hard to handle: they tend to accept the magical or theological ideas because the involvement—the spirituality, the group meeting, the moving symbols, the sheer fun of the practice—becomes so central to their lives. (1989, 178)

In contemporary witchcraft and magic, great emphasis is placed on visualization and meditation in ritual. The high priest or priestess may relate a story and ask the participants to imagine themselves in the story; it may be a walk through a moonlit wood or a voyage with Sir Francis Drake around the Horn of Africa. After the ritual, people report actually experiencing the salt spray on their face or the pitching of the sea, and they experience fellow participants as shipmates aboard Drake's ship, the *Golden Hind*. In other words, the ritual not only dramatically depicts a metaphor, it teaches the participants how to experience the world as if the forces, gods, and spirits were truly real. Consequently, it is not unusual, in any belief system, for people to claim to have had a "mystical experience," to experience themselves as "one with the universe," or to be overwhelmed with love or light. Thus, ritual not only teaches us about the world depicted in our metaphors, it also teaches us how to feel within the universe we create.

Dorothy Meets Luke Skywalker

Contemporary witchcraft and magic draw heavily from myth and literature for their language, symbols, and metaphors. Luhrmann reports that many of the magicians she came to know were first attracted to their

I NEED A HERO

From what you remember about both *The Wizard of Oz* and *Star Wars*, how does each represent the process of coming of age? Are there key differences in the stories that are significant? Consider the following questions: What does each of these heroes, Luke and Dorothy, seek? From whom do they obtain their power? What form does the power take, and why are the differences significant? What helpers join the heroes, and what is the hero's relationship to them? How do the heroes destroy evil, and what is the reaction to their heroic deeds? Finally, what lesson does each hero learn, and in what way have their adventures transformed them?

beliefs when they read J. R. R. Tolkien's *The Lord of the Rings*, Ursula LeGuin's *Earthsea Trilogy*, or Marion Zimmer Bradley's *Mists of Avalon*. These books and movies contain **key scenarios**—stories or myths that, like ritual, portray certain values and beliefs. In the same sense that people act out and communicate their view of the world in ritual and come to learn how to feel in that world, they can be said to act out the scenarios contained in their myths.

Joseph Campbell spent most of his life studying the myths of people around the world. In one of his earlier books, *The Hero with a Thousand Faces*, Campbell concludes that myths from all over the world contain stories about a hero who embodies the most valued qualities of that society. The myths have a consistent scenario: a hero, separated from home, family, or society, embarks on a journey in search of something—knowledge, a magical object, a person, or even a vision. In the course of the journey, the hero encounters a mentor, someone who conveys some kind of power to the hero. When the hero encounters strange creatures or powerful forces that make it difficult to reach a goal, helpers appear to assist and protect the hero. Eventually the hero faces death but, with the help of the mentor's power, escapes and ultimately reaches the goal.

This scenario should sound familiar, since it has been the source for many stories, books, and films. George Lucas' *Star Wars*, based partly on Campbell's writings, tells of the rise of Luke Skywalker. Frank Baum's *Wizard of Oz* is a story about the heroic Dorothy. While the two stories differ in important details, both help people learn about growing up. Both emphasize the American value of finding oneself, both define the qualities that are required for success, and so, both provide to the reader scenarios for solving real problems.

key scenarios dominant stories or myths that portray the values and beliefs of a specific society

QUESTION 4.3

How do people come to believe what they do, and how do they continue to hold their beliefs even if they seem contradictory or ambiguous?

In 1992 a New York newspaper sent one of its reporters, Dennis Covington, to cover a murder case in Scottsboro, Alabama. The case was unusual because a man was accused of trying to murder his wife by forcing her to stick her hand into a box full of poisonous snakes. Covington discovered that both the accused husband and his wife were members of a religious group who believe that the Bible, specifically the Book

These signs will accompany those who believe: by using my name they will cast out demons; they will speak in new tongues; they will pick up snakes in their hands, and if they drink any deadly thing, it will not hurt them; they will lay their hands on the sick, and they will recover. (Mark 16:17-18)

of Mark, directs true believers to handle deadly snakes and to drink poisons:

> These signs will accompany those who believe: by using my name they will cast out demons; they will speak in new tongues; they will pick up snakes in their hands, and if they drink any deadly thing, it will not hurt them; they will lay their hands on the sick, and they will recover. (Mark 16:17–18)

The husband and wife were members of the Holiness Church, a group that started in 1909 when a Tennessee farmer, George Hensley, claimed that the above section of the book of Mark appeared to him in a vision. He interpreted the vision as a message to build a church in which people would test their faith with poisonous snakes and drinks.

During his research, Covington attended some Holiness services and was taken with the rituals, particularly the music. He observed people handling poisonous snakes, drinking poisonous drinks, and speaking in tongues. What he did not expect was that he would become a believer and a practitioner himself. But that is exactly what did happen. Dennis Covington became a member of the church for a time, handled poisonous snakes, and even daydreamed about becoming a traveling preacher.

interpretive drift the slow, often unacknowledged shift in someone's manner of interpreting events as he or she becomes involved with a particular activity

The Process of Interpretive Drift

Covington's experience raises the question of how it is that people come to believe what they do. What causes them to view the world through new lenses, to convert to a new way of interpreting their experience? Tanya Luhrmann (1989, 312) suggests that changing one's beliefs involves a process she calls **interpretive drift**: "the slow, often unacknowledged shift in someone's manner of interpreting events as they become involved with a particular activity." When someone begins to practice, even in play, some new belief, they become more skilled at seeing new patterns, new connections between things.

Magicians, Luhrmann says, enter magic with the vague notion that the mind can affect the material world. They may begin to read books on magic, or they may attend parties at which the host or hostess playfully pulls out a tarot deck and reads fortunes. At this point they may not be "believers," but they may find themselves playfully interpreting events in their lives according to the beliefs of magic, and they may begin to find the interpretations intellectually and emotionally satisfying. They may attend a ritual, find "energy surging through them," and attribute that feeling to the presence of some mystical force or power.

Luhrmann experienced interpretive drift herself. A few months after she first met magicians in London, she was reading a magic text on a train from Cambridge, and she thought she was beginning to understand the meaning of magical power:

> Indeed I imagined the force flowing through me and felt electrically vital, as if the magic current were pulsing through my body. In the midst of the phenomenological fantasy, a bicycle battery in the satchel next to me melted with a crisp, singed smell, and while no doubt coincidental it was disconcerting at the time. (1989, 318)

Later, while she was attending a ritual and again feeling a force, her watch stopped. Although it was, she admits, a cheap watch, watches are said to stop during magic rituals. She concludes:

> With the watch and the battery, I had ready-made, non-magical, culturally laudable explanations of both events: they were coincidental, and had I not been involved in magic they would have been unsurprising. But I had been thinking about magic, trying to "think like" a magician, and these events were striking because they made the alternative way of looking at the world seem viable. (1989, 318)

Interpretive drift continues when there are systematic changes in the way the believer begins to interpret experiences and events. He or she begins to identify evidence of the new belief, and soon the beliefs come to seem more natural; the person begins to "believe" in their truth. Once participation in a belief system begins, the person may seek and find additional compelling evidence for the viability of the belief. Instead of thinking that his or her beliefs have "changed," the believer begins to believe that the new beliefs are simply "true."

The intellectual changes that accompany the adoption of a new belief are, says Luhrmann, illuminating, and the fact that they are illuminating makes the belief and its practice seem effective. That is, the new beliefs provide a sense of discovery and confirmation; they work to help believers make sense of themselves, events in their lives, and the world around them.

Robert was vacationing in Brussels when he met Françoise. As they toured the city, Françoise confided to him that she was epileptic and that the medicine that her doctor prescribed seemed to have no effect. After he returned to England, Robert wrote Françoise that he and his friends practiced spiritual healing and that if she would send a photograph and a lock of hair and pray to the Virgin Mary, they would attempt a cure. After the first ritual, Françoise wrote that she was only having minor seizures. Robert and his friends repeated the ritual, and in her next letter she reported feeling a tremendous inflow of energy.

Later, Robert wrote Françoise asking if he could visit. She met Robert with her family, who expressed great pleasure in meeting the man who had "cured" their daughter. "When were you cured?" Robert asked, and Françoise told him it was after a car accident when she had been hurled through the windshield. They attributed this "healing" event to the power of the ritual. Robert and Françoise found additional confirmation for their beliefs in the fact that the accident occurred at full moon on the pagan festival of Candlemas, exactly thirteen weeks after the first ritual was performed. For Robert, this event was a central piece of evidence of the efficacy of magic.

secondary elaboration a term suggested by E. E. Evans-Pritchard for people's attempts to explain away inconsistencies or contradictions in their beliefs

Luhrmann says that the key element in becoming a believer is actual involvement with the practices of a specific belief. In other words, people don't first come to believe something and then practice the beliefs; rather, they first practice, and then they come to believe. Dennis Covington first attended services, spoke with the people, and played with the ideas, and only then did he begin to find or seek evidence that converted him to the belief. His evidence was the power he felt and the visions he had while handling snakes, a power he attributed to the presence of the Holy Spirit. The power of practice might be expressed by saying that people do not go to church because they believe in God; rather they believe in God because they go to church.

Adopting new beliefs, however, does not remove what others may see as contradictions, ambiguities, or just plain absurdities. And it doesn't remove alternative metaphors, theories, or beliefs for interpreting events. Consequently, people must have ways of protecting their beliefs, ways to defend them against skeptics. In other words, once a belief system is adopted, once it seems as though it is true, how can the believer continue to protect these beliefs, even if they might seem foolish to others?

Explaining Why the Sun Moves around the Earth

For almost 2,000 years, Europeans believed that Earth was the center of the universe. They envisioned a two-sphere cosmos consisting of a vaulted heaven—on which were located the sun, planets, and stars that circled eastward across the heavens—and an earthly sphere that was at the center of the universe. This belief was reinforced by language; then, as now, people spoke of the sun rising and setting. The idea of an Earth-centered universe fit well with a society in which humankind was afforded the central place in the universe.

In spite of the extent to which people took for granted an Earth-centered universe, there were problems with understanding the system. It was difficult to explain the behavior of planets that revolved around Earth because they sometimes seemed to reverse their course or increase or decrease in brightness. Moreover, some early scholars, such as Aristarchus, a Greek grammarian, were aware of alternative views. But people were generally able to explain away apparent contradictions.

The history of astronomy illustrates some of the ways by which people are able to sustain belief in spite of contrary evidence. The behavior of the planets was a problem for medieval astronomers. Sometimes the planets could be observed reversing direction. In modern astronomy, this phenomenon is explained as a consequence of the differing speed of rotation of the planets around the sun. In the ancient system, however, the inconsistency was rationalized by proposing that planets moved in figure-eight loops around the earth. The epicycle concept also explained why a planet could vary in brightness, because during its loops its distance to the earth would vary. This method of rationalizing a belief in spite of evidence is known as **secondary elaboration**.

British anthropologist E. E. Evans-Pritchard illustrated secondary elaboration in his account of divination among the Azande of Zaire. An Azande who needs to make an important decision consults a diviner, who feeds poison to chickens and addresses questions to the oracle that is thought to be manifest in the poison. The poison sometimes kills the chicken and sometimes does not, so the questions are put to the oracle in the form: if such is the case, kill (or don't kill) the chicken. The procedure is done twice to check its accuracy. Sometimes the oracle is wrong. But instead of doubting the power of the oracle to predict, they excuse the error by saying that the wrong poison was used, witchcraft interfered with the oracle, the poison was old, ghosts were angry, or the diviner was incompetent.

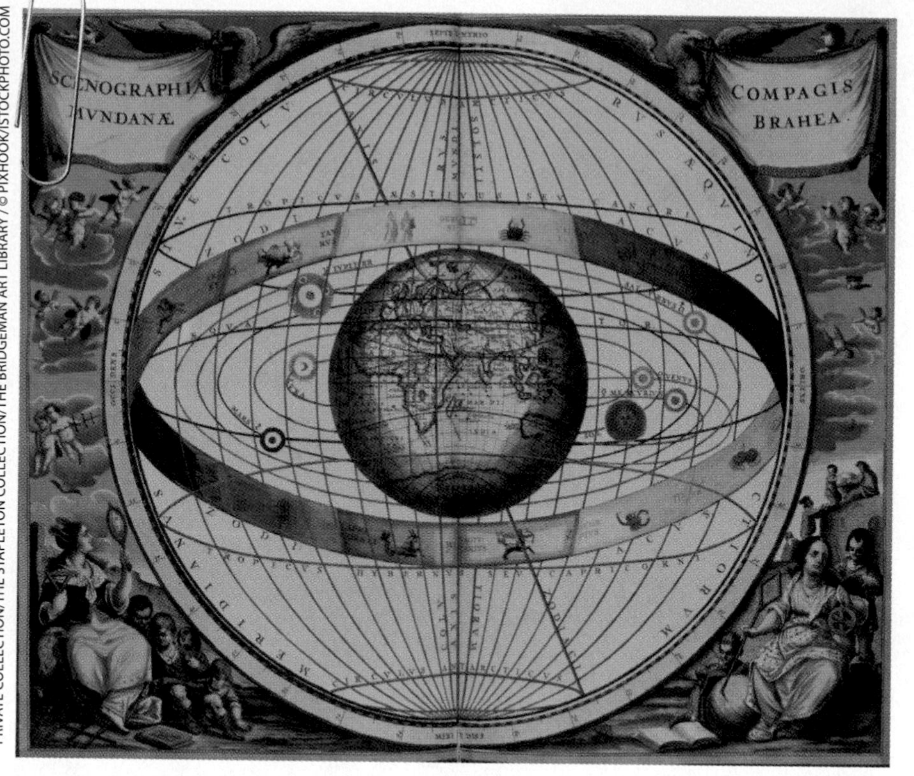

selective perception the tendency of people to see and recognize only those things they expect to see or those that confirm their view of the world

suppressing evidence the tendency to reject or ignore evidence that challenges an accepted belief

Beliefs can also be sustained by **selective perception**, seeing only what we want to see. The Earth-centered universe was easily confirmed by the evidence of the senses. There was certainly nothing to indicate that Earth moved. In fact, the senses indicated just the opposite: if you dropped an object, it fell straight down. If Earth moved, the object should fall to the right or left of the spot where it was dropped.

A belief can also be sustained by **suppressing evidence**—not allowing evidence that contradicts a cherished belief. In the Middle Ages, the Catholic Church denounced as heresy any attempt to suggest that Earth moved around the sun, and astronomers would simply ignore evidence that suggested otherwise.

Beliefs can also be sustained by an appeal to faith or mystery. The belief in an Earth-centered universe was sustained by an appeal to faith. If there were questions about it, people could be told that it was wrong to ask too many questions about the universe, that God sometimes worked in mysterious ways.

Beliefs can also be sustained by appeals to authority. The authority of Scripture supported the idea of an Earth-centered universe. And, if all else fails, it is possible to use violence or deceit to protect a belief that is threatened. In the seventeenth century, when Galileo

ONE OF THE MOST PERSISTENT CONTRADICTIONS IN JUDEO-CHRISTIAN THOUGHT HAS TO DO WITH THE NATURE OF GOD. The Judeo-Christian God is thought to be omnipotent, controlling everything, but also all good. But if God is both good and powerful, why do evil, suffering, and injustice exist in the world? If evil exists, he must allow it, in which case he is not all good. Or if he is all good, and evil, suffering, and injustice exist, he must not be omnipotent. How might this contradiction be resolved? How can it be explained away while maintaining the idea of an all-powerful, all-good deity?

CASE: I Am Your Father

After Barack Obama was elected president in late 2008, there was hope that he could end "politics-as-usual" . . .

. . . and help bring much-needed changes that would help steer the United States out of a crippling recession. These hopes were quickly dashed, however, as seemingly irresolvable conflicts arose between Democrats and Republicans on virtually every issue: taxes, health-care reform, regulation of financial markets, and economic stimulus packages. For us, the question is how people can hold such conflicting views on issues when they are faced with the same "facts."

George Lakoff, a linguist at the University of California at Berkeley, offers an answer—frames. He defines **frames** as mental structures that shape the way we see the world. They shape our goals, plans, and actions, and determine our values. In short, frames are metaphors that structure our view of the world.

frames mental structures that shape the way we see the world

Lakoff begins with the idea that people in the United States often use the metaphor of family to talk about their country. This is evident in phrases such as "founding fathers," "Uncle Sam," and even "Big Brother." He further argues that while both liberals and conservatives talk about the nation as a family, they use fundamentally different conceptions.

According to Lakoff, conservative politics are based on a strict-father notion of family. This metaphor conceives of a traditional nuclear family in which the father has the prime responsibility for protecting the family and the authority to set strict rules for children's behavior. Children must honor and obey their parents, and doing so builds character, self-discipline, and self-reliance. The goal of the strict-father family is to produce children who, when mature, are self-reliant, self-disciplined, and able to survive on their own.

Liberal politics, meanwhile, are based on a nurturant-parent metaphor, which emphasizes love, empathy, and nurturance, with the goal of producing children who are responsible, self-reliant, and care for others. Children are obedient not because they fear punishment but because they love and respect their parents.

At the root of each family model is a set of assumptions about the world. In the strict-father metaphor, the world is inherently dangerous and the family needs a father who can protect the family and teach right and wrong. The metaphor of the nurturant parent family, on the other hand, assumes that the world is basically good, that it can be made better, and that it is one's responsibility to work toward that goal. Children are born good, and parents can help them become nurturing and caring adults—just as, in the world, cooperation and shared responsibility can make the world a better place. These contrasting worldviews, rooted in contrasting metaphors of family, then lead to conflicting perspectives on the role of government. For liberals, government should nurture and help people. For conservatives, the government should be a moral authority that teaches discipline and self-reliance.

To see how these family metaphors lead to political positions, let's take a brief look at a key point of contention between conservatives and liberals, same-sex marriage. For conservatives, the idea of same-sex marriage does not fit the strict-father family model. In this view, the father must be manly, strong, and decisive, a model for his children to look up to. There must also be a mother, who must take care of the house, raise the children, and uphold the father's authority. Thus, the idea that two men or two women can marry and form a family runs counter to the basic elements of the strict-father family model. Additionally, recall that one of the key roles of the father in this model is to teach morality and discipline. This view contributes to the conservative argument that same-sex marriage is immoral and that it is the government's responsibility to establish moral standards.

There is nothing in the nurturant parent model to rule out same-sex marriage. In liberals' view, there is nothing about same-sex marriage that threatens heterosexual marriage. As a nurturing parent, it is the role of the government to support and help people, which means, in part, that the government should support (or at least not oppose) people's desires to marry whomever they want. According to Lakoff, activists for same-sex marriage need to ask people whether they think it is the government's place to tell people whom they can or cannot marry. In this view, same-sex marriage is about equal rights under the law; it permits people who are in love to make a lifetime public commitment to each other.

For conservatives, the idea of same-sex marriage does not fit the strict-father family model. There is nothing in the nurturant parent model to rule out such marriages.

proposed to support the idea that Earth revolves around the sun, he was imprisoned and tortured by church officials until he finally recanted. He spent the rest of his life under house arrest.

These are, of course, only some of the ways that people use to justify their beliefs. They may produce testimony, make an appeal to great men and women of the past, or even claim that all beliefs are subjective. The main point is that if people choose to adopt and defend a given set of beliefs, there are many ways they can do so.

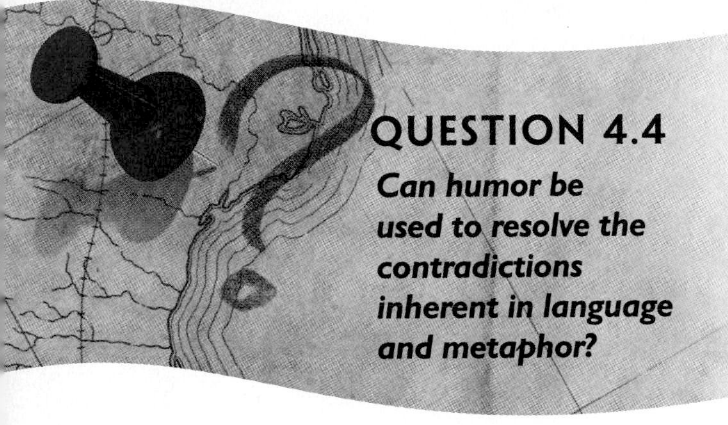

> A couple of Texas hunters are out in the woods when one of them falls to the ground. He doesn't seem to be breathing, and his eyes are rolled back in his head.
>
> The other guy whips out his cell phone and calls 911. He gasps to the operator, "My friend is dead! What can I do?"
>
> The operator, in a calm soothing voice says, "Just take it easy, I can help.
>
> First, let's make sure he's dead."
>
> . . . There is a silence, then a shot is heard . . .
>
> The hunter says, "OK, now what?"

What makes jokes funny? Often they seem absurd, with people doing or saying some very strange things. Yet, to a great extent, all language, ritual, myth, and other forms of symbolic action are, in a sense, absurd. Metaphors are highly inexact ways of understanding things—after all, courtship is not a sporting event—and life rarely follows the neat formulas laid out in ritual and myth. In real life, solutions are not as neat as they are in myths. Magic rituals often fail. Moreover, the meanings incorporated in language, ritual, and myth are problematic, and people often express considerable skepticism, doubt, and uncertainty about their beliefs. The area of human behavior in which these doubts and uncertainties gain expression is humor.

At first glance the subject of humor seems out of place in a discussion of the social processes of language, ritual, and myth. But social scientists, beginning with Sigmund Freud, have long recognized jokes as expressions of anxieties, doubts, and uncertainties. The joke depends on an abrupt switch or change of interpretation that allows a person, situation, or experience to take on a new, sometimes incongruous meaning. The switch in interpretation may also overcome some anxiety or fear.

A great illustration of the serious side of humor, and the ambiguities of language, is the pun. The joke in the pun rests on a basic ambiguity found in all languages, the fact that a word or expression can mean two things at the same time. "Tell me, Mr. Fields," a reporter once asked W. C. Fields (an actor who claimed to despise working with child stars), "do you approve of clubs for children?" "Only," said Fields, "when kindness fails." Here the humor focuses on the ambiguity of the term *club*, which can refer to a social organization or a weapon.

Did you hear about the guy whose whole left side was cut off? He's all right now.

As anthropologist Edmund Leach put it:

> A pun occurs when we make a joke by confusing two apparently different meanings of the same phonemic pattern. The pun seems funny or shocking because it challenges a taboo which ordinarily forbids us to recognize that the sound pattern is ambiguous. (Leach 1979, 207)

Ludwig Wittgenstein Meets Alice in Wonderland

The ambiguities that make humor possible are the same as those that philosophers struggle with in earnest. In fact, Ludwig Wittgenstein, perhaps the foremost philosopher of the twentieth century, once remarked that a

good, serious philosophical work could be written that consisted entirely of jokes. An example of how ambiguities in language can be the source of both philosophical concern and humor is found in George Pitcher's comparison of the work of Wittgenstein and the humor of Lewis Carroll in *Alice in Wonderland* and its sequel, *Through the Looking Glass*.

The basic assumption behind the use of metaphor is that if we know what something means in one context, we know what it means in another context. That is, if we know how to "measure" length, then we also know how to "measure" time. Wittgenstein claims that this simply isn't so; a person who knows what "W" means in one context does not necessarily know what it means in another context.

Carroll illustrates this idea in his description of the trial of the Knave of Hearts in *Alice in Wonderland*:

> . . . one of the guinea-pigs cheered, and was immediately *suppressed* by the officers of the court. (As that is rather a hard word, I will explain to you how it was done. They had a large canvas bag, which tied up at the mouth with strings: into this they slipped the guinea pig, head first, and then sat upon it.) "I'm glad I've seen that done," thought Alice. "I've so often read in the newspapers, at the end of trials, 'there was some attempt at applause, which was immediately *suppressed* by the officers of the court', and I never understood what it meant until now." (quoted in Pitcher 1965, 598; italics added)

Alice, in effect, wrongly assumed that since she understood what "suppressing a guinea pig" meant, she also knew what "suppressing applause" meant. Yet our entire mode of knowing is based on the assumption that if we know what something means in one context, we know what it means in another, just as Alice thought she did.

Wittgenstein points out the absurdity of the metaphors used to describe time as an object:

> We say that "the present event passes by" (a log passes by), "the future event is to come" (a log is to come). We talk about the flow of events; but also about the flow of time—the river on which the logs travel. Here is one of the most fertile sources of philosophic puzzlement: we talk of the future event of something coming into my room, and also of the future coming of this event. (quoted in Pitcher 1965, 609)

Carroll used this absurdity in our language as a rich source of humor. During the tea party with the Mad Hatter:

> . . . Alice sighed wearily. "I think you might do something better with the time," she said, "than wasting it in asking riddles that have no answers." "If you knew time as well as I do," said the Hatter, "you wouldn't talk about wasting *it*. It's a *him*. "I don't know what you mean," said Alice. "Of course you don't!" the Hatter said, tossing his head contemptuously. "I dare say you never even spoke to Time!" "Perhaps not," Alice cautiously replied; "but I know I have to beat time when I learn music." "Ah! That accounts for it," said the Hatter. "He won't stand beating. . . " (quoted in Pitcher 1965, 609)

A central doctrine in Wittgenstein's philosophy is that similarities in grammar cause confusion in our use of language. For example, the sentence "Nobody is here" is grammatically similar to the sentence "John is here," suggesting that "Nobody" can be interpreted as a name. Here is what Wittgenstein says about this:

> Imagine a language in which, instead of "I found nobody in the room," one said, "I found Mr. Nobody in the room." Imagine the philosophical problems which would arise out of such a convention. (quoted in Pitcher 1965, 610)

Alice's conversation with the King of Hearts builds on Wittgenstein's philosophical dilemma:

> "Just look along the road, and tell me if you can see either of them."
>
> "I see *nobody* on the road," says Alice.
>
> "I only wish I had such eyes," the king remarked in a fretful tone. "To be able to see *Nobody*! And at that distance too! Why it's as much as I can do to see real people, by this light!
>
> "Who did you pass on the road?" the king went on, holding out his hand to the messenger for some hay.
>
> "*Nobody*," said the messenger.
>
> "Quite right," said the king: "this young lady saw him too. So of course *Nobody* walks slower than you."
>
> "I do my best," the messenger said in a sullen tone. "I'm sure *nobody* walks much faster than I do!"
>
> "He can't do that," said the king, "or else he'd have been here first." (quoted in Pitcher 1965, 610, italics added)

Carroll's routine is, of course, a precursor to the Abbott and Costello's classic routine "Who's on First?" In sum, both Wittgenstein and Carroll draw attention to the fact that our languages are imperfect vehicles of meaning. They contain contradictions and ambiguities that are sources of confusion—and humor.

Apache Humor: Laughing at the Whiteman

The ambiguities and contradictions in language are not our only source for humor. Often people create humor out of everyday life problems or events. The humor created by the Western Apache is a good example. Like most indigenous peoples of North America, they suffered greatly at the hands of Anglo-Americans. Their lands were taken from them and they were confined to reservations in 1872. Even now whites, often insensitive to Apache culture, impose themselves and their values on them. This has led to a highly negative view of whites among Native Americans.

The biggest of all Indian problems is the Whiteman. Who can understand the Whiteman? What makes him tick? How does he think and why does he think the way he does? Why does he say one thing and do the opposite? Most important of all, how do you deal with him? Obviously he is here to stay. Sometimes it seems like a hopeless task. (quoted in Basso 1979, 3)

Paradoxically, one of the richest sources of humor for the Western Apache is the Whiteman. As anthropologist Keith Basso describes it, most Whiteman jokes take the form of little skits or performances in which an Apache imitates a white talking to an Apache. This example involves J, a cowboy (age 40+), his wife K (age 37), and L, a kinsman of J (age 35+). J and K have just finished a meal, and K is doing dishes while J is repairing a bridle. There is a knock on the door. J answers it, and greets L:

J: Hello my friend! How are you doing? How are you feeling L? You feeling good?

[J now turns to K and addresses her]

Look who's here everybody! Look who just came in. Sure, it's my Indian friend L. Pretty good all right!

[J slaps L on the shoulder and, looking him directly in the eyes, seizes his hand and pumps it wildly up and down.]

J: Come right in, my friend! Don't stay outside in the rain. Better you come in right now.

[J now drapes his arm around L's shoulder and moves him in the direction of a chair.]

J: Sit down! Sit right down! Take your loads off your ass. You hungry? You want some beer? Maybe you want some wine? You want crackers? Bread? You want some sandwich? How 'bout it? You hungry? I don't know. Maybe you get sick. Maybe you don't eat again long time.

[K has stopped washing dishes and is looking on with amusement. L has seated himself and has a look of bemused resignation on his face.]

J: You sure looking good to me, L. You looking pretty fat! Pretty good all right! You got new boots? Where you buy them? Sure pretty good boots! I glad...

[At this point J breaks into laughter. K joins in. L shakes his head and smiles. The joke is over.]

K: White men are stupid!

(Quoted from Basso 1979, 62–64)

The humor in this performance is rooted in mocking the behavior of whites toward Native Americans. Every bit of white behavior, for an Apache, was totally wrong and inappropriate. The greeting "Hello my friend" is an expression used by whites that Apaches find irresponsible and presumptuous. Apaches think whites use it even when they meet someone for the first time, or even if they hold a person in contempt. "How are you feeling" is an unsolicited and intrusive inquiry into a person's emotional or physical health that would never be asked of one Apache by another. "Look who's here everybody": An Apache who enters or leaves a group does so unobtrusively, never calling attention to himself or herself or others. J addresses L by his name; Apaches rarely do that. J slaps L on the back, stares him in the eye, and guides him to a seat; Apaches, especially adult males, rarely touch each other in public. And staring at someone is an aggressive act, as is forcibly moving somebody to another spot. "Come right in my friend! Sit down!" is viewed by the Apache as "bossing someone around." "Maybe you get sick": Apaches believe that talking about adversity and trouble may increase their chance of occurrence. "You hungry? You want some beer? Maybe you want some wine? You want crackers? Bread? You want some sandwich? How 'bout it? You hungry?": Except in an emergency, the Apache think it rude to ask a question more than once, and since it is polite to give people time to respond, demanding an answer is considered boorish behavior.

From an Apache perspective, J's behavior was all wrong. The joke, as Basso puts it, is a dramatized denunciation "of the ways in which Anglo-Americans conduct themselves in the presence of Indian people." These performances give visible expression to Apache views of whites, and to the problems they face when they interact with them. Basso also points out that the content of the humor has changed to incorporate different groups of whites that, over time, have appeared on the reservations. In the 1960s the Whiteman was portrayed as a hippie, mumbling and effeminate; in the 1970s, when VISTA volunteers arrived on the reservations, whites were portrayed as "gushingly altruistic," hopelessly incompetent at the simplest task, and, for some reason, always out of breath. When doctors arrived to stamp out diarrhea in infants and to "teach women how to breast feed," they were labeled "those-who-play-with-babies'-shit."

Like Lewis Carroll, Apache humorists highlight areas of experience that are somehow problematic. But there is a paradox. How can forms of expression—humor in this case—that draw our attention to absurdities help us find meaning in our experience? Shouldn't humor make us even more skeptical and doubtful of the meanings contained in our language and ritual performances?

Humor and Life's Incongruities

Anthropologists have long noted the association of humor and ritual performance. For the Hopi, the clown was an important part of all ritual performance. Rituals are said to have the power to heal, and some people, such as writer Norman Cousins, claim that humor also has therapeutic qualities. However, whereas ritual seeks to mask the ambiguities and contradictions in our lives, humor highlights and draws attention to them. In a very real sense, humor is anti-ritual. But the key is that when we laugh at the meanings in jokes, we laugh at the problems and contradictions of life.

Most societies have their clowns who, in one way or another, make fun of what otherwise are very serious things. The clown serves as a guide to the incongruities and absurdities in our beliefs. But clowns play a dangerous game. If they get us to laugh at a problem, they succeed in helping us negate our doubts. But if they fail to make us laugh, they have succeeded only in making us aware of our failings. The clown must make us laugh at the joke in the same way that the priest must prevent us from laughing at the ritual.

The clown serves another important purpose. By definition, the clown is not someone we take seriously, and when he or she points out the incongruities and

revitalization movements the term suggested by Anthony F. C. Wallace for attempts by a people to construct a more satisfying culture

absurdities in our lives, they lose some of their credibility through their association with the clown. That may be why the clown is inevitably an asocial, and often asexual, figure that exists on the fringes of society. The clown becomes, as psychologists have claimed, the butt of our aggressions, a cathartic figure who encapsulates all our fears and anxieties. The clown and the joke are, in effect, receptacles in which we store our fears and anxieties about threatened disorder, receptacles we conveniently trash by our laughter.

There is in humor, as John Allen Paulos points out, a sense of the mathematical proof that takes the form "to prove A, show not-A is nonsense." This is a form of proof popular with theologians who wish to prove the existence of God. If they cannot prove that God exists, they try to prove that existence without God is impossible. In the same way, humor, by making jokes about the very real ambiguities and contradictions in our lives, makes the problems they represent seem nonsensical and, consequently, less threatening.

QUESTION 4.5

How can people reorder their view of the world if it becomes unsatisfactory?

The meanings that people assign to their experiences do not change easily. We very much take for granted that the view of the world created by the interaction of our own experiences with the mediums of language, symbolic actions, humor, and collective judgments is the right view. But beliefs do change. These changes are often triggered by social upheavals, in which the old way of looking at the world, for whatever reason, is no longer satisfactory. If sufficient numbers of people share this unease, they may try to change both their view of the world and the organization of society. Anthropologist Anthony F. C. Wallace suggests the term **revitalization movements** for these attempts to construct a more satisfying culture.

Generally, a period of upheaval or oppression leads to the development of a new or revised belief system that offers a new vision of the world that will relieve the oppression. During such upheavals, the usual explanations for events are unsatisfactory, traditional solutions to problems no longer work, and rituals may be abandoned. Doubt engendered by upheaval is replaced with a new certainty born of religious fervor or conversion. An example of this kind of revitalization movement is the Shakers.

Mother Ann Lee and the Shakers

During the first half of the nineteenth century, hundreds of religious movements warning of the coming end of the world established religious communities. This was a period of great social change as the United States evolved from a rural agricultural to an urban industrial society. It was marked by considerable population movement, the spread of poverty, and the breakdown of the family as the guardian of societal norms. Revitalization movements represented an attempt to reformulate society in ways that remain relevant today. Virtually all of them reacted to poverty by eliminating private property and requiring communal ownership of all things; reacted to inequality by recognizing the equality of men and women; and reacted to what they perceived as the breakdown of the larger society by requiring a separation of their communities from the larger society.

The Shakers, or the United Society of Believers in Christ's Second Appearing, were one of the most notable of these groups. The group was founded by Ann Lee. We know little of her life other than information obtained from early-nineteenth-century accounts written by her followers. These sources tell us that she was born in Manchester, England, in 1736. At 8 years of age she was working 12 to 14 hours a day in the textile mills of Manchester, one of the worst urban slums in England. When she was 22, she attended a series of religious revival meetings led by Jane and James Wardley. The Wardleys had been Quakers but broke away to form the Wardley Society, developing an expressive kind of worship characterized by emotional chanting, shouting, and shaking, from which they got the name, the "Shaking Quakers."

Lee is reported to have exhibited an antipathy to sex early in her life and had been reluctant to marry. But when she was 25, pressured by her family, she married a blacksmith, Abraham Standerin. In a rare decision for its time, she continued to call herself by her maiden name. Her first three children died in infancy, and the fourth was stillborn. The chronicle of her life states that she was paralyzed by grief and guilt and became convinced that sex and marriage were the root of all evil and the cause of her misery. She gained support (over the objections of her husband) from the Wardleys and declared her celibacy.

The Wardleys preached that the second coming of Christ was near, and, because God was both male and female, the manifestation of Christ's second coming would be female. The movement embraced the public confession of sin, so Lee poured out all her transgressions and then joined the Wardleys to preach. She and her father, brother, and husband, all of whom had joined her, were arrested for causing a public nuisance. While in jail, she had a vision of Adam and Eve "committing the forbidden sexual act" and began publicly preaching against it. During one of her jail terms, she claimed to have had a vision in which Jesus appeared to her and revealed that she was his chosen successor, that she was to be the Word of God, the second coming of Christ as a woman.

The Wardleys accepted her vision, and stories began to circulate about the miraculous healing power of Mother Ann Lee, as she came to be called. One woman claimed that she had a cancer of the mouth, and when Lee touched it, it disappeared. She later had another vision that told her to take her religion to America. In 1774, along with her husband, brother, niece, and four others, she journeyed to America to establish a church. Escaping New York City just ahead of the British in 1776, they journeyed to upstate New York and established a settlement just outside Albany.

The turning point for the Shakers in the United States came in 1780. There was a religious revival of Baptists in the nearby community of New Lebanon, and Calvin Harlow and Joseph Meacham, Baptist ministers, heard about the Shakers and traveled to see Mother Ann Lee. They were so impressed with her and what she had to

THE GHOST DANCE

During the 19th century, the social fabric of Native American societies was being torn apart by war and expansion. In the midst of this social upheaval arose a revitalization movement led by a Paiute named Wovoka. In 1889 Wovoka had a vision in which he was taken up to heaven, where he saw God and all the deceased tribes performing traditional activities. God gave him instructions for a dance. If it were performed for five days and nights, peace would be restored, and people would be reunited with their deceased friends and relatives.

As Wovoka's message was spread over North America, it evolved. In some versions, the dance would destroy the white man and all Native Americans would be resurrected. In others, the dance would bring back the buffalo. The Sioux believed that Wovoka was the resurrected son of God, who would punish whites for their wickedness. Whatever the interpretation, the Ghost Dance, as it became called, was adopted by numerous groups who were seeking a revival of a way of life disrupted by Euro-American expansion.

THE GHOST DANCE, SOUTH DAKOTA, 1890 (B/W PHOTO) BY AMERICAN PHOTOGRAPHER (19TH CENTURY) PRIVATE COLLECTION/PETER NEWARK AMERICAN PICTURES/THE BRIDGEMAN ART LIBRARY

SHAKERS DANCING AND SHAKING, 1836 (COLOUR LITHO) BY AMERICAN SCHOOL (19TH CCENTURY) PRIVATE COLLECTION/PETER NEWARK PICTURES/THE BRIDGEMAN ART LIBRARY

say that Meacham became her first notable convert in the United States.

Mother Ann Lee died in 1784, perhaps as a result of a journey she and members of her group undertook in 1781 to bring her message to others in New England. The journey was marked by persecution and beatings. But the movement continued to spread, and at its height in the 1840s there were more than 6,000 members spread over 25 communities, from Maine to Florida and into the Ohio Valley.

The message of the Shakers was relatively simple. Sexual relations were banned, both men and women shared authority, members were required to publicly confess their sins, and property was held in common. There was also a prohibition on eating pork, and most Shakers ate no meat at all. The Shakers professed pacifism and sought to maintain a separate government apart from the rest of society. Each community was organized into groups called families and had a ministry consisting of males and females, usually two of each. Their religious principles included the idea that God is a dual being, male and female, that Mother Ann Lee was the second coming of Christ as spirit, and that the millennium had commenced with the establishment of their church.

It is difficult to speculate what led the people who joined the Shakers to accept their beliefs. Women were attracted to the movement because of its promise of equality, and all may have been attracted to the strong group support offered in Shaker communities. In many ways the physical layout, rituals, and rules of the Shaker communities seemed to be a denial of anything urban, anything suggesting economic or social exploitation. The communities thrived from 1800 to 1850, but began to decline after the Civil War as fewer and fewer people were attracted to the message. A small community of believers in Sabbathday Lake, Maine, remains to carry on the Shaker tradition.

WHAT DO WE NEED TO KNOW BEFORE WE CAN UNDERSTAND THE DYNAMICS OF FAMILY LIFE IN OTHER SOCIETIES?

Chapter 5
Patterns of Family Relations

If ever thou purpose to be a good wife, and to live comfortably, set down this with thyself: mine husband is my superior, my better; he hath authority and rule over me; nature hath given it to him . . . God hath given it to him.

W. Whately

The Bride Bush, London, 1617

A woman needs a man like a fish needs a bicycle.

"Tryin' To Throw Your Arms Around The World"

U2

* * *

QUESTIONS

In examining this problem, we will consider the following questions:

5.1 What is the composition of the typical family group?

5.2 How are families formed and ideal family types maintained?

5.3 What are the roles of sexuality, love, and wealth?

5.4 What threatens to disrupt the family unit?

INTRODUCTION

Soap Operas and Family Relations

If you decided to learn enough about family life in another society so that you could write a plausible soap opera, you would probably understand a good deal about the dynamics of their family life.

Could a foreign visitor to the United States learn anything about American family life from watching soap operas? Consider this plot from a recent episode of a popular soap:

> Holden is having an affair with Lilly while his wife Angel is undergoing psychiatric treatment because she had been sexually molested by her father, who was shot and killed by Kalib, Holden's brother. In the meantime Darryl is having an affair with Francine while he and his wife, Carol, are arranging to have a child through a surrogate mother. Francine's sister Sabrina has run off with Antonio, an apparent drug dealer who has shot Bob, the sister's father.

A visitor certainly might conclude from the popularity of this soap opera that Americans like to watch stories of illicit love, incest, infidelity, greed, and family conflict. And though the behaviors of these characters may not really represent the daily lives of Americans, they must represent enough of reality to allow viewers to identify with the characters and situations. In some ways, the plots and the relationships between the characters must seem plausible and reveal something about the dynamics of American lives. Our assumption in this chapter is that a person who understands and appreciates soap operas in America would have a good understanding of the dynamics of American life. But what relevance does that have for understanding family life in other societies?

Americans are not alone in their fascination with soap operas. Most societies have fictional dramas and real-life tales about family life that reveal people's concerns. Like Americans, Brazilians are fanatical soap opera watchers, but the characters, situations, and plots are completely different from those on American television, reflecting differences in family structure and dynamics in Brazil. The focus in Brazilian soap operas tends to be on the **family of orientation**—father, mother, self, and siblings—rather than on the **family of procreation**—husband, wife, and their children. The theme of class mobility, such as poor, rural women marrying wealthy men from the city, dominates Brazilian soaps. Love is depicted as dangerous and unrequited.

Soap operas reveal the reasons for domestic

family of orientation the family group that consists of father, mother, self, and siblings

family of procreation the family group that consists of a husband, a wife, and their children

bilateral kinship a system in which individuals trace their descent through both parents

strife. They depict individuals with choices to make—choices that impact others. They reveal character motivation and development. In whatever form they take—traditional dramas, real-life tales, or soap operas—stories are an interesting way to learn about family life in different societies. If you decided to learn enough about family life in another society so that you could write a plausible soap opera, you would probably understand a good deal about the dynamics of their family life.

What, then, would we need to know in order to write a good soap opera about families in other societies? First, we explore the composition of a typical family—how it is formed and maintained. We examine how the themes of sexuality, love, and wealth are dealt with, and what kinds of situations or conflicts can disrupt family life. Finally, we explore how the understanding of patterns of family relations can be relevant for careers.

To make this task more manageable, we focus on family life in three societies: the Ju/wasi, the Trobriand Islanders of the South Pacific, and a traditional Chinese farm family.* These societies have been selected for three reasons. First, they represent very different levels of social, cultural, and technological complexity. The Ju/wasi were gatherers and hunters living in nomadic groups, the Trobriand Islanders were horticulturists living in small villages, and the Chinese family represents a large, agricultural society. Second, family structure and roles vary significantly among the three, but together they depict family types and relations that are representative of many, if not most, societies around the world. Finally, the three societies have been studied in detail in anthropological literature.

*The actual descriptions of the Ju/Wasi, the Trobriand Islanders, and the traditional Chinese family will mostly refer to situations from the past, since these groups are very different today than when they were the object of anthropological study. We will, however, refer to them in the ethnographic present; that is, though we are talking about past situations, we will describe them as if they sill exist today.

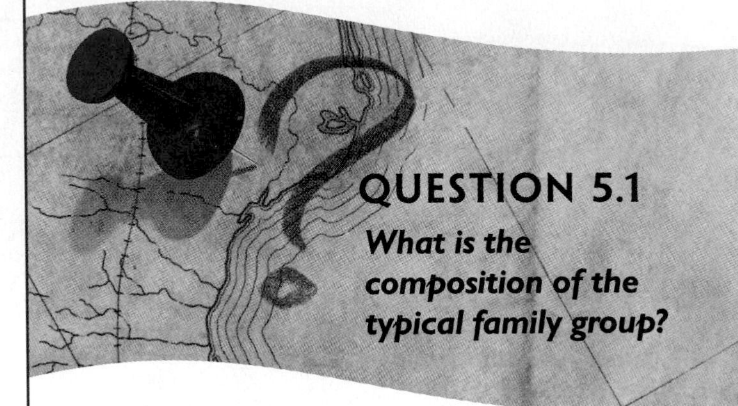

QUESTION 5.1
What is the composition of the typical family group?

To understand family composition in different societies, we need certain concepts and tools. One place to begin is by examining how most unmarried Americans would respond if asked about the composition of their families. They would probably list their mother, father, brothers, and sisters. If asked who else, they would likely add grandparents, aunts, uncles, and cousins. If they were married, they would add their husbands or wives and children. Figure 5.1 shows how this family structure would be diagrammed using genealogical notations.

Certain features of the typical American family stand out. Americans consider themselves equally tied by kinship to both their mother and father and to their maternal and paternal kin. In other words, Americans observe **bilateral kinship**, tracing their descent through both parents. This, as we shall see, is not true of all societies. Second, Americans make no linguistic distinction between their mothers' siblings and their fathers' siblings; both are referred to as aunts or uncles. Nor do they distinguish linguistically between the children of aunts and of uncles; all are referred to as cousins. For most Americans, the most important family

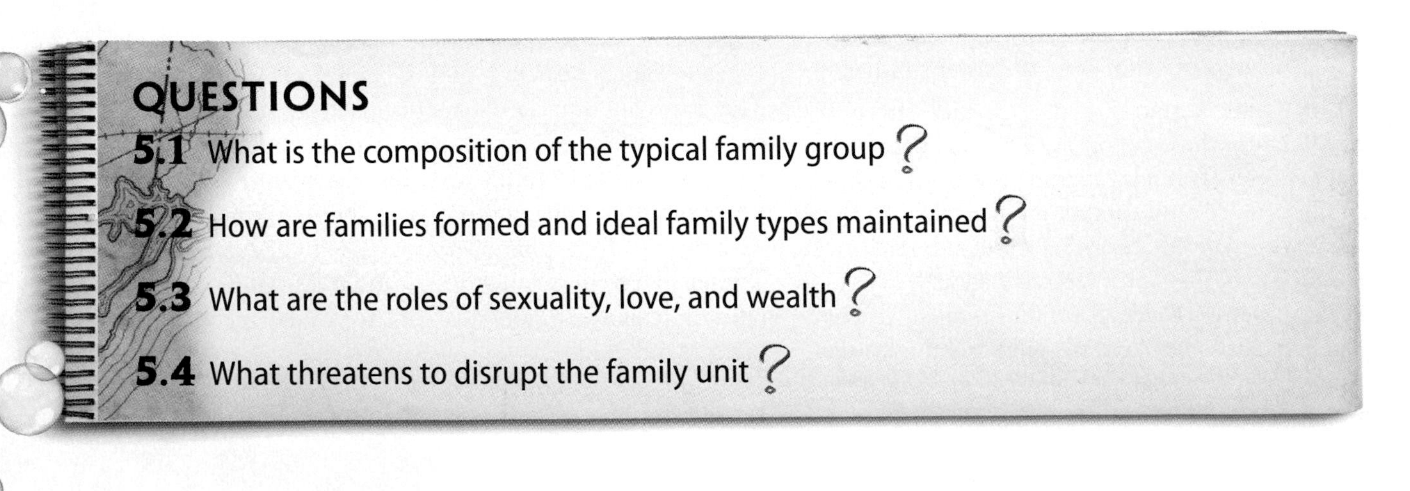

Figure 5.1

Composition and Development of the American Nuclear Family

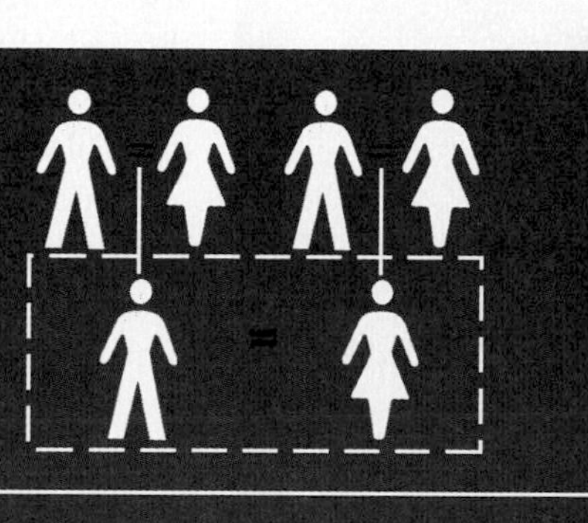

nuclear family the family group consisting of a father, a mother, and their biological or adopted children

matrilineal kinship a system of descent in which persons are related to their kin through the mother only

patrilineal kinship a system of descent in which persons are related to their kin through the father only

grouping is the **nuclear family**—the group consisting of a father, a mother, and their biological or adopted children.

Families in other societies may be composed very differently. For example, although Americans give equal recognition to their ties to mother and father, other societies place greater emphasis on ties to one parent. In some cases, only people related through either the mother or the father are considered family. Societies that emphasize persons' ties to their mother are said to have **matrilineal kinship** systems; those that emphasize persons' ties to their father are said to have **patrilineal kinship** systems. However, in few societies is an individual's relationship to one side of the family or the other totally ignored. Rather, relationships with mothers' families and fathers' families are viewed differently. For example, Americans traditionally inherit their surnames from their fathers, thus embracing the patrilineal principle, but in case of divorce, the American legal system usually gives priority to the matrilineal principle by awarding custody of children to their mother.

The three examples of societies used in this chapter—the Ju/wasi, Trobriand Islanders, and traditional Chinese—each define the composition of the family and relations between members differently.

The Family Composition of the Ju/wasi

For most of the year, the Ju/wasi live in groups numbering from 10 to 40 people, related bilaterally (through both parents), who hunt and gather in a territory associated with a particular waterhole. Camp groups are often organized around a brother-and-sister pair who claim ownership of the waterhole (see Figure 5.2 on the next page). They bring their spouses and children into the group. Their spouses, in turn, might bring in their siblings or parents.

Figure 5.2

Composition and Development of the Ju/wasi Camp

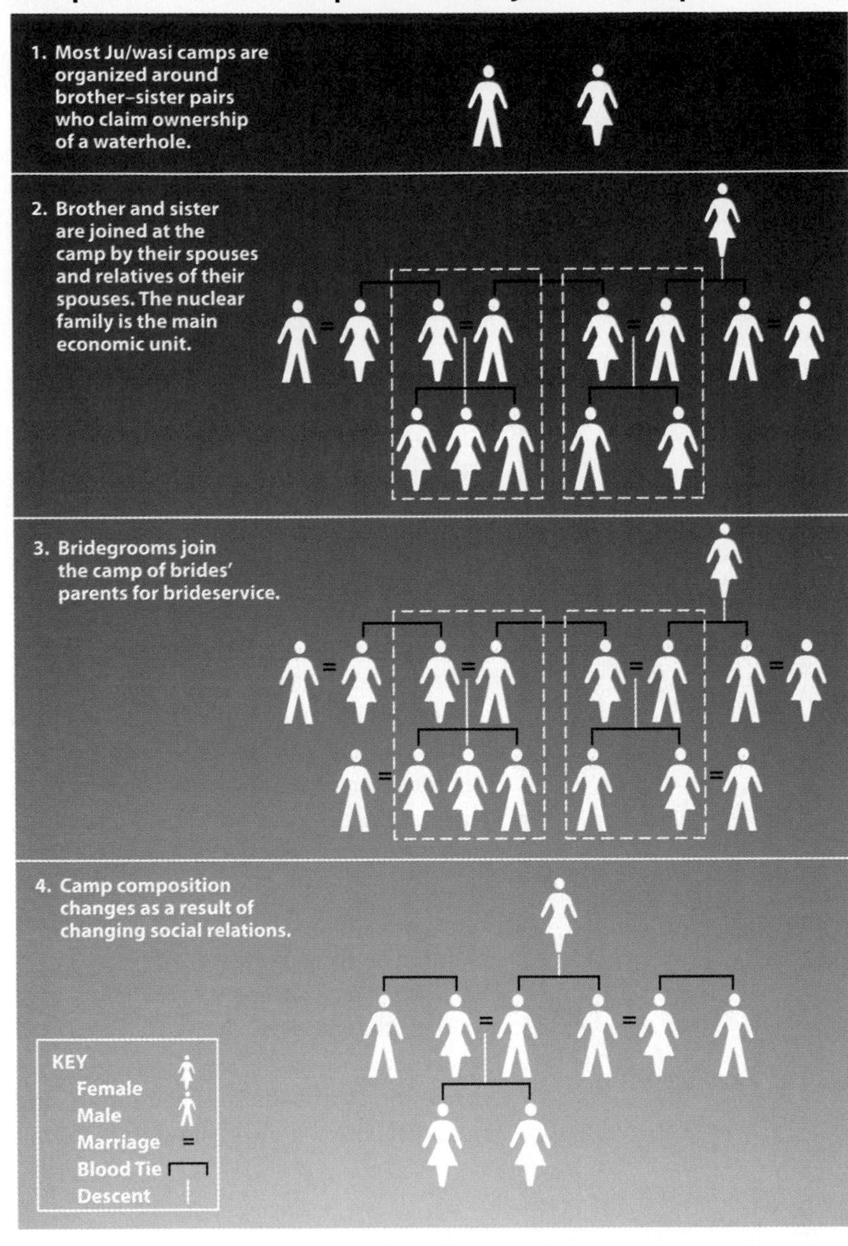

Membership in a camp is fluid. People move freely from camp to camp based on hunting alliances or because conflict develops in the group. Within the camp, however, the basic group is the nuclear family of husband, wife, and children. Children spend most of their time with their mothers. The Ju/wasi acknowledge the fact that pregnancy results from sexual intercourse (not all societies do). They also believe that conception takes place at the end of the woman's menses, when the man's semen joins with the last of the menstrual blood.

brideservice the requirement that when a couple marries, the groom must work for the bride's parents for some specified period of time

matrilineage a lineage that is formed by tracing descent in the female line

One feature of Ju/wasi society that figures prominently in the dynamics of family life is the custom of **brideservice**. When a couple marries, the groom is expected to come and live in the bride's parents' camp and work for her parents for as long as ten years. Tales of family life among the Ju/wasi are often built around the effects of this arrangement on family dynamics.

The Family Composition of the Trobriand Islanders

The people of the Trobriand Islands live in about 80 villages, with populations ranging from 40 to 400. Each village is surrounded by cultivated fields, waterholes, fruit trees, and palm groves. Each village is divided into hamlets, and each hamlet ideally consists of a **matrilineage**, or *dala*, as the Trobrianders call it: a group of men related to each other through the female line, along with their wives and unmarried children (see Figure 5.3).

The matrilineages are ranked relative to one another, and each village has a chief who is the eldest male of the highest-ranking matrilineage. Because each person is a member of the lineage of his or her mother, neither a man's wife nor his children can be members of his own *dala*.

The Trobrianders' mythology and beliefs about procreation dramatically depict the matrilineal element in their lives. Their mythology contains stories of how, a long time ago, pairs of brothers and sisters emerged from the ground to begin each *dala*. *Dala* members trace their descent back to their mythological ancestors, and they base their claims to specific plots of land on the fact that it was thence that their ancestors emerged. There is obviously an incestuous theme in Trobriand myth, because the originators of each lineage were brothers and sisters. However, Trobriand theories of procreation ostensibly deny a role to men in conception. They reinforce the matrilineal principle as well as the tie between brothers and sisters.

The Trobrianders say that when a person dies, the person's soul or spirit becomes young and goes to live on an island called Tuma. There the soul ages, but it regenerates itself by bathing in the sea. As the skin is sloughed off, a spirit child, or *baloma*, is created. It returns to the world of the living and enters the womb of a woman of the same matrilineage as itself. In effect, a Trobriand matrilineage exists in perpetuity, because souls and spirits travel back and forth between the land of the living and the island of the dead.

The *baloma* may enter the woman through her head, or it may be carried by water into her womb. In some areas of the Trobriand Islands, if a woman wishes to become pregnant, her brother brings a pail of water to her dwelling. In fact, a woman cannot conceive without the "permission" of her brother. Consequently, the act of conception among the Trobrianders is a matter of three agencies—a woman, the spirit or *baloma* of a deceased ancestor, and the woman's brother. Although sexual intercourse is said to play no role in conception, it does play a role in the development and growth of the fetus. Trobrianders believe that the man's semen provides food and nourishment for the fetus and that is why children physically resemble their fathers. Sexual intercourse is also said to open the womb for the child to emerge.

The Trobrianders can rationalize and "prove" their beliefs about procreation very easily. Bronislaw Malinowski, who spent four years studying the people of the Trobriand Islands, tells of their response when he suggested to them that sexual intercourse plays a role in procreation:

> I sometimes made myself definitely and aggressively an advocate of the truer physiological doctrine of procreation. In such arguments the natives would quote, not only positive instances of women who have children without having intercourse; but would also refer to the many cases in which an unmarried woman has plenty of intercourse and no children. This argument would be repeated over and over again, with specially telling concrete examples of childless persons renowned for profligacy, or of women who lived with one white trader after another without having any baby. (1929, 185–86)

To what extent the Trobrianders really deny a role to men in procreation is a matter of some debate. Annette Weiner, who worked with them in the early 1970s, some 50 years after the pioneering work of Malinowski, reported that they no longer denied the direct role of men in conception. However, she also reported a case in which a grandmother claimed that she had used magic to make her granddaughter pregnant when the woman conceived while her husband was away.

Regardless of the extent to which the Trobrianders recognize the role of coitus, their ideas about descent and procreation reflect important features

Figure 5.3

Composition of the Trobriand Island *Dala* and Household

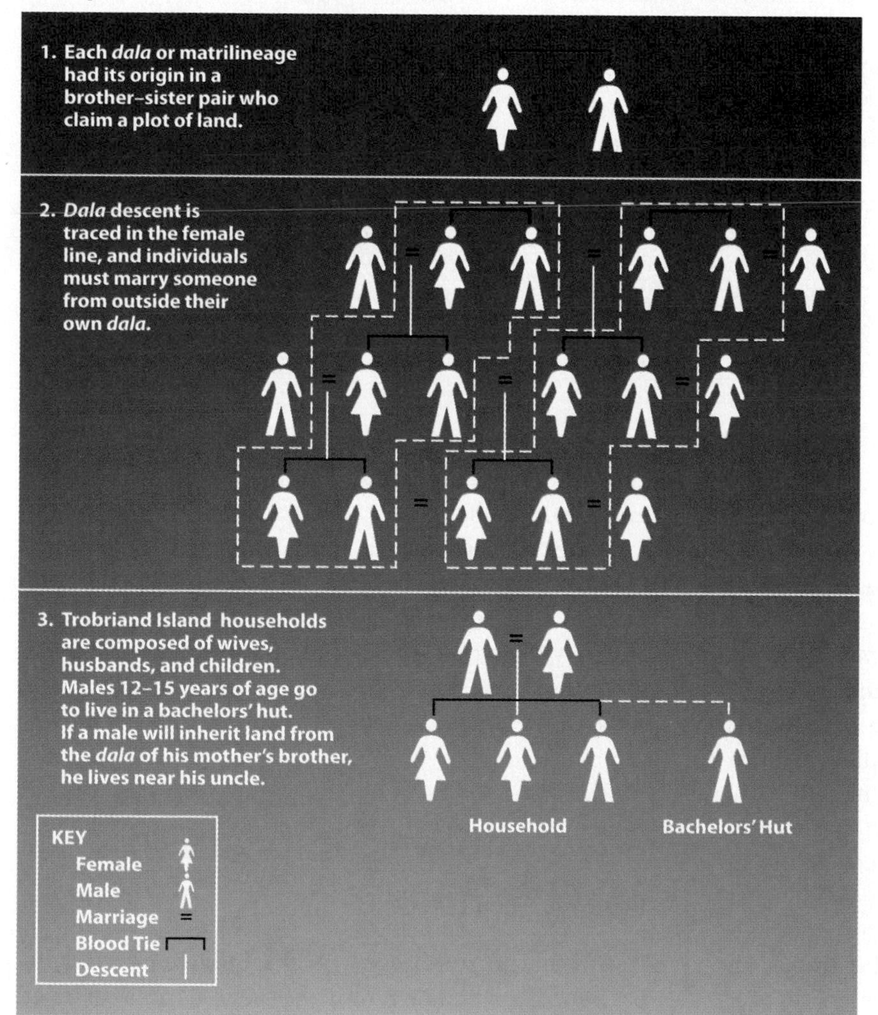

WHAT WOULD YOU DO?

The procreation beliefs of the Trobriand Islanders prompted debate among anthropologists. Did they really believe that men played no role in reproduction, or did they pretend not to acknowledge the man's role in order to emphasize the matrilineal principle? In either case, we would expect to find in societies that emphasize the patrilineal principle a de-emphasis on a woman's role in reproduction. What kind of belief about reproduction can you think of that would deny the importance of the female? How does this compare with the biological roles of men and women in American society?

of the composition of their families. First, the key family relationship for them is between brother and sister. Second, the father of the family is an outsider to his children, a member of another family group. His interest, ideally, is in his sister's children, because it is they who are members of his matrilineage. Third, because the matrilineal **extended family** group, the *dala*, is more important than the nuclear family, the Trobrianders merge certain people under the same kin term. A Trobriander refers to all women of his or her matrilineage of the same generation by the same term. A man refers to his mother as well as his mother's sisters by the term *ina*. A woman refers to her brother and to all other men of her matrilineage and generation as *luta*. Thus, a man has many "sisters," and a woman has many "brothers."

extended family a family group based on blood relations of three or more generations

Another consequence of matrilineal kinship is that a man inherits property not from his father but from his mother's brothers, and it is ideally in his maternal uncle's village that a young man goes to live. The fact that these ideal conditions are not always met creates some of the drama in Trobriand family life.

The Family Composition of the Chinese

Family life in traditional rural China centers on the patrilineal extended family household of a married

Figure 5.4

Composition and Development of the Traditional Chinese Family

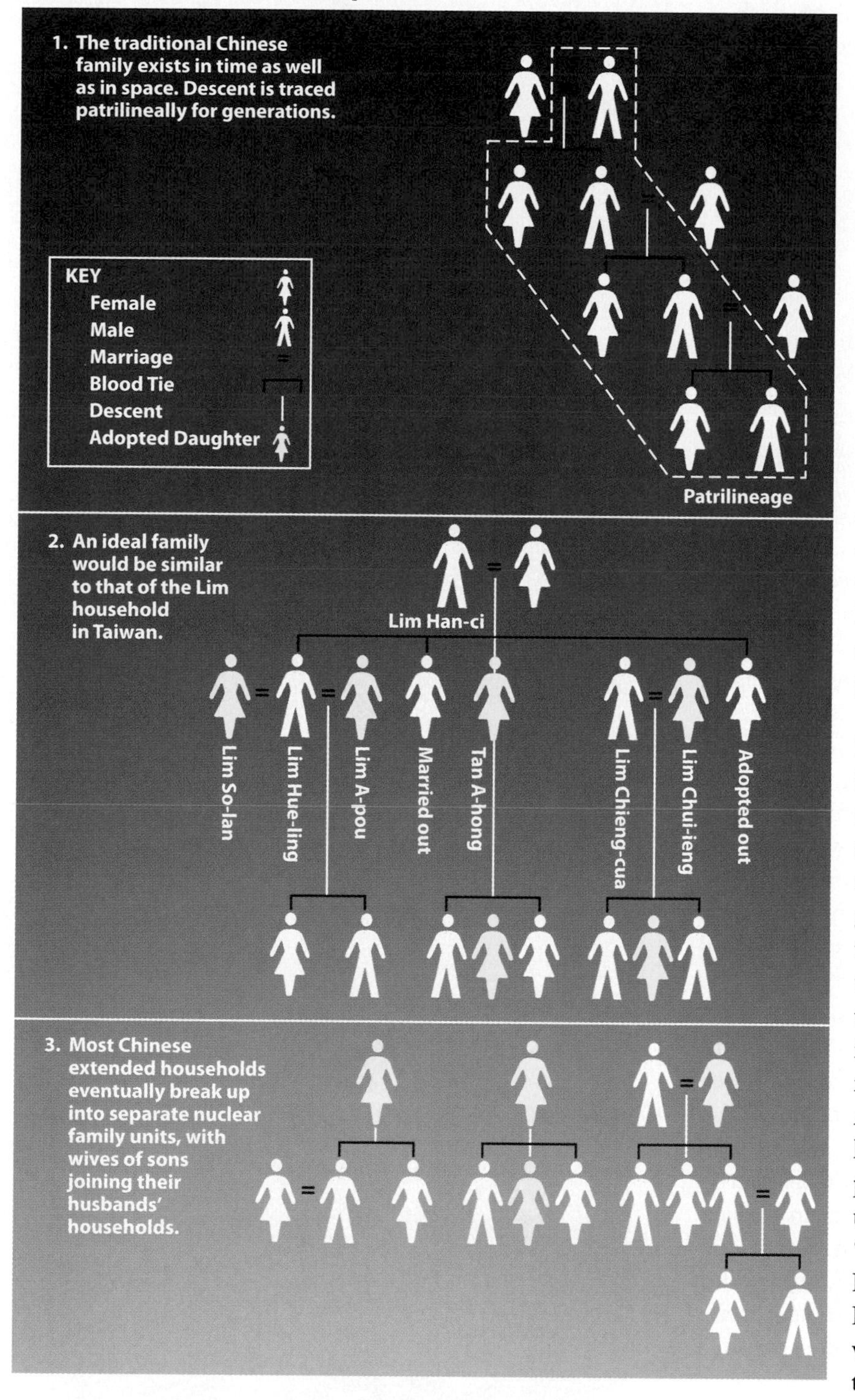

patrilineage a lineage that is formed by tracing descent in the male line

couple, their married sons and daughters-in-law, and their grandchildren and unmarried daughters (see Figure 5.4). To understand the traditional Chinese family, you have to understand the idea of temporal depth, for in China the **patrilineage** exists as much in time as it does in space. When Americans speak of family, they generally limit it to the living. In traditional China, the family includes a long line of patrilineal ancestors. Anthropologist Francis L. K. Hsu notes that the identity of each male is defined by his relations to the dead as much as it is by his relations to the living. His social worth and destiny are but reflections of the actions of his ancestors. He thus exists, as Hsu says, "under the shadow of his ancestors." Likewise, the spirits of the dead depend on the contributions of the living. These contributions are ceremonially made at altars, prominently positioned in each home, from which people send gifts to their ancestors by burning paper money, paper clothes, or other paper articles.

Given the interdependence between living and dead men of the patrilineage, it is apparent why it is essential for Chinese men to have male descendants to look after their well-being and provide for them in the afterworld. Male children and grandchildren are living proof to a man that his line will continue. For this reason, unlike the Ju/wasi or Trobriand Islanders, the Chinese express a marked preference for male children. Males are needed to maintain the patrilineal descent group. A son, as the Chinese put it, is a major happiness; a daughter is but a small happiness. Here is how one woman summed up the Chinese attitude toward daughters: "Why should I want so many daughters? It is useless to raise your own daughters. I'd just have to give them away when they were grown, so when someone asked for them as infants I gave them away. Think of all the rice I saved" (Wolf 1968, 40).

In addition to a long line of male ancestors, an ideal Chinese household should include several generations of fathers and sons sharing a common hearth or cooking stove and an ancestral altar, the symbols of the household. In the architecture of Peihotien, houses are constructed in such a way that they can easily be extended to accommodate additional sons and grandsons who bring their wives to live in the family home. In reality it is very difficult to maintain this ideal; most households in villages such as Peihotien are small, consisting of a married couple and several dependent patrilineal relatives.

QUESTION 5.2

How are families formed and ideal family types maintained?

Regardless of the size of family units or descent systems, in virtually all societies families require the socially recognized union of a male and female. Generally, this takes the form of marriage, a publicly recognized joining of two people or two families. Although marriage makes or sustains families, the manner in which such an arrangement comes about varies significantly. In American society, for example, children begin learning about courtship and marriage at an early age: 5- and 6-year-olds are teased about their "boyfriends" or "girlfriends," and playing house together is a popular preschool pastime. Americans begin serious courting in their early teens and usually go through a series of relationships before choosing a partner for their first marriage, most often when they are between the ages of 18 and 30. Although the choice of a marriage partner is supposedly based on feelings of love and sexual attraction, other factors are also important. Americans, like people in virtually all societies, are prohibited by the **incest taboo** from marrying their siblings, children, parents, and certain cousins. Ideally, a spouse should also be chosen from an appropriate income, ethnic, gender, and racial group. The conflict that may arise when an inappropriate marriage partner is chosen is often depicted in soap opera plots.

incest taboo a rule that prohibits sexual relations within certain categories of kin, such as siblings, children, parents, and certain cousins

The marriage ceremony in American society is traditionally hosted and financed by the bride's family, and after the honeymoon, the couple ideally

Ju/wasi family

Trobriand Islander family

Chinese family

establishes an independent residence. Their relationship, based on love expressed in regular sexual intercourse, is later transformed by the arrival of one or more children—a wife is transformed into a mother, a husband is transformed into a father.

The cycles of events that create or sustain the family among the Ju/wasi, Trobriand Islanders, and traditional Chinese illustrate the diversity of such arrangements. The soap opera themes of these groups would be quite different.

The Family Cycle of the Ju/wasi

Ju/wasi men and women, like Americans, begin to learn about courtship, sex, and marriage early in life. Because there is little privacy in a Ju/wasi camp and children sleep with their parents, they play "marriage" and imitate the bodily movements of parents making love at a young age. Most young men and women have had sexual experiences by the time they are 15. A Ju/wasi man usually marries for the first time between the ages of 18 and 25, when he is able to hunt and work for his wife's parents. Marriage is important to a man for a number of reasons. It marks him as an adult worthy of taking part in Ju/wasi public life, he gains a sex partner, and he gains a mate to provide his food. Although men are obligated to share and formally distribute the meat they obtain in the hunt with everyone in the camp, women, who obtain the majority of the camp's food, are not obligated to share what they gather.

© ROGER DE LA HARPE/GALLO IMAGES/CORBIS / © STEFAN KLEIN/ISTOCKPHOTO.COM

Women often marry as early as 12 to 14 years of age, generally before their first menstruation. Girls have fewer reasons to marry than men. Single or married men are always available as sex partners, and because the product of male labor, meat, is widely shared, a woman need not have a husband to ensure her share of the hunt. However, a girl's parents have good reasons for getting her married as soon as possible. The earlier she is married, the longer she and her husband will remain with her parents until she is of age, and the longer her husband will work for her parents. Moreover, the bride's family gains an alliance with another family and is less likely to get involved in open conflict between men over their daughter.

A couple's parents almost always arrange their marriage. Typically, the mother or father of the male approaches the family of the girl with a proposal for marriage. If the girl's parents approve of the match, the families exchange gifts to indicate their agreement. An appropriate husband for a daughter is a man who is not too much older, is not yet married, is a good hunter, and is willing to accept responsibility. The prospective groom should also be cooperative, generous, and unaggressive.

The Ju/wasi not only avoid choosing a spouse who is a close kinsperson, they are also restricted in the choice of a marriage partner by their naming system. There are only about 30 to 40 names that can be chosen for newborns, and people with the same first name consider themselves connected, regardless of their actual kinship relation. Suppose there are two people named Toma. Everyone related by kinship to one Toma will be considered to be related to the other Toma in the same way. Therefore, a marriage partner should occupy neither an actual prohibited kinship category nor one created by the naming system. A woman could not marry a man with the same name as her father or a man whose father had the same name as her father, because she and the man would refer to themselves as brother and sister.

Once a suitable match is made, one more obstacle to the marriage remains. Perhaps because they have little to gain or much to lose, young women often object strenuously to the marriage or to their parents' choice of a husband. If they protest long and hard enough, the marriage will be called off; if the protest is not sufficient, a marriage ceremony takes place. Members of both families build a hut for the couple that is set apart from the bride's family village.

A Ju/Wasi woman, Nisa, cried so much during her wedding and objected so strongly to spending the night with her new husband, Bo, that her parents asked a female relative, Nukha, to sleep between Nisa and Bo. She soon discovered that Nukha was having sex with Bo, and after a few nights she told her parents. They took her and moved to another waterhole, leaving Nukha and Bo behind. Nisa's second marriage, to Tashay, followed the same lines as her first; on her wedding night she cried and cried and finally ran away into the bush. Relatives tried to explain the benefits of marriage and to convince her to accept Tashay. When she finally agreed, Tashay took Nisa to his parents' home to live, and Nisa's parents followed. But not until Nisa and Tashay had been living together for a long time did they have sex. Nisa remembers the aftermath of their first lovemaking as being painful, and it was a long time before she allowed it again and began to enjoy it.

clan a unilineal descent group whose members claim descent from a common ancestor

exogamy a rule that requires a person to marry someone outside one's own group

Friends bring the couple to the hut, and the girl, with her head covered, is placed inside. Coals from the fires of both families are brought to start a fire in the couple's hut. Friends stay, joking, singing, and dancing, while bride and groom stay apart. Often, especially if the girl is young, a relative stays with them in the hut until she begins to adjust to her new status. These "honeymoons" are often the source of continuing conflict. Typically, half of all first marriages fail among the Ju/wasi, and they may enter several marriages over the course of their lives.

The Family Cycle of the Trobriand Islanders

Courtship and sexual play begin early in the Trobriand Islands. Children play erotic games at the age of 7 or 8 and begin seeking sex partners at ages 11 to 13. Trobriand adolescents are permitted to display their affection for each other openly. Girls scratch, beat, thrash, or even wound their lovers; boys accept this treatment as a sign of love and display their wounds as signs of success in courtship. They sing about love, both successful and unrequited, and take great pains with their physical appearance.

Because sexual activity before marriage is common and expected among the Trobrianders, marriage often simply formalizes an existing relationship. Although the couple may take the initiative in arranging a marriage, parents approve or disapprove of the choice of a spouse and sometimes arrange matches. There are certain categories of people a Trobriander may not marry. All Trobrianders belong to one of four **clans**, groups whose members consider themselves to be descended from a common ancestor. They must observe **exogamy**—that is, marry out of their own clan, into another. In addition, the incest taboo applies to all close relatives, particularly brothers and sisters, including all members of a matrilineage of the same generation. Trobriand myths tell of disastrous consequences of brother–sister incest that resulted in both parties' committing suicide. Sexual relations between a father and daughter are prohibited, although Trobrianders tell stories about it and joke about the idea of a father being overwhelmed by the beauty of his daughter. From the Trobriand point of view, fathers are not related by kinship to their daughters. The best marriage for a man is to a woman from his father's clan, for then his children, who will trace their descent from their mother, will be members of his father's clan. Consequently, the close relationship a man has with members of his father's clan will continue into the next generation.

There is no formal marriage ceremony; the girl simply stays overnight in her boyfriend's house. The next morning the bride's mother brings the couple

An adolescent gets definitely attached to a given person, wishes to possess her, works purposefully toward his goal, plans to reach fulfillment of his desires by magical and other means, and finally rejoices in achievement. I have seen young people of this age grow positively miserable through ill-success in love. (Malinowski 1929, 63)

cooked yams to indicate the bride's family's approval of the marriage. If girl's parents don't approve, they demand that their daughter return home with them. Significantly, the Trobrianders consider sharing food to be more intimate than having sex. Later, the wife's mother and maternal uncle bring raw yams for the couple, while the groom's father and maternal uncle begin collecting **bridewealth**—valuables such as stone ax blades, shells, and money—to give to the wife's kin and her father. The requirement of bridewealth makes young men dependent on members of their matrilineage.

During the first year of marriage, the couple lives in the hut that served as the groom's adolescent retreat, and during that year the groom's mother brings meals for them to share. At the end of the year, the groom's mother builds a stone hearth for the couple, and at that point the wife becomes responsible for the cooking.

The end of the first year of marriage marks a dramatic change in the husband–wife relationship. They no longer eat together, and the sexuality that bound them together as adolescents must be publicly submerged. After the first year of marriage, it is shameful for anyone to refer to the couple's sex life together. People may tease each other with such sexual taunts as "fuck your mother" or "fuck your father," but the epithet "fuck your wife" could get a person killed. In public, a husband and wife never hold hands or display affection. Their lives become segmented into a private domain, in which affection and emotion can be displayed, and a public domain, in which the meaning of their relationship is dictated by their obligation to help ensure the continuity and honor of their respective matrilineages.

The matrilineal principle in the life of a Trobriander husband and wife requires each to have a continued involvement with others outside the nuclear family. In addition to his ties to and concerns for his wife and children, the husband is also involved in the family life of his matrilineage—his sisters and their children. The wife is continually involved with her and her children's matrilineage—particularly her brothers. This involvement is economic and centers around wealth, particularly yams, banana-leaf bundles, and skirts, all of which women ultimately control.

One reason men marry is to obtain yams. Yams are more than food in the Trobriand Islands; they are valuable objects of wealth and are used as gifts to create and sustain relationships among people. They are particularly important in marriage transactions and in the continued tie of a woman to her matrilineage. Trobriand family yam gardens belong to the wife, but they are tended first by her father and later by a "brother." Each year at harvest time, the yams grown in her garden by her father or brother are ceremoniously taken to her. The amount and quality of the yams grown by a woman's brother are usually proportional to the bridewealth given to the wife's family by the groom's family when the couple was married. Early in the marriage these yams are stored in the rafters of the couple's hut, and the husband uses them as valuables to be redistributed to his kin who contributed the bridewealth. Later—often 10 to 15 years later—if the kin of a man's wife recognize him as important, they construct a yam house for him to store the yams they bring each year. The amount and quality of the yams stored and displayed by a man are indications of the regard in which his wife's kin hold him, and of his status in the community. The yam house is like a public bank account.

As a man seeks a wife to obtain the yams grown for him by his wife's brother, brothers seek husbands for their sisters, not only for the children nurtured by the husbands for their wives' matrilineage but for the brother-in-law's

bridewealth the valuables that a groom or his family are expected or obligated to present to the bride's family

CASE: How to Fight AIDS

Since the discovery of HIV/AIDS in the 1980s, the United States has developed a range of education programs intended to slow the deadly epidemic.

These programs, which educate the public about how HIV is spread and how to prevent infection, shared the assumptions that if sexual partners openly discuss the dangers of HIV/AIDS and the means to prevent infection, they will take necessary precautions. Thus, they emphasized the health risks of HIV/AIDS, the need for open communication between sexual partners, and the critical importance of using condoms. While these programs had measured success in the United States, similar programs in other countries have not had the same impact. What do medical practitioners and those working in AIDS prevention need to know to design effective prevention programs, and what can anthropologists do to help?

In his book *The Night Is Young: Sexuality in Mexico in the Time of AIDS*, Hector Carrillo argues health workers need to understand people's attitudes toward sexuality, love, and family, in order to implement successful HIV/AIDS programs in Mexico.

AIDS prevention specialists in the United States advise sex partners to communicate openly about their concerns over infection. According to Carrillo, this violates the "code of silence" about sexual matters in Mexican families. Children and parents in Mexican homes rarely talk about sex. Most of Carrillo's informants never had a conversation about sex with their parents. They learned about sex primarily on their own, with inputs from friends and popular media. The code of silence especially hindered gay men and women from discussing their sexual orientation with parents. While some revealed their sexual orientation to parents, there were attempts to hide the fact from others. Others assumed that their parents knew about their homosexuality but preferred to maintain silence, seeing it as tacit acceptance. They feared that they would withdraw that acceptance if anyone openly broached the subject.

Another cultural barrier is the traditional relationship in which women are supposed to be submissive to men both within the family and outside it. Mexican families are patriarchal, and *machismo*, an exaggerated masculinity, requires the subordination of women but grants sexual freedom to men. The difference in power between sex partners is a major cause of HIV risk, particularly for women when their male partners do not want to use protection. Further, when a woman requests a condom, she implies that she is sexually experienced and is assumed to be "loose." Consequently, many women are reluctant to request that a partner use a condom for fear of being stigmatized as promiscuous. Men who assume the submissive role in gay sex tend also to be reluctant

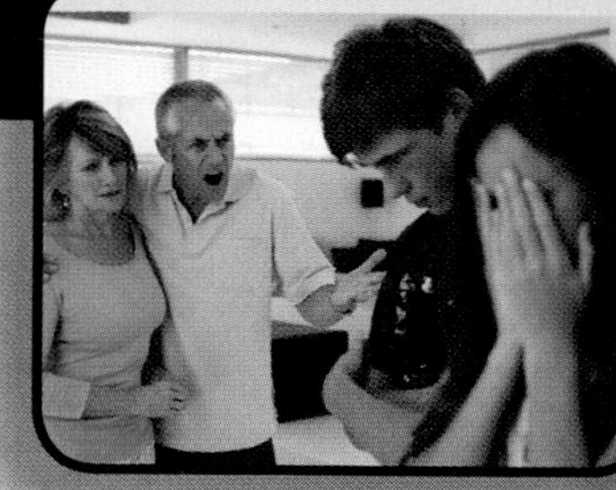

to insist that their partners use a condom, in much the same way that women are reluctant to insist on condom use by their male partners.

Another hindrance to condom use is the fear that the request for a condom may carry implications of mistrust or infidelity. Asking for a condom, says Carrillo, could be construed as meaning "I don't trust you" or "I have been unfaithful." The danger of this kind of misunderstanding is increased if partners have not used a condom on previous occasions or if sexual partners have known each other for some time. As a result, a partner might consent to unprotected sex rather than face issues of suspicion, mistrust, infidelity, and dishonesty.

Finally, attitudes about sex, love, and passion also pose barriers to condom use. Successful sexual encounters require abandonment or surrender (*entrega*), said Carrillo's informants. In the sexual encounter, lovers must suppress "rational" thinking, because rationality could destroy the sexual moment. As one informant put it, "It's necessary to allow yourself to be taken by the moment, by the caresses, not think that you are in a relationship, not pressure yourself [to think], because then it all dies." In this sense, the sexual experience requires what Carrillo calls an "altered state." According to one informant, safe sex was advisable for health reasons but the "irrationality" of passion and surrender was preferred. The implication is that the introduction of preventive measures would cause the whole sexual interaction to collapse.

Carrillo suggests...

. . . that there are two conflicting views of the sexual moment. One involves an emphasis on sexual desire, sexual passion, and love. This viewpoint emphasizes the value of emotions, the dynamics of the sexual relationship, and the value of seeking validation, satisfaction, and communion with sex partners. The second view, articulated in HIV-prevention literature, is highly medicalized and places priority on rationality, informed decision making, self-control, and sexual health. As Carrillo puts it, "In Mexico, while the former view of sex highlights spontaneity, mutual surrender, and abandonment, the latter has stressed self-control and the need to contain sexual passion." The question is how to reconcile these competing views of sex so as to develop a more effective means of preventing infection. That is, how can one introduce the awareness of disease risk and preventive measures without inhibiting the spontaneity of sex?

A yam house, which acts like a public bank account, displaying a man's status.

Bundles of banana leaves.

help in obtaining banana-leaf bundles. Sisters are obligated, with the help of their husbands, to prepare bundles of banana leaves to be used to finance the funerals of members of their matrilineage. The woman makes some, but her husband may have to purchase additional bundles. Members of the deceased's matrilineage give them away at funerals to people who were important in the life of the deceased. The more important the person was to the deceased, the greater the number of banana-leaf bundles he or she receives. In this way, members of a matrilineage uphold their honor and status; to fail to fulfill these obligations would bring dishonor to the matrilineage.

The development of Trobriand family life, then, must be understood in the context of the movement of such goods as yams and banana-leaf bundles between husband and wife and members of the wife's matrilineage. It is the successful completion of the cycle of exchanges of yams and banana-leaf bundles that ensures the stability of a marriage and a matrilineage.

The Trobriand nuclear family promotes stable bonds between husband and wife, although divorce is both frequent and easy to obtain. The wife usually takes the initiative. Most divorces occur in the first year of marriage; they are rare after the couple has been together for a few years.

Although fathers are not technically members of their children's family, they are very important in the lives of the children. Once children are weaned, they sleep with their fathers, and later fathers are responsible for enhancing their beauty with presents of shells, necklaces, and tiny tortoise-shell earrings. These objects are evidence of a father's presence in the life of his child. In fact the term for a child with unpierced ears is translated as "fatherless." So important is the tie that develops between a man and his son that when the son marries, the father may try to convince him to remain in his village rather than moving to the village of his maternal kin, as expected.

The Family Cycle of the Chinese

In China, the family centers on the relationship between father and son. Marriage in traditional China is less a matter of a man getting a wife than of bringing a childbearer into the household. As Hsu (1967, 57) describes it, "A marriage is made in the name of the parents taking a daughter-in-law, not in the name of the son taking a wife."

Because marriage has far less to do with relations between husband and wife than with those between the husband's family and a daughter-in-law, marriages in traditional China are almost always arranged, often far in advance, and there is little if any courtship. When a boy is 6 or 7 years old, his parents might hire a matchmaker to find a girl who will eventually be an appropriate bride. Because they believe that the time of a person's birth influences his or her personality and fate, the parents might also enlist the services of a diviner to make the appropriate match. The matchmaker takes a piece of red paper with the time and date of a girl's birth to a prospective groom's family. The boy's mother brings this paper (or papers, if there is a choice of brides) to a fortune-teller, who predicts the compatibility of the boy and girl. If the fortune-teller deems a girl appropriate, the matchmaker tries to convince the girl's parents to accept the match. If she is successful, the bridewealth, the marriage gifts of the husband's family to the wife's parents, is then negotiated.

Another way parents can obtain a wife for their son in traditional China is to adopt an infant girl, who will be reared in the household and later will marry the son. Although this kind of arrangement is not as prestigious as bridewealth marriage, it has two advantages. Because the prospective bride is raised in the household of her future mother-in-law, she is more likely to be obedient, and it is not necessary to pay a brideprice. The major disadvantage is that the prospective bride and groom are raised virtually as brother and sister and often find it difficult to make the transition to husband and wife.

The adoption of a boy to serve as a husband for a daughter is a third way to arrange a marriage. Adoption occurs only when a family has no sons. The adopted boy then assumes the family name, so that his sons continue the line of his adopted father. Such marriages are not as respected as others, and a man who is adopted into his wife's family bears the stigma of having abandoned his parents and ancestors. For poor or orphaned boys, however, the prospect of heading a thriving household might outweigh such stigma.

Compared to the Ju/wasi or Trobriand marriage ceremony, the Chinese wedding is very formal and, for the groom's family, very expensive. A diviner determines the date and hour of the wedding, and even the exact time the bride will arrive in her sedan chair. The day before the wedding, the girl's **dowry** is sent to the groom's home in a procession accompanied by a band, drummers, and ushers. The dowry consists of such goods as leather chests, tables, stools, cosmetics, housewares, or clothing and cloth, but never land or a house. On the day of the wedding, the groom is carried in a sedan chair to the house of the bride. When he arrives, she shows token resistance, and she and her mother weep. Then she is carried to the groom's house in a red sedan chair decorated to suggest the early birth of sons. Offerings are made at the ancestors' altar to ensure the success of the marriage. Then the couple is taken to pay respects to the boy's parents—the formal introduction of the bride to the groom's household. Feasting and dancing accompany the wedding, sometimes lasting for three or four days.

After the wedding, there is little time or place for romantic relations between husband and wife. According to Hsu, husband and wife sleep in the same bed for only seven days, and there is no public expression of affection between them. Once the wife enters into her husband's family, she finds herself among strangers, virtually cut off from her parents and siblings. She must treat her mother-in-law with respect and acquiesce to the demands of sisters-in-law or other members of her husband's family. She occupies the lowest place at the table. She occasionally can go back to her mother and sob at her change of status, but, as the Chinese proverb puts it, spilled water cannot be gathered up. She does not acquire full status in her husband's family until she produces a male child. Until then, the husband must show indifference to his wife,

dowry the goods and valuables a bride's family supplies to the groom's family or to the couple addressing her through a third party. After the birth of a son, he can refer to her as the mother of his child. It is as if a man's wife is related to him only through his children. For the groom, marriage is simply a continued expression of his duty to his father and his ancestors. In no way is his new relationship with a wife to interfere with that duty; rather, the marriage is an expression of his filial devotion and obligation to produce male heirs.

Whereas divorce is a fairly common among the Trobrianders and among the Ju/wasi, it is virtually unheard of in traditional China. A husband can take mistresses with impunity, but, in theory, he can murder an adulterous wife. Wives have no rights of divorce. Other than flight or suicide, a woman who wants to leave her husband and in-laws has few options.

QUESTION 5.3

What are the roles of sexuality, love, and wealth?

The themes of sex, love, and wealth are pervasive in American life, as well as in American soaps. Young men and women use their sexuality and appearance to influence one another and to gain potential partners and spouses. Later, as husbands and wives, they attempt to manage their wealth to fulfill social obligations and to rise in status. Often they seek to cement their status both as individuals and as a family by having children. As mothers and fathers, they face the task of guiding their children and trying to ensure their success and happiness.

The manipulation and negotiation of sexuality, love, and wealth dominate many of the plots of American soap operas. The ideas about romantic love expressed in these plots, however, often are not shared in other societies. Examining these ideas among the Ju/wasi, Trobriand Islanders, and Chinese—and imagining how they might be expressed in soap operas—can help us understand our own beliefs about these things.

Sex, Love, and Wealth among the Ju/wasi

Wealth plays virtually no part in the lives of the Ju/wasi, but, for women especially, sex, love, and beauty are very important. Sexuality is important first for the woman's well-being. Nisa told Marjorie Shostak that if a girl grows up not learning to enjoy sex, her mind doesn't develop normally; if a grown woman doesn't have sex, her thoughts are ruined and she is always angry. A Ju/wasi woman's sexuality also maximizes her independence. Sex attracts lovers, and a love relationship, being voluntary, recognizes the equality of the participants. By taking lovers, a Ju/wasi woman proclaims her control over her social life, because she can offer her sexuality to men as a means of vitalizing them. Nisa talked candidly about sex, male impotence, and the contributions women make to men:

> A woman can bring a man life, even if he is almost dead. She can give him sex and make him alive again. If she were to refuse, he would die! If there were no women around, their semen would kill men. Did you know that? Women make it possible for them to live. Women have something so good that if a man takes it and moves about inside it, he climaxes and is sustained. (Shostak, 1983, 288)

There is one trade-off for Ju/wasi women who use their sexuality—men see them as sources of conflict and consequently as potentially dangerous.

Motherhood, unlike sexuality, is not easily bartered by Ju/wasi women. In other societies, including our own, parents are apt to stress how much they have sacrificed or suffered for their children, thus using motherhood or fatherhood as a way of creating obligations and ties. It makes little sense for a Ju/wasi woman (or man, for that matter) to make such a claim. Children owe their parents little; there is no need for bridewealth or dowries for marriage, and food and kin to care for them are plentiful. The dynamics of Ju/wasi families are built on the need of individuals to avoid permanent ties and obligations and to maintain their independence.

Sex, Love, and Wealth among the Trobriand Islanders

Whereas the maintenance of sexuality is important throughout life among the Ju/wasi, among the Trobriand Islanders it is important for women only prior to marriage. Armed with the magic and bodily adornments contributed by her father, but without the wealth—yams, banana-leaf bundles, and other valuables—she will later acquire, an unmarried woman uses her sexuality to negotiate her relationships with others. Once married, she ceases to emphasize her beauty and sexual attraction and instead emphasizes her fertility and motherhood. A woman's worth, once measured by her father's concern for her and her sexuality, is determined after marriage by her ability to collect yams for her husband, produce children, and provide banana-leaf bundles for her matrilineage.

Men's sexuality is viewed very differently. Because the Trobrianders claim that men play no role in reproduction, their sexuality is not important. Their physical attractiveness, however, is important, for this is what attracts lovers and later a wife to collect the yams by which a man measures his status. Beauty is especially important for chiefs. They must maintain an aura of sexual attractiveness in order to attract more wives, whose fathers and brothers will supply the wealth they need to maintain their position of influence.

Wealth also forms different kinds of links for Trobrianders. Because the Ju/wasi have little wealth to contend for and what there is (e.g., meat) is widely shared, the links men create with their wives' families are based not on wealth but on labor. Among the Trobrianders, however, a man who wants to marry must use the wealth of members of his matrilineage as bridewealth payments to his wife's family. He is required to return this wealth to members of his family by redistributing the yams he later receives from his wife's brothers. Moreover, the yams he receives from his brothers-in-law are in some ways payment for the children his wife produces, who are members of the wife's and brother-in-law's matrilineage.

Sex, Love, and Wealth among the Chinese

The themes of sexuality, love, and wealth are played out very differently in the traditional Chinese rural family. Whereas both Ju/wasi and Trobriand adolescents have considerable freedom to use their sexuality to attract and influence others, quite the opposite is true in China. If a girl comes from a family that is influential and wealthy enough to make an attractive match for her, she will have little to do with boys. Virginity is both valued and necessary for a Chinese bride. If a girl has been mixed up in an affair, her only chance of marriage is to wed someone in a distant village.

Romantic love and sexuality are also irrelevant in the relations between traditional Chinese husbands and wives. A wife's function is to produce children. A man who can afford it takes concubines. A man who can't afford it, but does so anyway, is criticized not for his infidelity to his wife but for squandering the wealth of his ancestors and descendants.

In fact, sexuality figures very little in the life of a Chinese woman either before or after her marriage. It is as a mother that most Chinese women establish significant relations. Her value consists in her potential to become the mother of a boy. Becoming a mother cements her relations with her husband, her father-in-law, and her mother-in-law, and it is her motherhood that secures her life.

It is as a mother that most Chinese women establish significant relations.

The only exception to the motherhood-over-sexuality rule is the woman who is unable to obtain a husband or who loses one. Such a woman may become a concubine or prostitute. Margery Wolf tells the story of Tan A-Hong in the Taiwanese village of Peihotien, who was adopted by Lim Han-ci to be the wife of a son who later died. When this happens, adopted daughters are often sold as slaves or prostitutes. Lim Han-ci arranged to have Tan A-Hong adopted into another family, but for whatever reason, the adoption didn't work out. Tan A-Hong moved to southern Taiwan and became a prostitute. She ultimately moved back to Peihotien, bringing with her an adopted daughter whom she reared in her way of life to care for her. It should be noted that the Chinese do not condemn women who choose prostitution. According to Margery Wolf, prostitutes are said to be "more interesting" than other women, but people rarely make judgments about them because too many village girls "go out to work" to support family members.

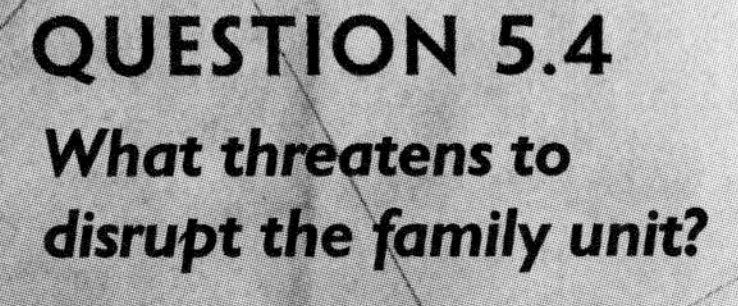

QUESTION 5.4
What threatens to disrupt the family unit?

polygamy a form of marriage in which a person is permitted to have more than one spouse

polygyny a form of marriage in which a man is permitted to have more than one wife

polyandry a form of marriage in which a woman is permitted to have more than one husband

Threats to family formation and maintenance are, as might be expected, major sources of soap opera drama. If soap operas are in any way accurate reflections of American life, infidelity, sickness, authority struggles, and economic hardship are the principal threats. Moreover, as our soap operas constantly remind us, any threat to an established marriage endangers the continued existence of the family unit.

There are also threats to the stability and maintenance of Ju/Wasi, Trobrian and traditional Chinese families, but they differ from those that threaten the American family.

Threats to the Ju/wasi Family

The major threat to family stability among the Ju/wasi is conflict between husband and wife over infidelity or the efforts of a husband to secure a second wife. Like many societies around the world, the Ju/wasi allow **polygamy**. Men are allowed to have more than one wife (**polygyny**), and apparently women are permitted to have more than one husband (**polyandry**), though this is rare. Though it's allowed, polygamy is the exception rather than the rule. A survey conducted by Lee in 1968 of 131 married Ju/wasi men found that 93 percent were living monogamously, 5 percent were living in polygynous unions, and 2 percent were living in polyandrous relationships.

One reason why polygamy is rare, even though having more than one wife is a sign of prestige, is the family difficulties it creates. According to Marjorie Shostak, a popular saying among the Ju/Wasi is "there is never any peace in a household with two women in it." Stories of the complications resulting from polygamous unions are an endless source of humor for those who are single or monogamous:

> When a man married one woman, then marries another and sets her down besides the first so there are three of them together at night, the husband changes from one wife to another. First he has sex with the older wife, then with the younger. But when he goes to the younger wife, the older one is jealous and grabs and bites him. The two women start to fight and bite each other. The older woman goes to the fire and throws burning wood at them yelling "What told you that when I, your first wife, am lying here that you should go and sleep with another woman? Don't

After the death of her second husband, Tashay, Nisa married Besa. Nisa says that even though they began fighting soon after the marriage, she became pregnant. Besa then abandoned her and she miscarried. Shortly after, she met some people from Besa's village and told them to tell Besa that their marriage was over. She began a relationship with Twi, an older man, who asked her to live with him. Besa returned, saying he had come to take her back with him. Nisa refused. Besa and Twi fought, and Besa, the younger man, pushed Twi down. Later Nisa and Twi separated because Nisa's brother Dau liked Besa and sent Twi away.

Nisa still refused to return to Besa and resumed an affair with a past lover that lasted until he died. Then she began to see another man named Bo, but Besa returned to renew his claim over her. Violence again erupted, this time between Besa and Bo; they pushed each other and called each other insulting names, such as "Big Testicles" or "Long Penis." In an almost final confrontation with Besa, Nisa publicly stripped off her apron and cried, "There! There's my vagina! Look Besa, look at me! This is what you want!" Besa, consoled by a man who accompanied him, left. Soon after, Nisa and Bo married. Besa also remarried, but later he approached Nisa again about renewing their relationship.

> I have a vagina? So why do you just leave it and go without having sex with me? Instead you go and have sex with that young girl!" Sometimes they fight like that all night, until dawn breaks. A co-wife is truly a terrible thing. (Shostak 1983, 172)

Although polygamy is rare, marital infidelity is not. At one waterhole with 50 married couples, Lee recorded 16 couples in which one or another of the partners was having an affair. The Ju/wasi recognize certain benefits in taking lovers. For a woman, extramarital affairs add variety, as well as economic insurance.

> When you are a woman, you just don't sit still and do nothing—you have lovers. You don't just sit with the man of your hut, with just one man. One man can give you very little. One man gives you only one kind of food to eat. But when you have lovers, one brings you something and another brings you something else. One comes at night with meat, another with money, another with beads. Your husband also does things and gives them to you. (Shostak 1983, 271)

Men say that the emotion and passion of extramarital affairs are wonderful: "Hearts are on fire and passions great," as the Ju/wasi say. When Shostak asked a young married man about his lover, he said they fantasized about running away. She asked what it would be like, and he smiled and replied, "The first few months would be wonderful!" Extramarital affairs are likely to be threatening to a husband, however, and they are the most common cause of conflict and violence among the Ju/wasi. Wives are important to Ju/wasi men, because as long as they have wives they are dependent on no one. Male adulthood requires acquiring and demonstrating a willingness to fight for a secure marital status.

Threats to the Trobriand Island Family

Among the Trobriand Islanders, it is not threats to the husband–wife relationship that are critical but threats to the matrilineage. Because the matrilineage is the major social unit, the honor of that family group is a central concern to all members. Lineages among the Trobriand Islanders are ranked according to the closeness of their genealogical connection to the founders of the lineage. Each lineage must be able to maintain its position vis-à-vis others through the ceremonial presentation of valuables, particularly yams and banana-leaf bundles. So important are yams in the relative ranking of matrilineages that groups try to demonstrate their wealth by giving more yams to others than they receive. Because giving may be taken as a claim of superiority, however, it can be dangerous; as the Trobrianders put it, "When you give too much, people worry."

Although it may seem implausible, yams could become the focus of a Trobriand soap opera plot. For example, a man's political power, measured in yams, is a direct result of the support he receives from his wife's kin—it is her yams, grown for her by her father and brother, that create status for her husband. However, the annual yam gifts received by a husband can also be a source of conflict. If the amount or size of yams harvested does not live up to a husband's expectations, he may be insulted. On the other hand, if a woman's brother is unhappy over the bridewealth he received from the husband's family or the support given by the husband to his sister in collecting banana-leaf bundles, he may purposely communicate his unhappiness by not working hard in his sister's yam gardens. Other plots could be devised about unrequited love, attempts of fathers to convince their sons to remain in their father's villages, and even about incest. But a theme that would be sure to attract a Trobriand audience would be about sorcery.

A person who uses sorcery against another is dominating that person.

The Trobrianders claim to know spells that can kill. Generally, only chiefs have this power, but others can seek out a chief and, for a price, convince him to use his power against their enemies. Someone who is believed to have this power is both feared and respected; Trobrianders tell of instances in which they were challenged and retaliated with sorcery. Vanoi, an important Trobriand chief, told Weiner about being challenged by a Christian convert who openly mocked Vanoi's knowledge of sorcery. Vanoi offered the man a cigarette, saying that he should smoke it if he doubted the chief's knowledge of sorcery. The man did; he became ill later that night and died a week later.

© LJUPCO/ISTOCKPHOTO.COM

A person who uses sorcery against another is dominating that person, and because each person's fate is tied to that of the matrilineage, a threat to one is considered a threat to all. That is why any death among the Trobrianders is a serious matter. Because death is attributed to sorcery, every death is a sign that someone from another lineage is challenging the power of a matrilineage. Each funeral marks an attempt by the members of a matrilineage to reassert its power; at the same time, the mourners assert their innocence of sorcery. The matrilineal kin of the deceased do this by distributing banana-leaf bundles and other valuables to those who have come to publicly mourn the passing of the deceased and to assist with the funeral arrangements by decorating and carrying the corpse. In recognition of their contribution to the life of the deceased, they receive gifts. The deceased's matrilineage empties its treasury to announce its strength in the face of the threat to its integrity that is signaled by a death. Here is how Weiner sums up the meaning of death for them:

> Because of the expanding possibilities in a person's life, each Trobriander represents her or his matrilineal identity—originally conceived through a woman and an ancestral *baloma* spirit—as well as the accumulation of all the other relationships that parenthood and marriage made possible. Therefore, a death demands attention to this full totality, as the members of a matrilineage seek both to repay all "others" for their past care and to hold on to them now that this death has occurred. (1988, 161)

Threats to the Chinese Family

The biggest threat to the traditional rural Chinese family is, of course, the absence of a son. The lack of a male heir endangers not only the continuance of a household but the entire patrilineage through time. A man without sons, a spirit without descendants, has no one to offer incense for him and no altar on which his spirit can find refuge and honor. The existence of a son is no guarantee of smooth family relations, however. Fathers have enormous authority and power over sons, and sons are obligated to worship, respect, obey, and care for their fathers. But fathers often become overbearing or use force to assert their authority. Margery Wolf says that Lim Han-ci in the village of Peihotien was unusual in how frequently he beat

Lim Han-ci adopted Lim A-pou, then 9 months old, to be reared as a wife for his son Hue-ling. A-pou was a model daughter-in-law. She accepted reprimands without becoming sullen, she did not complain, and she was a hard worker. However, her relationship with her prospective husband was not a happy one. When Hue-ling was 19, he committed an act of moral violence by leaving home and severing ties with his father. Hue-ling was able to leave home only because he had become a leader in the lo mue, a secret criminal society.

Years later, Hue-ling returned to Peihotien, reconciled with his father, and went through a simple ceremony to marry his adopted sister A-pou. Although it must have been obvious to her that Hue-ling would be less than an ideal husband, A-pou did not protest, for she had no other alternatives. She could not return to her biological family, and it would be impossible to stay in the Lim household after refusing to marry Hue-ling. Moreover, marrying the eldest son would give her status in the household. When Hue-ling took a succession of mistresses after the marriage, A-pou complained very little. Because she had a son by Hue-ling, her status in the family was secure.

partible inheritance a form of inheritance in which the goods or property of a family is divided among the heirs

impartible inheritance a form of inheritance in which family property is passed undivided to one heir

his sons. However, regardless of how harshly a person may be treated, breaking away from one's father is considered a violent act.

Dramatic splits between fathers and sons are rare in traditional China. More frequent is conflict between brothers over the division of an inheritance. In most other rural, peasant societies around the world, the male head of the household designates his heirs before death. He might divide his property among his offspring—**partible inheritance**—or he may leave all of it to one descendant—**impartible inheritance**. In China the ideal is for brothers to continue to live together and share the inheritance, usually under the direction of the eldest son, thus avoiding the division of property. In fact, however, brothers rarely continue to share, and ultimately conflict between them leads to a division of household property.

Wolf documents the ultimate disintegration of the Lim household after the death of Lim Han-ci and the resulting arguments over property by the sons and their wives. When Wolf went to live in the Lim household, Lim Han-ci and his oldest son, Hue-ling, had already died. The two remaining family units consisted of the family of the second-oldest son, Chieng-cua, and the family of Hue-ling's widow, A-Pou. While Lim Han-ci was alive, his control over the family's wealth was enough to maintain the extended family. Once he died, conflict between A-pou and her son, on the one hand, and Chieng-cua, on the other, led to the division of family property. The wealth that had held the extended family together served, finally, to drive it apart.

AN INTERNATIONAL TELEVISION PRODUCTION COMPANY HAS HIRED YOUR COMPANY, CREATIVITY ENTERPRISES, TO WRITE A PILOT EPISODE OF A SOAP OPERA TO BE MARKETED IN RURAL CHINA. The plot of the soap you will create will revolve around the Wang family. The Wangs are a relatively well-off farming family who live in rural China. The characters in the soap opera are to include the following family members:

Wang Zhou, the 55-year-old male head of the family

Wang Lim, the wife of Wang Zhou

Wang Xiao, the eldest son of Wang Zhou

Wang Lao, the wife of Wang Xiao

Wang Jiang, the second son of Wang Zhou

Wang Jane, the wife of Wang Jiang

Wang Sally, the 20-year-old unmarried daughter of Wang Zhou

Wang Nai-Nai, the mother of Wang Zhou

Xiao and Lao have four children, two boys and two girls.

Jiang and Jane have two children, both girls.

You may, if you wish, add other characters to the story. The story line should be simple but clear, and you are free to embellish the characters in any way you want, but keep in mind that the soap must appeal to a rural Chinese audience.

PRODUCTION

DIRECTOR

CAMERA

DATE SCENE TAKE

Cultural ANTHRO was built on a simple principle: to create a new teaching and learning solution that reflects the way today's faculty teach and the way you learn.

Through conversations, focus groups, surveys, and interviews, we collected data that drove the creation of the current version of Cultural ANTHRO that you are using today. But it doesn't stop there—in order to make Cultural ANTHRO an even better learning experience, we'd like you to SPEAK UP and tell us how Cultural ANTHRO worked for you.

What did you like about it?
What would you change?
Are there additional ideas you have that would help us build a better product for next semester's students?

At **www.cengagebrain.com** you'll find all of the resources you need to succeed—**videos, flash cards, interactive quizzes,** and more!

Speak Up! Go to **www.cengagebrain.com.**

PROBLEM 6

HOW DO PEOPLE DETERMINE WHO THEY ARE, AND HOW DO THEY COMMUNICATE WHO THEY THINK THEY ARE TO OTHERS?

Chapter 6 The Cultural Construction of Identity

When an individual enters the presence of others, they commonly seek to acquire information about him or to bring into play information about him already possessed. They will be interested in his general socioeconomic status, his conception of self, his attitude toward them, his competence, his trustworthiness, etc. Although some of this information seems to be sought almost as an end in itself, there are usually quite practical reasons for acquiring it. Information about the individual helps to define the situation, enabling others to know in advance what he will expect of them and what they may expect of him. Informed in these ways, the others will know how best to act in order to call forth a desired response from him.

Erving Goffman

QUESTIONS

In examining this problem, we will consider the following questions:

6.1 How does the concept of personhood vary from society to society?

6.2 How do societies distinguish individuals from one another?

6.3 How do individuals learn who they are?

6.4 How do individuals communicate their identities to one another?

6.5 How do individuals defend their identities when they are threatened?

INTRODUCTION

The Importance of Self

As we become who we are, we learn how we stand in relation to others. We learn how we relate to others as son, daughter, student, friend, or lover.

Of all the products of our culture, the one we most take for granted is our self. We are not born knowing who we are or what our place is on the social landscape; we learn to be American or Japanese, male or female, husband or wife. As we become who we are, we learn how we stand in relation to others. We learn how we relate to others as son, daughter, student, friend, or lover. In this sense, society is a collection of **social identities**. Individuals strive to arrive at some identity/destination from which they can relate to other social identities while they seek confirmation from others that they occupy the position on the social landscape that they claim to occupy.

To appreciate the importance of the self, try to imagine a society in which every person is physically indistinguishable from every other person. How would people in such a society know how to behave toward each other? Whenever we interact with another person, the interaction must be based on some idea of who the other is—Friend? Stranger? Family member? Teacher? At the same time, the other person must have some idea of who we are, a conception of the relationship that exists between us. The necessity of knowing the social identity of others is apparent when strangers meet and, directly or indirectly, seek to elicit information from each other. Each tries to place the other in some identity at some spot on the social landscape.

Imagine next a society in which every person is completely unique. In this case, every interaction would be different, and there would be no way to learn from one situation how to behave in another situation. Each person would need to have an infinite variety of behaviors with which to interact with an infinite number of types of people. We avoid this situation by categorizing people, placing them in groups, so that not everyone in our social universe is unique. We group them into categories based on criteria such as gender, ethnicity, or personal characteristics.

social identities views that people have of their own and others' positions in society. Individuals seek confirmation from others that they occupy the positions on the social landscape that they claim to occupy

Try to imagine, also, a social landscape in which no person communicates in any way who he or she thinks the other person is. This, too, would represent an impossible situation. People would have no way of acquiring from others confirmation that they occupy the social identities they think they occupy. In reality, much of our social identity is based on what others confirm about our position in the landscape. Put another way, nobody is anybody except in relation to somebody else.

Finally, try to imagine a social landscape in which everyone communicates to everyone else that they occupy the wrong spot on the landscape. Every person actively disagrees with every other person about his or her identity. This situation would be, if not impossible, at least chaotic.

To examine how people in a society determine their identities and communicate who they think they are to others, we explore the ways different societies define the person, the ways individuals are differentiated from others, the manner in which individuals find out who they are, how they convey to others who they are, and the consequences of disagreements over identity. Finally, we consider how we can apply what we learn about identity to solve problems regarding body image.

QUESTION 6.1

How does the concept of personhood vary from society to society?

In most societies, names are intimate markers of the person, differentiating individuals from others. Names can also reveal how people conceive of themselves and their relations to others, and whatever form it takes, a name represents the self. How much is revealed by a name varies by culture and situation. When American businesspeople meet, they exchange first names, last names, and business titles, revealing how they are connected to their organizations. When Moroccans from different towns meet, they not only give their names, but the names of their home towns. The Moroccan self is embedded in family and place of origin. Among the Gitksan of British Columbia, the names people use depend on their social position; when they enter adulthood, get married, or assume a higher rank in Gitksan society, they change their names. The Gitksan self is inseparable from one's position in society.

The differences in naming practices reveal the different ways societies conceptualize what a person is and how that person relates to the group. Most Americans believe that individuals are stable, autonomous entities who exist more or less independent of whatever situation or status they occupy. As Americans move from status to status or place to place—from student to husband or wife to employee to father or mother—they

The holistic view of the self is expressed in Gandhi's metaphor of individuals as drops in the ocean; the drops cannot survive without the ocean, and the ocean loses its identity without the drops.

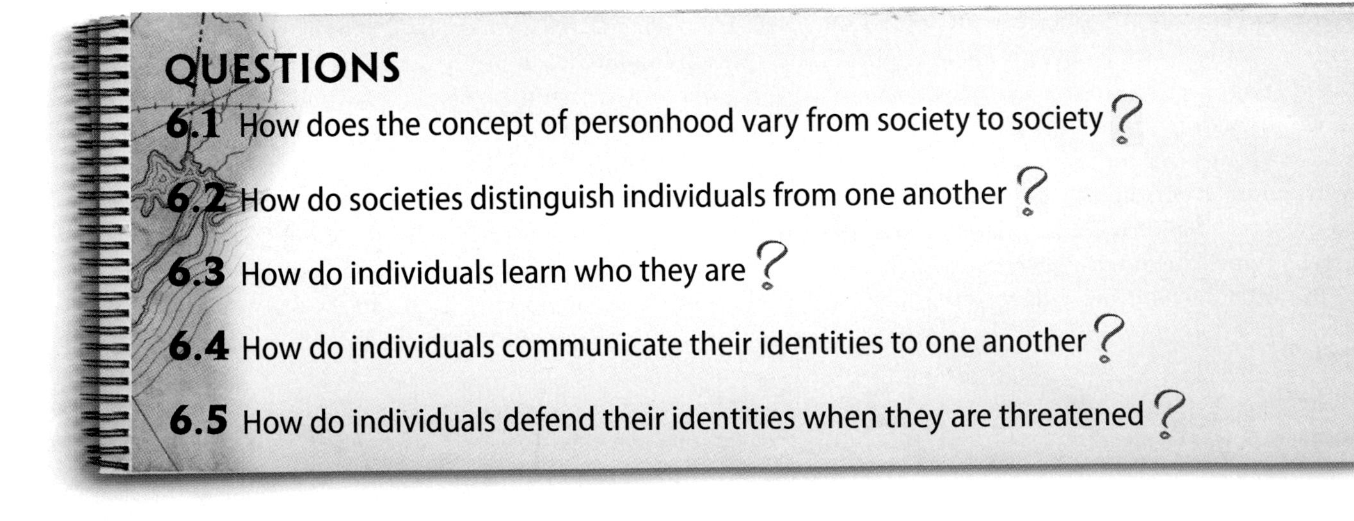

believe themselves to be the same person. In this regard, Americans are highly **individualistic**.

This does not seem to be the case in other societies in which individuals are not seen as entities distinct from their social position or group. In these societies, such as the Gitksan, the relationship between the person and the group or the person and social position is **holistic**. There is no separation between the person and the rest of society, and his or her status within that society.

The Egocentric and Sociocentric Self

The differences between individualistic and holistic conceptions of the self led Richard A. Shweder and Edmund J. Bourne to identify two distinct ways in which the person is conceived in different societies: the **egocentric** and the **sociocentric** views of self. In the egocentric view, each person is defined as a replica of all humanity, the locus of motivations and drives, capable of acting independently from others. This view is pervasive in the U.S., where the individual is viewed as the center of awareness, a distinct whole set against other wholes. Social relations are regarded as contracts between autonomous, free-acting beings. Individuals are free to negotiate their places in society, and the dominant idea is that everyone is responsible for what and who he or she is.

In contrast to the egocentric view of the person, the sociocentric view of the self depends on context. The self exists as an entity only within the concrete situation or role occupied by the person, in much the same way that Gitksans' names are linked to their position in society and not to some autonomous, separate self. From a sociocentric view, there is no intrinsic self that can possess enduring qualities such as generosity, integrity, or beauty. Such qualities apply only to concrete social situations. Instead of saying that a man is generous, a sociocentric perspective would say that he gives money to his friends.

individualistic a view of the self in which the individual is primarily responsible for his or her own actions

holistic a view of the self in which the individual cannot be conceived of as existing separately from society or apart from his or her status or role

egocentric a view of the self that defines each person as a replica of all humanity, the locus of motivations and drives, capable of acting independently from others

sociocentric a view of the self that is context dependent; there is no intrinsic self that can possess enduring qualities

"How to Succeed in Life"

As detailed in the recent book *Habits of the Heart*, the ideal American self pursues happiness and satisfies wants individually. The individual needs to demonstrate that she can stand on her own two feet and be self-supporting. This ideal of a self-reliant, independent self underlies the belief in success as the outcome of free and fair competition among individuals. Most successful Americans claim that they achieved success through their own hard work and seldom their families, their schooling, or their social position. They view their success primarily as the fruits of their own efforts. It is as if they believe that they have given birth to themselves.

Personhood in Japan and the U.S.

The anthropologist Christie Kiefer attributes a sociocentric view of the self to the Japanese. She explains that the Japanese are more apt to include within the boundaries of the self the social groups of which the person is a member. In contrast to children in the U.S., Japanese children are taught that interdependence between the person and the family or group is more important than independence.

The sociocentric Japanese also differ from the egocentric Americans in their approach to social interaction. Americans believe it is desirable to assert themselves; some even undergo assertiveness training. The Japanese believe that social interaction should be characterized by restraint or reserve. This attitude is best summed up in a Japanese proverb—The nail that sticks up shall be hammered down.

It should be noted that the Japanese do conceive of themselves as separate entities. They are as attached to their personal names as Americans are, if not more so.

Do I Say "Ohayo" or "Ohayo Gozaimasu?"

Robert Smith shows how the interdependent view of the self is expressed in Japanese language. In English, you would use the word "I" no matter who you were speaking to. The same goes for other pronouns like "you" or "they." In Japanese, the pronouns are much more complex. You would, for example, use a different word for "I" or "you" depending on your age, your gender, as well as the age and gender of the person you are speaking with.

The specific pronoun you use also depends on social status. Japanese speakers use different forms of address depending on their social position relative to the person to whom they are speaking. When conversing with someone in a superior social position, the speaker must linguistically acknowledge his or her inferiority.

© SANDRAMO/ISTOCKPHOTO.COM

identity toolbox
features of a person's identity (such as gender, age, or personal appearance) that he or she chooses to emphasize in constructing a social self

Moreover, the Japanese believe in self-development. But for the Japanese, the autonomy of the individual is not established by actively distinguishing themselves from others, as it is for Americans. Instead, it takes place away from society, where self-reflection and introspection are legitimate. It is through introspection that the Japanese are put in touch with their true nature.

In the remainder of this chapter, we will look at the self less from our own egocentric perspective and more from the sociocentric perspective, as something contingent and relative to the situation. Our focus will be on that part of the self that is defined by social relations and social processes and that is subject to change and redefinition.

QUESTION 6.2

How do societies distinguish individuals from one another?

Differences and similarities among persons are the materials from which we construct social landscapes that allow us to distinguish individuals from one another. From these similarities and differences, we construct our social identities. However, not all societies use the same similarities and differences to construct a social code, nor do they use these similarities and differences in the same way. Some characteristics of persons, or the **identity toolbox**, so to speak, are almost universally used to differentiate and group people. Family membership, gender, and age, for example, are used in every society as categories of a social code. Other characteristics, such as ethnic group membership, skin color, and wealth, figure prominently only in some societies.

Consider the variety of personal characteristics that students and teachers in a suburban New York high school use to construct a social landscape. They include performance in sports, participation in extracurricular activities, dress, scholastic achievement, will to achieve, disruptive behavior, willingness to cooperate with teachers, gender, ethnicity, wealth, health, age, grade, and so on.

Perhaps the most important set of characteristics used to define the self is related to kinship and family membership. In traditional societies, kinship is the central organizing principle—the main determinant of a person's social identity. Anthropologists working with traditional societies are often "adopted" by a family. This act, although also a signal of acceptance, serves the practical purpose of assigning an outsider a social

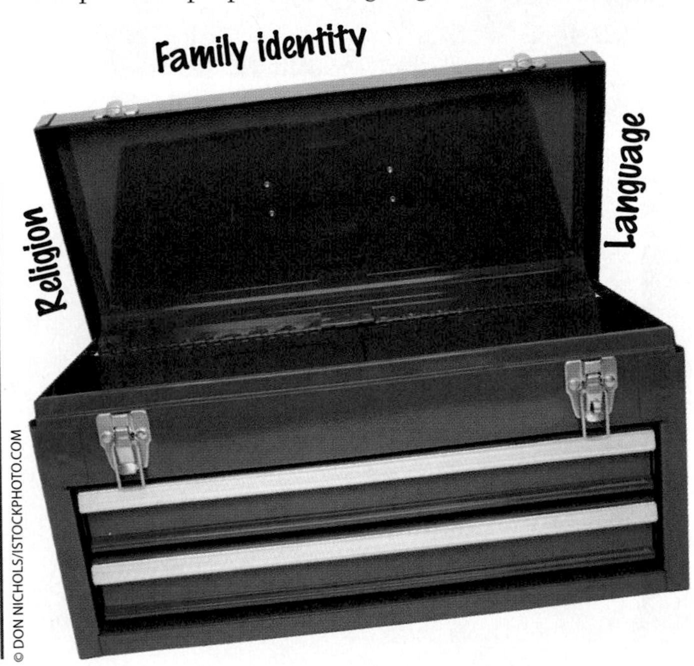

© DON NICHOLS/ISTOCKPHOTO.COM

People begin to learn from childhood the ways in which their self relates to others and their groups. That is, from the behavior of others toward them, they come to see themselves as distinct entities or as beings intimately linked to others. Schools in America are significant environments for learning about the self. Try to list the ways in which American school settings, and how children act in them, convey to children their degree of individuality and responsibility for their actions. Are there ways in which individualism is submerged? Might school settings differ in the extent to which the egocentric, as opposed to the sociocentric, self is developed?

identity through which others can approach him or her. To have no kinship label or designation in such societies is to have no meaningful place in the social landscape.

Language is another important identity marker that is often viewed as essential for the maintenance of a group identity. Even the way the same language is spoken is often important. Think of how Americans use dialect and accent to identify people as being New Englanders, southerners, or British. Language is often strongly tied to a national identity, and many countries have established institutions to oversee the "purity" of the national language. The Académie Française is charged with keeping the French language free of foreign borrowings, such as "le hot dog" or "le hamburger." In some countries, language causes conflict between groups. In Canada, for example, a large group of Quebec residents view French as essential to their group identity and seek independence from the English-speaking remainder of the country.

In other countries, religious affiliation is an important marker of group identity. In Northern Ireland, being Protestant or Catholic is possibly the most important defining feature of social identity. This is reflected in the joke about a man who is stopped on a Belfast street and asked his religion. "Jewish," he replies. "Yes," says the questioner, "but are you a Catholic Jew or a Protestant Jew?" Northern Ireland also illustrates the importance of having either a **positive identity** or a **negative identity**. Members of each group attempt to build a positive identity, to attribute to themselves characteristics they believe are desirable, and to construct a negative identity for others by attributing undesirable characteristics to them. In Northern Ireland, people often do this by comparing themselves with the other religious group. Catholics build a positive identity by emphasizing their Celtic heritage and their "decency," whereas Protestants emphasize their past military triumphs and their loyalty to Great Britain. Protestants believe themselves to be "neater" and "cleaner" than Catholics; Catholics think of themselves as the only true Irish.

Constructing Male and Female

Although some personal attributes are used to construct identities in almost all societies, they are not always used in the same way. Gender is a good example. Most Americans take gender for granted, assuming that it is biologically determined. But in fact, gender may be a cultural creation; that is, different standards apply to being male and being female.

Let's consider how gender is constructed in the U.S. Gender assignment begins at birth with the announcement that the baby is a girl or boy. Once the announcement of gender is made, the infant is given a gender-appropriate name, dressed in properly colored clothing, and spoken to in gender-appropriate language. Parents use more diminutives (cutie, honey) when speaking to girls than to boys; they use more inner-state words (happy, sad) with girls than with boys; and they use more direct prohibitives (no! no! no!) with boys than with girls.

Parents and other caregivers then teach male children that it is manly to be tough and endure pain. Male children are discouraged from expressing discomfort and encouraged when they can withstand it. They are also encouraged to be aggressive and competitive; they learn to compete in games and play with toys that require aggressive behavior. Female children, on the other hand, are comforted when they hurt themselves. They are taught to be caring and helpful; they are given toys such as dolls that encourage "feminine" behavior.

Societies differ not only in terms of gender

positive identity the attribution to people of personal characteristics believed to be desirable

negative identity the attribution of personal characteristics believed to be undesirable

roles, but in the number of gender categories. Many Native American societies traditionally recognized a third gender—called *berdache* among the Cheyenne and Lakota and *nadle* among the Navajo. The *berdache* or *nadle* is a biological male who does not fill a standard male role. Such individuals are not seen as men, nor are they defined as women. They occupy a third role, one that is culturally defined, accepted, and—in some cases—revered. Male children in the Navajo, Lakota, Cheyenne, and other groups could thus choose from two gender categories rather than learning that gender roles are defined by physiology. Among the Lakota, male children learned that if they desired, they could adopt the dress and work roles of women and have sex with men. The *berdache* or *nadle* did not play only women's roles, however; some were noted for their hunting skills and exploits in war. In American society, in contrast, persons who do not assume the gender roles associated with their anatomy are defined as deviant, abnormal, or nonconformist.

Anthropologist Harriet Whitehead suggests that Americans have difficulty recognizing a third gender in part because they make ethnocentric assumptions about what characteristics are most important in defining gender roles. Americans define gender largely by sexual preference—whether a person prefers to have sex with a male or a female. They pay less attention to preferences in dress, behavior, and occupation. Native North Americans traditionally placed a different emphasis on these characteristics. Groups that included the socially legitimate identity of *berdache* or *nadle* defined gender primarily by choice of occupation; the gender of a sexual partner was least important.

Language, Gender, and Race

As Penelope Eckert and Sally McConnell-Ginet point out in their book *Language and Gender*, people use language to present themselves as a certain kind of person. This not only includes a certain kind of attitude, but their conception of gender, as well.

Many children will unconsciously lower or raise the pitch of their voice to conform to gender expectations. A lisp is sometimes associated with femininity. Grammar can signal gender. Thus in French, there are male and female forms of nouns; in English, the third person singular *he* or *she* forces us to differentiate gender. In Japanese there are sentence-final particles that add to or soften the force of an utterance, with so-called women's language characterized as milder.

The contents of what is said can convey gender. Profanity is reserved largely for males and is prohibited to women and children. There are still laws in certain states that ban the use of "foul" language in the presence of women and children, and as late as 1999 a man was indicted and convicted in Michigan on such a charge.

Conversational styles may also convey gender. Linguist Robin Lakoff was one of the first to draw attention to the way that a woman's identity in society influences how she speaks. Women, says Lakoff, are constrained to minimize their expression of opinion with various linguistic devices such as tag questions (This election mess is terrible, *isn't it*?), rising intonations on declaratives (When will dinner be ready? *Six o'clock*?), the use of hedges (That's *kinda* sad, or It's *probably* dinnertime), boosters or amplifications (I'm *so* glad you're here), and indirection (e.g., saying "I've got a dentist's appointment then," thus conveying an inability or reluctance to meet at that time and asking the other person to propose another time).

The general thrust of Lakoff's argument has to do with the relative powerlessness of women, stemming from their relatively weak social position. Speaking "as a woman," Lakoff suggests, requires avoiding firm commitment or expressing strong opinions and, in general, being constrained to use a "powerless" language.

Some very simple linguistic devices can be used to change identity. Imagine, suggests Eckert and McConnell, an adolescent girl who begins to use profanity. She may be trying to demonstrate autonomy from her teachers or other adults or distinguish herself from her "preppy" peers. She may be trying to project the air of a grownup or of a rebellious, assertive, or angry person. The point is that she has drawn from her identity toolbox some linguistic symbols that serve to position her in a specific part of the social landscape. Through her language, she is active in projecting the way that she wants others to see her.

Can you imagine a football team named the New York Negroes? With cheerleaders dressed up in blackface, eating watermelon and fried chicken on the sidelines? With halftime ceremonies featuring cotton picking contests? The shock and outrage against this would be unimaginable. And yet, as Ward Churchill points out, the same kind of racist degradation is tolerated, and even celebrated, when it comes to Native Americans. The Cleveland Indians, Washington Redskins, and Chicago Blackhawks (just to name a few) feature mascots and logos that are an insulting parody of Native American groups and their rich cultural heritage. Over the years, there have been many attempts to have these names changed, but to no avail. Are concerns over these names just too much political correctness, or a realization of how language is used to belittle a minority group?

Language can also be used to construct the identity of others, groups from which people want to separate themselves. In a classic article, "Racism in the English Language," Robert B. Moore discusses how judgments about race are coded into the way we speak. References to the color black are scattered throughout the English language, generally with negative meanings: having a black outlook, to blackball or blacklist someone, or to be a black sheep. The word *tribal* is often applied to discussions of African politics but not European affairs. Rivalries between Hutu and Tutsi in Rwanda are referred to in the press as "tribal conflicts," but not the conflict between Basques and Spaniards.

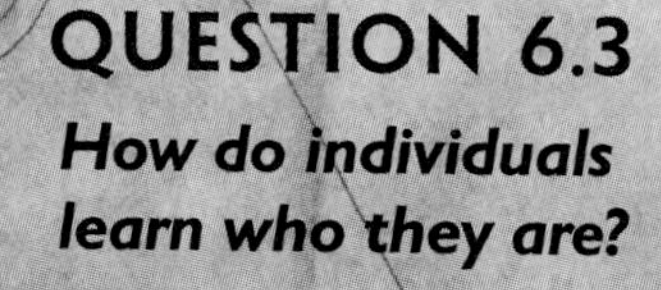

QUESTION 6.3
How do individuals learn who they are?

We are not born with an identity; it is something we learn. Moreover, identities are not static phenomena. In all societies, people are constantly changing their identities as they move through the life cycle. How are these changes announced?

In a classic work, Arnold van Gennep introduced the concept of **rites of passage**. These rituals mark a person's passage from one identity to another. Van Gennep identifies three phases of these rites: first, the ritual separates the person from an existing identity; next, the person enters a transition phase; finally, the changes are incorporated into a new identity. Different ceremonies emphasize different phases. The separation phase, for example, is a major part of funeral ceremonies designed to help the living let go of the deceased. Transition is a major part of ceremonies marking the passage of a person from childhood to adulthood. Incorporation is emphasized in marriage ceremonies that mark the transfer of a person from one social group to another.

Three phases of rites of passage:
1. separation
2. transition
3. incorporation

Anthropologists have shown how modern businesses use ritual to define a person's identity. At Mary Kay Cosmetics, sales personnel are given annual awards in a setting that has been compared to the Miss America pageant. Honorees, dressed in evening gowns, are seated on the stage of a large auditorium in front of a cheering audience. The ceremony celebrates the personal

rites of passage the term suggested by Arnold van Gennep for rituals that mark a person's passage from one identity or status to another

You must not budge; don't move a muscle or even blink. You can face only one direction until the operation is completed. The slightest movement on your part will mean you are a coward, incompetent, and unworthy to be a Maasai man.

saga of the founder Mary Kay, who was able to found her own company through personal determination and optimism. A bee-shaped pin with the legend "Everyone can find their wings and fly" symbolizes the ideology of the corporation.

The Transition to Adulthood

Most societies around the world have some sort of ceremony that marks a boy's transition to manhood. Many of these involve some test of courage. Anthropologist David Gilmore claims that one reason so many societies incorporate tests of masculinity and torturous initiation rituals for males is that the male identity is more problematic than the female identity. For every individual, there is in the beginning of life a subliminal identification with the mother, and men must make greater efforts to differentiate themselves from this connection. Consequently, societies incorporate rituals that symbolically separate the boy from his mother, while at the same time incorporating him into manhood.

The Maasai are a cattle-herding people of East Africa. For the Maasai, the road to being a man begins when the father looks for a sign that the boy is ready to assume the responsibilities of manhood. Tepilit Ole Saitoti tells in his autobiography how he begged his father to let him be initiated. One day Tepilit confronted a huge lioness that threatened the family's cattle and killed it. Shortly after, his father gathered the family and said, "We are going to initiate Tepilit into manhood. He has proven before all of us that he can now save children and cattle."

The central feature of the Maasai initiation is circumcision, a painful procedure that can last up to four minutes and is performed with no anesthetic. The boy, standing before male relatives and prospective in-laws, must remain absolutely still and silent. Tepilit Ole Saitoti describes how, shortly before his circumcision, he was told, "You must not budge; don't move a muscle or even blink. You can face only one direction until the operation is completed. The slightest movement on your part will mean you are a coward, incompetent, and unworthy to be a Maasai man."

Peggy Reeves Sanday, in her study of college fraternity gang rape, provides a vivid portrait of how male identity is defined and reinforced in American society. Gang rape, or "pulling train," as it is called in fraternities, begins with the coercion of a vulnerable young woman who is seeking acceptance. When she is too weak or intoxicated to protest, a "train" of men have sex with her. Gang rape is not limited to college campuses; it is also associated with sports teams, street gangs, and other groups of men for whom the act often serves, according to Sanday, as a male bonding ritual.

As Sanday and her associates interviewed fraternity members, women who were associated with them, and victims of rape, they sought to explain what it was about male identity that encourages these actions. Three things seemed to stand out in her account. First, there is a heavy emphasis in fraternities on male bonding and male-bonding behavior, to the extent that a college man's self-esteem and social identity are dependent on gaining entry to a fraternity and being accepted by the brothers. Fraternities confer status; on most college campuses they are recognized as places "where the action is." They also provide reassurance, security, and ready-made identities. Membership in a fraternity transforms outsiders into insiders.

Second, sex constitutes a major status and identity marker. Masculinity is defined and demonstrated by sexual conquest. In the fraternity in which the gang rape occurred, a major activity was persuading a woman to have sex. Men who had more success gained status, while those who often failed were in danger of being labeled "nerds" or, worse, "fags." Sex in this case is a public thing. Men in the fraternities that Sanday interviewed bragged publicly about their sexual conquests and arranged for brothers to witness them. Some fraternities posted weekly newsletters listing brothers' sexual conquests.

A third element in the identity of fraternity men concerns their attitudes toward women. Many of the fraternity members implied that women were sex objects to be abused or debased. A woman's identity among fraternity men was determined largely by her sexual interactions with them. Women who are sexually unresponsive are "frigid," women who allow advances only up to a point are "cockteasers," and women who have sex with many men are "sluts" or "cunts." Such labels indicate that the role of girlfriend is virtually the only role with no negative connotations that a woman can play. In one fraternity, brothers marked women who attended their parties with "power dots," black, red, yellow, white, or blue stickers they attached to a girl's clothing at parties to indicate how easy the girl was to pick up.

For fraternity men, the debasement of women is interwoven with the themes of male bonding and sexual conquest. Part of the reason men bond in college, says Sanday, is to achieve domination and power they think is owed to males. One fraternity man explained how verbally harassing a girl increases male bonding. "I mean, people come back the day after a party and say, 'You should have seen me abuse this girl.' They're real proud of it in front of everyone."

In her book on gang rape, Sanday also discusses the role of pornography in the definition of male and female identities in America. She suggests that pornography depicts women as subservient to men, reinforces sexist attitudes and encourages behavior toward women characteristic of men in fraternities. Do you agree or disagree, and why?

Sanday uses the term **phallocentrism**, "the deployment of the penis as a concrete symbol of masculine social power and dominance," to describe the use of sex and the debasement of women to demonstrate masculinity. Phallocentrism as well as the themes of male bonding, sexual prowess, and the debasement of women are all manifested in the act of pulling train. It is a form of bonding, it publicly legitimizes a male's heterosexuality, and it makes women an object of scorn and abuse.

Sanday is quick to emphasize that not all college men subscribe to the ideology of phallocentrism, and not all fraternity men measure their masculinity by sexual conquest. In the case that initiated her study, all the women who knew them described the six men charged with gang rape as "among the nicest guys in the fraternity." Individually, probably none of them would have committed the act they were charged with. In the context of the fraternity, however, gang rape is the credible outcome of a process of identity formation that is manifested in fraternity life in general and in the fraternity initiation ritual in particular.

The fraternity initiation ritual on most college campuses is the culmination of a period of pledging in which initiates are required to perform various demeaning acts. In general the ritual stigmatizes the initiates as infants, children, or girls and then proceeds to cleanse them of this negative identity before incorporating them into the fraternity as full-fledged brothers.

In one fraternity initiation described to Sanday, the initiates were blindfolded and stripped down to their jockstraps. Then they were told to drop their jockstraps and were ridiculed: "Look at the pin-dicks, pussies, fags. They're all a bunch of girls, it's amazing they don't have tits." As the brothers screamed at them, their testicles were rubbed with Ben-Gay. After about ten minutes a brother spoke, saying "Sorry we had to do that, but we had to cleanse you of your nerd sin." Then the pledges were put to tests of trust. In one case, a pledge was thrown to the ground; one brother placed a sword at his crotch and another brother placed a sword at his chest. The pledge was then asked if he trusted the brothers not to kill him. As the pledge nodded yes, the brother brought the sword down on his chest; since it was made of wood, it shattered. In another fraternity, initiates were taken blindfolded to a bathroom and told to eat some feces out of a toilet bowl and trust they would not become

phallocentrism a term coined by Peggy Sanday that refers to the deployment of the penis as a symbol of masculine social power and dominance

sick. As they picked it out and ate it, they realized they were eating bananas.

The final stage of most fraternity initiations generally includes a secret ritual in which the pledges come before the brothers, who are dressed in robes and hoods or other ritual paraphernalia. In one ritual reported to Sanday, a brother addressed the initiates with the following words:

> You have shown trust in the fraternity and trust in the brothers. We know we can trust you now. A bond has been formed between us. No one has experienced the hell you have except us and the brothers before us. Bonded by strength, loyalty, and trust we are one. Cleansed of weakness and filth, we are men. As men we stand tall. As men we stand for the fraternity, and [name of fraternity] stands for us. (Sanday 1990, 163)

In these ceremonies, the abusers of the initiates then gain credence by accepting those they have just heaped with abuse. One initiate described to Sanday how he felt at this point:

> I felt exhilarated. I kept saying, "Oh wow!" and hugging my big brother and shaking hands with everybody. I was incredibly happy. I was made to feel worthless by the fraternity as an individual, and now that it was all over, I was made to feel wonderful by the fraternity as a brother. My worth was celebrated by the same process that had previously denied it, because of the change that it had effected within me. I now saw myself as a brother, and what may feel terrible to an individual confronted by brothers feels tremendous to an individual who is a brother. (Sanday 1990, 149)

Sanday concludes that fraternity initiation rituals serve to solidify a fraternity man's identity by separating him from his previous identity as a member of a family and perhaps separating him from his mother. The ritual incorporates the man into a group whose activities reinforce a male identity, which is defined largely by the degradation of female identity through sexual conquest and physical abuse of women. Pulling train is both an expression of male sexuality and a display of the power of the brotherhood to control and dominate women. In other words, gang rape is but one instance of the abuse and domination that begin in the initiation and are continued later in relations with women and new pledges. Sanday says that once initiates have suffered abuse as a means of establishing their bond to the fraternity, they are obliged to abuse new generations of pledges and party women as a way to honor the original contract and renew the power of the brotherhood.

QUESTION 6.4

How do individuals communicate their identities to one another?

There is an episode in Jonathan Swift's 18th century classic *Gulliver's Travels* in which Gulliver learns of an experiment conducted by professors at the Academy of Lagado. They believe that because words are only names for things, they can abolish words by having people carry with them everything they need to engage in conversation with others. Gulliver describes such a "conversation": Two people meet, open their packs of things,

© MARIA TOUTOUDAKI/ISTOCKPHOTO.COM / © TYLER STALMAN/ISTOCKPHOTO.COM / © BRIAN DOTY/ISTOCKPHOTO.COM / © BRIAN FINKE/STONE+/GETTY IMAGES

"talk" by using them for an hour, pack up their things, and go off.

In many ways our interactions with others are similar. We communicate with things by using them to make statements about who we think we are or who we want to be. The clothes we wear, the cars we drive, and the people we associate with are all used to display an identity that we think we have or that we desire. For example, if gender is used as a criterion to distinguish individuals, there must be ways of displaying sexual differences so others can read them. In seventeenth-century Europe, men wore codpieces to emphasize their male anatomy. In areas of Africa, people from different villages have different hairstyles.

A Trobriand Islander shows the various gifts he received, and which he will give, through the *kula* ring.

One of the most influential works in the history of anthropology is a book written by Marcel Mauss, modestly entitled *The Gift*. Mauss identifies what he calls the **principle of reciprocity**: the giving and receiving of gifts. His major point is that gifts, which in theory are voluntary, disinterested, and spontaneous, are in fact obligatory. The giving of the gift creates a tie with the person who receives it and who, on some future occasion, is obliged to reciprocate. To Mauss, the types of things given and received signal the identities of the participants in the exchange and the kind of relationship that exists between them. If the gifts are roughly of equal value, the relationship is one of equality. If the gifts are unequal in value, the person who gives the more valuable gift is generally of higher status than the receiver.

Mauss' principles are illustrated in the *kula* ring of the Trobriand Islanders, the circulation of gifts among trading partners. The seagoing Trobrianders leave their homes on islands off the eastern coast of New Guinea and travel to other islands. Each man has trading partners on the islands he visits, and these partnerships are signaled with gifts of red-shell necklaces or white-shell armbands. As a man travels and trades, he also gives and receives necklaces and receives armbands. A man who receives either an armband or a necklace does not keep it but passes it along to another trading partner. There is a set pattern to the exchange: necklaces travel from island to island in a clockwise direction, whereas armbands move counterclockwise.

The *kula* ring serves as a concrete representation of the ties between individuals. Any change in the pattern of gift giving reflects a change in the nature of the social ties. In addition, special gifts that are individually owned are also circulated, and the owner's status and renown grow as the goods he owns circulate along predetermined paths. A successful *kula* operator participates in many such exchanges and can profit from them by keeping items for as long as he can before passing them along. Of course, if he keeps them too long, others will be reluctant to exchange, so a good deal of social skill is required to *kula* successfully.

Exchanges that convey recognition of identities needn't be limited to material goods; they may also consist of emotion and sentiment. The emotional qualities of a person's relationships are one criterion by which others judge, interact with, and respond to that person. For example, if you accept an offer of hospitality in Hawaii, it is a signal that you recognize the generous nature of the offer and you wish to maintain the social link. If you reject the offer of hospitality, it is seen as a hurtful sign that you do not recognize the generosity of the person and do not wish to maintain the relationship. Hawaiians attempt to keep social pathways open with altruistic exchanges of love, sincerity, feeling, and warmth.

Gifts and Commodities

An important characteristic of traditional *kula* goods is that they have a history. A Trobriander who received a necklace or armband could likely recite the history of the object, sometimes from its creation through all

principle of reciprocity the social principle that giving a gift creates social ties with the person receiving it, who eventually is obliged to reciprocate

the persons who had, at one time or another, possessed it. These goods are similar to heirlooms in our society: the family wedding ring that has been worn by brides for three generations; the watch that was owned by a great-grandfather; the quilt that was made by a great-aunt. The history of these kinds of objects, especially when they are given as gifts, forms a vital part of their identity and, consequently, of the identity of the person who gives them. They say something special about the relationship between the giver and the receiver of the gift.

The same is true to a lesser extent of gifts that are produced by the giver; they carry a special meaning apart from the object itself. However, in modern society, most of our gifts are mass-produced, largely impersonal goods available in department and chain stores. Herein lies a dilemma.

James Carrier, in his book *Gifts and Commodities: Exchange and Western Capitalism Since 1700*, argues that since the sixteenth and seventeenth centuries, the production and distribution of goods have become impersonal and that the spread of industrial and commercial capitalism has alienated objects and relations. In previous times, commodities were personalized in various ways. The relationship between the producer and/or the seller of goods was a personal one between relatives or friends. The buyer knew who made and sold the object purchased. Even when stores replaced home trade and markets, the buyer knew the storeowner, who personalized the goods by buying them in bulk and individually packaging and displaying them. The buyer–seller relationship was further personalized by the extension of credit from seller to buyer and by the customer loyalty expressed by the buyer to the seller. Today the buyer knows neither the producer nor the seller; if the item is bought on credit, it is through a credit card issued by some distant bank. There are no personal connections in the transaction.

Carrier labels goods that carry no special meaning **commodities**, distinguishing them from what he calls **possessions**. Gifts, says Carrier, must be possessions before they carry meaning in an exchange. Commodities involve a transfer of value and a countertransfer: A sells something to B, and the transaction is finished. But in a gift exchange, a more or less permanent link is established between giver and receiver. Gifts are inalienable—they are bound to people after the presentation. Commodities, on the other hand, are independent of their sellers (or producers). It is easy to return, destroy, or give away a commodity; it is a dilemma to do any of those with a gift.

commodities goods that carry little personal meaning (compare to *possessions*)

possessions goods that are associated in some personal way with their producer and/or distributor (compare to *commodities*)

The only gift is a portion of thyself. Thou must bleed for me. Therefore the poet brings his poem; the shepherd, his lamb; the farmer, corn; the miner, a gem; the sailor, coral and shells; the painter, his picture; the girl, a handkerchief or her own sewing. This is right and pleasing. . . when a man's biography is conveyed in a gift.

—Ralph Waldo Emerson

As mentioned previously, for Americans the contrast between commodities and gifts poses a special problem. Most of the items that we give as gifts are store-bought, mass-produced commodities. Their history is brief and undistinguished. Their meaning is contained in their worth or utility, in their materiality. The meaning of a gift is different; the perfect gift is priceless, its materiality is immaterial.

For Carrier the problem is how, in a world filled with impersonal, alienated commodities—goods without history—can we turn these things into personal items with meaning and history, into possessions that carry something of the buyer's identity? In gift giving, how do we turn commodities into items that say something about the relationship between the giver and the receiver?

According to Carrier, we convert commodities into possessions and gifts by a process of appropriation. When a person takes an impersonal space, a dorm room or a rented apartment, and decorates and modifies the space, he or she has appropriated it and given it meaning. Shopping itself, says Carrier, is a way of appropriating commodities; the "wise shopper" chooses what is "right" for him or her or what is "right" for the recipient of a gift.

Manufacturers and sellers try to aid the process of appropriation by stamping their products with a distinct identity. A good example is Harris tweed, which most buyers associate with some Harris Islander weaving on a loom in his shed, creating the item as his ancestors have done for centuries, and even giving each item its own serial number.

© LISA THORNBERG/ISTOCKPHOTO.COM

Displaying goods in catalogs in a way that helps the buyer appropriate commodities has become a fine art. For example, Carrier notes how the Smith & Hawken catalog for gardeners forges a personal link between object and producer by detailing the historical origins of the tools and linking them to historical figures, almost always English, and most from the eighteenth or nineteenth century. The text communicates this message by using words such as "origins," "can be traced back to," "was invented by," and so on. Lands' End catalogs display pictures of employees, thereby linking commodities to the people who work at Lands' End, even though these employees may not be the actual producers of the goods.

Gift Giving and Christmas in America

The dilemma of converting commodities into gifts is particularly acute during the Christmas season, when most gift giving takes place in America. Most social scientists who have written about Christmas agree that it is largely a celebration of the family, serving especially to distinguish the world of the family from the world of work. Christmas serves to affirm a person's membership in a specific family group, as the circle of kin with whom gifts are exchanged defines the boundaries of the family. Christmas heightens a person's sense of family identity, expressing how warm the family is and how cold the world outside may be.

Thus, it is within the family that the Christmas gift is most important and where the gift must contain something of the biography of the giver and the history of the relationship. It is in the family where the gift must be a possession rather than a commodity. The question is how do we resolve the problem of using commodities as family gifts? How do we transform commodities into statements about the special role that family and family relations play in defining our identity?

The appropriation of commodities takes place in a number of ways. First, we may simply say that the nature of the gift itself is immaterial, that "it's the thought that counts." Second, we purchase things that aren't very useful, giving frivolous or luxurious gifts, or items that are Christmas-specific, such as tree decorations. Third, and very important, there is the wrapping; the wrapping converts the commodity into a gift. Finally, says Carrier, there is the shopping itself—the time and worry we spend to get the "right" gift for the "right" person. Why, he asks, do we go through all this? It is onerous, it is stressful, and it is expensive.

In the face of this bother and complaint, why do Americans, even devout Christians, spend so much effort on Christmas shopping? Why not give homemade gifts? Indeed, why give presents at all? It is true that the giving of purchased gifts reflects a number of motives, ranging from displays of affluence to a desire to shower a loved one with lovely things. However, these more commonly recognized motives do "not explain the intensity of Christmas shopping and people's ambivalence towards it" (Carrier 1993, 62).

© ROMAN MILERT/ISTOCKPHOTO.COM / © COMSTOCK IMAGES/JUPITERIMAGES

identity struggles a term coined by Anthony F. C. Wallace and Raymond Fogelson to characterize interaction in which there is a discrepancy between the identity a person claims to possess and the identity attributed to that person by others

Carrier suggests that the answer to this riddle lies in the fact that shopping itself is a method of appropriation, of converting a commodity into a gift, as we exercise choice from among the mass of commodities presented to us. As Carrier puts it,

> Christmas shopping is an annual ritual through which we convert commodities into gifts. Performing this ritual indicates that we can celebrate and recreate personal relations with the anonymous objects available to us, just as it strengthens and reassures us as we undertake the more mundane appropriations of everyday life during the rest of the year. (1993, 63)

It also demonstrates to people, says Carrier, that they can create a world of family, a world of love, out of the impersonal commodities that flood the world "out there." Christmas is a time when Americans make a world of money into a world of family—a time of contrast between the impersonal world of commodities and the personal world of possessions and gifts.

QUESTION 6.5

How do individuals defend their identities when they are threatened?

In defining themselves and others, people sometimes disagree on their relative positions on the social map; they disagree on their respective identities. Anthony F. C. Wallace and Raymond Fogelson refer to these situations as **identity struggles**—interactions in which there is a discrepancy between the identity a person claims to possess and the identity attributed to her by others. Consider the medicine fight among the Beaver Indians of British Columbia. The Beaver believe that a man's identity relative to others is determined by the amount of supernatural power or "medicine" he possesses. This power determines a man's success in hunting and protects him and his family from illness and misfortune. Any personal misfortune a man experiences, such as illness or failure to kill game, is interpreted by others as a loss of supernatural power and, hence, a loss of prestige. However, the man experiencing the misfortune does not interpret it in the same way; for him, the misfortune is caused by someone using supernatural power against him. In other words, his view of his identity is different from what he believes is attributed to him by others. The person experiencing the misfortune will then dream the identity of the attacker and publicly accuse him. The accused may deny the charge, responding that his accuser is experiencing misfortune because he has committed some wrongful act. Thus begins the medicine fight, a series of accusations and counteraccusations that sometimes leads to violence.

Making *Moka* in Papua New Guinea

The Beaver claim or defend their social identities through spiritual means. More common is the manipulation of material goods. The Melpa, who live around the area of Mt. Hagen in the Central Highlands of Papua New Guinea, provide an example. The people of Mt. Hagen live by growing crops such as sweet potatoes and raising pigs. Pigs serve not only as a source of protein but also as signs of wealth that are required for gift exchange.

The most important identity on the Highlands social landscape is that of Big Man. Because they are leaders and among the wealthiest in terms of pig ownership, Big Men are the most independent from others. A man who is poor and dependent on others for food and sustenance is called by a term that translates into English as "rubbish man."

Becoming a Big Man requires courage in warfare as well as making peace. The greatest skill required of a Big Man, however, is making *moka*. As described by anthropologist Andrew Strathern, *moka* is a form of ceremonial gift exchange in which a man makes an initial gift to a trading partner and then receives in return more than he gave. These exchanges serve two purposes—they establish and maintain links between individuals and groups, and they establish a rank system that enables men to earn status and prestige and

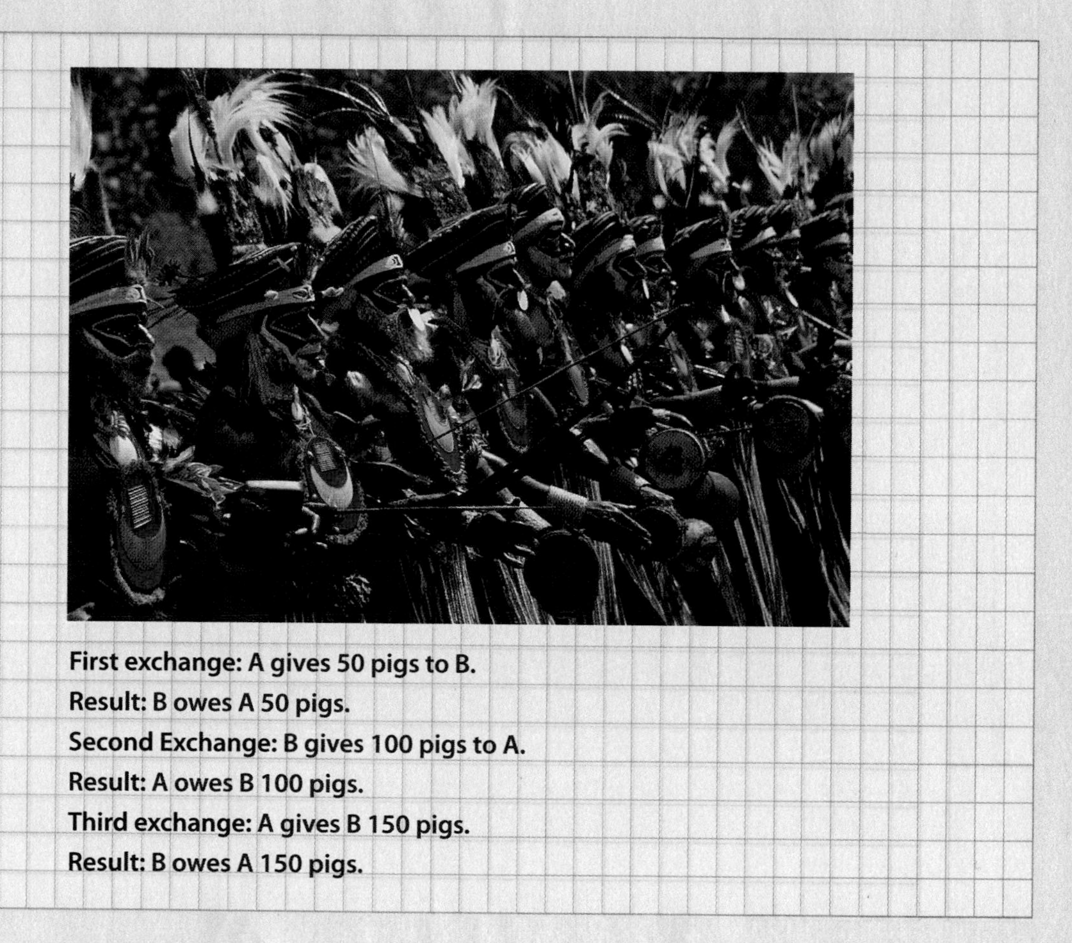

© KEREN SU/CHINA SPAN/ALAMY

become Big Men. Big Men from the same clan can make *moka* with each other, but it is most common for a man to have partners outside his clan and among ex-enemies or groups related by marriage. Items that are given in exchanges traditionally included pigs, shells, bird plumage, salt, decorating oil, and stone axe blades, but now also include Australian money, bicycles, cattle, and even trucks.

The major idea in making *moka*, and consequently establishing the status of Big Man, is for a man to give his trading partner more than he received at the last exchange. If A gives 100 pigs to B and B returns a countergift of 150 pigs that A cannot counter, then B is the Big Man because he gave the last gift.

In *moka*, the basic rule is to give more than you receive, the result being that one person always owes the other. The two participants never reach the point where things are even. It is this incremental change in the debt that allows a man to say he made *moka*.

The negotiation of identity between *moka* partners is never an isolated affair because a man rarely is able to make *moka* solely on the basis of what he possesses at a given time. If a man wants or is being pressured to make *moka* with a rival to whom he must give six pigs and he doesn't have that many, he must either get pigs from family and friends or call in outstanding *moka* obligations. Thus, any given exchange may involve a host of people and groups. A map of the circulation of *moka* goods around Melpa society would provide a pretty good idea of how different people and groups are related to others and would indicate the social identity of each person in the exchange network. These exchanges serve for the Melpa as public statements of social identities—the relations between people and groups—at any given time.

At a fairly typical *moka* exchange, many Big Men from different groups may make *moka* at once. The ceremony takes place at a ceremonial ground associated with a particular clan or lineage, usually built by the Big Man of that group. Preparations for the *moka* exchange begin months before the actual presentation, and Big Men of donor groups negotiate the timing of the exchange. Those who are ready can push the *moka* through, but those who are not ready and who do not have enough to give to their trading rivals in the other group risk defaulting to their partners. Those who do not possess enough wealth to give may try to delay the timing of a *moka* ceremony but may in turn be taunted as procrastinators or as "rubbish men."

Before making *moka*, each man reviews his partnerships and ties to others, perhaps dropping some and adding others. Men scheduled to receive gifts at the *moka* exchange make initiatory gifts to their *moka* partners. The men scheduled to give gifts set up stakes to indicate how many pigs they will give away to their partners. They also clear the ceremonial ground, make speeches, and review the history of the relations between the two groups. At each meeting the Big Men try to contract for more gifts, egging on their clanmates to give more pigs

One of our most important identity features is our body shape.

In most modern societies, a thin person is judged to be superior to a heavier person. When researchers asked children ages 6 to 9 to examine three body silhouettes and describe the kind of person represented by each body type, the children described the thinner figure as friendly, kind, happy, and polite, whereas they described the heavier figure as lazy, lying, and cheating. Later in life, people who are overweight face hostile work environments and job discrimination because workers judged unattractive by their peers, particularly women, are consistently described in more negative terms.

The relationship between self-image and body shape is particularly relevant for female adolescents, as anthropologist Mimi Nichter discovered in a three-year study among high school girls in Arizona. Adolescent girls are particularly vulnerable to body image issues because during adolescence, girls gain up to 25 pounds of body fat and hence are likely to be more critical of their own bodies. Young girls, says Nichter, are imbedded in a morality play in which thinness is good, fatness is bad, and dieting is the way to get in shape.

The concern about body image seems so great that even girls whose weight is normal or below normal seem to fear being fat. Nichter asked a thin girl if she ever felt fat. The girl responded by relating a dream in which she was looking in a mirror and appeared really fat, but when she looked down at herself, she looked skinny. It was as if, suggests Nichter, inside her was lurking a fat girl waiting to be seen and leaving her with feelings of shame.

As an anthropologist, Nichter could take a critical look at the cultural obsession with body image and examine the negative effects it had on adolescent girls. She concluded that schools and families were not providing girls with effective instructions on the developmental process, on eating well and exercising, and on critical thinking regarding media images. The few nutrition classes that were offered were ineffective because they did not connect "health work" with "beauty work." What is worse, schools provided easy access to fatty food and sodas.

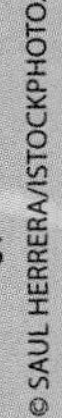

Having identified the needs, Nichter and her associates developed a program that would help adolescent girls address the anxiety over their appearance and, at the same time, promote a healthy lifestyle. There were two goals: (1) to expand the girls' notions of beauty beyond "Barbie beauty" and to help them develop the skills to work on themselves more holistically; (2) to help girls address their consumption habits and harmful dieting practices.

The first step would be to raise awareness of the unrealistic body images being promoted in the media. The girls needed to understand and appreciate the diversity of healthy body shapes in the real world. Consequently, on the first day of the program Nichter presented a slide show of images from magazine advertisements of white, Latino, and African American girls. The group discussed how the media attempted to limit the differences among the models and attempted to make them conform to some ideal body type and appearance. The discussion made it obvious to all participants that media images were marketing discontent, and even girls who were white, blond, and thin were driven to be dissatisfied with their appearance.

The program also helped girls of different backgrounds talk together about body image in the collective sense. The girls learned that what was desirable in white culture was not necessarily what was valued among African Americans. Consequently, they were able to expand on what it meant to be stylish.

Some classes were devoted to nutrition, with dietary assessment and cooking demonstrations. Students analyzed the foods they had eaten and discussed how and why they made the food choices they did. They also had sessions on the necessity of physical exercise. They discovered that some girls were reluctant to participate in physical activities because they were afraid that if they breathed hard or sweated, it would reveal that they were out of shape.

The program also helped define parental involvement. Very few parents had told the girls that weight gain was a normal part of puberty. Parents also tended to avoid talking about the topic because they were reluctant to discuss sensitive topics that might lead to arguments. Parents were made aware that excessive talk about dieting normalized girls' dissatisfaction with their bodies. Parents were also encouraged to provide more direction on diet. Family meals, the researchers discovered, were the exception rather than the rule. Most girls reported that their parents were just too tired after working all day to prepare family meals, leaving the girls to prepare their own meals. As a consequence, parents were less able to monitor their children's diets.

It is probably too early to know how effective Nichter's program was in helping the girls alleviate anxiety over their body shapes or in helping them develop healthier diets and exercise regimes. But clearly an anthropological perspective can illuminate issues that are not addressed in most health education classes and can identify issues that families need to address as part of their children's normal maturation process.

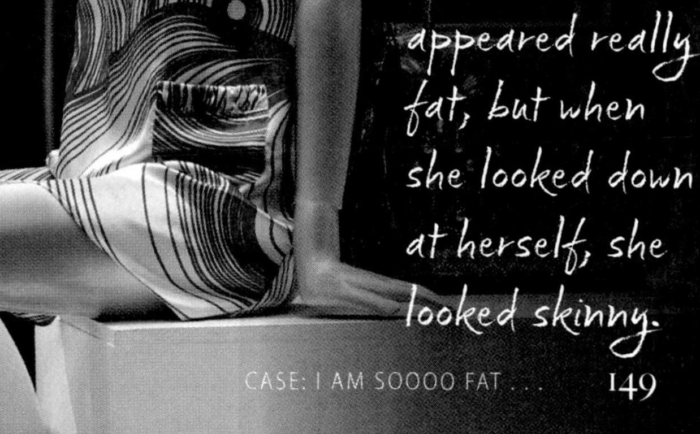

The girl responded by relating a dream in which she was looking in a mirror and appeared really fat, but when she looked down at herself, she looked skinny.

to their trading partners and increasing the competitive spirit. They insist that they must surpass the gifts they received from their partners the last time they received *moka*. The climax of these discussions is the showing of the gifts. Once this is done, the final transfer takes place with dancing and oratory.

When the presentation is made, the Big Men among the donors step forward and make speeches. On the final day, men and women of the recipient group converge on the ceremonial grounds while the donors decorate themselves with pearl shell pendants, fine bark aprons and belts, pig grease or tree oil, and charcoal and red ochre. At the ceremony, the donors run up and down the row crying "hoo-aah, hoo-aah" and performing a war dance. Their speeches are boasts, claiming that by the amount they have given, they have "won." Here is an excerpt of such a speech:

> My sister's sons, my cross-cousins. I am your true cross-cousin, living close to you. My sisters' sons, my cross-cousins, you say you see big pigs, big shells, well, now I have given you large pigs on the two *olka* stakes, given you a bicycle too, given you all the food you like to eat. Further, I have given you two steers, and so I win. I have given you all the things which are your food; I give you two steers also and so I win. (Strathern 1971, 241)

And the winner is....

Recipients who do not receive what they expect at the ceremony (and they never know exactly what they will get until the ceremony takes place) complain loudly and bitterly. Thus, the ceremony is an anxious occasion in which the honor and, consequently, the social identities of both donor and recipient are on the line. Sometimes actual fighting breaks out. If a man does not meet his commitments to his partner and does not give gifts commensurate with what he received at the last ceremony, his partner can do little but shout insults or physically attack him.

At the end of the ceremony, an orator counts the gifts while the recipient offers stylized thanks. The recipients of *moka* then gather their shells and pigs and knock over the pig stakes, except for one that is left standing as proof that the donors have made *moka* at their ceremonial ground.

PROBLEM 7

WHY ARE MODERN SOCIETIES CHARACTERIZED BY SOCIAL, POLITICAL, AND ECONOMIC INEQUALITIES?

Chapter 7 The Cultural Construction of Social Hierarchy

Every social hierarchy claims to be founded on the nature of things. It thus accords itself eternity; it escapes change and the attacks of innovators. Aristotle justified slavery by the ethnic superiority of the Greeks over the barbarians; and today the man who is annoyed by feminist claims alleges that woman is naturally inferior.

Robert Hertz, 1909

* * *

QUESTIONS

In examining this problem, we will consider the following questions:

7.1 How do societies rank people in social hierarchies?

7.2 Why do societies construct social hierarchies?

7.3 How do people come to accept social hierarchies as natural?

7.4 How do people living in poverty adapt to their condition?

7.5 Can a nonstratified community exist within a larger hierarchical society?

INTRODUCTION

The Rationale for Social Inequality

There are few, if any, modern nations in which one portion of the population does not in some way enjoy privileges that other portions do not share.

Unequal distribution of wealth, status, and privilege is a significant problem throughout the modern world. To Americans it is visible in the starving faces that stare out from our television screens on the evening news, interspersed with advertisements for luxury automobiles. Some people can purchase the finest amenities, whereas others lack the basic necessities of life, such as food, shelter, and health care. There are few, if any, modern nations in which one portion of the population does not in some way enjoy privileges that other portions do not share.

The most common figure used to measure inequality is income distribution. In the U.S., in 2006, the poorest 20% of the population earned 3.4% of the total income, whereas the richest 5% earned 22.3%. Examining income distribution historically (see Table 7.1), we find that in the United States income inequality grew from 1967 to 2002, with the lowest fifth of the population having a smaller share of the national income (decreasing from 4.0 percent to 3.4 percent) and the highest fifth having a greater share (increasing from 43.8 percent to 50.5 percent).

TABLE 7.1 HOUSEHOLD SHARES OF AGGREGATE INCOME
by Fifths on the Income Distribution: Selected Years, 1967–2006

Year	Lowest Fifth	Second Fifth	Third Fifth	Fourth Fifth	Highest Fifth	Top 5 Percent
2006	3.4	8.6	14.5	22.9	50.5	22.3
2001	3.5	8.7	14.6	23.0	50.1	22.4
1999	3.6	8.9	14.9	23.2	49.4	21.5
1995	3.7	9.1	15.2	23.3	48.7	21.0
1990	3.9	9.6	15.9	24.0	46.6	18.6
1985	4.0	9.7	16.3	24.6	45.3	17.0
1980	4.3	10.3	16.9	24.9	43.7	15.8
1975	4.4	10.5	17.1	24.8	42.2	15.9
1970	4.1	10.8	17.4	24.5	43.3	16.6
1967	4.0	10.8	17.3	24.2	43.8	17.5

Source: United States Census Bureau, Historical Income Tables—Income Equality, http://www.census.gov/hhes/www/income/histinc/h02ar.html

Gini coefficient a measure of variability, developed by Italian statistician and demographer Corrado Gini, used to measure income distribution

The **Gini coefficient** is another way to measure income distribution. The coefficient provides a way of measuring distribution. It produces a number between 0 and 1, where 0 corresponds to perfect equality and 1 corresponds to perfect inequality. In terms of income distribution, 0 would mean that everyone has the same amount of income, while 1 would mean that only one person has all the income.

The Gini coefficient is calculated using a Lorenz curve. Imagine a graph in which the vertical axis represents the number of households in a country and the horizontal axis represents the total income they receive. In this graph, a Lorenz curve will show what percentage of households has a given percentage of income. If every household had the same income, that is 20 percent of households had 20 percent of the income, 40 percent of households had 40 percent of the income and so on, the plotted line would rise evenly (see Figure 7.1a). This is the line of perfect equality. If, on the other hand, one person had 100 percent of the income, the graph would look like Figure 7.1b; this is the line of perfect inequality. In most cases, the Lorenz curve will look something like Figure 7.1c, since there is no perfect distribution of income. The Gini coefficient, then, is the area between the Lorenz curve and the line of perfect equality, and reflects the actual distribution of income.

Table 7.2 shows the Gini coefficient for selected countries as of 2008 (multiplied by 100). Various factors influence the Gini coefficient, such as the level of industrialization of different countries, the nature of their economic systems, and the extent to which tax systems seek to redistribute income.

TABLE 7.2

GINI COEFFICIENT OF SELECTED COUNTRIES

Country	Gini coefficient
Sweden	23
Denmark	24
Albania	26.7
Ethiopia	30
Pakistan	30.6
Canada	32.1
Morocco	40
United States	45
Costa Rica	49.8
Papua New Guinea	50.9
Central African Republic	61.3
Namibia	70.7

Source: https://www.cia.gov/library/publications/the-world-factbook/fields/2172.html

Some people believe that the hierarchical ordering of people and groups is unavoidable. In their view, scarce resources, occupational specialization, and the power of elite groups necessarily result in some form of social stratification. Others maintain that stratification is not only avoidable, but is counter to human nature. According to anthropologist Thomas Belmonte:

> Since the emergence of stratification, man's history (his changing ways of relating to nature and other men) has stood opposed to his humanity. The emergence of power-wielding elites laid the basis for a new kind of anti-collective society whose vastly accelerated growth was founded, not on the reconciliation of antagonisms between men, but

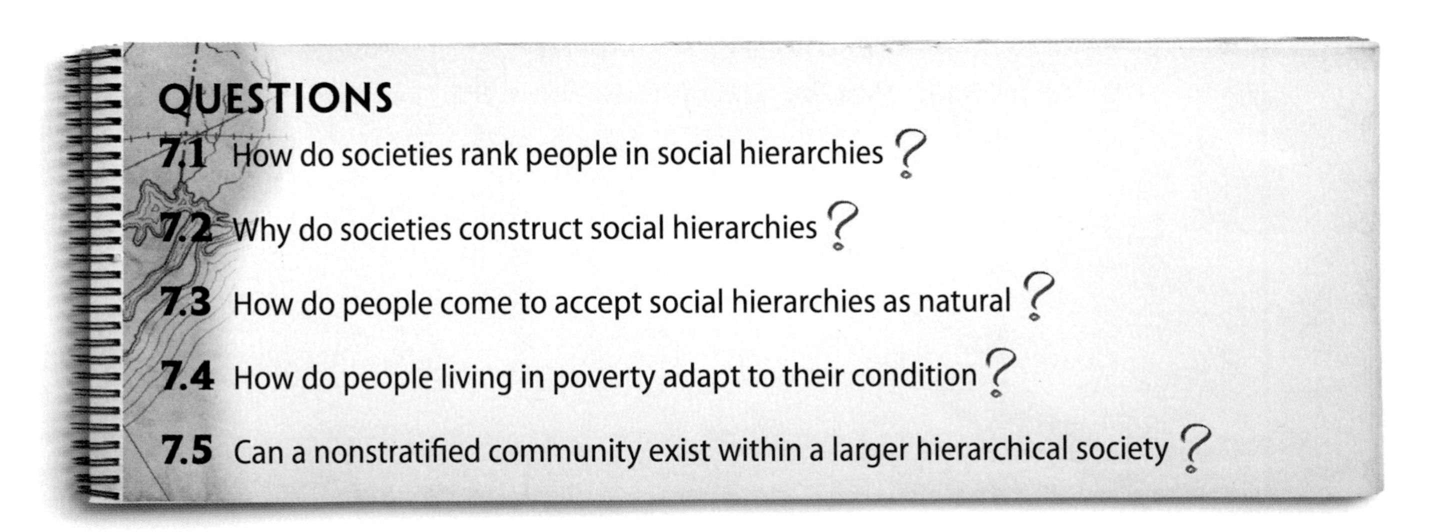

Figure 7.1
The Lorenz Curve and the Gini Coefficient

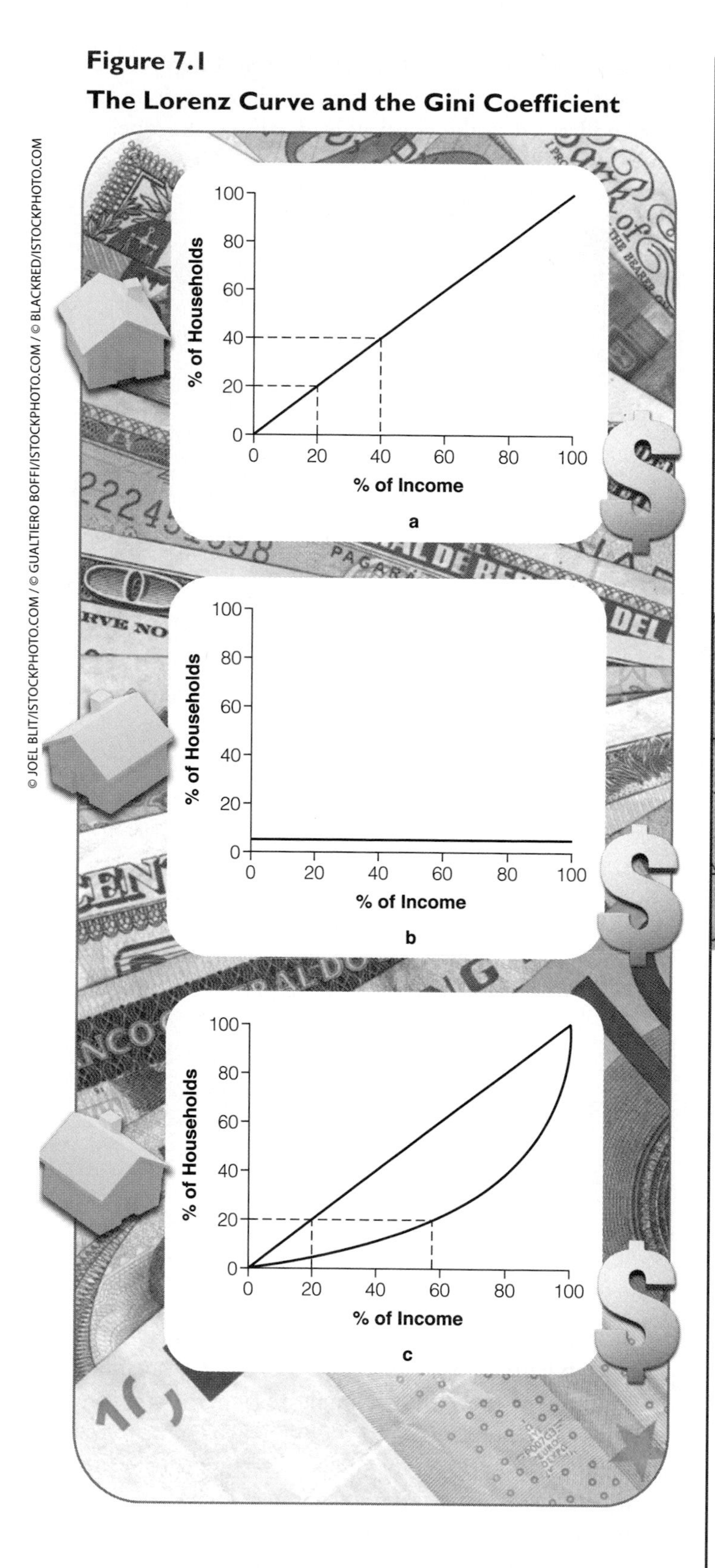

on their origination and amplification in slavery, caste, and class. (1989, 137)

Those who support Belmonte's view note that in societies such as those of the Ju/wasi and Inuit, there are no "poor," "rich," "inferior," or "superior" people. This is not to say that these societies are totally egalitarian. Rather, the question is why modern societies are characterized by such extremes of poverty and wealth.

In this chapter we examine how societies construct social hierarchies and why some groups erect social edifices that encompass social dominance and submission, high and low status, and oppressors and oppressed. We examine why most people in stratified societies—both those at the top and those at the bottom—consider social ranks to be "in the nature of things." We ask how people at the bottom levels of the hierarchy—those in poverty, for example—adapt to their conditions, and we explore whether a nonstratified community can exist within a large-scale society.

QUESTION 7.1

How do societies rank people in social hierarchies?

Social hierarchies vary along several dimensions—the criteria used to differentiate people into one level of society or another, the number of levels that exist, the kinds of privileges and rights that attach to people at different levels, and the strength of the social boundaries that separate the different levels. In American society, people are stratified by income and personal possessions into **social classes** (e.g., lower class, middle class, and upper class). They are classified by cultural or family background into ethnic groups (e.g., Italian, Jewish, or Hispanic), or by physical appearance or skin color into racial categories (e.g., black or white). They are also classified by gender and age, as well as by standards such as education.

In any stratified society, people's access to jobs, wealth, and privilege is determined largely by their position in the hierarchy. In India, the population is stratified

social classes a system of social stratification based on income or possession of wealth and resources. Individual social mobility is possible in a class system

Below is a list of personal attributes. Your task is to rank them by number (1–11) from most to least important to you in judging a person's social or personal worth—no ties allowed.

_____Personal appearance

_____Monetary income

_____Gender

_____Age

_____Religion

_____Ethnic or community origin

_____Family background

_____Intelligence (as indicated by school performance)

_____Athletic ability

_____Personal possessions (clothes, car, etc.)

_____Personality

by a **caste** system, in which individuals are assigned at birth to the ranked social and occupational groups of their parents. The various castes are based on traditional roles. The Brahmins, priests whose lives were devoted to worship and teaching, occupy the top of the caste hierarchy. Directly under them were the Kshattriya, whose members comprised the soldiers, politicians, and administrators. Next were the Vaisya, made up of farmers and merchants. At the bottom of the hierarchy were the Sudra, which were devoted to the service of other castes. In addition, there is a fifth caste, the "untouchables," who were believed to be polluting to others because of their occupations as tanners, sweepers, or shoemakers.

castes a system of social stratification based on assignment at birth to the ranked social or occupational groups of parents. There is no mobility from one caste to another, and intermarriage may be forbidden

Youth and Class

In 1999, the frozen bodies of Yaguine Koita and Fode Tounkara, 14-year-old boys from Conakry, Guinea, were found in the landing gear of a plane at Brussels International Airport. Along with the bodies, authorities found a note addressed to the political leadership of Europe:

Gentlemen, members and leaders of Europe, we appeal to your solidarity and kindness to help Africa. Please help us, we are suffering enormously in Africa, we have problems, and some weaknesses with regard to children's rights . . . we have war, disease, lack of food, etc. . . . In Guinea we have many schools but a big absence of education and training. Therefore, if you see that we are sacrificing ourselves, and expose our lives it is because we are suffering a lot in Africa, and we need your support to fight poverty and end war in Africa. Nevertheless, we want to study and we ask you to help us study so that we can live like you but in Africa. Finally, we beg you to accept our apologies for taking the liberty to address you this letter because you are eminent personalities, which we ought to respect. (quoted in de Boeck and Honwana 2005, 7)

There is a lot to be learned from that incident—the global gap between rich and poor, the desire of the poor to emulate the rich, the rationale for migration from poor to rich countries, and so on. But it also points to the emergence of youth as a major social category. They are, in the words of Alcinda Honwana and Filip de Boeck, "makers and breakers." They are makers in the sense of the cultural contributions they make and the innovations they introduce. They are breakers in the form of alcohol use, unprotected sex, violence, and crime.

Jean and John L. Comaroff note that there are startling similarities among youth all over the world. On the one hand, they are excluded from local economies, particularly the shrinking blue-collar sectors, and cut off from state assistance as neoliberal policies reduce government expenditures on the unemployed. Cut off from wage-earning citizenship, they take to the streets. They are overwhelmingly male, and their exclusion marks what the Comaroffs call a "crisis of masculinity" evidenced in African gang rape, soccer violence, and school shootings such as that at Columbine High School.

On the other hand, youth has gained unprecedented autonomy. Its disenfranchisement has led to the creation of a kind of "counter nation" with its own spaces, its own forms of recreation, and its own forms of illicit enterprise like drug trafficking and computer hacking. The young, say the Comaroffs, "have felt their power, born partly of the sheer weight of numbers, partly of a growing inclination and capacity to turn to the use of force, partly of a willingness to hold polite society to ransom" (2001, 18).

There is among the genteel mainstream, they say, a nightmare image of a youth as a larger-than-life figure wearing expensive sneakers, blaring headsets spewing gangsta rap, and a cell phone tied to the global underground economy. Is this not, they ask, a "sinister caricature of the corporate mogul," the "dark side of consumer capitalism"? It is this image that led U.S. Representative William McCollum of Florida to exclaim that contemporary youth "are the most dangerous criminals on the face of the earth." Of course, such descriptions and actions are generally applied to juveniles from poor or "high-crime" neighborhoods. Thus, in the United States, three-quarters of youth in jail are black or Hispanic; a black teenager is 6 times more likely than a white teen to be sent to jail for a first-time violent offence, and a black teenager is 48 times more likely to be jailed for a drug offence than a white teen.

To some extent, the congressman is correct; by criminalizing behaviors associated with marginalized groups, by criminalizing certain drugs (such as cocaine and marijuana) while legalizing others (alcohol), society creates a marginalized criminal class that legal authorities are then justified in watching closely. Is it so surprising, then, that juveniles see themselves, as the Comaroffs put it, as "mutant citizens of a new world order"?

Status and the Petty Cruelties of High School

The dilemma of youth as a marginalized social category is also evident in the obsession with social structures that they create. These are particularly evident in the American high school. In one high school, Murray Milner, Jr. identified six primary groups arranged in a status hierarchy: the "Preps" (image-conscious types), the "Jocks" (usually involved in at least two sports), the "Rockers" (alternative/grunge, skateboard types), the "Nerds" (academic, studious), the Punks/Weirdos (nonconformists, apathetic to the school social hierarchy), and the "G's" (gangsters, "wannabe" gangsters). Everyone agreed that two groups in particular distinguished themselves from the rest—the Preps and the Jocks.

These groups used a variety of symbols to differentiate themselves, including clothing, music, activities, and even gathering places. Status, according to Milner, was such an obsessive concern of these students that who they sat with at lunch was a greater concern than school grades.

Milner concludes that high school students are so obsessed with status because making judgments about each other is the only power they really have. They have little economic or political power; they must attend school all day and have very little say in what goes on there; they are pressured into learning esoteric subjects that have little immediate relevance to them. The one power they do have is to create their own hierarchy by evaluating each other with criteria very different from those promoted by teachers and parents.

Because status is relatively finite, Milner points out that the only means that students have to increase or maintain their social standing is by lowering the status of others. That is, you move up by putting others down through petty cruelties like gossip, ridicule, and even bullying.

The concern for status is evident also in the degree of sexism in schools. Sexism is prevalent in many formal school rituals, such as the prom with its glorification of romance that empowers men and the elevation of male sporting events with female cheerleaders. You also see it in the acceptance of misogyny in rap lyrics. Interestingly, while racism in schools seems to have declined significantly, sexism is as strong as ever. The question is, why?

Paul Willis's study of working class youth in Great Britain offers an interesting explanation. His book, *Learning to Labor: How Working Class Kids Get Working Class Jobs*, is about how a class reproduces itself from generation to generation. Why do working-class kids tend to end up in working-class jobs? It is not, says Willis, solely because of the ideology of the school and its middle-class biases (see Question 7.3). The kids themselves, by their behavior, essentially do the job of

"The dilemma of youth as a marginalized social category is also evident in the obsession with social structures that they create. These are particularly evident in the American high school."

© DAVID FRANKLIN/ISTOCKPHOTO.COM / © DAN BACHMAN/ISTOCKPHOTO.COM / © RYAN LANE/ISTOCKPHOTO.COM / © PASCAL GENEST/ISTOCKPHOTO.COM

funneling themselves into the working class. They do this by refusing to follow the agenda of the school, rebelling against its discipline, and rejecting what they see as "mental" labor, as opposed to "manual" labor. Their own behavior dooms them to failure in the one institution that might lead to better jobs.

Working class youth glorify manual labor as manly. Mental labor, on the other hand, is seen as feminine. And to be feminine, for working-class youth, is to be an "ear'oles," "pouf," or "wanker," all sexually laden insults. Thus, to be masculine, working-class youth must reject the educational agenda of the school. In rejecting school work as effeminate, the "lads," as they called themselves, must also reject anything associated with women and demonstrate their control and domination over them physically and sexually.

QUESTION 7.2

Why do societies construct social hierarchies?

The construction of social hierarchy is not a necessary feature of all human societies. There seems to be no universal inclination to rank people by one criterion or another. Groups such as the Ju/wasi or Inuit, for example, are not totally egalitarian, but people go out of their way not to appear better than others. In some societies, skin color makes a difference; in others, it doesn't. In some societies, men are accorded far greater status than women; in others, there is little difference in gender rank. The only general rule that seems to hold is that as societies become more complex and populous, their propensity for social stratification increases.

Integrative and Exploitative Theories of Social Hierarchy

Various explanations have been offered for the existence of social hierarchies. Some claim that social stratification emerged with the origin of private property; others claim it was created to satisfy the organizational needs of war. We explore two explanations here: the **integrative theory of social stratification**, based on the assumption that social hierarchy is necessary for the smooth functioning of modern society; and the **exploitative theory of social stratification**, which presumes that hierarchy exists because one group of individuals seeks to take advantage of another group for economic purposes.

integrative theory of social stratification a theory based on the assumption that social hierarchy is necessary for the smooth functioning of society

exploitative theory of social stratification a theory based on the assumption that social stratification and hierarchy exist because one group of individuals seeks to take advantage of another group for economic purposes

Proponents of the integrative theory of social stratification assume that as societies grow and there are more people to feed, house, and clothe, more efficient or sophisticated means are required to produce enough food and other necessities and to erect the necessary infrastructure. Unlike the smaller societies of hunters and gatherers, larger-scale societies require individuals to specialize in certain tasks or occupations, as noted in Chapter 2. This results in a division of labor that requires greater coordination of tasks, more efficient management, and more complex leadership systems, all of which inevitably lead to some form of social stratification. In addition, as societies become more complex, they need to organize systems of defense against other groups. The development of a military organization requires the centralization of power, which again leads to the emergence of an elite group. As resources become scarce, an internal policing system may also be required to prevent crime. Thus, the integrative theory of social stratification is based on the assumption that society's need for greater integration, along with the need to assert greater controls on individual behavior, necessitates some form of centralized authority that offers its citizens security, a means of settling disputes, defense against other groups, and sustenance. All these are offered in exchange for the people's acceptance of and loyalty to authorities and officials.

In the integrative theory, society is compared to a living organism, the parts of which must be regulated by a controlling device if they are to function efficiently for the survival of the whole. The nineteenth-century

means of production the materials, such as land, machines, or tools, that people need to produce things

social philosopher Herbert Spencer suggested that complex societies, like complex living organisms, exhibit greater differentiation as they evolve. Greater differentiation leads to a greater degree of interrelation among parts, which in turn requires greater control by government, management, and the military. Without control, society, like a living organism, would cease to exist.

In American society, proponents of the integrative theory of hierarchy might point to the military to illustrate the necessity for stratification. Without generals or commissioned officers, soldiers would argue, privates, corporals, and sergeants could not do their jobs, and the military would therefore disintegrate. As for societies with no hierarchy, like the Ju/wasi, integrationists might say because each person or family is self-sufficient, there is no need for the coordination of activities.

Proponents of the exploitative theory of social stratification dispute the claim that integration requires social hierarchy. They argue that stratification arises when one group seeks to exploit the resources or labor of others. The exploitation might take various forms of manipulation and control, such as military conquest or enslavement. During the Spanish conquest of South America, thousands of indigenous people were forced to labor on farms or in mines to increase the wealth of Spanish conquerors.

Karl Marx, 1818–1883

THE ART ARCHIVE/KARL MARX MUSEUM TRIER/ALFREDO DAGLI ORTI / © STEFAN KLEIN/ISTOCKPHOTO.COM

Karl Marx and the Origin of Class

The most influential and controversial proponents of the exploitative theory of social stratification are Karl Marx and Friedrich Engels. As witnesses to the squalor of British cities during the industrial revolution, Marx and Engels concluded that landlords and factory owners (capitalists, in their terms) were able to use their control of resources to exploit the unlanded laborers in the factories and mines of England. To understand how landlords and factory owners were able to exploit the masses, it is necessary to grasp the meaning of some key concepts in Marxist theory. The most important of these concepts is social class.

According to Marx, social classes are an outgrowth of capitalism, not a necessary feature of modern society. They arise when a group gains control of the **means of production**, which consists of the materials, such as

Friedrich Engels, 1850–1895

THE ART ARCHIVE/KARL MARX MUSEUM TRIER/ALFREDO DAGLI ORTI / © STEFAN KLEIN/ISTOCKPHOTO.COM

land, machines, or tools, that people need to produce things. A group that controls the means of production can maintain or increase its wealth by taking advantage of the **surplus value of labor**.

The idea of the surplus value of labor works something like this: suppose that the labor value of bricks on the open market is $300 per 1,000 bricks; that is, people are willing to pay $300 above the cost of materials for every 1,000 bricks they purchase. If the same people both make the bricks and sell 1,000 of them, they are getting a 100 percent return on their labor. But what if the person who controls the means of production hires others to make the bricks and pays them $30 for every 1,000 bricks they make? The value of the labor to produce the bricks remains $300 per 1,000, with the laborers are getting one-tenth ($30) of what their labor is worth and the person controlling the means of production keeping the other nine-tenths of the labor value of the bricks ($270). In other words, the capitalist—the person who controls the means of production—is expropriating $270 worth of labor from the worker who produced the bricks.

Why would a worker labor under such conditions? The reason is **political or social repression**, which occurs because the group that controls the means of production also makes the rules of the society. Members of this class elect or choose representatives who pass laws that serve their interests. Such laws may prohibit workers from organizing into labor unions, require them to accept whatever wages they are offered, or forbid them from protesting the working conditions the laws produce. Because the ruling class can enforce these rules with the threat of joblessness, jail, or even death, most people allow themselves to be exploited. Moreover, the workers readily accept their situation if the ruling class also controls the distribution of information, enabling it to create an **ideology of class** for its own benefit.

The ideology of class is a belief that the division of society into classes is both natural and right. According to Marx and Engels, if the ruling class controls the institutions that determine how people view the world (such as churches, schools, and newspapers), it can promote the view that their dominance of society is in the best interests of all. The church, for example, might encourage the lower class to accept its fate because it is "God's will." The ruling class may limit education to its own children, while also making education a requirement for membership in the ruling elite. The ruling class may use the media to tell people that the whole society would perish without it, or it may promote an ideology based on the belief that if you are poor, it's your own fault. As a result of an ideology of class, members of the lower class come to believe that their position in society is as it should be and that there is nothing they can (or should) do about it.

The ideology of class thus produces a society in which a few people control the means of production through the expropriation of the surplus value of labor, maintaining their position of control through repression and the manipulation of ideology. The only way the lower class can rectify this situation, according to Marx and

surplus value of labor the term suggested by Karl Marx and Friedrich Engels for the portion of a person's labor that is retained as profit by those who control the means of production

political or social repression the use of force by a ruling group to maintain political, economic, or social control over other groups

ideology of class a set of beliefs characteristic of stratified societies that justifies the division of a society into groups with differential rights and privileges as being natural and right

Repression and poverty ultimately push the lower class, in desperation, to revolt to regain control of the means of production.

violent revolution the term suggested by Karl Marx and Friedrich Engels for the necessary response of workers to their repression by the ruling class

Engels, is through **violent revolution.** Violent revolution is necessary because the ruling class controls the means of repression (police, military) and won't relinquish its privileges unless it is violently overthrown. Thus, repression and poverty ultimately push the lower class (the workers), in desperation, to revolt to regain control of the means of production.

Two points from Marx and Engels' work are particularly relevant for modern society. First, the notion that class structure is very resistant to change seems to be corroborated by income distribution figures in the United States over the past few decades, as we saw earlier in Table 7.1. Second, there is the notion that people in class societies come to believe that social stratification is "natural." We examine that idea in more detail next.

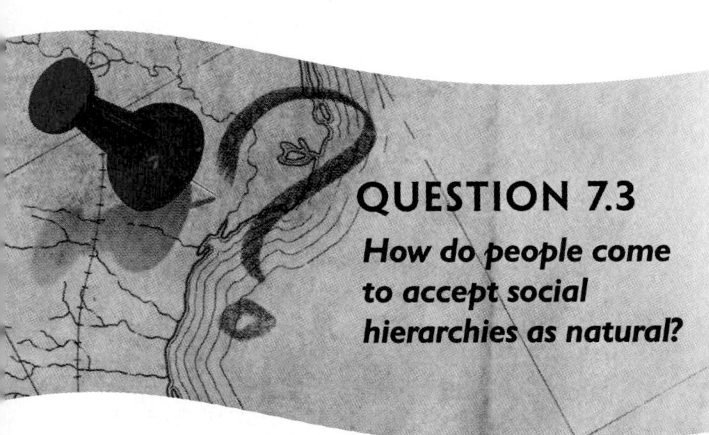

Understanding how societies legitimize social discrimination is one of the most important and, to some extent, the most difficult tasks of anthropology. Part of the problem is that discriminatory thoughts based on racism or sexism exist not only in popular culture, but also in scientific works, as well. It will be useful, then, to examine how such theories are constructed and how they are used to justify the ranking of people within the social hierarchy.

Constructing the Ideology of Racism

In the United States, the ideology of class is based on the assumption that a person's social position is determined largely by achievement or individual effort. Yet there are also attempts to justify social position in terms of a person's biological makeup, that is, by race, intelligence, and gender. The hierarchical ordering of society is thus seen as an expression of a natural law that some people are innately more fit to succeed than others.

For centuries, European and American societies have been characterized by racial stratification. Traditionally, membership in certain racial or ethnic groups was enough to define a person's social, political, and economic status. In the United States, for example, position in the racial hierarchy often determined whether a person could vote, hold political office, or attend certain schools. Until the second half of the twentieth century, racial stratification was written into the laws of many states.

Most people had little trouble constructing an ideology to justify racial stratification. Many claimed that racial stratification was God's will, that he deemed some people to be inferior to others. Others argued that members of one race were created to be intellectually or morally superior to others. Even the supposedly objective findings of scientists assisted in building a racist ideology. In the nineteenth century, reputable scientists devoted much time and energy to proving that the racial stratification of society was "in the nature of things."

Samuel George Morton was a scientist and physician who began to collect and measure skulls from all over the world in the 1820s. When he died in 1851, he left a collection of some 6,000 skulls. Like many in the nineteenth century, Morton believed that a person's intelligence was related to the size of his or her brain: the larger the brain, the more intelligent the person. Because the size of the brain could be determined by the size of the skull, he believed that a ranking of the races could be objectively achieved by a ranking of skull size.

He claimed that "white" skulls had a mean volume of 92 cubic inches; "American Indian" skulls 79 cubic inches; and "black" skulls from America, Africa, and Australia 83 cubic inches. Among "white" skulls, the largest were those of Germans and English people, in the middle were those of Jews, and at bottom were those of Hindus. Thus, "whites" (more specifically, northern European "whites") were not just socially superior, they were biologically superior. Morton believed he had provided objective evidence that the distribution of status and power in nineteenth-century America accurately reflected biological merit.

When Stephen Jay Gould, a Harvard biologist, reexamined Morton's published data in 1977, he concluded that Morton's summaries were a "patchwork of fudging and finagling" that supported the socially constructed

Samuel Morton believed that a ranking of the races could be achieved by a ranking of skull size.

hierarchy. Gould found no evidence of conscious fraud. He concluded that Morton had simply selected or rejected certain data to ensure that the results confirmed what he and most other Americans "knew": that whites were naturally more intelligent than everyone else.

Working with the same skulls Morton had used more than 150 years earlier, Gould discovered that the sample of 144 Native American skulls included proportionally more small-brained Inca skulls from Peru and fewer large-brained Iroquois skulls. This naturally produced a lower mean cranial capacity for indigenous Americans than would have occurred had Morton correctly adjusted for this discrepancy. Moreover, Gould discovered that Morton's failure to include the small-brained Hindu skulls with his "white" skulls had produced a higher average cranial capacity for white skulls. When Gould corrected for Morton's sample biases, he discovered that there was no difference between Euro-American and indigenous American cranial capacity. As for comparisons between "white" and "black" skulls, Gould discovered that Morton had ignored the facts that brain size is related to body size and that male skulls are larger than female skulls. Examination of Morton's "black" skulls indicated that the group included proportionally more female skulls. When Gould remeasured the "black" and "white" skulls, he discovered that the mean cranial capacity of black males was slightly higher than the mean for white males.

Gould does not believe that Morton consciously manipulated his skull measurements to prove that whites were intellectually superior to Native Americans or blacks. Rather, he thinks Morton simply assumed that this is what his measurements would prove and set about achieving the results he expected. Although Morton's measurements were obviously in error, as was his assumption that cranial capacity reveals intelligence, they were used well into the twentieth century to support an ideology that the racial ranking of persons in society could be justified on natural grounds.

The Social Construction of "Intelligence"

Morton's experiments represent just one example of efforts to show that social hierarchies are not the result of chance, but rather innate, natural ability. To believe otherwise would threaten a key assertion of American ideology—that all Americans enjoy an equal opportunity for success. Moreover, believing otherwise has serious political and economic consequences. If poverty and a low ranking in society are not the fault of the poor but the result of some failure of society, then there is strong reason to rework social and economic policies. Because such changes might lead to a loss of privilege for those who benefit from present policies, there is strong motivation to find some concept that legitimizes inherited privilege and lays the blame for poverty on the poor themselves.

The concept of intelligence neatly solves this problem. If people accept the idea that intelligence explains how well people do in life, then the fiction that people's rank in society depends solely on their own natural ability can be maintained. Moreover, if it can be shown that intelligence is inherited, then we can explain why it is that the children of successful people tend to be successful and why certain groups are disproportionately poor.

The failure of the cranial-capacity thesis did not end attempts to link intelligence to success, as well as to race and ethnicity. Instead, there have been continuing effort on the part of some members of the scientific community to marshal evidence to prove that intelligence is both inherited and racially conditioned. These efforts included, for example, the work of Arthur Jensen in the 1960s and 1970s and, more recently, *The Bell Curve* by Richard J. Herrnstein and Charles Murray, published in 1994. Missing from most of these accounts is any acknowledgment that the concept of intelligence itself is a social construct, an idea that is invented. Consequently, we need to look closely at our concept of intelligence. How did it evolve?

To begin, anthropologist Allan Hanson notes that the concept of intelligence contains a number of questionable assumptions. First, intelligence is assumed to be a single entity. Second, it is assumed to be measurable and unequally distributed in the population. Third, the amount of intelligence people have is assumed to be relatively fixed throughout life. Fourth, the amount is assumed to largely explain their degree of success in life. Finally, intelligence is assumed to be largely inherited.

False Assumptions About Intelligence

1. It's a single entity
2. It can be measured, and it is unequally distributed in society.
3. The amount people have is relatively fixed.
4. It explains the degree of success people have in life.
5. It is largely inherited.

Each of these assumptions is critical to the intelligence construct as most people think of it, and each has been the subject of enormous scientific attention and criticism. The first assumption requires that we accept the idea that someone who is intelligent in one way is also intelligent in other ways. The second assumption implies that we can somehow measure innate intelligence, as opposed to achievement, and the third presumes that we can show that whatever is measured does not vary throughout a person's life. The fourth is built on the idea that people who have more measurable intelligence are more likely to be successful, whereas the fifth assumption requires us to show that the children of people with high measurable intelligence also have high measurable intelligence.

In spite of the number of assumptions that lie behind the notion of intelligence and the studies that illustrate how questionable each of these assumptions really is, most Americans take the notion for granted. This is, however, a unique idea, one not shared by many other societies. Indigenous maritime navigators of the South Pacific, for example, learned to read wave patterns, wind direction, and celestial constellations to navigate vast distances in the ocean. Yet others in the same society who are unable to duplicate this feat don't view the navigators as somehow being smarter; they see them as people who can navigate.

We might learn something about the social construction of ideologies of class by briefly looking at the early history of the intelligence construct and reviewing how reputable scientists proceeded to develop it. Three pioneers—Francis Galton, Karl Pearson, and Charles Spearman—supplied the basic ideas and experimental proofs for the concept of intelligence as a fixed, "mental" entity that is differentially distributed in the population, is measurable, explains a person's educational and occupational success, and is inherited.

Francis Galton was one of the leading intellectual figures of the late nineteenth century. In his best-known work, *Hereditary Genius*, published in 1869, Galton sought to demonstrate that the "genius" of selected eminent men was largely inherited from their eminent parents. In his sample of 997 eminent British men, he found that 31 percent had eminent fathers, 48 percent had eminent sons, and 41 percent had eminent brothers, far higher percentages than one would expect by chance. Galton concluded that these statistics illustrate the power of heredity in the distribution of "genius." He was, of course, rightly criticized for ignoring the impact of environment. But he did something else that is more interesting, something that went largely unchallenged: he selected the eminent men from the British upper and upper-middle classes, ignoring the "captains of industry and finance" and, of course, women. Eminence was eminence only within a select range of activities and occupations. Galton, the nephew of Charles Darwin and of upper-middle-class background, was faithfully reproducing the judgments of his own status as to what constituted intelligence.

Much of Galton's later research was devoted to arguing that those characteristics he called "genius," "mediocrity," and "imbecility" were analogous to certain physical characteristics in their statistical distribution within a society. He developed a number of tests for cranial capacity and for sensory capacities—the ability to discriminate between colors or smells, for example. Galton was not the only one trying to do this; in Germany, the United States, and England, other researchers were trying to measure intelligence largely through the measurement of sensory and reflex activity, such as reading aloud rapidly, giving the colors of named objects, naming and classifying plants, and other tests of memory and spatial judgment. Around 1900 there was a move away from these kinds of measures, however, largely because they weren't showing any correlation with each other and, more importantly, because they showed only a low correlation with teachers' estimates of the mental capability of their students. Regardless, by 1900 the classic intelligence construct had been laid out, although its proof was somewhat wanting.

The next person in our story is Karl Pearson, a prolific author whose works include more than 400 articles on mathematical physics, statistics, and biology, as well as poetry, a passion play, art history, German history, and political essays. In 1901, Pearson published a study in the *Proceedings of the Royal Society of London* in which he concluded, "The mental characteristics in man are inherited in precisely the same manner as the physical. Our mental and moral nature is quite as much as our physical nature, the outcome of hereditary factors" (1901, 155).

It is instructive to look at how Pearson reached this conclusion. He took pairs of brothers and measured specific physical characteristics, such as stature, forearm length, hair color, eye color, and cephalic index. He found, not surprisingly, that there was a high correlation among brothers for these traits. Then he asked teachers, using another sample of brother pairs, to rank them on seven "mental characteristics": intelligence, vivacity, conscientiousness, popularity, temper, self-consciousness, and shyness. Teachers were asked to rate each child as "keen" or "dull" and to choose among six subdivisions of intelligence. When the teachers' evaluations of brother pairs were tabulated, Pearson again found a strong correlation between brother ratings, thereby proving the power of inheritance.

Much about this study is questionable, but of particular note is the role of teachers' judgments. Obviously, teachers were evaluating selected behavior patterns and personal characteristics that they judged to be evidence of various "mental characteristics." In other words, the teachers' judgments were highly subjective and, at best, questionable. But Pearson's work marked an important development in the construction of our concept of intelligence. Whatever intelligence was, he claimed to show that it was inherited at least as much as physical characteristics.

Let's move forward a couple of years to the next important stage in the construction of the intelligence construct, that of Charles Spearman and "general intelligence." Spearman's research, published in the *American Journal of Psychology* in 1904, was designed to prove that there were different degrees of correspondence between an individual's performance on different types of tests. Thus, one would expect to find a high degree of correspondence between one's performance on geometrical tests and tests of spatial perception and a low degree of correspondence between one's performance on, say, tests of musical ability and tests of weight discrimination. If there was some correlation among all the test results, this would indicate that there was some general factor, *g*, that would affect performance on all tests. Thus, tests that resulted in high correlation would be heavily saturated with *g*, whereas tests with little correlation would not be. To use an athletic analogy, if someone hits both a baseball and a golf ball a long way, we might assume that some general factor for athletic ability could account for both skills.

Spearman suggested that the *g* factor underlies all mental operations and that if it could be ascertained, it would approximate true intelligence. This was a major claim, for to prove the existence of *g* would result in the dismissal of the idea, widely held at the time, that different people could be intelligent in different ways.

To prove the existence of general intelligence, Spearman isolated four kinds of intelligence that, he claimed, when correlated would show a high degree of correspondence: "present efficiency," "native capacity," "general impression produced upon other people," and "common sense." "Present efficiency" referred to the "ordinary classification according to school order" in subjects such as Greek, Latin, or mathematics. "Native capacity" was arrived at by taking the difference between a child's rank in school and his age, whereas

© PAWEL GAUL/ISTOCKPHOTO.COM

CASE: Fight for Our Right

In 1948, the General Assembly of the United Nations adopted the Universal Declaration of Human Rights.

In this statement, the UN proclaimed that every person in the world had the right to life, liberty, security, freedom from torture, and freedom of expression. In addition, the UN declaration also included the right to a standard of living adequate for health and well-being, including food, clothing, housing, medical care, and necessary social services, along with the right to security in the event of unemployment, sickness, disability, widowhood, old age, or other lack of livelihood in circumstances beyond the person's control.

Similar rights are incorporated into various other international treaties and conventions. Unfortunately, most of these agreements are not enforced. In 1994, the signatories to the Convention on the Prevention and Punishment of the Crime of Genocide, including the U.S., all stood idly while more than 800,000 Rwandans were being exterminated. They justified their inaction by refusing to define what was taking place as genocide. Though governments may be unwillingly to take radical action, Carole Nagengast and Carlos G. Vélez-Ibáñez suggest that anthropologists are uniquely prepared for work on human rights. Anthropologists are most prepared to deal with cultural variation and to understand complex community struggles. They are trained to understand the workings of official bureaucracies and global processes; and they have "a strong penchant for supporting the underdog." The work of Paul Farmer in Haiti is especially instructive for what anthropologists can do to protect human rights.

While studying anthropology as an undergraduate, Farmer began working in Haiti, assisting agencies delivering health and social services. From this initial experience, Farmer learned the value of anthropology in addressing health problems. In one instance, a mother sought out a Voodoo priest to treat her child for malaria, while at the same time allowing Farmer to give her chloroquine. It was critical, Farmer says, to appreciate the role of Voodoo in the life of most Haitians. A doctor who knew nothing about local beliefs might end up at war with Voodoo priests. But a doctor with a background in anthropology could find a way to cooperate.

A second defining lesson came from liberation theology. During the 1960s, Catholic priests and theologians responded to oppressive, dictatorial governments by organizing movements that sought to empower the poor. It was an attempt to apply the message of the Bible to everyday life, with the hope of replacing the old, abusive order of things.

Farmer was attracted to liberation theology, which he described as "a powerful rebuke to the hiding away of poverty," because it was driven by a need to accomplish something concrete in the lives of the poor. It

was characterized by what Farmer calls "pragmatic solidarity" with the communities that it sought to assist by giving the poor preferential, rather than equal, treatment.

Farmer also gained an appreciation for understanding the context in which poverty and oppression occurred. He understood that "a minor error in one setting of power and privilege could have an enormous impact on the poor in another." During the 1950s, the U.S. Army Corps of Engineers built the Péligre dam, displacing thousands of Haitian farmers, who were forced to rebuild on the sides of mountains or move to cities for low-paying jobs. The few farmers that remained still had their pigs, but after an outbreak of swine fever in the Dominican Republic, the U.S. destroyed all the Haitian pigs to protect the American pork industry. The farmers were given pigs from Iowa, but most were unsuited for Haiti and died, leaving them with nothing. These are examples of what Farmer refers to as "structural violence," actions of remote groups that result in denial to the poor of basic rights of food, shelter, or livelihood.

What is needed, says Farmer, is a strategy to confront structural violence. The problem is that traditional government and nongovernmental organizations are restricted in addressing rights issues. They are constrained by the fact that they must work through governments, which also happen to be the major violators of rights. For this reason, Farmer suggests that, while NGOs and other groups must work with and through governments, they must also work in solidarity with the members of affected communities.

Farmer's own efforts provide a model for how to address human rights abuses. While he was in Boston, he tried to raise money to build a bread oven in the village of Cange. He approached a local charity, which gave him the money and also put him into contact with one of their regular donors, Tom White, a contractor who helped establish Partners In Health and a corresponding organization in Haiti called Zamni Lasante. Partners In Health has subsequently grown into a major provider of health care programs in Haiti, Peru, and Russia.

The Peligre dam displaced thousands of peasants and submerged acres of useful, productive farmland.

© PAVLEN/ISTOCKPHOTO.COM / © IGOR BYRKO/ISTSOCKPHOTO.COM

According to Charles Spearman, the *g* factor underlies all mental operations and approximates true intelligence.

"general impression produced on other people" was obtained by asking the teacher of a class who was the brightest pupil, the next brightest, and so on. "Common sense" was arrived at by asking the oldest child in a class to rank her fellow students on "sharpness and common sense out of school." As a check on the reliability of judgments, he also asked the rector's wife to rank the children, although as Spearman notes regretfully, she did not know some of them. Spearman, not surprisingly, found that children who ranked high on one kind of intelligence tended to rank high on others, thereby validating the existence of *g*.

Obviously the methodology of these classic studies was seriously flawed, relying on subjective and biased judgments. From Galton to Spearman, members of the professional middle class identified as intelligent those people whose behavior patterns and appearance most conformed to their own. Moreover, little effort was made to conceal the fact. Subjective judgments of the professional class were the major means by which intelligence was defined. Nonetheless, the intelligence construct as we know it was generally complete, and reputable scientists considered it to be experimentally validated. They defined intelligence as a singular trait, represented by *g*, that is inherited and is differentially distributed in the population.

Much more was to come, of course, in the social construction of intelligence, most notably the development of the Stanford-Binet IQ test and, later, the Scholastic Assessment Test (SAT). Additional and more sophisticated experiments were performed that some claimed supported the conclusions of early pioneers such as Galton, Pearson, and Spearman. But the most interesting feature is the dominance of social judgments—largely of teachers, psychologists, and school administrators—in determining what does or does not constitute intelligence. As late as the 1960s, results of intelligence tests were still being cross-checked with teachers' judgments and students' ranks in class. If the test scores failed to correlate with the teachers' judgments, the tests were changed.

In spite of the obvious flaws in this concept of intelligence—flaws that most scientists acknowledge—it continues to serve as a means of legitimizing the social order, making it seem as if a person's place in it is "in the nature of things." Clarence J. Karier put it particularly well:

> The many varied tests, all the way from IQ to personality and scholastic achievement, periodically brought up-to-date, would serve a vital part in rationalizing the social class system. The tests also created the illusion of objectivity, which on the one side served the needs of the "professional" educators to be "scientific," and on the other side served the need of the system for a myth which would convince the lower classes that their station in life was part of the natural order of things. (1976, 136)

Constructing Stratification by Gender

Looking back at the history of the social construction of intelligence, it is easy to condemn the biases that created a scientifically supported system of stratification by race and class. Yet the biases that falsely linked race to biology and intelligence to class also led to the belief that the superiority of men over women was not socially constructed but "natural." Many people believed that women's bodies defined both their social position and their role, which was to reproduce, as men's bodies dictated that they manage, control, and defend. At the beginning of the twentieth century, even the Supreme Court of the United States ruled that women should be prohibited from jobs that might endanger their reproductive function, concluding that a

WHAT DETERMINES SUCCESS?

According to Malcolm Gladwell, it is not just a person's intelligence, skill, or some other innate ability. In his 2008 book *Outliers*, Gladwell profiles Christopher Langan. With an estimated IQ of 195–210, Langan has been called by some the smartest man in America. He began speaking at six months, taught himself to read, and spent most of his high school years doing independent study on philosophy, advanced mathematics, and physics. But for all his intelligence, Langan hardly qualifies as a success. His "career" has consisted of a series of odd jobs—construction worker, farmhand, firefighter, and nightclub bouncer. Why was he unable to find success in life? Gladwell argues that it was because of his environment. Langan's life in an unstable home—his father died before he was born, his stepfather physically abused him, and his family lived in great poverty—did not give him the opportunities for success that others had. According to Gladwell, success is not just the product of extraordinary talent, but extraordinary opportunities.

"woman's physical structure and the performance of maternal functions place her at a disadvantage in the struggle for subsistence. Since healthy mothers are essential to vigorous offspring, the physical well-being of women becomes an object of public interest and care in order to preserve the strength and vigor of the race."

The view that the biology of females makes them lesser persons than males remains embedded in American culture, sometimes in very subtle ways. An example is the language used by professionals to describe menstruation and menopause. Anthropologist Emily Martin says that during the nineteenth century, Americans regarded the female body as if it were a factory whose job was to "labor" to produce children. Menopause was viewed negatively because it marked the end of productive usefulness, and menstruation was described as a sign of the failure of the implantation of a fertilized egg.

Martin says that the same attitudes toward female reproductive functions that existed in the nineteenth century persist today, encoded in contemporary medical and biology textbooks. Menopause is described in some texts as a breakdown of communication between the brain and the reproductive parts of the female body. In menopause, says one college textbook, the ovaries become unresponsive to hormonal stimulation and, as a result, regress. The hypothalamus, which controls hormone production, is addicted to estrogen from years of menstruation. Because of decreased estrogen at menopause, the hypothalamus gives inappropriate orders. Menopause is thus described as a breakdown of authority—functions fail and falter; organs wither and become senile. Our language still depicts the female body as a machine that in menopause is no longer able to fulfill its proper goal; it can no longer produce babies. In this view, at menopause the female body becomes a broken-down factory.

Menstruation is likewise described as a breakdown in the reproductive process. When an egg is not implanted, the process is described in negative terms as a disintegration or shedding. According to one college textbook, "When fertilization fails to occur, the endometrium is shed, and a new cycle starts. This is why it used to be taught that 'menstruation is the uterus crying for lack of a baby.'" Menstruation is depicted as a sign of an idle factory, a failed production system, a system producing "scrap" or "waste." Note the language used in the following passage from another textbook:

> If fertilization and pregnancy do not occur, the corpus luteum degenerates and the levels of estrogen and progesterone decline. As the levels of these hormones decrease and their stimulatory effects are withdrawn, blood vessels of the endometrium undergo prolonged spasms (contractions) that reduce the blood flow to the area of the endometrium supplied by the vessels. The resulting lack of blood causes the tissue of the affected region to degenerate. After some time, the vessels relax, and allow blood to flow through them again. However, capillaries in the area have become so weakened that blood leaks through them. This blood and the deteriorating endometrial tissue are discharged from the uterus as the menstrual flow. As a new ovarian cycle begins and the level of estrogen rises, the functional layer of the endometrium undergoes repair and once again begins to proliferate. (Martin 1987, 47)

Martin notes that very different language is used in the same textbooks to describe male reproductive functions. For example, the textbook from which the above description of menstruation is taken describes the production of sperm as follows: "The mechanisms which guide the remarkable cellular transformation from spermatid to mature sperm remain uncertain. Perhaps the most amazing characteristic of spermatogenesis is its sheer magnitude: the normal human male may manufacture several hundred million sperm per day" (Martin 1987, 48).

This text, which describes menstruation as "failed production," fails to mention that only about one of every 100 billion sperm ever makes it far enough to fertilize an egg. Moreover, other bodily processes that are similar to menstruation are not spoken of in terms of breakdown and deterioration. Seminal fluid picks up shredded cellular material as it passes through the male ducts, and the stomach lining is shed periodically. Why are these processes not also described in the same negative terms as menstruation? Martin says the reason is that both men and women have stomachs, but only women have uteruses. The stomach falls on the positive side, the uterus on the negative.

Rather than describing menstruation as failed production, Martin suggests that it might be more accurate to describe it as the successful avoidance of an egg implant. If a couple has done anything to avoid the implantation of an egg, is it still appropriate to talk of the reproductive cycle in terms of production? The following description of menstruation offered by Martin portrays it not as a failure to reproduce, but as the successful avoidance of a pregnancy:

> A drop in the formerly high levels of progesterone and estrogen creates an appropriate environment for reducing the excess layers of endometrial tissue. Constriction of capillary blood vessels causes a lower level of oxygen and nutrients and paves the way for a vigorous production of menstrual fluids. As a part of the renewal of the remaining endometrium, the capillaries begin to reopen, contributing some blood and serous fluid to the volume of endometrial material already beginning to flow. (1987, 52)

Emily Martin's analysis reveals that in contemporary American society, the ideology of gender stratification remains embedded in our language and in our scientific ideas about the bodily functions of males and females. Describing the bodily processes of women in negative terms makes women seem to be lesser human beings. Moreover, describing menstruation and menopause in negative terms leads women themselves to believe that their bodily functions are less clean and less worthy than those of men.

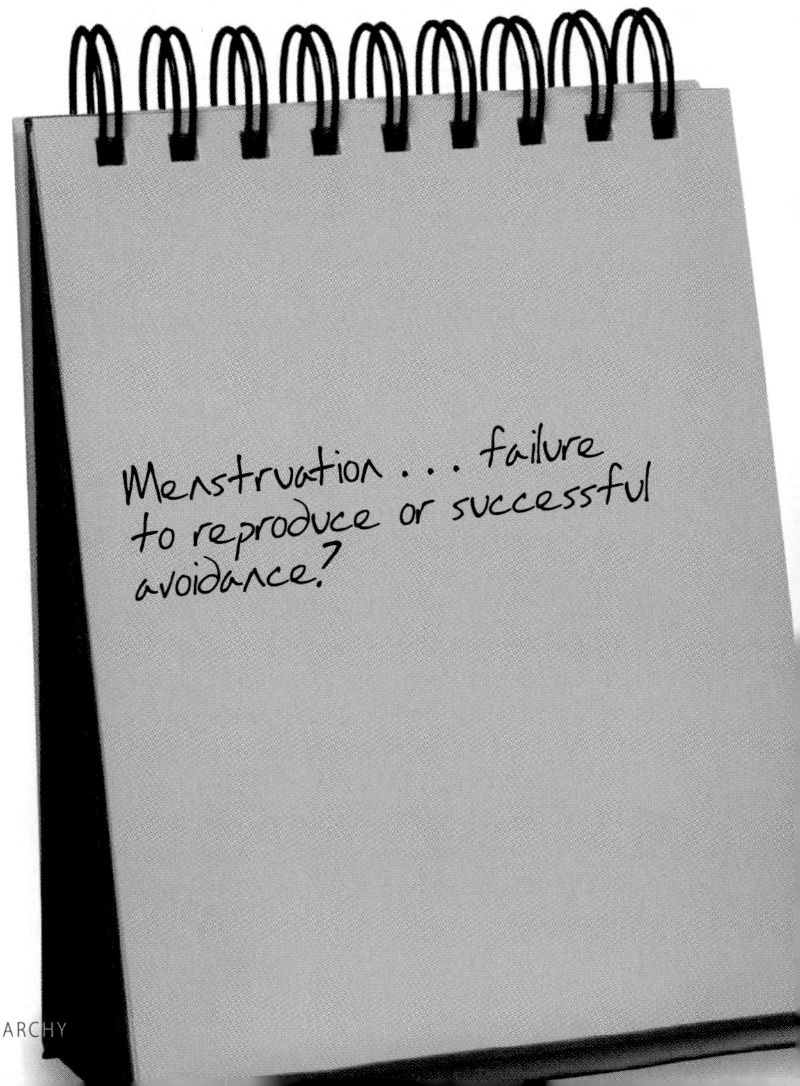

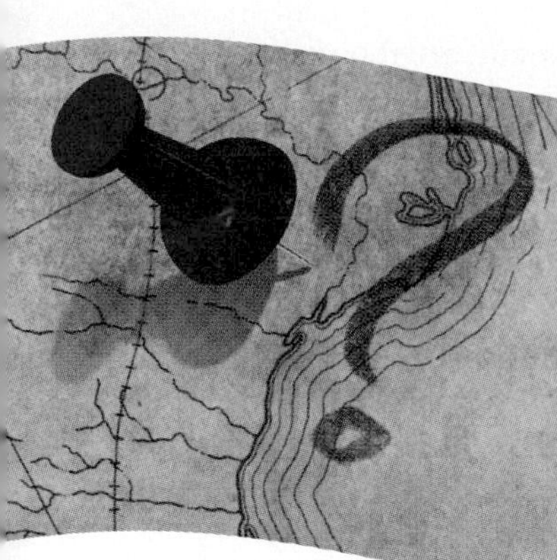

QUESTION 7.4

How do people living in poverty adapt to their condition?

The position in a social hierarchy that each person occupies is like a window to the world. In order to survive in the impoverished conditions that exist in the lower tiers of society, people adopt specific adaptive strategies. Anthropologist Oscar Lewis coined the term **culture of poverty** to describe the lifestyle and worldview of people who inhabit urban and rural slums.

Some anthropologists object to that term because it implies that poverty is somehow rooted in the subcultural values passed on between generations rather than in the social and cultural values of the larger society. The implication is that if it weren't for the culture of poverty, the poor would have no culture at all. Modifying that view, some anthropologists maintain that the behavior of people in poverty represents their adaptations to their socioeconomic condition. These conditions are the result of inequality, usually reinforced by racism, and further buttressed by an economic system that requires a source of cheap labor. Moreover, descriptions of poor families as broken, fatherless, or female-centered are misleading. Many of the behaviors of the poor that are viewed negatively by the dominant society are actually resilient responses to the socioeconomic conditions of those living in poverty.

More recent views confirm that conditions of poverty and oppression that exist in U.S. cities do require a cultural adaptation built on efforts to compensate for living at the economic and social margins of society. This poverty and marginalization of inner cities has spawned, says Philippe Bourgois, an "inner-city street culture,"

> a complex and conflictual web of beliefs, symbols, modes of interaction, values, and ideologies that have emerged in opposition to exclusion from mainstream society. . . . This "street culture of resistance" is not a coherent, conscious universe of political opposition but, rather, a spontaneous set of rebellious practices that in the long term have emerged as an oppositional style. (1995, 8)

In fact, much of this culture has been commercialized by the mainstream U.S. culture through fashion, music, film, and television and adopted by middle- and upper-class youth.

culture of poverty a phrase coined by Oscar Lewis to describe the lifestyle and worldview of people who inhabit urban and rural slums

generalized reciprocity a form of exchange in which people share what they have with others but expect them to reciprocate later

balanced reciprocity a form of exchange in which items of equal or near-equal value are exchanged on the spot

negative reciprocity a form of exchange in which the object is to get something for nothing or to make a profit

Kinship as an Adaptation to Poverty

In the late 1960s, anthropologist Carol B. Stack conducted one of the classic studies of how families cope with poverty. She worked closely with a predominantly black community she called The Flats, a section of a small, Midwestern city of some 55,000 people. Unemployment in The Flats was higher than 20 percent, and 63 percent of the jobs held were in low-paying service occupations such as maids, cooks, and janitors. Although only 10 percent of whites in the city lived in housing classed as deteriorating, 26 percent of blacks did. Moreover, blacks had inadequate access to health care, and their infant mortality rate was twice that of whites.

Stack's interest was in how the residents responded to their impoverished conditions. She discovered that they fostered kinship ties and created fictive kinship links to form close, interlocking, cooperative groups that would ensure economic and social support in times of need. Few people earned enough to provide them or their families with enough to eat or a place to stay on a regular basis; even welfare payments could not always guarantee food and shelter for a family. Accordingly, people in The Flats regularly "swapped" food, shelter, child care, and personal possessions. In this respect, the community resembled societies such as the Ju/wasi, in which a person shares with others but expects them to reciprocate at some later time. Anthropologists call this type of sharing **generalized reciprocity**, as distinguished from **balanced reciprocity**, in which items are exchanged on the spot. **Negative reciprocity** is an attempt to get something for nothing or make a profit.

The advantage of generalized reciprocity is that widespread sharing ensures that nobody lacks the basic needs for survival. People in The Flats cultivated diffuse kinship and friendship relations by giving when they could, so that others would give to them when they were in need. These networks were often framed in a kinship idiom, even though no biological kin tie existed.

Another adaptation to poverty in The Flats involved child care. Given the unpredictability of employment, the young age at which many women had children, and the need to respond to unpredictable living conditions and substandard housing, a child might reside with three or four different adults. Often, different people performed the roles of provider, discipliner, trainer, curer, and groomer. Stack points out that those who provided child care did so because they considered it a privilege as well as a responsibility. Children were valued, and they were considered the responsibility of a wide network of kin and friends.

Male–female relations were most affected by the difficulty that men had in finding steady employment. Generally a couple in The Flats would not marry unless the man had a steady job. Men in The Flats had accepted the mainstream American model of the male provider, and the inability to find regular employment prevented their assumption of that role. Moreover, marriage removed people from the widespread sharing network, because after marriage their major obligations belonged to their husbands or wives. In addition, because a woman was cut off the welfare rolls if she married, kinship networks and welfare benefits offered more security than a husband could. Nevertheless, men and women in The Flats did form intimate relationships, out of which children were born. Moreover, the fathers took considerable pride in their children, as did the paternal grandparents, to whom the children often went for help. However, the mothers often regarded the fathers as friends who had failed to fulfill their paternal obligations. Thus, the conditions of poverty drew people into kinship and friendship networks rather than the nuclear family patterns valued by the larger society.

In Search of Respect: Selling Crack in El Barrio

Although people make creative adaptations to impoverished conditions, they also attempt to resist the patterns of oppression and discrimination that are the roots of the poverty. The resistance itself can often lead to self-destructive behavior. Philippe Bourgois, in his study of drug use in the East Harlem section of New York City, also known as El Barrio, portrays a culture that emerges out of people's search for dignity and their rejection of racism and marginalization. However, because this culture centered on drugs, it led people into violence, substance abuse, and internalized rage.

El Barrio, says Bourgois, must be seen in the historical context of a colonized island—Puerto Rico. In the late nineteenth and early twentieth centuries, the island was taken over by American sugar growers who dispossessed thousands of rural farmers, forcing them to seek wage labor on coastal sugar plantations.

After World War II, hundreds of thousands of people migrated from Puerto Rico to the United States, many to New York City and East Harlem. Overall, some 1.5 million left the sugarcane fields, shantytowns, and highland villages for New York City. In two or three generations, these migrants went from being semisubsistence peasants on private plots to agricultural laborers on foreign-owned, capital-intensive plantations to factory workers in export-platform shantytowns, to sweatshop workers in ghetto tenements, to service sector employees living in public housing.

East Harlem has long been home to poor minorities. After a period when it was the site of elite farms and country houses, the building of cheap transportation in the late nineteenth century turned it into the home of wave after wave of immigrant groups, creating what some called the most ethnically diverse area in the United States. In the mid-twentieth century, "slum clearance" programs destroyed functioning Italian working-class communities and replaced them with concentrated populations of poor Puerto Ricans. But what brought people, in this case from Puerto Rico, to live in this neighborhood?

By the 1970s, many of the new migrants were faring relatively well, having obtained employment in various manufacturing jobs. But once again the global economy disrupted their lives. Taking advantage of cheap labor and tax incentives, many companies moved manufacturing jobs overseas, leaving millions of workers in the U.S. out of work. In New York City alone, from the 1960s to the early 1990s, some 800,000 manufacturing jobs were lost.

Thus, over the course of the past century, the global economy, combined with systematic racism and discrimination, has produced high rates of unemployment, substance abuse, broken families, and deteriorated health. No group in the United States other than Native Americans fare as badly statistically as Puerto Ricans. In 1993, the median household income for Puerto Ricans was $14,000 less than for whites and more than $4,000 less than for other Latino groups. But perhaps the greatest irony is that, in spite of this history, most members of El Barrio see their violent actions and deteriorated lives as a result of their own actions and their own choices.

The area in East Harlem where Bourgois worked had a poverty rate of almost 40 percent, and more than half the population, given their incomes, should not have been able to meet subsistence requirements. That many do, says Bourgois, is a tribute to the underground economy that allows people to meet basic food and clothing needs. Underground economic activities for women include babysitting, working "off the books" as seamstresses, tending bar at social clubs, and taking in boarders. Men's jobs tend to be more visible: street-corner car repairs, unlicensed contractors, selling "numbers," or selling drugs. Drugs are the multibillion-dollar foundation of the underground economy, with cocaine, crack, and heroin the most prevalent.

These drugs are easily accessible. Bourgois says that within a two-block radius of the tenement in which he lived with his family, he could obtain heroin, crack, powder cocaine, hypodermic needles, methadone, Valium, angel dust, and marijuana. Within 100 yards of his stoop were three competing crack houses selling vials at $2, $3, and $5. And just a few blocks away in what was called a "pill mill," one doctor wrote $3.9 million worth of Medicaid prescriptions, 94 percent of which was on the NYC Department of Social Services' list of frequently abused prescription drugs.

Crack, a combination of cocaine and baking soda that can be smoked for an instant high, was by far the most in demand. Selling crack enabled some members of El Barrio to amass both wealth and prestige. One of the most notable dealers that Bourgois came to know was Ray. Ray built his business, which required him to balance discipline and the threat of violence with respect, around the Game Room. Ray formed special ties with workers, serving as godfather to children of his workers and friends in much the same way as local landlords in Puerto Rico would use godfather or *compadrazgo* ties to ensure the loyalty of their farm workers. Ray also bestowed special benefits on his employees, including bail money, lawyer fees, holiday bonuses, family gifts, and special dinners.

Some workers employed by Ray would earn hundreds of dollars a night running a crack house, and others earned considerable sums serving as lookouts. Yet Bourgois found that in spite of the amount of money they earned, most in the crack trade were almost always penniless. He discovered that whatever they earned they would spend on expensive gifts, consumption behavior that is mirrored by rapidly upward mobile persons in the legal economy.

Furthermore, says Bourgois, when you calculate the risks of the drug trade, such as getting shot, arrested, or beaten up, the off-time spent in jail or when the police shut down the crack house, and the poor working conditions, employment in the crack economy is generally much worse than legal employment. For these reasons, most workers in the drug trade prefer legal employment. In fact, most drug workers have had legal work experience, often beginning at the age of 12. But by the time they reach the age of 21, few residents of El Barrio have fulfilled their dreams of finding stable, well-paying jobs. Instead, they settle for low-paying service-sector jobs.

Many of the people involved in the crack house economy alternate between street-level crack dealing and minimum-wage jobs in the legal economy. But most, says Bourgois, either quit or are fired from the legal jobs because of a refusal to be exploited or because of the racist or condescending attitudes of the predominantly white, middle-class employers and supervisors. Often they view their return to the streets as a triumph of free will and resistance.

Yet, says Bourgois, there is much self-reproach at not being able to hold a steady, legal job. Often, failure at legal employment or the inability to find a job at all drove people to more substance abuse. It also became harder to explain to prospective employers the reasons for their periods of unemployment. They became what economists call "discouraged workers," those who no longer seek employment and are no longer counted in the unemployment statistics. But this discouragement leads to a spiral of depression, increased substance abuse, evictions, and fractured social relations.

In this environment of little economic opportunity, drugs play economic, psychological, and social functions. They provide income; they provide a respite and escape from the conditions of El Barrio; and they constitute a form of symbolic resistance to the racism, discrimination, and subordination in the larger society. But, says Bourgois, this adaptation is self-destructive. Drug use, of course, destroys bodies. But additionally, because male drug users feel powerless as their role in households diminishes, they lash out at the women and children they can no longer control as their wage-earning fathers and grandfathers did.

Women in El Barrio face their own special problems. Many, particularly those involved in the drug economy, must be able to balance the demands of the two state agencies that dominate their lives—the penal system and the welfare system. Given the federal and state budget cuts of the past two decades, it is virtually impossible to support a family on welfare alone. Women had to supplement their welfare income with off-the-books jobs, maintain two or more social security cards, or sell drugs. Making matters worse, welfare rules required people to requalify every six months or be cut off.

The dilemma of women in El Barrio is exemplified by Maria, whose boyfriend, Primo, was one of Bourgois's closest friends. Maria, who shared an apartment with her mother, became pregnant and was overjoyed. It was, writes Bourgois, precisely her terrible living conditions that made motherhood so attractive. It offered her, he says, a romantic escape from her difficult surroundings and cemented her love for Primo, who at the time faced the prospect of a four- to six-year jail sentence.

Having a child also symbolized economic independence. Mothers are eligible for desired public housing, which has an 18-year waiting list for others. Once their romantic ideals disappear, as they often do when people lack the financial resources to enact this ideal, children become a woman's main focus in life.

For children, however, life in El Barrio is especially destructive, given the poverty, the lack of day-care support, the deteriorating schools, the prevalence of drugs, and a life centered on the streets. Bourgois witnessed the metamorphosis of cute, bright 8-year-old girls into pregnant, crack-using 13-year-old "teenagers"; of bright, energetic 9-year-old boys into juvenile inmates accused of "assault with a deadly weapon." For many children, the crack house is the only space that is heated in the winter and air-conditioned in the summer. Children become socialized into the street culture and take it for granted.

In many ways, says Bourgois, East Harlem resembles the poverty of Third World countries, where infants and children die at a rate 10 to 100 times that of developed countries. But it is not a lack of calories and potable water that are killing them. Instead it is substance abuse, racism, a withdrawal of public services, and the exodus of jobs to other countries. The death and destruction of inner-city children, says Bourgois, occurs in adolescence rather than infancy. In the mid-1990s in East Harlem, 18- to 24-year-olds had a greater risk of violent death than soldiers on active duty in World War II.

Although crack dominates the economic, social, and psychological life of men, women, and children in El Barrio, it is not the root of the problem. As Bourgois puts it,

> Self-destructive addiction is merely the medium for desperate people to internalize their frustration, resistance, and powerlessness. In other words, we can safely ignore the drug hysteria that periodically sweeps through the United States. Instead we should focus our ethical concerns and political energies on the contradictions posed by the persistence of inner-city poverty in the midst of extraordinary opulence. In the same vein, we need to recognize and dismantle the class- and ethnic-based apartheids that riddle the U.S. landscape. (1995, 319)

The studies by Carol Stack in The Flats and by Bourgois in El Barrio provide convincing evidence that people do not passively accept their position at the bottom of a stratified society. Rather, they adapt to their circumstances as best they can. They have the same social and economic aspirations as those who have greater income and opportunity. Although Stack, like others, emphasizes this, she concludes,

> those living in poverty have little or no chance to escape from the economic situation into which they were born. Nor did they have the power to control the expansion or contraction of welfare benefits or of employment opportunities, both of which have enormous effect on their daily lives. In times of need, the only predictable resources that can be drawn upon are their own children and parents, and the fund of kin and friends obligated to them. (1974, 107)

QUESTION 7.5

Can a nonstratified community exist within a larger hierarchical society?

Many people who are convinced of the harmful effects of social stratification believe nevertheless that it is inevitable in a modern industrial state. Yet for thousands of years, some groups in stratified societies have attempted to create classless, egalitarian, utopian social settings.

Christianity began as a utopian dream of universal equality, and the idea of a real-life utopia emerged with the idea that man, under God, has the power to create an earthly paradise. Among the earliest expressions of this idea was Christian communalism, which led to the founding of monastic orders—isolated, virtually self-sufficient communities in which the work was collective and egalitarian. In the nineteenth century, industrialists such as Robert Owen attempted to build utopian factory communities, and Karl Marx's goal was to build a national utopian society. In the middle of the twentieth century, psychologist B. F. Skinner outlined a utopian society based on scientific technology in *Walden Two*, a controversial novel that inspired the community of Twin Oaks in Virginia. All these attempts to construct utopian societies are evidence of the long history of the search for an egalitarian social order.

Anthropologist Charles Erasmus examined hundreds of utopian communities in an effort to discover why most of these ultimately failed. He concluded that the main problem was motivating community members to work and contribute to the common good without the promise of individual material rewards, status, or prestige. Some groups, however, did succeed, the most notable being the Hutterites, a Protestant sect that originated in Moravia in the sixteenth century. Why did the Hutterites succeed while so many others failed? Is it possible to use their community as a model for modern egalitarian communities?

The Hutterites and the Colony of Heaven

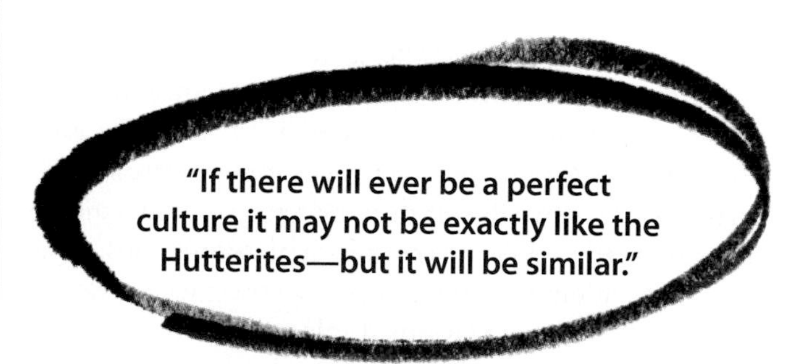

These words of a member of a Hutterite colony express the feeling that the group has succeeded in building utopian communities. In fact, the Hutterite colonies are among the most successful products of the Christian communal movement, which includes the Mennonites and the Amish.

The Hutterites originated during the Protestant Reformation. In 1528 they began to establish colonies throughout what are now Germany, Austria, and Russia. Their pacifism and refusal to perform military service brought them into conflict with European governments, and in 1872, to avoid conscription, they immigrated to South Dakota. During World War I, a confrontation over military conscription with U.S. authorities led them to move to Canada. But their successful agricultural techniques were valued in the United States during the Great Depression of the 1930s, and state governments persuaded them to return and establish new colonies in the U.S. By the early 1970s, there were more than 37,000 Hutterites distributed among 360 colonies in the United States and more than 9,000 in 246 colonies in Canada.

The goal of the Hutterites is to create a "colony of heaven." Drawing their inspiration from the Old and New Testaments, the Hutterites believe in the need for communal living and the proper observance of religious practice. They reject competition, violence, and war and believe that property is to be used but not possessed. They respect the need for government, but they do not believe they should involve themselves in it or hold public office. An elected board that includes the religious leaders and the community teacher govern a Hutterite colony, so authority is group-centered. It is a family-based, agricultural community in which everyone is expected to contribute to the work and to share equally in the bounty. Unlike the Amish, the Hutterites accept and use modern technology; they are acknowledged to be among the most successful agriculturists in North America.

The Hutterites are not totally egalitarian. Their society is ranked by age and gender. Members cannot participate in the decision-making process until they are married, and women are considered intellectually and physically inferior to men. However, they reject unequal distribution of wealth and competition among members for status, prestige, or personal possessions. The Hutterites minimize competition by renouncing private adornment and ostentatious displays of wealth and by practicing collective consumption. There is little difference in dress, and adornment is usually frowned upon. All the housing is plain and utilitarian. And, as in most Christian communes, they are careful to indoctrinate their children against competition. Children are taught to avoid seeking honors or placing themselves above others. They are taught never to envy others.

One way the Hutterites build commitment to the group is through frequent face-to-face interaction. Members eat together in a communal dining hall, work together, and meet frequently to discuss the affairs of the community. Almost every evening the entire community gathers for church service. Although the Hutterites have no formal means of punishing those who violate group rules, they do practice a form of ostracism called *den Frieden nehmen*, "taking away the individual's peace of mind." An ostracized man is not allowed to talk to other members, including his own wife. He may also be assigned a special room in which to sleep apart and may be required to eat alone.

Erasmus points out that social movements have difficulty maintaining long-range goals, especially as wealth accumulates. The Hutterites address this problem by dividing the communities, or branching, every 15 years. Each community saves a portion of its earnings to purchase additional land, build houses and barns, and accumulate the necessities for starting a new colony. When the new physical facilities are complete, members of the community draw lots to determine which families will relocate. Branching provides each Hutterite community with a tangible goal. "Wealthier" colonies that delay branching are often disrupted by internal quarrels and become examples of the danger of failing to branch on schedule. Branching also has a built-in renewal factor, as new communities reproduce the founding enthusiasm and ideals. If there is competition, it is between colonies rather than individuals.

A Hutterite community in North Dakota.

The Hutterites have resisted specialization, unlike other groups that have evolved into industries producing specific goods such as the Oneida community of New York, known for their silverware. The Hutterites have also resisted hiring outside labor. Instead, they exchange labor among colonies and use technology to further agricultural production.

In sum, the Hutterites, by a collective effort, have created within the larger society a community without poverty, without economic classes, with little or no crime, where each person, without the promise of material reward, contributes to the common good. There are, however, some negatives. The Hutterites are a Bible-based religious community that teaches male supremacy and severely limits individual freedom. The question is whether these negatives outweigh the benefits of creating nonstratified communities. There is also a question of whether cooperative communities such as the Hutterites can serve as a model for the poor in the larger society. Does the establishment of closed, collective communities offer a solution to the endemic poverty of those at the bottom level of modern society? Does the success of the Hutterites suggest that it is within our means to build societies without poverty?

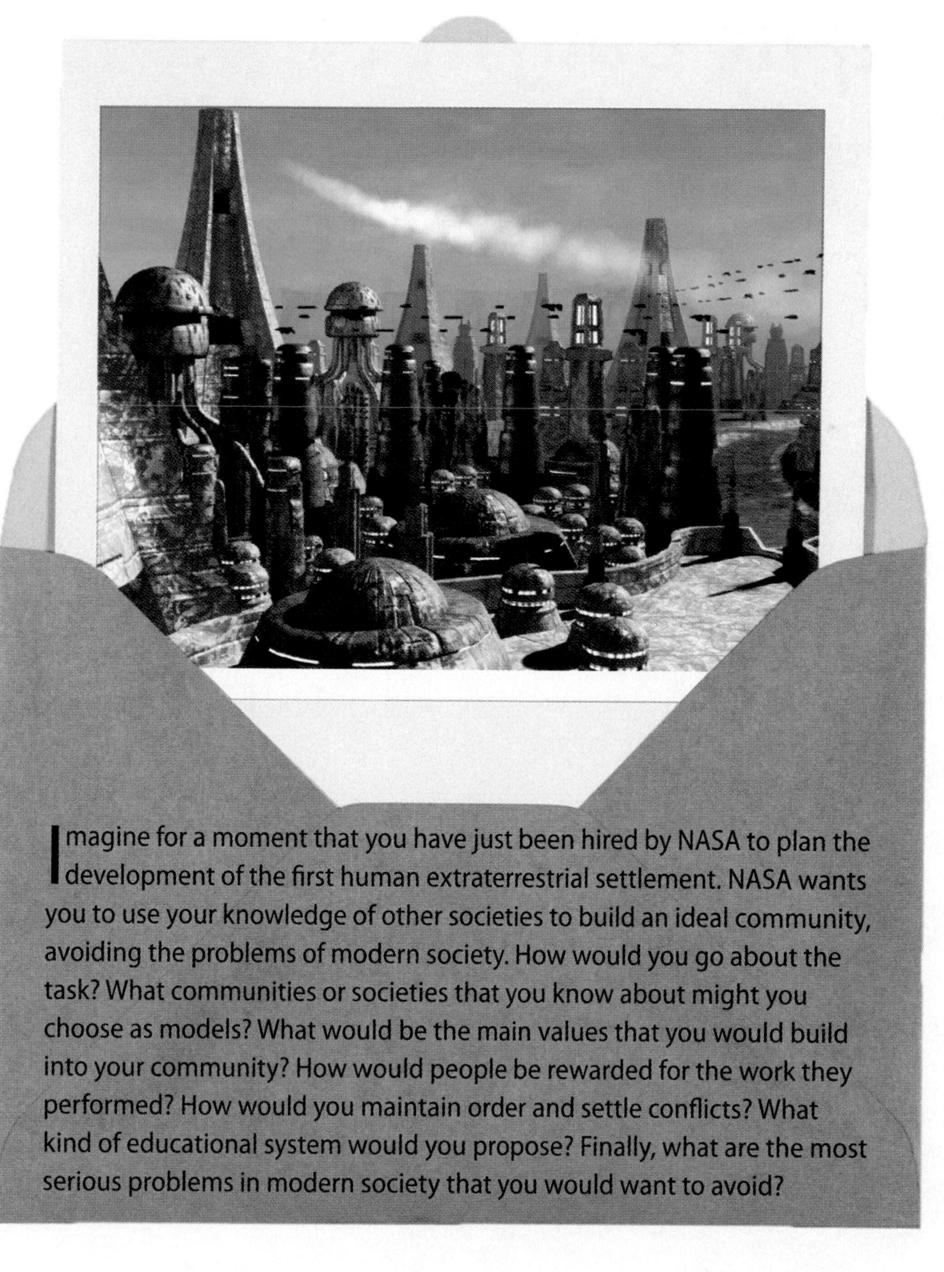

Imagine for a moment that you have just been hired by NASA to plan the development of the first human extraterrestrial settlement. NASA wants you to use your knowledge of other societies to build an ideal community, avoiding the problems of modern society. How would you go about the task? What communities or societies that you know about might you choose as models? What would be the main values that you would build into your community? How would people be rewarded for the work they performed? How would you maintain order and settle conflicts? What kind of educational system would you propose? Finally, what are the most serious problems in modern society that you would want to avoid?

Chapter 8

The Cultural Construction of Violent Conflict

What a cruel thing is war: to separate and destroy families and friends, and mar the purest joys and happiness God has granted us in this world; to fill our hearts with hatred instead of love for our neighbors, and to devastate the fair face of this beautiful world.

Robert E. Lee

Father, father, we don't need to escalate.
You see war is not the answer,
for only love can conquer hate.
You know we've got to find a way,
to bring some lovin' here today.

"What's Going On?"

Marvin Gaye

USS WEST VIRGINIA AND USS TENNESSEE ON FIRE DURING THE JAPANESE ATTACK ON PEARL HARBOR, 7TH DECEMBER, 1941 (PHOTO), AMERICAN PHOTOGRAPHER, (20TH CENTURY)/PRIVATE COLLECTION/PETER NEWARK MILITARY PICTURES/ THE BRIDGEMAN ART LIBRARY

* * *

QUESTIONS

In examining this problem, we will consider the following questions:

8.1 How do societies create a bias in favor of collective violence?

8.2 How do societies create a bias against violent conflict?

8.3 What are the economic, political, or social differences between peaceful and violent societies?

8.4 What are the effects of war on societies?

8.5 How is it possible to justify the creation of weapons of mass destruction?

INTRODUCTION

The Justification of Violent Conflict

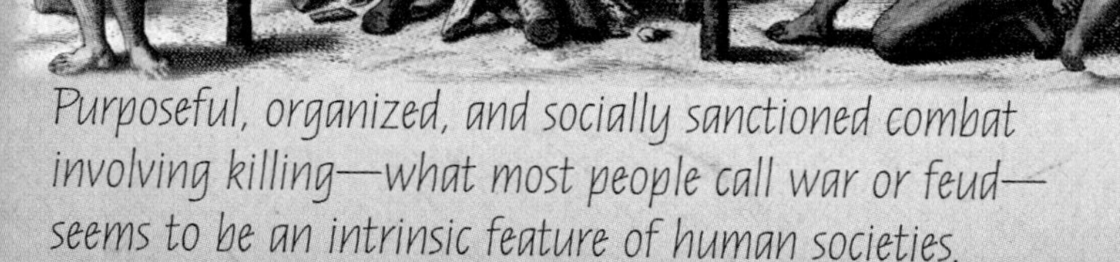

Purposeful, organized, and socially sanctioned combat involving killing—what most people call war or feud—seems to be an intrinsic feature of human societies.

When the Spaniards invaded the New World, they met fierce resistance from the Carib, a warlike people that inhabited the northeast portion of South America near what is now Venezuela and Guyana. The Carib were fierce people, cannibals, whom their neighbors called "sons of the tiger's teeth." To prepare for war, a Carib chief would hold a feast at which women urged warriors to be fierce and avenge their dead. The warriors danced to encourage the tiger spirit, Kaikusi-yuma, to take possession. When they went to war, it was Kaikusi-yuma who killed, not them. A warrior could rid himself of the possession only by tasting the blood and flesh of a dead enemy.

From our perspective, the acts of the Spanish and the Carib were horrific. The Spanish murdered and enslaved thousands of people; the Carib devoured human flesh. But both considered their actions to be moral and proper. The Spanish justified their killing as the work of God, and the Carib defined their killing as the result of spirit possession. Both constructed meanings for their acts that distanced them from the consequences of their violence. Although we may condemn these acts, we live in a world in which governments construct systems of meaning that allow them to plan and execute the use of weapons that

are infinitely more deadly than what the Carib and Spanish used.

Purposeful, organized, and socially sanctioned combat involving killing—what most people call **war** or **feud**—seems to be an intrinsic feature of human societies. In fact, it is difficult to find societies that do not sanction violence for one reason or another. Why is collective violence so universally sanctioned? Some suggest that human beings have an innate instinct toward aggression and that the roots of war lie in the biological mechanisms that animals and humans have in common. Others contend that collective violence is a cultural construction with roots

war see *feud*

feud purposeful, organized, and socially sanctioned combat involving killing

in the human mind. Although there may be some innate aggressive impulse, human beings choose how that impulse is expressed.

The fact that people construct systems of meaning to justify violent conflict and distance themselves from its consequences suggests that it has little to do with a natural aggressive impulse. Acts of collective violence are rationalized as purposeful, noble, or inevitable. The problem is to discover how societies construct meanings for violent conflict that mask its consequences and convince people that it is right and proper.

To evaluate this issue, the first question to be addressed is how societies create a bias in favor of collective violence. What kinds of meanings are constructed to encourage people to commit violence against others? Then, if there are societies without collective violence, how do they create a bias against it? If violent conflict is not simply natural but culturally constructed, it may be possible to learn from societies in which there is little, if any, violence. Are there significant social, economic, or political differences between violent and peaceful societies? Next, we examine the effects of violent conflict on societies to determine whether war serves some useful purpose. Because collective violence is sanctioned in American society, it is instructive to ask how we have created a bias toward conflict and constructed meanings that allow us to plan for and pursue the destruction of millions of people. Finally, we examine how an anthropological perspective can better help us understand the rhetoric of war and violence.

Horses, Rank, and Warfare among the Kiowa

One way societies create a bias toward collective violence is to reward it. Among the Native Americans of the western plains, horses symbolized wealth and importance. Horses were not indigenous to North America; they were brought to the continent by the Spanish in the 1500s. Native American groups acquired horses either by trading with the Spanish or raiding other tribes. Among many groups, including the Kiowa, these raids became a way for a man to rise in status.

Among the Kiowa, the rank of a man was determined in two ways: by the number of horses he owned and the honors he earned in battle. Kiowa society was divided into four ranks. At the top were *ongop*, men who were generous, owned considerable wealth, and,

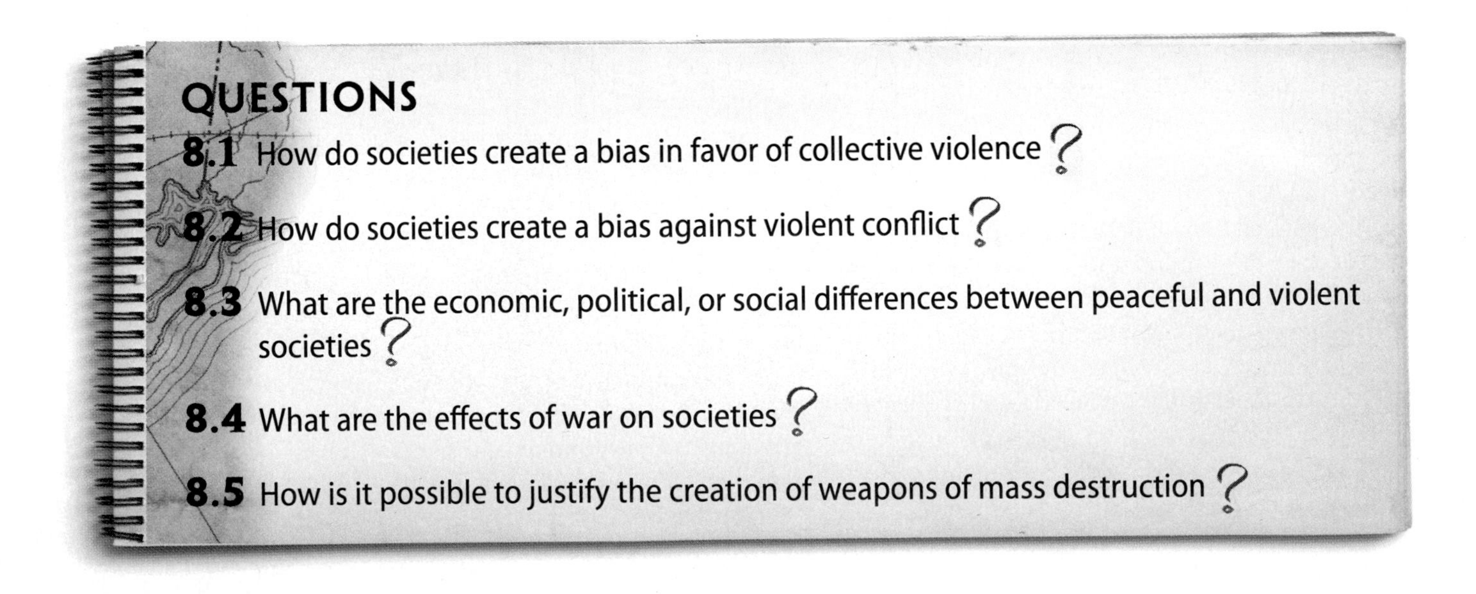

most importantly, had distinguished themselves in war. In the second rank were *ondeigupa*, men who had property, especially horses, and were generous but had not yet distinguished themselves in war. The lower ranks of Kiowa society were occupied by *keen* or *dupom*, people who were poor, propertyless, or helpless.

To rise in status, a young Kiowa male needed to acquire horses. Often he would begin his climb through the ranks of Kiowa society by borrowing a horse from a kinsperson to go on a raid, hoping to repay the loan with another horse he captured. With a horse of his own, he could participate in more raids, gradually obtaining enough horses to rise to the rank of *ondeigupa*. Several years of raiding might bring him twenty or thirty horses, at which point people would begin speaking of him with respect.

To rise to the top rank of *ongop*, however, required the accumulation of war honors. The Kiowa had a very elaborate system of battle honors divided into three groups of brave deeds, with group I being the most honored (see Table 8.1). The number of heroic exploits that a man accomplished would be reflected by the number of feathers in his headdress. Anthropologist Bernard Mishkin estimates that approximately 10 percent of the men would rise to the top rank of Kiowa society by obtaining a significant number of horses and accumulating sufficient battle honors.

TABLE 8.1

KIOWA RANKING AND HONORS

Group I	Group II	Group III
1. Counting first coup	1. Killing an enemy	1. Dismounting, turning horse loose, and fighting on foot
2. Charging an enemy while the party is in retreat, thus covering the retreat	2. Counting second coup	2. Counting third and fourth coup
3. Rescuing a comrade while the party is retreating before the enemy	3. Receiving a wound in hand-to-hand combat	3. Serving as raid leader
4. Charging the leading man of the enemy alone before the parties have met		4. Success in stealing horses
		5. Efficiency in war camp life

Source: Information from Bernard Mishkin, *Rank and Warfare Among the Plains Indians* (Seattle: University of Washington Press, 1940).

Good Hosts among the Yanomamö

Another way societies create a bias for collective violence is to make it a way of protecting valuable resources. The Yanomamö of Venezuela live in villages of 40 to 250 people and practice slash-and-burn (swidden) agriculture. Intervillage warfare is endemic to the Yanomamö. Anthropologist Napoleon Chagnon, who has worked with the Yanomamö since 1964, reports that one village of 200 people was attacked 25 times during a period of 15 months. He estimates that some 20 to 25 percent of all male deaths are the result of warfare.

Yanomamö men believe that, to protect their resources they must demonstrate their ferocity through raids. They may attack other villages to avenge the death of a family member, or to capture women and children, which are the most prized resources in their society. The threat of raids often forces villages to move frequently, and sometimes take refuge in their allies' villages. This practice is risky, however, since host villages generally expect sexual access to the wives of their guests or expect unmarried female guests to marry men of their village. These expectations often lead to open hostilities between hosts and guests.

Expressions of ferocity may be directed between members of the same village as well. Men often demonstrate their ferocity to others by beating their wives. A man who accuses another of cowardice or making excessive demands for

goods or women may challenge his opponent to a chest-pounding duel, in which they take turns hitting each other in the chest as hard as they can. The duel generally ends when one of the contestants is too injured to continue. Fights with clubs are another form of settling disputes between men; these fights generally result in free-for-alls that can be deadly.

In this environment, in which each man strives to acquire females from others, it is necessary to adopt an antagonistic stance toward others, encouraging the development of what the Yanomamö call *waiteri* (ferocity). The *waiteri* complex, as Chagnon calls it, is evidenced in ways other than direct conflict. The Yanomamö express it in their origin myth, which tells how the original people were created from the blood of the moon, which had been shot with an arrow by beings who believed that it had devoured their children's souls. The first Yanomamö, born of the blood of the moon, were exceptionally fierce and waged constant war on one another.

The Yanomamö also socialize male children to be hostile. Boys are teased to strike tormentors and bully girls. Chagnon witnessed one gathering in which all the boys between the ages of 8 and 15 were assembled and forced them to fight one another. At first, the boys were reluctant and tried to run away, but their parents dragged them back and insisted that they hit each other. As the fight progressed, fear became rage, and they ended up pounding each other while they screamed and rolled in the dirt, drawing cheers and admiration from their fathers.

Defending Honor in Kohistan

Another way societies create a bias toward collective violence is by making it part of a code of honor. The Kohistani, villagers in the mountains of northwest Pakistan, follow a code that demands vengeance against any threat to a man's honor. The men of Thull view each other with guarded suspicion, and relationships of friendship can easily slip into *dushmani*, blood feud. They believe that if another person wrongs them, they must retaliate, with the act of revenge not exceeding the original wrong. However, any unwarranted behavior toward a man's daughter, wife, or unmarried sister requires deadly retaliation. Even staring at these female relatives requires death for the offender.

Anthropologist Lincoln Keiser, who worked in the Kohistani village of Thull, relates what happened to a man named Omar. According to Keiser's friend, Omar's brother, Omar had been killed by a neighbor while he was bringing some food, since he had heard that the neighbor's family had none. "But why," asked Keiser, "would a man kill his neighbor who only tried to help him?" "Who knows?" the friend replied. "But I will take vengeance." Keiser says he had no doubt he would. Looking into the incident further, Keiser heard gossip that Omar was killed because he really went to the house to stare at his neighbor's wife and brought the food only as a ruse. Keiser himself was ultimately forced to leave Thull because of a rumor that in taking a photograph of a goatherd he was actually trying to photograph the herd owner's wife.

The Kohistan are mostly farmers and herders. As Muslims, they have constructed a system of meaning in which vengeance is a religious act. Central to their beliefs is the idea of *ghrairat*, a man's personal worth, integrity, or character. *Ghrairat* is given to men by God and can be lost if they fail to protect it. In this perspective, women's behavior is also a matter of *ghrairat* because men must control their women. Any act of a woman—or a person toward a woman—that threatens to bring shame is a direct attack on the man's *ghrairat* and must be avenged. Women must never walk outside their father's or husband's house without an escort, must never speak to an unrelated man, and must always comport themselves with modesty, hiding and minimizing their sexuality. Men who allow their women freedom are *baghrairatman*, "men without personal integrity."

The Yanomamö

Defending *ghrairat*, however, is more than simply the concern of an individual. Because of the webs of kinship, friendship, and political ties, it often involves whole groups within the community in violence against one another. Men in Thull constantly ally themselves with others in kinship or political groups. A man seeking vengeance for a wrong may enlist the help of others with whom he is allied. More important, an act of vengeance may be taken not only against the man who committed the wrong but also against a kinsperson or a member of his faction. Because of the threat of violence, the men of Thull habitually walk around armed, design their houses for defense against gunfire, and spend most of their money on rifles and arms. A prized possession is a Russian-made AK-47 assault rifle.

Two young men, Mamad Said and Amin, were herding goats together. One day, in response to a friendly shove, Mamad Said playfully swung a stick at Amin, hitting him in the face and drawing blood. Amin went to his uncle, Shah Hajji Khan, who got revenge by beating Mamad Said with some men. Friends and relatives of Mamad Said attacked Shah Hajji Khan's group in revenge and caused great injuries; Shah Hajji Khan's son almost died. Now, Shah Hajji Khan needed to avenge two injuries: the original blow to Amin and the beating inflicted upon his friends and son. Some time later, Shah Hajji Khan hatched a plot to ambush Mamad Said, who escaped by hiding in an irrigation ditch. Six months later Mamad Said died from tuberculosis, which might be expected to bring an end to the feud. But Mamad Said's brother, Qui Afsal, claimed that he had died from sickness contracted while hiding from Shah Hajji Khan. In revenge he killed Shah Hajji, Khan's friend's son. Qui Afsal was later shot in revenge but survived.

Constructing Religious Justifications for Violence

Another way to justify violence is to frame it as a cosmic struggle between good and evil. Most modern religions contain sacred texts with accounts of such confrontations. The book of Revelation of the New Testament, describing the battle between the forces of Satan and the forces of God, is one of the best (and most violent) metaphors of war and redemption in Western literature. As Elaine Pagels notes, the characterization of one's enemies as "satanic," and oneself as God's people, has long been a formula for justifying hatred and mass slaughter.

Virtually all major religions have their violent militants. The Army of God is a militant group of Protestant fundamentalism dedicated to, among other things, halting abortions. Its doctrine is outlined in an underground manual, *Army of God*, whose authorship is attributed to Reverend Michael Bray. Bray, a staunch opponent of abortion, defends the killing of abortion providers, and in 1985, was convicted of setting fire to seven abortion clinics. According to Bray, Americans live in a state of "hidden warfare," comparable to that of Nazi Germany, and a dramatic event, such as an economic collapse, would reveal the demonic role of the government. At that point believers would take up a revolutionary struggle and establish a new moral order based on biblical law. Until then, he and others must have the moral courage to resist, particularly by defending unborn babies and killing those who threaten them. For members of the group, killing abortion providers is "justifiable homicide."

Mark Juergensmeyer asks under what conditions people are likely to use religious justifications for violence. He suggests that by locating a struggle on a cosmic scale and invoking legendary battles between good and evil, aggressors elevate its importance beyond local concerns. Michael Bray defended the need to kill and, if necessary, die over the issue of abortion by pointing to a great cosmic war. This rhetoric has even entered the United States political mainstream with terms such as "axis of evil." There is real power, suggests

Juergensmeyer, in elevating a political conflict to a cosmic war. To live in a state of war, he says,

> is to live in a world in which individuals know who they are, why they have suffered, by whose hand they have been humiliated, and at what expense they have persevered. The concept of war provides cosmology, history, and eschatology and offers the reins of political control. Perhaps most important, it holds out the hope of victory and the means to achieve it. In the images of cosmic war this victorious triumph is a grand moment of social and personal transformation, transcending all worldly limitations. One does not easily abandon such expectations. To be without such images of war is almost to be without hope itself. (2000, 154–55)

QUESTION 8.2

How do societies create a bias against violent conflict?

Anthropologist Thomas Gregor suggests that because war is so widespread in human societies, the task of the social scientist is not so much to explain war as to explain peace. In his view, peaceful societies, those not involved in internal collective violence and in which there is little interpersonal violence, are difficult to find. Societies that have been characterized as relatively peaceful include the Ju/wasi, the Semai of Malaysia, and the Inuit.

There is real power in elevating a political conflict to a cosmic war.

THE ARCHANGEL MICHAEL DEFEATING SATAN (OIL ON CANVAS), RENI, GUIDO (1575–1642)/PRIVATE COLLECTION/THE BRIDGEMAN ART LIBRARY / © ELIZA SNOW/ISTOCKPHOTO.COM

Characteristics of Peaceful Societies

Peaceful societies avoid conflict over resources by emphasizing sharing and cooperation. It is expected that everyone in the group has a legitimate claim to what the group possesses. The Semai of West Malaysia are known for their nonaggressiveness and avoidance of physical conflict. Understanding Semai nonviolence, says anthropologist Clayton Robarchek, requires understanding the notion of *pehunan*, a state of being in which a person is unsatisfied in regard to some need such as food or sex. The Semai believe that denying a person in need intensifies the danger to both the individual and the group. For that reason, the group is obligated to help. The idea of *pehunan* encompasses a depiction of the community as nurturant caregivers. The Semai believe that it is the obligation of all members of the community to help others. Thus, Semai values stress affiliation, mutual aid, and the belief that violence is not a viable option for settling disputes.

Another way people in peaceful societies create a bias against violence is by condemning those who boast or make claims that can be interpreted as a challenge to others. Among the Ju/wasi, no one is praised for gathering food or making a kill, and people go out of their way to minimize their accomplishments. Those who make boastful claims are ridiculed. Anthropologist Richard Lee painfully learned this lesson himself when, to show his appreciation for the help the Ju/wasi had given him, he brought an ox to be slaughtered and distributed at a feast. The Ju/wasi, much to Lee's chagrin, ridiculed the ox, claiming it was thin and unappetizing. Lee later realized that they were letting him know that he wasn't as important as the gift made him think he was.

People in peaceful societies also avoid telling others what to do and carefully control their emotions in order to maintain goodwill. The Inuit fear people who do not demonstrate goodwill by smiling or laughing because someone who is unhappy may be hostile. The Inuit believe that strong thoughts can kill, so they go to great pains to satisfy other people so that resentment does not build up. Anthropologist Jean Briggs describes the Inuit as people who emphasize kindness and concern and never, under any circumstances, demonstrate anger. So great is their fear of causing conflict that they make requests indirectly to avoid being refused or to avoid embarrassing someone by making them refuse a request. So great is the crime of losing one's temper that someone who does so may be ostracized from the group.

Peaceful societies also minimize violence and conflict through ceremony. The Ju/wasi believe that everyone has *n/um*, a substance in the pit of the stomach that can keep people healthy and cure the sick. Most importantly, *n/um* can be transferred from someone who is acting as a healer to others through the trance dance. The idea behind the dance is for a person to "heat up" *n/um* by dancing. As the person dances, the *n/um* in the stomach is vaporized and travels up the spinal cord into the brain, which causes the dancer to go into a trance. The dancer then goes from person to person laying on hands and transferring healing power. Anyone can be a healer among the Ju/wasi; in a lifetime, each person is likely to serve as a healer at one time or another.

Trance dances are most frequent when large numbers of people come together (from about once a month in small groups to four times a week in large camps) and during certain occasions such as the arrival of visitors to a camp, the presence of meat, or sickness. The gathering of large numbers of people, the presence of meat, and the arrival of new people are all occasions that in one way or another create the potential for interpersonal conflict. The frequency of trance dances during such times may indicate that they serve to heal social conflict in addition to individual maladies. By bringing people together in the ceremony, through the sharing of *n/um* and the ritual recognition of common threats, the trance

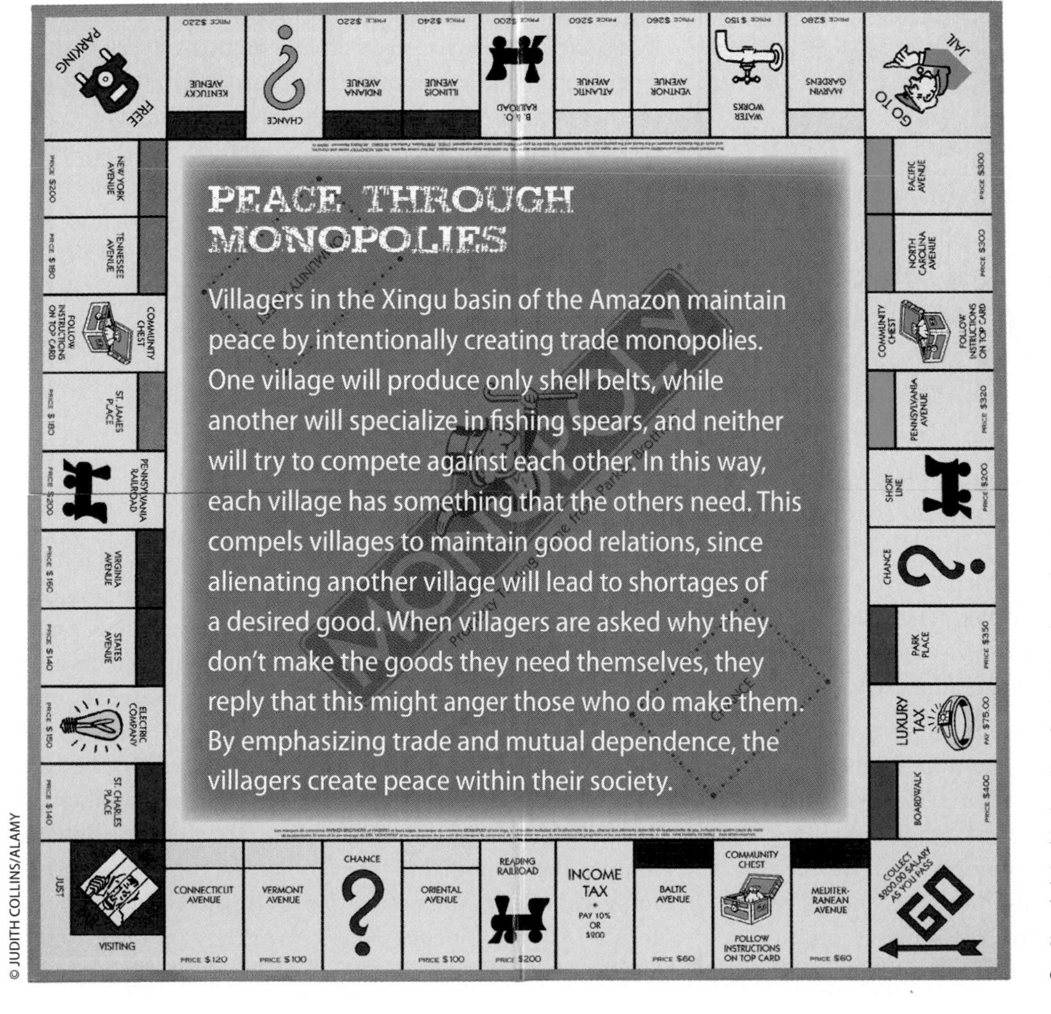

PEACE THROUGH MONOPOLIES

Villagers in the Xingu basin of the Amazon maintain peace by intentionally creating trade monopolies. One village will produce only shell belts, while another will specialize in fishing spears, and neither will try to compete against each other. In this way, each village has something that the others need. This compels villages to maintain good relations, since alienating another village will lead to shortages of a desired good. When villagers are asked why they don't make the goods they need themselves, they reply that this might anger those who do make them. By emphasizing trade and mutual dependence, the villagers create peace within their society.

© JUDITH COLLINS/ALAMY

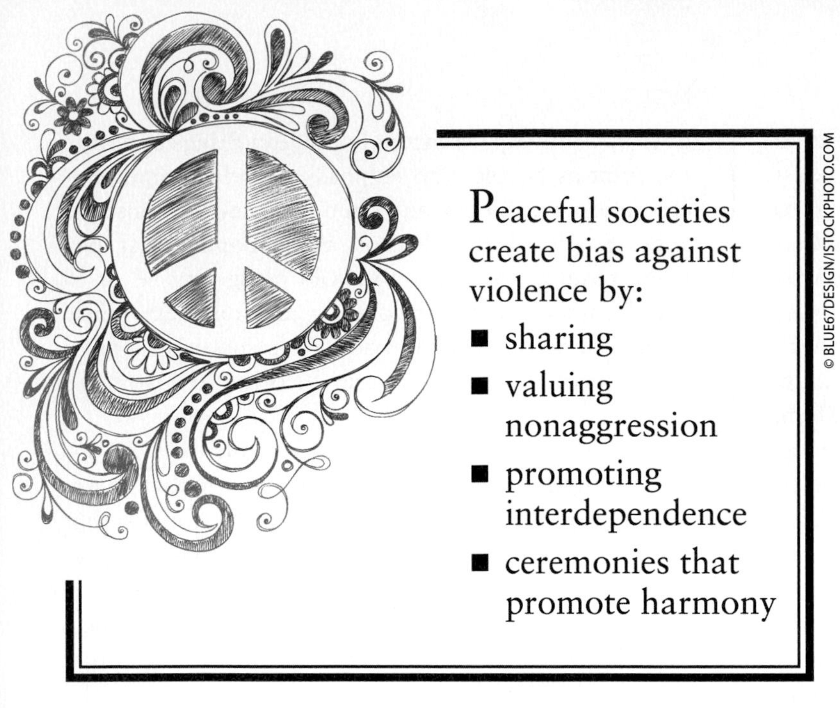

dance unites people and serves to symbolize the relationship between group harmony and individual well-being.

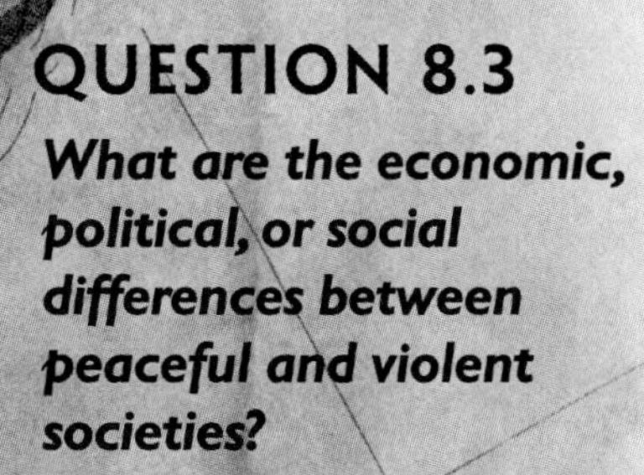

QUESTION 8.3

What are the economic, political, or social differences between peaceful and violent societies?

Thomas Hobbes, a seventeenth-century philosopher, proposed that human beings in their natural state, without government or laws, are driven by greed. Without some common power to keep them in awe they live in a state of war, every person against every other person. Here is one of the more famous passages from *Leviathan*, in which Hobbes describes his vision of life before civilization:

> Whatsoever therefore is consequent to a time of warre, where every man is enemy to every man; the same is consequent to a time, wherein men live without other security, than what their own strength and their own invention shall furnish them withall. In such a condition there is no place for Industry; because the fruit thereof is uncertain; and consequently no Culture of the Earth [agriculture]; no navigation, nor use of the commodities that may be imported by sea; no commodious Building; no Instruments of moving, and removing such things as require much force; no Knowledge of the face of the Earth; no account of Time; no Arts; no Letters; no Society; and which is worst of all, continual feare, and danger of violent death; And the life of man, solitary, poore, nasty, brutish, and short. (Hobbes 1651/1881, 94–96)

Hobbes saw human beings as having a natural inclination for violence, which could only be controlled by some centralized authority. However, as anthropologists have discovered, societies with little formal government, such as the Ju/wasi, Inuit, and Semai, are among the most peaceful in the world (see Question 8.2). These peaceful societies are small in scale, relatively isolated, and lack formal mechanisms for resolving conflict. Because there is little that people in these societies can do once violence begins, they go to great lengths to avoid it.

Had Hobbes known the Yanomamö, however, he might have found verification for his vision of a stateless society, "where every man is enemy to every man." Their social and economic life closely resembles that of the Semai, and they live in virtually the same environment and are neighbors of the peaceful Xinguano. But Yanomamö society creates attitudes favoring collective violence in order to protect its women and children (see Question 8.1). In this case, the lack of a centralized authority results in unrestrained violence rather than the avoidance of conflict.

The Need to Protect Resources and Honor

In societies without centralized control and a bias for collective violence, such as those of the Yanomamö and the Kohistani, individuals must protect their own resources through force. Because the Yanomamö do not control intravillage conflict, men are constantly seeking to seduce others' wives. Consequently, the men, individually or in groups, must build a reputation for fierceness in order to protect themselves and their families.

The conditions that give rise to violent conflict among the Yanomamö are similar to those that promote violence among street gangs in the United States. In the 1960s, Lincoln Keiser worked with the Vice Lords, a Chicago street gang. From his research, he concluded that boys joined gangs because they could not protect themselves from shakedowns or safeguard their interests in girls on their own. Whereas the Yanomamö encouraged *waiteri*—fierceness—the Vice Lords valued heart—a willingness to follow any suggestion regardless of personal risk. Whereas a Yanomamö demonstrated fierceness in chest-pounding duels and raids against enemy villages, the Vice Lords confirmed heart in fights against other gangs. Street gangs even formed alliances with each other against other gangs, as Yanomamö villages do with each other. The similarities in the dynamics and values of violent conflict among the Yanomamö and among street gangs in the United States illustrate how under certain conditions individuals form groups to protect themselves against other groups. To discourage attacks from others in the absence of protection from other agencies, these groups cultivate a reputation for violence.

The social and political conditions that characterize the societies of the Vice Lords and the Yanomamö are such that in each group, individuals must mobilize and use force to protect or acquire desired resources. In neither case is there any effective centralized authority to guarantee the safety of resources or stop violence once it begins. There is a centralized force in Chicago—the police—but they rarely intervene in gang violence, because they are unwilling or do not have the resources to do so or because local residents are afraid or reluctant to report violence.

The idea that violence may erupt because of a lack of centralized control to protect valued resources is evident also among the Kohistani in Thull. Good land is scarce, and ownership of land is often questioned because there is no system of land recording registration. Land is usually acquired by inheritance, but there is little to stop anyone from saying that one of their ancestors was wrongfully denied ownership of a particular plot in the past. Whether such a claim is won or lost may depend on which of the claimants has greater firepower. In Thull also, an ideology that encourages collective violence may be attributable to a need to protect resources in the absence of any effective centralized authority.

. . . an ideology that encourages collective violence may be attributable to a need to protect resources in the absence of any effective centralized authority.

Creating the Conditions for Violence

Napoleon Chagnon characterized Yanomamö warfare as a "truly primitive cultural adaptation . . . . before it was altered or destroyed by our culture." It was, he said, the normal state of affairs before it was suppressed by colonial governments. However, there is considerable evidence that Yanomamö warfare and aggression were less a product of their "primitive" nature than a consequence of Western contact.

Brian Ferguson maintains that the period of Chagnon's fieldwork (1964–1972) was one of the most turbulent periods in Yanomamö history. Violence and aggression, says Ferguson, were a product of three major changes: (1) the presence of new outpost settlements of government agents, missionaries, and researchers; (2) competition for Western manufactured goods, particularly steel cutting tools, and (3) a breakdown of social relations brought about by epidemics and depletion of food resources.

The Yanomamö, Ferguson points out, had been in contact with outsiders for centuries. Europeans captured the Yanomamö for slaves from the mid-seventeenth century until around 1850. In the late nineteenth century, the rubber boom in the Amazon brought the Yanomamö into increased contact and conflict with other indigenous groups. After the rubber boom collapsed in the 1920s, the area in which the Yanomamö lived was relatively peaceful until the 1950s and 1960s, when influenza and measles epidemics swept the area, leaving only one-quarter of the children with both parents. But even more disruptive was the presence of new Western outposts.

The new outposts made manufactured items, such as steel knives and shotguns, available to the Yanomamö. The Yanomamö could obtain these items in various ways. They could relocate their villages near the outposts, they could send trading parties on long voyages, or they could raid other groups. The greatest advantage went to what Ferguson called "anchor villages," those that relocated near outposts. The result was a hierarchy of settlements, ranging from anchor villages whose members were able to monopolize the new desired goods to more isolated settlements whose members had fewer and lower-quality goods.

Yanomamö in anchor settlements traded Western items to distant groups for local handicrafts such as cotton hammocks, spear points, or manioc flour. But trading parties were also the targets of raids. To protect themselves and their monopoly, Yanomamö groups found it advantageous to cultivate reputations for violence and aggression.

The Yanomamös aggression may be due to their contact with Westerners and access to Western goods.

In addition to access to desired goods, proximity to Western outposts incited violence in other ways. Once people relocated their village near an outpost settlement, they were reluctant to move. One way that small-scale, mobile societies such as the Yanomamö avoided conflict was by moving villages away from enemies when conflict was threatened. But because moving would mean giving up exclusive access to Western goods, members of anchor villages were reluctant to move and hence needed to find other ways to protect themselves. In addition, more permanent settlements quickly depleted game resources, resources that had been used in reciprocal exchanges with other people and groups. Thus, sharing patterns, which we noted in Question 8.2 are crucial for maintaining peaceful relations, began to break down, leading to more conflict.

In addition to promoting aggression, access to Western goods also helps explain the attitudes of Yanomamö men to women. Traditionally the Yanomamö practiced brideservice; a groom was obligated to work for his bride's family for one to four years. But families of grooms in anchor villages were able to substitute Western goods for brideservice. This led many women to move to villages with greater access to Western goods. Combined with the Yanomamö practice of female infanticide and polygamy, the result was a shortage of and greater competition for females and more frequent raiding of other villages for women. In sum, many of the patterns of Yanomamö warfare, violence, and aggression cannot be understood without knowledge of their contact with Western society. Ferguson concludes:

> If villages were not anchored to outposts but were able to move freely, if long-established marital alliances were not disturbed by massive mortality, if communal sharing of meat were still the norm, and, above all, if necessary technology were widely and equally available, my theoretical expectation is that there would be little collective violence among the Yanomami. (1992, 225)

Sexism and Violent Conflict

Another difference between peaceful and violent societies has to do with gender roles. Among the Ju/wasi, Xinguano, and Semai, men and women are relatively equal, and there is little institutionalized violence against women. In contrast, the Yanomamö and Kohistani (and the Vice Lords) are characterized by male dominance; they all sanction violence against women. Several reasons have been given to support this link. First, it is men that make war. Although there are societies in which women engage in armed combat, such instances are the exception rather than the rule. Second, there is a strong link between patriarchy and violent conflict. After examining more than 1,000 societies, William Tulio Divale and Marvin Harris concluded that the intensity of collective violence is significantly higher in societies characterized by a strong male bias. Finally, there is evidence that societies characterized by sexual violence against women tend to be more warlike and prone to collective violence. Peggy Sanday's study of 95 societies in which there was evidence of frequency of rape supports this conclusion. The question is, then, does a sexist ideology promote violent conflict, or does the incidence of violent conflict promote sexism?

Those who claim that sexism promotes violent conflict make that connection in various ways. Betty Reardon and Leslie Cagan suggest that societies that relegate women to an inferior position explicitly or implicitly sanction violence against women. Moreover, violence toward women serves as what they call a "primal" paradigm for violent warfare against other peoples.

According to Peggy Sanday and others, both sexism and violent conflict have their roots in competition over scarce resources. She says women are generally associated with fertility and growth, whereas men are associated with aggression and destruction. During periods in which resources are not scarce, both males and females are valued equally. When there is a shortage of resources, however, males become of greater value, females become objects to be controlled, and sexual violence becomes one way that men demonstrate their dominance.

In sum, factors such as a lack of centralized control, competition over scarce resources, private property, and sexism may lead societies to construct an ideological bias toward violence. Examining the effects of violent conflict to see if some of them could be beneficial may provide further insights into the factors that promote violent conflict.

QUESTION 8.4

What are the effects of war on societies?

Are there any benefits to violent conflict? Biologists studying animal populations suggest that predators help the species they prey on by limiting population growth and eliminating the weak from the breeding population. Some anthropologists suggest that war may play a similar function for the human species by limiting population and influencing the biological composition of the human species through natural selection.

The Impact of War on Population

In his book *The Statistics of Deadly Quarrels*, mathematician Lewis F. Richardson examines the effects that violent conflicts had on world population between 1821 and 1945. During that period, there were 282 wars that had battle fatalities ranging from 300 to 20 million people. To this figure, Richardson adds an estimate of the number of murders committed during this period and of the number of deaths caused by disease due to war conditions, and concludes that deadly quarrels account for about 10 percent of all deaths that occurred between 1821 and 1945.

This certainly appears to reflect the great toll of war. According to Frank Livingstone, however, war seems to have little appreciable effect on population growth. During World War II, about 9 percent of the Russian population and 5 percent of the German population died. Yet this had almost no effect on their rates of population growth, since both countries had recovered within a decade to the level at which they would have been had there been no war.

CASE: How to Win Hearts and Minds

U.S. ARMY PHOTO BY STAFF SGT. MICHAEL L. CASTEEL/DEPARTMENT OF DEFENSE/ DEFENSEIMAGERY.MIL

In 2005, Montgomery McFate published an article in the Military Review arguing that there is a "culture gap" in our understanding of the conflict in Iraq . . .

. . . caused by "the almost total absence of anthropology within the national-security establishment." She argued that successful counter insurgency requires a total understanding of local culture. To be victorious, the U.S. must understand traditional authority structure and the competing interests of different groups such as the Shia, Sunni, and Kurds. In a second article, co-written with Andrea Jackson, McFate outlined a proposal to establish an "Office for Operational Cultural Knowledge," which would train teams to provide battlefield commanders with knowledge of local culture, or as it was being called, the "human terrain."

The emphasis on cultural knowledge was echoed in the military sphere. According to retired Major General Robert H. Scales, Jr., these new conflicts require not technological superiority but "an exceptional ability to understand people, their culture, and their motivation."

One outcome of this interest in cultural knowledge is the development of Human Terrain Systems (HTS). The centerpiece of the program is Human Terrain Teams (HTTs), which consist of five people: an army officer serving as team leader, a cultural analyst, a regional studies analyst, a Human Terrain (HT) research manager, and an HT analyst. Each team would study local culture, interview natives, and provide valuable information to the battalion commander.

Anthropologists who joined the HTS project explain their service as an attempt to do something meaningful. Marcus Griffin wrote "I have an obligation to use my skills to learn about people and to share what I learn." Working as a member of an HTT in Iraq, Griffin sees his job as finding out what Iraqis need and helping them fulfill those needs.

Not everyone, however, shares this positive assessment of HTS. The American Anthropological Association issued a formal statement in 2007 condemning the project, arguing that it will lead anthropologists to violate ethical standards, and that it poses a danger to both the anthropologist and the people they study. Another notable critic, Roberto Gonzales, points out a number of dangers to HTS. First, is it possible for informants to give consent as to whether or not they wish to participate? Second, what type of information will be gathered by anthropologists and how will it be used? Third, how well will informants be protected from retaliation from hostile groups or political rivals?

What bothers so many critics of HTS is that regardless of the efforts of the military and others to put a humanitarian face on the contributions of social scientists, it is clear that the information gathered by HTTs will be used for military purposes. HTS advocates want to make whatever information is gathered available to other agencies and to the governments of Iraq and Afghanistan, to "enable them to more fully exercise sovereignty over their country" (Gonzalez 2009, 74). This reminds many anthropologists of the disastrous CORDS program, implemented during the Vietnam War. Like HTS, CORDS was designed to gather cultural knowledge in order to win "hearts and minds." Using information from social scientists, military personnel exploited Vietnamese superstitions and religious beliefs to frighten and terrorize civilians. When CORDS data was given to the South Vietnamese government, it was used to target political opponents and dissidents. What sort of precaution is being taken to ensure that the Iraqi and Afghan government does not use HTT information to target political rivals, or create a blacklist for personal vendettas?

© JOHN NAIRNE/ SHUTTERSTOCK

© STOCKCAM/ ISTOCKPHOTO.COM

The use of social scientists for HTTs in Iraq and Afghanistan raises the larger issue of the responsibility of anthropologists and other social scientists to be aware of how their research and data may be used. The Pentagon, for example, is developing computer programs using data, which includes those collected by social scientists, to help users identify dangerous neighborhoods in Baghdad or Kabul. They would predict which neighborhoods are at risk for riots, gun violence, or bombings, often providing the names of possible participants along with their addresses, fingerprints, ID photos, and the names of relatives, friends, and associates.

U.S. ARMY PHOTO BY SPC. BENJAMIN BOREN/DEPARTMENT OF DEFENSE/DEFENSEIMAGERY.MIL

Perhaps more ominous is the number of grants that have been awarded to social scientists and engineers by the military to forecast human behavior. The Department of Defense has a budget item dated February 2007 called the Human Social and Culture Behavior Modeling (HSCB) project scheduled for development between 2008 and 2013. Much of this work will be contracted out to private corporations eager to secure lucrative government contracts. One corporation, Aptima, in conjunction with Carnegie Mellon University, developed "Social Network Analysis" (SNA) software. SNA has been used by the U.S. military "to predict a state's potential for instability of civil unrest in terms of nine key factors" ranging from "lack of essential services" to "corruption level" to "tension."

One danger, of course, is that the philosophy of HTS, and the development of elaborate surveillance technologies using vast quantities of information now available on citizens, will move from military applications in places such as Iraq and Afghanistan, to domestic uses that seriously undermine democratic freedoms. Gonzalez concludes his critique of HTS as follows:

What comes across from the accounts of many social scientists supporting counterinsurgency initiatives in Iraq and Afghanistan is a fundamental acceptance of modern warfare in general and the U.S.-led occupations in particular. Furthermore, they generally accept the false notion that counterinsurgency—the "graduate level of war" to quote one military enthusiast—is more antiseptic, more humane, less damaging than conventional warfare. As technicians of power, some adhere to Machiavellian principles: do not question the prince or his war, but instead use the most efficient means to help him achieve victory. War's inevitability is taken for granted. Basic assumptions are left unquestioned. Missing from these accounts is the question of whether war is appropriate at all today. (Gonzalez 2009, 123–124)

Livingstone points out that violent conflict may have had a much greater impact on population of small-scale societies. Among the Murngin of Australia, about 28 percent of male deaths were due to war; among the Enga and the Dani of New Guinea, about 25 percent. Livingstone notes, however, that it is hard to see where any of this has affected the biology of the species. The killing seems to have been more or less random. Moreover, because males are the most frequent victims and because the incidence of polygyny (marriage to multiple wives) increases in societies that suffer losses, the number of children born remains more or less constant.

William Tulio Divale and Marvin Harris address the problems posed by Livingstone by proposing that violent conflict does regulate population growth by encouraging the killing of infant girls. The incidence of violent conflict, they reason, is associated with a preference for male children along with female infanticide or the neglect of female infants. This is evidenced in either direct reports of female infanticide or the skewed sex ratios of children under the age of 14 in societies characterized by violent conflict.

If war or violent conflict is frequent in a society, Divale and Harris reason, the group that raises the most fierce, aggressive warriors will be at an advantage. Consequently, the existence of violent conflict encourages a strong preference for rearing male children, supports restrictions on the rearing of female children, and, in general, creates an ideology of male supremacy. Thus, they conclude, war and violent conflict do encourage sexism, but only because they serve to promote selective population control.

The Evolution of the Nation-State

Anthropologists also suggest that violent conflict may encourage certain forms of political organization. Robert Carneiro argues that in the course of human history, violent conflict has been the primary agent in the development of complex nation-states. Carneiro reasons that war promotes the consolidation of isolated, autonomous villages into chiefdoms of united villages and into states. War began as an effort to oust a rival from a territory but soon evolved into an effort to subjugate and control an enemy. Later, war became the mechanism by which the number of political units in the world began to decline.

The rise of the Zulu state in Africa illustrates Carneiro's theory of how war leads to the coalescence of separate political units into a larger state. The Zulu state took form in southeast Africa in the early nineteenth century. Prior to that time, the region was inhabited by small, sometimes warring groups. About 100,000 people lived in an area of about 80,000 square miles, practicing agriculture and cattle herding. While there were separate entities labeled tribes by Westerners, the largest political unit was the clan.

Warfare increased between 1775 and 1800 as the population of southeast Africa increased. The process of state formation, combining these separate groups into a larger political unit, was begun by a leader of the Mtetwa tribe named Dingiswayo. He developed new ways to organize his troops and took control of the territory of those he defeated. Using new techniques of war

Shaka Zulu united various tribal groups to form the Zulu Kingdom.

and political control, he achieved dominance over a wide area. Part of the reason why he extended his control was to promote peace among warring groups. Dingiswayo, it was said, "wished to do away with the incessant quarrels that occurred amongst the tribes, because no supreme head was over them to say who was right or who was wrong" (Service 1975, 108–109).

By the early 1800s, Dingiswayo had conquered and united some thirty different groups. He was aided by a young officer named Shaka Zulu, the son of the chief of the Zulu clan. When the Zulu chief died, Dingiswayo installed Shaka as the head of the clan, and when Dingiswayo was killed by a rival, Shaka took over the army and established his Zulus as the dominant clan. By 1822, Shaka had defeated every rival and was master of all of the present South African province of Kwa-Zulu Natal.

There is some suggestion of a link between militarism and competitive sports; that is, societies that are prone to collective violence are more likely to value games in which men aggressively compete against other men. How does this apply to American society? Which sports in America most closely resemble or promote the values of militarism and war? Does the language of these sports reflect militaristic values? Do gender roles reflect these values?

Violence and Male Solidarity

In addition to controlling population and uniting tribal societies into large-scale states, violent conflict may also be valued as a means of promoting group solidarity. Male solidarity seems to be enhanced by collective violence. Societies in which there is frequent violence often have more men's clubs, men's sports teams, or special men's houses. Anthropologist Ralph L. Holloway suggests that the psychological attributes that allow human beings to create sentimental bonds between members of a group are the same attributes that, when turned outward, promote violent conflict against nongroup members. That is, collective violence is simply the other side of group togetherness.

QUESTION 8.5

How is it possible to justify the creation of weapons of mass destruction?

Because the ability to conceal the consequences of violent conflict may be one of the reasons for its frequency, it is useful to examine how people manage to mask the consequences of planning what now would be the ultimate form of violence—the unleashing of nuclear weapons.

The Anthropology of a Nuclear Weapons Laboratory

Anthropologist Hugh Gusterson, who had been an antinuclear activist, wanted to know how nuclear weapons scientists could justify conducting research on and testing weapons of mass destruction. What could create a worldview that would enable people to justify performing that kind of work? To answer that question, he set out to study the culture of the Lawrence Livermore National Laboratory in Livermore, California.

Gusterson suggests that those who justify nuclear weapons and question nuclear disarmament make four assumptions about the world. First, unlike national systems in which a monopoly on the use of force guarantees stability, they claim that anarchy characterizes international relations. Second, they assume that states must rely on self-help since no one else is going to offer them protection. Third, they assume that nuclear weapons are the ultimate form of self-help, because they vastly increase the cost of aggression against them. And fourth, they assume that relatively little can be done in the short term to change the anarchistic nature of the international system.

Critics of nuclear weapons make very different assumptions. They argue that international relations are not as anarchistic as they are made out to be, and that rules and norms that control aggression exist. Many critics see the nuclear arms race as "objective social madness." People who work in the area, they assume, must be in denial and must demonize the other to justify their work. Gusterson wanted to find out not so much who was "right," but rather how people came to hold such divergent opinions.

When he began his research, Gusterson was surprised to find the variety of political and religious viewpoints of people working at Livermore. Political views ran the gamut from conservatives to active environmentalists, civil rights supporters, and women's rights advocates. How, he asked, could such a diverse population all agree on the value of nuclear weapons development, an agreement so profound that "they often asked me in puzzlement to explain why antinuclear activists were so afraid of nuclear weapons"?

Nuclear weapons scientists did not, says Gusterson, avoid the ethical concerns of their research. Most, however, accept the central axiom that nuclear research is necessary to make the world safe. To some, working on nuclear weapons is more ethical than working on conventional weapons, since conventional weapons are more likely to be used. Nuclear weapons, the scientists assume, are simply symbolic chips in a game, the goal of which is to avoid using them. When asked if he would ever foresee a circumstance in which nuclear weapons would be used, one scientist said "no, even if we were under attack." In this view, the only reason you have nuclear weapons is for deterrence; once you are being attacked, the whole thing has failed. Others rationalize their work more baldly, saying they are not responsible for how what they design is used. "Are automobile designers," they ask, "responsible for deaths caused by drunk drivers?"

The W88 warhead is almost 40 times more powerful than the atomic bomb dropped on Hiroshima, Japan in 1945. Eight of these warheads are equipped onto a single Trident II missile; the U.S. operates 14 submarines that each carry 24 of these missiles. Each sub has more than 7,500 times the power of the first atomic bomb. With so many powerful weapons, why do nations keep expanding their arsenals? The answer lies in a strategy known as MAD—mutually assured destruction. Suppose there are two nations at war, both with nuclear weapons. According to MAD, if one nation used its weapons, the other would quickly respond with its own, resulting in the destruction of both countries. Thus, the central tenet of MAD is that the proliferation of nuclear weapons is essential to prevent another group from using those same weapons.

When Gusterson asked people why they chose to work at Livermore, most cited the intellectual freedom they enjoyed working in a weapons laboratory. Almost all compared Livermore favorably to working in universities (which they characterized as "stodgy," "cutthroat," or "high-pressure") or in private organizations. Some also cited the challenge of weapons research and the opportunity to work with state-of-the-art equipment. Livermore also paid about twice as much as a university position.

Once a person is hired, secrecy plays a major role in forging a person's identity. Livermore employees are investigated before being given security clearance to laboratory facilities. Personnel are divided into different security categories and given colored badges indicating their level of clearance. "Q" clearance (a green badge) is necessary for classified research; "L" clearance (yellow badge) allows access to classified areas but not to classified information. The labs themselves are divided into areas of lesser and greater security. As Gusterson puts it, the laboratory is "an enormous grid of tabooed spaces and tabooed topics."

Without a green badge, says Gusterson, a weapons scientist is not considered a full adult in the lab. But the process involved in getting "Q" clearance is elaborate and may take from six months to two years. Virtually every aspect of a person's life is subject to investigation in search of clues that the person is unfit to handle classified material. But most people pass, and, because secrecy is not that well guarded in practice, the security clearance process may function mostly as a rite of passage that adds to the mystique of weapons research and disciplines the initiate.

Knowing secrets serves to mark a person as a member of a special group.

Secrecy, says Gusterson, is one of the main ways that the diverse population of the lab is brought together. Knowing secrets, regardless of how mundane they might be, serves to mark a person as a member of a special group and lends an air of dramatic importance to one's work. Secrecy also serves to limit discussion that could change a person's view of the work that they do. As Gusterson puts it,

> the laboratory's culture of secrecy does tend to produce certain effects in its scientists: it segregates laboratory scientists as a privileged but somewhat isolated elite; it inculcates a sense of group loyalty; and it thrusts on laboratory scientists an amorphous surveillance, which can become internalized. (1995, 68)

The process of testing nuclear weapons, says Gusterson, is in many ways the critical step in creating the nuclear scientist. Any Livermore scientist can propose a weapons test, but reviewers (senior scientists at the laboratory) select only about 1 out of 20 ideas for testing. Approval of an idea for testing further reaffirms the scientist's membership in the group. Nuclear tests, says Gusterson, have elements of myth and ritual. Rarely in narratives that he collected on testing did anyone note the importance of testing nuclear reliability. Instead, people spoke of the fulfillment of personal ambition, the struggle to master a new technology, the drama of creating something new, and the experience of community that each test created.

Testing, says Gusterson, produces not only weapons, but weapon designers. It is a way of producing the elite. The more tests one participates in, the greater the prestige and power that accrues. A successful test validates status and credentials and brings forth congratulatory support and reinforcement. The test provides what Gusterson calls a symbolic simulation of the reliability of the whole system of deterrence:

> Each time a nuclear test is successfully carried off, the scientists' faith in human control over nuclear technology is further reinforced. Seen in this light, the "reliability" the tests demonstrate has an expandable meaning, extending out from the reliability of the particular device being tested to the entire regime of nuclear deterrence. (1995, 161)

The Language of Nuclear Destruction

Carol Cohn spent one year studying the culture of a strategic studies institute, or "think tank," for government defense analysts who plan nuclear strategy. She began her study with this question: How are people whose job it is to plan nuclear destruction able to do it? One of her conclusions is that language is used to distance the planners from the consequences of the actions they are planning. The language they use obfuscates and reassembles reality in such a way that what is really being talked about—the destruction of human lives—is hidden behind metaphors and euphemisms.

During her first weeks at the center, as she listened to the participants talking matter-of-factly about nuclear destruction, she heard language that she labeled *technostrategic*. This language includes expressions such as *clean bombs* (fusion bombs that release more energy than fission bombs), *penetration aids* (technology that helps missiles get through enemy defenses), *collateral damage* (human deaths), and *surgical strikes* (bombing that takes out only military targets). Domestic metaphors are common in the technostrategic language; missiles are based in *silos*, piles of nuclear weapons in a submarine are *Christmas tree farms*, bombs and missiles are *reentry vehicles* or *RVs*, and massive bombing is *carpet bombing*. Cohn says that the domestic images are more than a way for people to distance themselves from the grisly reality they are discussing. Calling the pattern in which a bomb falls a *footprint* removes the speakers from any position of accountability for the acts they are contemplating.

Cohn also discovered that the language and metaphors of those working at the institute seemed incapable of expressing certain realities. The aftermath of a nuclear attack is described in technostrategic language as "a situation bound to include EMP blackout, brute force damage to systems, a heavy jamming environment, and so on" (Cohn 1987, 707). Cohn contrasts this with eyewitness accounts of the bombing of Hiroshima (see below).

There is, says Cohn, no way of describing this experience with the language of technostrategic. It removes the speakers from having to think about themselves as victims of nuclear war.

Cohn also discovered that she could not use ordinary language to speak to the defense analysts. If she tried, they acted as if she were ignorant or simpleminded. To communicate at all, she had to use terms like *subholocaust engagement* and *preemptive strikes*. The word *peace* was not a legitimate part of the vocabulary; to use it was to brand oneself as a softheaded activist. The closest she could come to *peace* in the language of technostrategic was *strategic stability*.

Cohn encountered descriptions of nuclear situations that made little sense until she realized that different realities were being discussed. For example, the following passage describes a nuclear exchange in a situation in which missiles with more than one warhead are mutually banned:

> The strategic stability of regime A (a scenario) is based on the fact that both sides are deprived of any incentive ever to strike first. Since it takes roughly two warheads to destroy the enemy silo, an attacker must expend two of his missiles to destroy one of the enemy's. A first strike disarms the attacker. The aggressor ends up worse off than the aggressed. (Cohn 1987, 710)

By what type of reasoning, asks Cohn, can a country that has dropped a thousand nuclear bombs 10 to 100 times more powerful than the one dropped on Hiroshima end up "worse off" than the country it dropped the bombs on? This would be possible only if winning depends on who has the greatest number of weapons left.

To an anthropologist, the fact that people are limited by their culture, their language, and their point of view is, of course, no surprise. All cultures give a characteristic meaning to violent conflict, whether it is viewed as the act of an animal in possession of a human body, the will of God, or a game. The more serious implication of Cohn's observations is that as scientists and academics, nuclear planners give weight to their claim that their perspective is "objective" and therefore has greater truth value than other perspectives. Moreover, says Cohn, if one can speak to defense analysts only in the language of technostrategic, and if the language is constructed in such a way as to be incapable of expressing different realities, then there is no way for these analysts to appreciate or understand the other realities involved in the use of nuclear weapons.

Everything was black, had vanished into the black dust, was destroyed. Only the flames that were beginning to lick their way up had any color. From the dust that was like fog, figures began to loom up, black, hairless, faceless. They screamed with voices that were no longer human. Their screams drowned out the groans rising everywhere from the rubble, groans that seemed to rise from the very earth itself.

—Hisako Matsubara (Cohn 1987, 708)

References

A

Adams, John W. 1973. *The Gitksan Potlatch: Population Flux, Resource Ownership and Reciprocity.* Toronto: Holt, Rinehart and Winston of Canada.

Alford, Richard D. 1988. *Naming and Identity: A Cross-Cultural Study of Personal Naming Practices.* New Haven, CT: HRAF Press.

American Anthropological Association. 2005. *Anthropology News* 6(1).

Anelauskas, Valdas. 1999. *Discovering America as It Is.* Atlanta: Clarity Press.

Angeloni, Elvio. 1990. *Anthropology 90/91.* Guilford, CT: Dushkin Publishing Company.

Arens, William. 1976. "Professional Football: An American Symbol and Ritual." In *The American Dimension: Cultural Myths and Social Realities.* Edited by William Arens and Susan P. Montague. Port Washington, NY: Alfred Publishing Company.

B

Baker, Dean, and Mark Weisbrot. 2001. *Social Security: The Phony Crisis.* Chicago: University of Chicago Press.

Barlow, Maude. 2001. *Blue Gold: The Global Water Crisis and the Commodification of the World's Water Supply.* International Forum on Globalization. Available online at http://www.thirdworldtraveler.com/Water/Blue_Gold.html.

Barnes, Barry. 1974. *Scientific Knowledge and Sociological Theory.* London: Routledge & Kegan Paul.

Basso, Keith. 1979. *Portraits of "The Whiteman": Linguistic Play and Cultural Symbols among the Western Apache.* Cambridge: University of Cambridge Press.

Bean, Susan. 1976. "Soap Operas: Sagas of American Kinship." In *The American Dimension: Cultural Myths and Social Realities.* Edited by William Arens and Susan P. Montague. Port Washington, NY: Alfred Publishing Company.

Beaud, Michel. 1983. *A History of Capitalism, 1500–1980.* New York: Monthly Review Press.

Belmonte, Thomas. 1989. *The Broken Fountain.* New York: Columbia University Press.

Benedict, Ruth. 1934. *Patterns of Culture.* New York: Houghton Mifflin.

Boas, Franz. 1966. *Kwakiutl Ethnography.* Edited by Helen Codere. Chicago: University of Chicago Press.

Boas, Franz, and George Hunt. 1905. *Kwakiutl Texts. Memoir of the American Museum of Natural History,* vol. 5. Leiden, The Netherlands: E. J. Brill.

Bodley, John. 1985. *Anthropology and Contemporary Problems,* Second Edition. Palo Alto, CA: Mayfield Publishing Company.

Bodley, John. 1994. *Cultural Anthropology: Tribes, States, and the Global System.* Mountain View, CA: Mayfield Publishing Company.

Bodley, John. 1999. *The Victims of Progress.* Mountain View, CA: Mayfield Publishing Company.

Bohannan, Laura. 1966. "Shakespeare in the Bush." *Natural History Magazine,* August/September.

Bohannan, Paul, editor. 1970. *Divorce and After.* New York: Doubleday.

Bourdieu, Pierre. 1986. "The Forms of Capital." In *Handbook of Theory and Research for the Sociology of Education.* Edited by John G. Richardson. New York: Greenwood Press.

Bourgois, Philippe. 1995. *In Search of Respect: Selling Crack in El Barrio.* Cambridge, UK: Cambridge University Press.

Braudel, Fernand. 1982. *Civilization and Capitalism, 15th–18th Century: Vol. II. The Wheels of Commerce.* New York: Harper & Row.

Briggs, Jean. 1970. *Never in Anger.* Cambridge, MA: Harvard University Press.

Burton, Thomas. 1993. *Serpent-Handling Believers.* Knoxville: University of Tennessee Press.

C

Cagan, Leslie. 1983. "Feminism and Militarism." In *Beyond Survival: New Directions for the Disarmament Movement.* Edited by M. Albert and D. Dellinger. Boston: South End Press.

Cairns, Ed. 1982. "Intergroup Conflict in Northern Ireland." In *Social Identity and Intergroup Relations.* Edited by Henri Tajfel. New York: Cambridge University Press.

Campbell, Joseph. 1949. *The Hero with a Thousand Faces.* Princeton, NJ: Princeton University Press.

Campion, Nardi Reeder. 1990. *Mother Ann Lee: Morning Star of the Shakers.* Hanover, NH: University Press of New England.

Carneiro, Robert. 1978. "Political Expansion as an Expression of the Principle of Competitive Exclusion." In *Origins of the State.* Edited by Ronald Cohn and Elman Service. Philadelphia: Institute for the Study of Human Issues.

Carneiro, Robert. 1979. "Slash-and-Burn Cultivation among the Kuikuru and Its Implications for Cultural Development in the Amazon Basin." In *The Evolution of Horticultural Systems in Native South America: Causes and Consequences. Anthropologica,* Supplement 2. Edited by J. Wilbert. Caracas, Venezuela.

Carneiro, Robert. 1990. "Chiefdom-Level Warfare as Exemplified in Fiji and Cauca Valley." In *The Anthropology of War.* Edited by Jonathan Hass. New York: Cambridge University Press.

Carrier, James G. 1993. "The Rituals of Christmas Giving." In *Unwrapping Christmas.* Edited by Daniel Miller. Oxford, UK: Clarendon Press.

Carrier, James G. 1995. *Gifts and Commodities: Exchange and Western Capitalism since 1700.* London: Routledge.

Carrillo, Hector. 2002. *The Night Is Young: Sexuality in Mexico in the Time of AIDS.* Chicago: University of Chicago Press.

Carroll, John B. 1956. *Language, Thought, and Reality: Selected Writings of Benjamin Lee Whorf.* New York: John Wiley and Sons.

Carsten, Janet E. 1989. "Cooking Money: Gender and the Symbolic Transformation of Means of Exchange in a Malay Fishing Village." In *Money and the Morality of Exchange.* Edited by J. Parry and M. Bloch. Cambridge, UK: Cambridge University Press.

Cathcart, Dolores, and Robert Cathcart. 1985. "Japanese Social Experience and Concept of Groups." In *Intercultural Communication: A Reader,* Fourth Edition. Edited by Larry A. Samovar and Richard E. Porter. Belmont, CA: Wadsworth Publishing Company.

Chagnon, Napoleon. 1983. *The Fierce People,* Third Edition. New York: Holt, Rinehart and Winston.

Chagnon, Napoleon. 1990. "Reproductive and Somatic Conflicts of Interest in the Genesis of Violence and Warfare among Tribesmen." In *The Anthropology of War.* Edited by Jonathan Hass. New York: Cambridge University Press.

Chin, Elizabeth. 2001. *Purchasing Power: Black Kids and American Consumer Culture.* Minneapolis: University of Minnesota Press.

Chomsky, Noam. 1984. *Turning the Tide: U.S. Intervention in Central America and the Struggle for Peace.* Boston: South End Press.

Chomsky, Noam. 2003. *Hegemony or Survival: America's Quest for Global Dominance.* New York: Metropolitan Books.

Churchill, Ward. 1994. *Indians Are Us?* Monroe, ME: Common Courage Press.

Clay, Jason W. 1984. "Yahgan and Ona—The Road to Extinction." *Cultural Survival Quarterly* 8:5–8.

Cohen, Mark. 1977. *The Food Crisis in Prehistory.* New Haven, CT: Yale University Press.

Cohen, Mark. 1989. *Health and the Rise of Civilization.* New Haven, CT: Yale University Press.

Cohn, Carol. 1987. "Sex and Death in the Rational World of Defense Intellectuals." *Signs* 12:687–718.

Cohn, Carol. 1991. "Decoding Military Newspeak." *Ms,* March/April, 88.

Collier, Jane E., and Michelle Rosaldo. 1981. "Politics and Gender in Simple Societies." In *Sexual Meanings: The Cultural Construction of Gender and Sexuality.* Edited by Sherry B. Ortner and Harriet Whitehead. New York: Cambridge University Press.

Comaroff, Jean, and John L. Comaroff. 2001. *Millennial Capitalism and the Culture of Neoliberalism.* Durham, NC: Duke University Press.

Conklin, Beth. 2001. *Consuming Grief: Compassionate Cannibalism in an Amazonian Society.* Austin: University of Texas Press.

Cousins, Norman. 1991. *The Anatomy of an Illness.* New York: Bantam.

Covington, Dennis. 1995. *Salvation on Sand Mountain: Snake Handling and Redemption in Southern Appalachia.* New York: Addison-Wesley.

Cowell, Daniel David. 1985–1986. "Funerals, Family, and Forefathers: A View of Italian-American Funeral Practices." *Omega* 16:69–85.

Crick, Malcolm R. 1982. "Anthropology of Knowledge." In *Annual Review of Anthropology,* vol. 11, pp. 287–313. Palo Alto, CA: Annual Reviews.

Crotty, James. 2008. "Structural Causes of the Global Financial Crisis: A Critical Assessment of the 'New Financial Architecture.'" *Cambridge Journal of Economics* 33.

Crowley, Aleister. 1985. *The Book of Thoth.* Stamford, CT: U.S. Games Systems.

Culler, Jonathan. 1977. "In Pursuit of Signs." *Daedalus* 106:95–112.

D

D'Andrade, Roy. 1995. "Moral Models in Anthropology." *Current Anthropology* 36:399–408.

Davis, D. L., and R. G. Whitten. 1987. "The Cross-Cultural Study of Human Sexuality." In *Annual Review of Anthropology,* vol. 16, pp. 69–98. Palo Alto, CA: Annual Reviews.

de Vries, Jan and Ad van der Woude. 1997. *The First Modern Economy: Success, Failure, and Perseverance of the Dutch Economy, 1500–1815.* Cambridge: Cambridge University Press.

Delaney, Carol. 1991. *The Seed and the Soil: Gender and Cosmology in a Turkish Village Society.* Berkeley: University of California Press.

DeLind, Laura B. 1998. "Parma: A Story of Hog Hotels and Local Resistance." In *Pigs, Profits, and Rural Communities,* pp. 23–38. Edited by Kendall Thu and E. Paul Durrenberger. Albany: State University of New York Press.

Desai, Ashok V. 1972. "Population and Standards of Living in Akbar's Time." *Indian Economic and Social History Review* 9:42–62.

Divale, William Tulio, and Marvin Harris. 1976. "Population, Warfare, and the Male Supremacist

Complex." *American Anthropologist* 78:521–38.
Douglas, Mary. 1966. *Purity and Danger.* New York: Frederick A. Praeger.
Douglas, Mary, and Aaron Wildavsky. 1983. *Risk and Culture: An Essay on the Selection of Technological and Environmental Dangers.* Berkeley: University of California Press.
Doyle, Arthur Conan. 1930. "The Sign of the Four." In *The Complete Sherlock Holmes*, vol. 1. New York: Doubleday.
Drèze, Jean, and Amartya Sen. 1991. *Hunger and Public Action.* New York: Cambridge University Press.
Dumont, Louis. 1970. *Homo Hierarchicus: An Essay on the Caste System.* Chicago: University of Chicago Press.
Durham, William H. 1990. "Advances in Evolutionary Culture Theory." In *Annual Review of Anthropology,* vol. 19, pp. 187–210. Palo Alto, CA: Annual Reviews.
Durkheim, Émile. 1961. *The Elementary Forms of the Religious Life.* New York: Collier. (Originally published 1912)

E

Eckert, Penelope, and Sally McConnell-Ginet. 2003. *Language and Gender.* Cambridge, UK: Cambridge University Press.
Eisler, Riane. 1987. *The Chalice and the Blade.* New York: Harper & Row.
Erasmus, Charles. 1977. *In Search of the Common Good.* Glencoe, IL: Free Press.
Ervin, Alexander M. 2005. *Applied Anthropology: Tools and Perspectives for Contemporary Practice.* Boston: Allyn & Bacon.
Escobar, Arturo. 1995. *Encountering Development: The Making and Unmaking of the Third World.* Princeton, NJ: Princeton University Press.
Evans-Pritchard, E. E. 1937. *Witchcraft, Oracles and Magic among the Azande.* London: Oxford University Press.
Evans-Pritchard, E. E. 1940. *The Nuer: A Description of the Modes of Livelihood and Political Institutions of a Nilotic People.* Oxford, UK: Clarendon Press.
Evans-Pritchard, E. E. 1965. *Theories of Primitive Religion.* Oxford, UK: Clarendon Press.
Ewen, Stuart. 1996. *PR: A Social History of Spin.* New York: Basic Books.

F

Farmer, Paul. 2003. *Pathologies of Power: Health, Human Rights, and the New War on the Poor.* Berkeley: University of California Press.
Fausto-Sterling, Anne. 1993. "The Five Sexes: Why Male and Female Are Not Enough," *The Sciences* 33(March/April):20–24.
Fei, Hsiao-Tung. 1939. *Peasant Life in China: A Field Study of Country Life in the Yangtze Valley.* London: Routledge & Kegan Paul.
Ferguson, R. Brian. 1992. "A Savage Encounter: Western Contact and the Yanomami War Complex." In *War in the Tribal Zone: Expanding States and Indigenous Warfare.* Edited by R. Brian Ferguson and Neil L. Whitehead. Santa Fe, NM: School of American Research Press.
Ferguson, R. Brian. 1995. *Yanomami Warfare: A Political History.* Santa Fe, NM: School of American Research Press.
Fernandez, James W. 1978. "African Religious Movements." In *Annual Review of Anthropology,* vol. 7, pp. 195–234. Palo Alto, CA: Annual Reviews.
Foer, Franklin. 2004. *How Soccer Explains the World: An Unlikely Theory of Globalization.* New York: Harper Perennial.
Foucault, Michel. 1979. *Discipline and Punishment: The Birth of the Prison.* New York: Vintage Books.
Fried, Morton. 1967. *The Evolution of Political Society: An Essay in Political Anthropology.* New York: Random House.
Fried, Morton, Marvin Harris, and Robert Murphy, editors. 1967. *War: The Anthropology of Armed Conflict and Aggression.* Garden City, NY: Natural History Press.
Friedman, Benjamin. 2006. *The Moral Consequences of Economic Growth.* New York: Vintage Books.

G

Galton, Francis. 2006. *Hereditary Genius: An Inquiry into Its Laws and Consequences.* New York: Prometheus Books. (Originally published 1869)
Geertz, Clifford. 1972. "Deep Play: Notes on the Balinese Cockfight." *Daedalus* 101:1–37.
Geertz, Clifford. 1973. "The Impact of Culture on the Concept of Man." In *The Interpretation of Cultures.* New York: Basic Books.
George, Susan, and Fabrizo Sabelli. 1994. *Faith and Credit: The World Bank's Secular Empire.* Boulder, CO: Westview Press.
Gibson, Thomas. 1990. "Raiding, Trading and Tribal Autonomy in Insular Southeast Asia." In *The Anthropology of War.* Edited by Jonathan Hass. New York: Cambridge University Press.
Gilmore, David D. 1990. *Manhood in the Making: Cultural Concepts of Masculinity.* New Haven, CT: Yale University Press.
Ginsburg, Faye, and Rayna Rapp. 1991. "The Politics of Reproduction." In *Annual Review of Anthropology,* vol. 20, pp. 311–43. Palo Alto, CA: Annual Reviews.
Glanz, James. 2007. "Iraqi Factories, Aging and Shut, Now Give Hope." *New York Times,* January 18. http://www.nytimes.com/2007/01/18/world/middleeast/18factory.html.
Goffman, Erving. 1959. *The Presentation of Self in Everyday Life.* New York: Doubleday.
Gonzales, Roberto. 2009. *American Counterinsurgency: Human Science and the Human Terrain.* New York: Prickly Paradigm Press.
Gould, Stephen Jay. 1981. *The Mismeasure of Man.* New York: W. W. Norton.
Green, Nancy. 1995. "Living in a State of Fear." In *Fieldwork under Fire:*

Contemporary Studies of Violence and Survival. Edited by Carolyn Nordstrom and Antonius C. G. Robben. Berkeley: University of California Press.

Greenhouse, Carol. 1987. "Cultural Perspectives on War." In *The Quest for Peace: Transcending Collective Violence and War among Societies, Cultures and States.* Edited by R. Varynen. Beverly Hills, CA: Sage Publications.

Gregor, Thomas. 1990. "Uneasy Peace: Intertribal Relations in Brazil's Upper Xingu." In *The Anthropology of War.* Edited by Jonathan Hass. New York: Cambridge University Press.

Gusterson, Hugh. 1995. *Nuclear Rites: A Weapons Laboratory at the End of the Cold War.* Berkeley: University of California Press.

Guttmann, Robert. 1994. *How Credit-Money Shapes the Economy: The United States in a Global System.* London: M. E. Sharpe.

Gwynne, Margaret A. 2003. *Applied Anthropology: A Career-Oriented Approach.* Boston: Allyn & Bacon.

H

Hall, Edgar T. 1966. *The Hidden Dimension.* Garden City, NY: Doubleday.

Hanson, Allan. 1993. *Testing Testing.* Berkeley: University of California Press.

Harris, Marvin. 1977. *Cannibals and Kings: The Origins of Culture.* New York: Vintage Books.

Harris, Marvin. 1987. *Sacred Cow and the Abominable Pig.* New York: Touchstone Books.

Harris, Marvin, and Eric Ross. 1987. *Food and Evolution: Toward a Theory of Human Food Habits.* Philadelphia: Temple University Press.

Hartwick, Elaine, and Richard Peet. 2003. "Neoliberalism and Nature: The Case of the WTO." *Annals of the American Academy of Political and Social Science* 590:188–211.

Hayden, Dolores. 1981. *Seven American Utopias: The Architecture of Communitarian Socialism, 1790–1975.* Cambridge, MA: MIT Press.

Henderson, Paul. 1976. "Class Structure and the Concept of Intelligence." In *Schooling and Capitalism: A Sociological Reader.* Edited by Roger Dale, Geoff Esland, and Madeleine MacDonald. London: Routledge & Kegan Paul in association with Open University Press.

Henle, Paul. 1958. *Language, Thought and Experience.* Ann Arbor: University of Michigan Press.

Hernandez-Giron, C. A., A. Cruz-Valdez, M. Quiterio-Trenado, F. Uribe-Salas, A. Peruga, and M. Hernandez-Avila. 1999. "Factors Associated with Condom Use in the Male Population of Mexico City." *International Journal of STD & AIDS* 10(2):112–17.

Herrnstein, Richard J., and Charles Murray. 1994. *The Bell Curve: Intelligence and Class Structure in American Life.* New York: Free Press.

Hertz, Robert. 1960. *Death and the Right Hand.* Translated and edited by Claudia and Rodney Needham. Glencoe, IL: Free Press. (Originally published 1909)

Hobbes, Thomas. 1881. *Leviathan.* London: Oxford University Press. (Originally published 1651)

Hobsbaum, Eric. 1959. *Primitive Rebels: Studies in Archaic Forms of Social Movement in the 19th and 20th Centuries.* New York: Frederick A. Praeger.

Holloway, Ralph, Jr. 1968. "Human Aggression: The Need for a Species-Specific Framework." In *War: The Anthropology of Armed Conflict and Aggression.* Edited by Morton Fried, Marvin Harris, and Robert Murphy. Garden City, NY: Natural History Press.

Honigmann, John J. 1976. *The Development of Anthropological Ideas.* Homewood, IL: Dorsey Press.

Honwana, Alcinda, and Filip de Boeck, 2005. *Makers and Breakers: Children and Youth in Postcolonial Africa.* Trenton, NJ: Africa World Press.

Hostetler, John. 1974. *Hutterite Society.* Baltimore: Johns Hopkins University Press.

House, James S., Karl R. Landis, and Debra Umberson. 1988. "Social Relationships and Health." *Science* 241:540–45.

Howell, Signe, and Roy Willis, editors. 1989. *Societies at Peace: An Anthropological Perspective.* London: Routledge.

Hsu, Francis L. K. 1967. *Under the Ancestors' Shadow.* New York: Anchor Books.

I

Ikerd, John E. 1998. "Sustainable Agriculture, Rural Economic Development, and Large-Scale Swine Production." In *Pigs, Profits, and Rural Communities,* pp. 157–69. Edited by Kendall Thu and E. Paul Durrenberger. Albany: State University of New York Press.

Inhorn, Marcia C., and Peter J. Brown. 1990. "The Anthropology of Infectious Disease." In *Annual Review of Anthropology,* vol. 19, pp. 89–117. Palo Alto, CA: Annual Reviews.

J

Johnson, Chalmers. 2004. *The Sorrows of Empire: Militarism, Secrecy, and the End of the Republic.* New York: Metropolitan Books.

Johnson, Norris Brock. 1985. *Westhaven: Classroom Culture and Society in a Rural Elementary School.* Chapel Hill: University of North Carolina Press.

Juergensmeyer, Mark. 2000. *Terror in the Mind of God: The Global Rise of Religious Violence.* Berkeley: University of California Press.

K

Karier, Clarence J. 1976. "Testing for Order and Control in the Corporate Liberal State." In *Schooling and Capitalism: A Sociological Reader.* Edited by Roger Dale, Geoff Esland, and Madeleine MacDonald. London: Routledge & Kegan Paul

in association with Open University Press.
Kearney, Michael. 1991. "A Very Bad Disease of the Arms." In *The Naked Anthropologist: Tales from Around the World.* Edited by Philip Devita. Belmont, CA: Wadsworth Publishing Company.
Keesing, Roger. 1991. "Not a Real Fish: The Ethnographer as Inside Outsider." In *The Naked Anthropologist: Tales from Around the World.* Edited by Philip Devita. Belmont, CA: Wadsworth Publishing Company.
Kehoe, Alice. 1989. *The Ghost Dance: Ethnohistory and Revitalization.* New York: Holt, Rinehart and Winston.
Keiser, Lincoln. 1969. *The Vice Lords: Warriors of the Streets.* New York: Holt, Rinehart and Winston.
Keiser, Lincoln. 1991. *Friend by Day, Enemy by Night: Organized Vengeance in a Kohistani Community.* New York: Holt, Rinehart and Winston.
Kelly, John D., and Martha Kaplan. 1990. "History, Structure, and Ritual." In *Annual Review of Anthropology,* vol. 19, pp. 119–50. Palo Alto, CA: Annual Reviews.
Kennedy, Paul. 1993. *Preparing for the Twenty-first Century*. New York: Random House.
Kets de Vries, Manfred F. R., and Danny Miller. 1987. "Interpreting Organizational Texts." *Journal of Management Studies* 24:233–47.
Kidder, Tracy. 2003. *Mountains beyond Mountains.* New York: Random House.
Kindleberger, Charles P. 2000. *Manias, Panics, and Crashes: A History of Financial Crisis*. New York: John Wiley and Sons.
Kinkade, Kathleen. 1973. *A Walden Two Experiment: The First Five Years of Twin Oaks Community.* New York: William Morrow.
Klein, Naomi, 2004. "Baghdad Year Zero: Pillaging Iraq in Pursuit of a Neocon Utopia." *Harper's Magazine,* September. http://harpers.org/BaghdadYearZero.html.
Kopytoff, Igor. 1986. "The Cultural Biography of Things." In *The Social Life of Things: Commodities in Cultural Perspective*. Edited by Arjun Appadurai. Cambridge, UK: Cambridge University Press.
Kotlowitz, Alex. 1991. *There Are No Children Here.* New York: Anchor Books.
Kottak, Conrad Phillip. 1990. *Prime Time Society: An Anthropological Analysis of Television and Culture.* Belmont, CA: Wadsworth Publishing Company.
Kroeber, Alfred L. 1948. *Anthropology.* New York: Harcourt, Brace.
Kuhn, Thomas. 1957. *The Copernican Revolution: Planetary Astronomy in the Development of Western Thought.* Cambridge, MA: Harvard University Press.

L

La Barre, Weston. 1962. *They Shall Take Up Serpents: Psychology of the Southern Snakehandling Cult.* Minneapolis: University of Minnesota Press.
Lakoff, George. 1996. *Moral Politics: What Conservatives Know That Liberals Don't.* Chicago: University of Chicago Press.
Lakoff, George. 2004. *Don't Think of an Elephant: Know Your Values and Frame the Debate.* White River Junction, VT: Chelsea Green Publishing.
Lakoff, George, and Mark Johnson. 1980. *Metaphors We Live By.* Chicago: University of Chicago Press.
Lakoff, Robin. 1975. *Language and Woman's Place*. New York: Harper & Row.
Lappé, Frances Moore, and Joseph Collins. 1977. *Food First: Beyond the Myth of Scarcity.* New York: Random House.
Layard, Richard. 2005. *Happiness: Lessons from a New Science*. New York: Penguin Books.
Lear, Jonathan. 2006. *Radical Hope: Ethics in the Face of Cultural Devastation*. Cambridge, MA: Harvard University Press.
Lee, Richard. 1969. "Eating Christmas in the Kalihari." *Natural History Magazine,* December.
Lee, Richard. 1984. *The Dobe !Kung*. New York: Holt, Rinehart and Winston.
Levi-Strauss, Claude. 1974. *Tristes Tropiques*. New York: Atheneum Publishers.
Lewis, Oscar. 1959. *Five Families: Mexican Case Studies in the Culture of Poverty.* New York: Basic Books.
Linderman, Frank B. 1962. *Plenty Coups: Chief of the Crows*. Lincoln: University of Nebraska Press.
Livingstone, Frank B. 1968. "The Effects of Warfare on the Biology of the Human Species." In *War: The Anthropology of Armed Conflict and Aggression*. Edited by Morton Fried, Marvin Harris, and Robert Murphy. Garden City, NY: Natural History Press.
Longres, John F. 1990. *Human Behavior in the Social Environment.* Itasca, IL: F. E. Peacock Publishers.
Lorber, Judith. 1995. *Paradoxes of Gender*. New Haven, CT: Yale University Press.
Lowie, Robert H. 1983. *The Crow Indians*. Lincoln: University of Nebraska Press.
Luhrmann, Tanya M. 1989. *Persuasions of the Witch's Craft: Ritual Magic in Contemporary England*. Cambridge, MA: Harvard University Press.

M

Maddison, Angus. 2003. *The World Economy: A Millennial Perspective*. Paris: Development Centre of the Organization for Economic Co-operation and Development.
Malinowski, Bronislaw. 1929. *The Sexual Life of Savages in North-Western Melanesia*. New York: Halcyon House.
Malinowski, Bronislaw. 1961. *Argonauts of the Western Pacific*. New York: E. P. Dutton. (Originally published 1922)
Mandelbaum, David G., editor. 1949. *Selected Writings of Edward Sapir in Language, Culture, and Personality.* Berkeley: University of California Press.
Marshall, Lorna. 1976. *The !Kung of Nyae Nyae*. Cambridge, MA: Harvard University Press.

Martin, Emily. 1987. *The Woman in the Body: A Cultural Analysis of Reproduction.* Boston: Beacon Press.

Marwick, Max. 1965. *Sorcery in Its Social Setting.* Manchester, UK: University of Manchester Press.

Matsubara, Hisako. 1985. *Cranes at Dusk.* New York: Dial Press.

Mauss, Marcel. 1967. *The Gift: Forms and Functions of Exchange in Archaic Societies.* Translated by Ian Cunnison. New York: W. W. Norton. (Originally published 1925)

Maybury-Lewis, David. 1997. *Indigenous Peoples, Ethnic Groups, and the State.* Boston: Allyn & Bacon.

McCauley, Clark. 1990. "Conference Overview." In *The Anthropology of War.* Edited by Jonathan Hass. New York: Cambridge University Press.

McElroy, Ann, and Patricia Townsend. 1979. *Medical Anthropology.* North Scituate, MA: Duxbury Press.

McFate, Montgomery. 2005. "Anthropology and Counterinsurgency: The Strange Story of Their Curious Relationship." *Military Review,* March–April.

McFate, Montgomery, and Andrea Jackson. 2005. "An Organizational Solution for DOD's Cultural Knowledge Needs." *Military Review,* May–June.

McKibben, Bill. 2007. *Deep Economy: The Wealth of Communities and the Durable Future.* New York: Times Books.

Milner, Murray, Jr. 2006. *Freaks, Geeks, and Cool Kids: American Teenagers, Schools, and the Culture of Consumption.* New York: Routledge.

Mintz, Sidney W. 1985. *Sweetness and Power: The Place of Sugar in World History.* New York: Viking Press.

Mishkin, Bernard. 1940. *Rank and Warfare among the Plains Indians.* Monograph No. 3, American Ethnological Society. Seattle: University of Washington Press.

Moffatt, Michael. 1989. *Coming of Age in New Jersey: College and American Culture.* New Brunswick, NJ: Rutgers University Press.

Montague, Susan P., and William Morais. 1976. "Football Games and Rock Concerts: The Ritual Enactment of American Success Models." In *The American Dimension: Cultural Myths and Social Realities.* Edited by William Arens and Susan P. Montague. Port Washington, NY: Alfred Publishing Company.

Moore, Robert B. 1976. *Racism in the English Language.* New York: Council on Interracial Books for Children.

Moos, Robert, and Robert Brownstein. 1977. *Environment and Utopia.* New York: Plenum Press.

Morgan, Lewis Henry. 1964. *Ancient Society.* Cambridge, MA: Belknap Press. (Originally published 1877)

Mukhopadhyay, Carol C., and Patricia J. Higgins. 1988. "Anthropological Studies of Women's Status Revisited: 1977–1987." In *Annual Review of Anthropology,* vol. 17, pp. 461–95. Palo Alto, CA: Annual Reviews.

Munoz-Laboy, Miguel, Vagner de Almeida, Luis Felip Rios do Nascimento, and Richard Parker. 2004. "Promoting Sexual Health through Action Research among Young Male Sex Workers in Rio de Janeiro, Brazil." *Practicing Anthropology* 26(2):30–34.

Myers, Fred R. 1988. "Critical Trends in the Study of Hunters-Gatherers." In *Annual Review of Anthropology,* vol. 17, pp. 261–82. Palo Alto, CA: Annual Reviews.

N

Needleman, Jacob. 1991. *Money and the Meaning of Life.* New York: Doubleday.

Nichter, Mimi. 2000. *Fat Talk: What Girls and Their Parents Say about Dieting.* Cambridge, MA: Harvard University Press.

Nigh, Ronald. 1995. "Animal Agriculture for the Reforestation of Degraded Tropical Rainforests." *Culture and Agriculture* 51/52:2–5.

Nordhoff, Charles. 1966. *The Communistic Societies of the United States.* New York: Dover Publications. (Originally published 1875)

O

Ocaya-Lakidi, Dent. 1979. "Manhood, Warriorhood and Sex in Eastern Africa." *Journal of Asian and African Studies* 12:134–65.

Oldfield-Hayes, Rose. 1975. "Female Genital Mutilation, Fertility Control, Women's Roles, and the Patrilineage in Modern Sudan: A Functional Analysis." *American Ethnologist* 2:617–33.

Omohundro, John T. 2001. *Careers in Anthropology.* Mountain View, CA: Mayfield Publishing Company.

Ortner, Sherry B. 1973. "On Key Symbols." *American Anthropologist* 75:1338–46.

P

Pagels, Elaine. 1995. *The Origin of Satan.* New York: Vintage Books.

Palgi, Phyllis, and Henry Abramovitch. 1984. "Death: A Cross-Cultural Perspective." In *Annual Review of Anthropology,* vol. 13, pp. 385–417. Palo Alto, CA: Annual Reviews.

Parry, J., & M. Bloch, editors. 1989. *Money and the Morality of Exchange.* Cambridge, UK: Cambridge University Press.

Parsons, Talcott, Edward Shils, Kaspar D. Naegele, and Jesse R. Pitts. 1961. *Theories of Society.* Glencoe, IL: Free Press.

Pasternak, Burton. 1976. *Introduction to Kinship and Social Organization.* Englewood Cliffs, NJ: Prentice Hall.

Paulos, John Allen. 1980. *Mathematics and Humor.* Chicago: University of Chicago Press.

Payne, David. 1989. "The Wizard of Oz: Therapeutic Rhetoric in a Contemporary Media Ritual." *Quarterly Journal of Speech* 75:25–39.

Pearson, Karl. 1901. "On the Inheritance of Mental Characteristics in Man." *Proceedings of the Royal Society of London* 69:153–55.

Philips, Susan U. 1980. "Sex Differences and Language." In *Annual Review of Anthropology,* vol. 9, pp. 523–44. Palo Alto, CA: Annual Reviews.

Pitcher, George. 1965. "Wittgenstein, Nonsense and Lewis Carroll." *Massachusetts Review*, vol. 6: 591–611.

Polanyi, Karl. 1957. *The Great Transformation.* Beacon Press: Boston. (Originally published 1944)

Putnam, Robert D. 2000. *Bowling Alone: The Collapse and Revival of American Community.* New York: Simon & Schuster.

R

Read, Kenneth E. 1965. *The High Valley.* New York: Columbia University Press.

Reardon, Betty. 1985. *Sexism and the War System.* New York: Columbia University Teachers College Press.

Rich, Bruce. 1994. *Mortgaging the Earth: The World Bank, Environmental Impoverishment, and the Crisis of Development.* New York: Beacon Press.

Richardson, Lewis. 1960. *The Statistics of Deadly Quarrels.* Pacific Grove, CA: Boxwood Press.

Ridington, Robin. 1968. "The Medicine Fight: An Instrument of Political Process among the Beaver Indians." *American Anthropologist* 70:1152–60.

Rindos, David. 1984. *The Origins of Agriculture.* New York: Academic Press.

Rivoli, Pietra. 2005. *The Travels of a T-Shirt in the Global Economy: An Economist Examines the Markets, Power, and Politics of World Trade.* Hoboken, NJ: John Wiley.

Robarchek, Clayton. 1989. "Hobbesian and Rousseauan Images of Man: Autonomy and Individualism in a Peaceful Society." In *Societies at Peace: An Anthropological Perspective.* Edited by Signe Howell and Roy Willis. London: Routledge.

Robarchek, Clayton. 1990. "Motivations and Material Causes: On the Explanation of Conflict and War." In *The Anthropology of War.* Edited by Jonathan Hass. New York: Cambridge University Press.

Robbins, Richard H. 2008. *Global Problems and the Culture of Capitalism,* Fourth Edition. Boston: Allyn & Bacon.

Rosaldo, Michelle, and Jane Monnig Atkinson. 1975. "Man the Hunter and Woman: Metaphors for the Sexes in Ilongot Magical Spells." In *The Interpretation of Symbolism.* Edited by Roy Willis. New York: John Wiley & Sons.

Roy, Ramashray. 1985. *Self and Society: A Study in Gandhian Thought.* Beverly Hills, CA: Sage Publications.

Rubel, Arthur. 1964. "The Epidemiology of a Folk Illness: Susto in Hispanic America." *Ethnology* 3:268–83.

Rummel, R. J. 1994. *Death by Government.* New Brunswick, NJ: Transaction Press.

S

Saitoti, Tepilit Ole. 1986. *The Worlds of a Maasai Warrior.* New York: Random House.

Sanday, Peggy Reeves. 1981. "The Socio-Cultural Context of Rape: A Cross-Cultural Study." *Journal of Social Issues* 37:5–27.

Sanday, Peggy Reeves. 1990. *Fraternity Gang Rape: Sex, Brotherhood, and Privilege on Campus.* New York: New York University Press.

Scaglion, Richard. 1990. "Ethnocentrism and the Abelam." In *The Humbled Anthropologist: Tales from the Pacific.* Edited by Philip Devita. Belmont, CA: Wadsworth Publishing Company.

Scheper-Hughes, Nancy. 1992. *Death without Weeping: The Violence of Everyday Life in Brazil.* Berkeley: University of California Press.

Scheper-Hughes, Nancy. 1995. "The Primacy of the Ethical: Propositions for a Militant Anthropology." *Current Anthropology* 36:409–20.

Schieffelin, Bambi B., and Elinor Ochs. 1986. "Language Socialization." In *Annual Review of Anthropology,* vol. 15, pp. 163–91. Palo Alto, CA: Annual Reviews.

Schrire, Carmel. 1984. "Wild Surmises on Savage Thoughts." In *Past and Present in Hunter Gatherer Studies.* Edited by Carmel Schrire. New York: Academic Press.

Schwartz, Gary, and Don Merten. 1968. "Social Identity and Expressive Symbols." *American Anthropologist* 70:1117–31.

Service, Elman R. 1975. *Origins of the State and Civilization: The Process of Cultural Evolution.* New York: W. W. Norton.

Shipton, Parker. 1990. "African Famines and Food Security." In *Annual Review of Anthropology,* vol. 19, pp. 353–94. Palo Alto, CA: Annual Reviews.

Shore, Chris, and Susan Wright. 1997. *Anthropology of Policy: Critical Perspectives on Governance and Power.* London: Routledge.

Shostak, Marjorie. 1983. *Nisa: The Life and Words of a Ju/wasi Woman.* New York: Vintage Books.

Shweder, Richard A., and Edmund J. Bourne. 1984. "Does the Concept of the Person Vary Cross-Culturally?" In *Cultural Conceptions of Mental Health and Therapy.* Edited by A. J. Marsella and G. M. White. Boston: D. Reidel Publishing Company.

Sipes, Richard G. 1973. "War, Sports, and Aggression: An Empirical Test of Two Rival Theories." *American Anthropologist* 74:64–86.

Skocpol, Theda. 2003. *Diminished Democracy: From Membership to Management in American Civic Life.* Norman: University of Oklahoma Press.

Smith, Adam. 1994. *The Wealth of Nations.* Edited by Edwin Cannan. New York: Modern Library. (Originally published 1776)

Smith, Arthur H. 1970. *Village Life in China.* Boston: Little, Brown and Company.

Smith, Raymond T. 1984. "Anthropology and the Concept of Social Class." In *Annual Review of Anthropology,* vol. 13, pp. 467–94. Palo Alto, CA: Annual Reviews.

Smith, Robert J. 1983. *Japanese Society: Tradition, Self and the Social Order.* New York: Cambridge University Press.

Spearman, Charles. 1904. "General Intelligence." *American Journal of Psychology* 115:201–92.

Spindler, George, and Louise Spindler. 1983. "Anthropologists View American Culture." In *Annual Review of Anthropology*, vol. 12, pp. 49–78. Palo Alto, CA: Annual Reviews.

Stack, Carol. 1974. *All Our Kin: Strategies for Survival in a Black Community.* New York: Harper & Row.

Stein, Stephen J. 1992. *The Shaker Experience in America: A History of the United Societies of Believers.* New Haven, CT: Yale University Press.

Stern, Jessica. 2003. *Terror in the Name of God: Why Religious Militants Kill.* New York: HarperCollins.

Stiglitz, Joseph. 2002. *Globalization and Its Discontents.* New York: Norton.

Stone, Lawrence. 1977. *The Family, Sex and Marriage in England, 1500–1800.* New York: Harper & Row.

Strathern, Andrew. 1971. *The Rope of Moka: Big Men and Ceremonial Exchange in Mount Hagen, New Guinea.* London: Cambridge University Press.

T

Tett, Gillian. 2009. *Fool's Gold: How the Bold Dream of a Small Tribe at J. P. Morgan Was Corrupted by Wall Street Greed and Unleashed a Catastrophe.* New York: Free Press.

Thomas, Elizabeth. 1959. *The Harmless People.* New York: Alfred A. Knopf.

Thompson, E. P. 1967. "Time, Work-Discipline and Industrial Capitalism." *Past and Present* 38:56–97.

Trice, Harrison M., and Janice M. Beyer. 1984. "Studying Organizational Cultures through Rites and Ceremonials." *Academy of Management Review* 9:653–69.

Turner, Victor. 1967. *The Forest of Symbols: Aspects of Ndembu Ritual.* Ithaca, NY: Cornell University Press.

Tylor, Edward. 1871. *Primitive Culture.* London: Murray Publishers.

U

Underhill, Paco. 1999. *Why We Shop: The Science of Shopping.* New York: Simon & Schuster.

Underhill, Paco. 2004. *Call of the Mall.* New York: Simon & Schuster.

United Nations. 1951. *Measures for the Economic Development of Under-Developed Countries.* New York: United Nations.

V

Valentine, Charles A. 1968. *Culture and Poverty: Critique and Counter-Proposals.* Chicago: University of Chicago Press.

van den Berghe, Pierre L. 1965. *South Africa: A Study in Conflict.* Middletown, CT: Wesleyan University Press.

van den Berghe, Pierre L. 1970. *Race and Ethnicity.* New York: Basic Books.

van den Berghe, Pierre L., and George P. Primov. 1977. *Inequality in the Peruvian Andes: Class and Ethnicity in Cuzco.* Columbia: University of Missouri Press.

van Gennep, Arnold. 1960. *The Rites of Passage.* Translated by Monica B. Vizedom and Gabrielle L. Chaffe. Chicago: University of Chicago Press. (Originally published 1906)

W

Wagner, Roy. 1984. "Ritual as Communication: Order, Meaning, and Secrecy in Melanesian Initiation Rites." In *Annual Review of Anthropology*, vol. 13, pp. 143–55. Palo Alto, CA: Annual Reviews.

Walens, Stanley. 1981. *Feasting with Cannibals: An Essay on Kwakiutl Cosmology.* Princeton, NJ: Princeton University Press.

Wallace, Anthony F. C. 1966. *Religion: An Anthropological View.* New York: Random House.

Wallace, Anthony F. C., and Raymond D. Fogelson. 1965. "The Identity Struggle." In *Intensive Family Therapy.* Edited by I. Boszormenyi-Nagy and J. L. Framo. New York: Harper & Row.

Wallerstein, Immanuel. 1989. *The Modern World-System III: The Second Era of Great Expansion of the Capitalist World-Economy, 1730–1840s.* New York: Academic Press.

Weatherford, Jack. 1997. *The History of Money: From Sandstone to Cyberspace.* New York: Crown.

Weiner, Annette B. 1988. *The Trobrianders of Papua New Guinea.* New York: Holt, Rinehart and Winston.

White, Leslie. 1949. *The Science of Culture.* New York: Farrar, Straus and Giroux.

White, Leslie. 1959. *The Evolution of Culture.* New York: McGraw-Hill.

Whitehead, Harriet. 1981. "The Bow and the Burden Strap: A New Look at Institutionalized Homosexuality in Native North America." In *Sexual Meanings: The Cultural Construction of Gender and Sexuality.* Edited by Sherry B. Ortner and Harriet Whitehead. New York: Cambridge University Press.

Whitehead, Neil Lancelot. 1990. "The Snake Warriors—Sons of the Tiger's Teeth: A Descriptive Analysis of Carib Warfare, ca. 1500–1820." In *The Anthropology of War.* Edited by Jonathan Hass. New York: Cambridge University Press.

Williams, Walter L. 1986. *The Spirit and the Flesh: Sexual Diversity in American Indian Culture.* Boston: Beacon Press.

Willis, Paul. 1977. *Learning to Labor: How Working Class Kids Get Working Class Jobs.* New York: Columbia University Press.

Wilmsen, Edwin N., and James R. Denbow. 1990. "Paradigmatic History of San-speaking Peoples and Current Attempts at Revision." *Current Anthropology* 31:489–512.

Wolf, Eric. 1966. *Peasants.* Englewood Cliffs, NJ: Prentice Hall.

Wolf, Eric. 1982. *Europe and the People without History.* Berkeley: University of California Press.

Wolf, Margery. 1968. *The House of Lim.* Englewood Cliffs, NJ: Prentice Hall.

Woodburn, James. 1968. "An Introduction to Hadza Ecology." In *Man the Hunter.* Edited by Richard Lee and Irven DeVore, with the

assistance of Jill Nash. Chicago: Aldine Publishing Company.
World Commission on Environment and Development. 1987. *Our Common Future*. Oxford, UK: Oxford University Press.
Worsley, Peter. 1982. "Non-Western Medical Systems." In *Annual Review of Anthropology*, vol. 11, pp. 315–48. Palo Alto, CA: Annual Reviews.
Wright, Quincy. 1965. *A Study of War*. Chicago: University of Chicago Press.

Y

Yanagisako, Sylvia Junko. 1979. "Family and Household: The Analysis of Domestic Groups." In *Annual Review of Anthropology*, vol. 8, pp. 161–205. Palo Alto, CA: Annual Reviews.
Young, Allan. 1982. "The Anthropologies of Illness and Sickness." In *Annual Review of Anthropology*, vol. 11, pp. 257–85. Palo Alto, CA: Annual Reviews.

Z

Zechenter, Elizabeth. 1997. "In the Name of Culture: Cultural Relativism and the Abuse of the Individual." *Journal of Anthropological Research* 53: 319–48.

Index

A

B

C

D

E

F

G

H

I

R

S

T

U

V

W

X

Y

Z

DESIGN PHOTO CREDITS

Chapter Opener green & gold map background: © thisorder/iStockphoto.com
Chapter Opener white open book: © Christa Brunt/iStockphoto.com
Chapter Opener orange map background: © DNY59/iStockphoto.com
Pushpin in various colors: © David Franklin/iStockphoto.com
Polaroid frames: © David Franklin/iStockphoto.com
Introduction orange & yellow hands background: © pamspix/iStockphoto.com
Introduction passport & airplane boarding pass: © Richard Cano/iStockphoto.com
Questions spiral notebook: © Stefanie Timmerman/iStockphoto.com
Questions sepia map background: © Tyndrya/iStockphoto.com
Question mark in chalk: © Nigel Carse/iStockphoto.com
Margin blue globe: © Comstock Images/Jupiterimages
Margin & background cave painting: © Terry Katz/iStockphoto.com
What Would You Do? card with emblem: © Duncan Walker/iStockphoto.com
Case blue map heading background: © Will Evans/iStockphoto.com
Case video phone heading background: © pavlen/iStockphoto.com
Case blue & orange globe background: © DNY59/iStockphoto.com
Pull quote marker circle: © ranplett/iStockphoto.com
Graph paper background: © thumb/iStockphoto.com
Caption scrap of paper: © Uyen Le/iStockphoto.com

CHAPTER 1 PREP CARD

Culture and Meaning

What's Inside: introduction to cultural anthropology; differences in beliefs and behaviors; judging the beliefs and behaviors of others; the ethnocentric and relativistic fallacy; objectivity and morality; the ethnographic method; interpreting cultural texts; analyzing football and happy meals

Problem 1

The central problem of this chapter is: How can people begin to understand beliefs and behaviors that are different from their own? To examine this problem, we pose the following questions:

- Why do human beings differ in their beliefs and behaviors?
- Why do people judge the beliefs and behaviors of others?
- Is it possible to see the world through the eyes of others?
- How can the meanings that others find in experience be interpreted and described?
- What can learning about other people tell Americans about themselves?

Chapter Outline

Key Terms

Multimedia

Title: What Is Culture?

Topic: Culture

Run Time: 2:41

Ask Your Students: How do culture and society differ? What types of shared characteristics tie an ethnic group together? Why is Oaxaca Mexico a pluralistic society?

Title: Medical Anthropology: Nurses Helping Nurses

Topic: Culture

Run Time: 6:19

Ask Your Students: How do globalization and cultural differences show up in emergency room environments? What did the research with nurses uncover about the need for breaks and vacations? What anthropological skills can be applied in a multi-level environment such as a hospital?

Internet Resources

- The culture concept: http://www.umanitoba.ca/faculties/arts/anthropology/courses/122/module1/concept.html
- Ethics in anthropology: http://www.aaanet.org/committees/ethics/ethics.htm
- The basics of fieldwork: http://www.alanmacfarlane.com/DO/filmshow/film30.htm
- A trailer for *Blood and Incense*, a documentary about cockfighting and ritual in Bali, Indonesia: http://hotdocs.bside.com/2008/?mediaAutoplay=true&_view=_filmdetails&mediaTab=video&mediaIdx=0&filmId=51988294
- An anthropological study of Silicon Valley: http://www.sjsu.edu/depts/anthropology/svcp/

Exercises

Finding Common Ground

Divide the class into groups of four to six, and have them individually record whether they agree or disagree with each statement that follows. The group should then convene and review each statement to see if any one member disagrees with any of the statements being considered. If even one person disagrees, the groups should revise the statement so that it is acceptable to all members. In this exercise, group members cannot agree to disagree. The revised statements should be recorded and shared with the rest of the class.

This exercise is a modified version of one posted on the e-mail list XCULT-L by Kerry Kind of the University of Kentucky. It is an effective way to introduce students to the subtleties of ethnocentrism. It works very well in groups and takes about 15 minutes of group work, with another 10 to 20 minutes (depending on class size) for each group to present its views.

1. The fact that the United States was able to place people on the Moon proves its technological superiority.
2. Foreigners coming to live in the United States should give up their foreign ways and adapt to American culture as quickly as possible.
3. Many of the world's cultures remain "underdeveloped" because they do not take enough initiative to develop themselves.
4. Minority members of any population should be expected to conform to the customs and values of the majority.

Fieldwork among the Alphans and Betans

Divide the class into two groups, the Alphans and the Betans, and give them the corresponding instructions below. Ideally, the two groups should be placed in separate rooms. You will also need to supply the Alphan group with chips or pieces of paper of the color listed in the instructions below.

Once each group begins enacting its culture (about 5 minutes), ask each to select an observer to visit the other culture and report their findings. After they make their reports, each group selects another observer to send and report back. After a number of observer exchanges, the groups should re-gather and report to one another their interpretation of the others' culture.

Instructions to the Alphans: You are a member of the Alphans. Your society is very egalitarian and resource oriented. The people freely interact with one another and are trade oriented. They are obsessed with collecting colored tokens and believe it desirable to have tokens only of one color. Whenever you meet others you give them a gift (chip). If they return a gift, you give them another; if not, you turn your back on them and try to find someone who will exchange with you.

The Alphan language is very simple; it consists of four words: red, white, blue, gold. Alphans use these words to seek appropriate trading partners.

To summarize the rules:

1. Freely give gifts of tokens, but expect tokens back.
2. If you don't get what you want, seek another partner.
3. Try to collect tokens of the same color.
4. Speak only Alphan.

Instructions to the Betans: You are a member of the Betans. As a people you are very easygoing and friendly, although there are interaction rules that must be followed. Betans stand very close to each other when interacting—no more than six inches apart. Anyone who stands farther away is being impolite and should be ignored. In addition, Betans initiate conversations with a light touch on the left shoulder. Someone who fails to do that is being rude.

Betans like to talk about the weather. They value women more than men and eagerly recruit new women into their groups by trying to convince them that the weather for their group is better than that for others. Foreign men are usually ignored. A woman leads each group. A person who desires to speak to her must first ask her permission by tapping himself or herself on the left shoulder. Failure to do so is a flagrant violation of the rules, and anyone doing that is immediately ostracized. Sometimes the group leader will grant permission to speak, sometimes not.

To summarize the rules:

1. Initiate interaction with a touch.
2. Stand no more than six inches away from the person you are addressing.
3. Make sure to ask permission by tapping your left shoulder before addressing the group leader.
4. Avoid foreign men, but try to recruit foreign women to your group.
5. Talk about the weather.

In this exercise, Alphans may react to the gender discrimination of the Betans and the propensity to stand very close, while Betas tend to focus on the trade orientation and "rudeness" of the Alphans. With very large classes, certain groups of students can be asked to enact the Betan and Alphan roles, with others being asked to record their observations of the interactions.

CHAPTER 2 PREP CARD

The Meaning of Progress and Development

What's Inside: life as a hunter-gatherer; population density as a factor in the transition to agriculture; the British textile industry and its effects on India, China and the United States; economic development in underdeveloped economies; the price of progress; inequality in modern medical treatments; interpersonal theory of disease; the disappearance of simpler societies; cultural change for the Crow

Problem 2

The central problem of this chapter is: How do we explain the transformation of human societies over the past 10,000 years from small-scale, nomadic bands of hunters and gatherers to large-scale, urban-industrial states? To examine this problem, we pose the following questions:

- Why did hunter-gatherer societies switch to sedentary agriculture?
- Why are some societies more industrially advanced than others?
- Why don't poor countries modernize and develop in the same way as wealthier countries?
- How do modern standards of health and medical treatment compare with those of traditional societies?
- Why are simpler societies disappearing?

Chapter Outline

Key Terms

sedentary 29
progress 29
culture change 30
slash-and-burn (swidden) agriculture 30
state 30
irrigation agriculture 30
population density 35
Industrial Revolution 39
"putting out" system 39
factory system 39
economic development 43
World Bank 43
factory model 45
agroecological approach 45
pathogen 48
vector 48
interpersonal theory of disease 50

Multimedia

Title: Diet, Lifestyle, and Consequences

© COAST COMMUNITY COLLEGE DISTRICT

Topic: The Impact of Agriculture on Cultural Evolution

Run Time: 7:12

Ask Your Students: How does agriculture affect settlement patterns? What are the other affects of agricultural development?

Title: Ancient Lives: Marsh Arabs

Topic: Extinct People
Run Time: 5:21
Ask Your Students: What are some of the reasons that the Marsh Arabs are disappearing? On a more global scale, why do you think simpler, indigenous societies are becoming extinct?

Internet Resources

- How do countries get into debt, and what can be done about it?
  - Debt Initiative for the Heavily Indebted Poor Countries—IMF: http://www.imf.org/external/np/hipc/hipc.htm
  - Debt Relief Web Site: http://www.worldbank.org/hipc/index.html
  - Readings on the Capitalist: http://faculty.plattsburgh.edu/richard.robbins/legacy/capitalist_readings.htm
- Readings on Health and Disease: http://faculty.plattsburgh.edu/richard.robbins/legacy/disease_readings.htm
- Definition of "indigenous people": http://www.un.org/esa/socdev/unpfii/documents/workshop_data_background.doc
- Human rights of indigenous peoples: http://www.earlham.edu/~pols/17Fall97/indigenous/index.html
- Cultural Survival, an organization that sponsors research, forums and publications dedicated to helping protect indigenous peoples: http://www.cs.org

Exercises

A Loan for Brazil?

It is 1960. You are a consultant to the World Bank, assigned to evaluate a loan proposal made by the government of Brazil. The country is predominantly agricultural—nearly 70 percent of the population lives in rural areas. Virtually all settlement is along the Atlantic coast, while the vast tropical forests of the Amazon are undeveloped, inhabited by indigenous peoples and itinerant rubber tappers. Most farms consist of subsistence plots worked by small family groups. Per capita income is very low, only about $200 per year. The democratically elected government seeks a loan to make the nation an economic and industrial power. Its proposals include:

1. The construction of hydroelectric plants to attract industry and modernize agriculture.
2. The building of roads into the Amazon valley to encourage new settlements.
3. Funds to resettle people who are displaced by the new roads.
4. Funds to develop new crops for export and expand sugar production.

Your task is to evaluate each proposal, consider the impact it will have on the nation, and make your decision on whether it should be approved or rejected. If the proposal is unacceptable, you should propose revisions that would make it acceptable.

Contacting Alien Worlds

Marilyn vos Savant, famed for having an extremely high IQ, writes a weekly column for *Parade* magazine in which she answers a wide variety of questions from readers. In one particular column, she responds to a letter from a man who recommends that we stop trying to contact alien worlds through programs such as SETI (Search for Extra Terrestrial Intelligence). "It is very likely," he writes, "that any civilization we find will be far more advanced than our own. History has shown that whenever a more advanced civilization comes into contact with a less advanced one, it leads to the destruction of the latter, even if the intent of the former is not hostile." In her response, Ms. vos Savant says, "In my opinion we should continue the search . . . . While it may be true that less advanced civilizations are absorbed into advanced ones, we usually call this progress, not destruction. Few of us would wish to return to our ancestors' way of living, unless we've romanticized them beyond reality." Continue the exchange with Ms. vos Savant. What might you say to her in response?

Introducing Wage Labor to the !Kung

You are members of a film group from Cambridge University that has, for the last 20 years, produced and marketed various film studies of the !Kung. By selling and renting these films to colleges, the media, and private groups, your group has earned hundreds of thousands of dollars. And the money is still flowing in.

Your group has been asked by various anthropologists what should be done with the profits. More specifically, they ask if some of the royalties should not be given to the subjects of the film, because even a small percentage is likely to have a huge positive financial impact. You are charged with making a three-minute presentation to the governing board of the film company on whether it should share revenue with the indigenous people it films. What are the potential benefits and drawbacks of either sharing the money or not sharing the money? If you choose to share, how will you distribute the money?

This exercise introduces students to the impact of fieldwork, filmmaking, and other forms of cultural contact. It can produce great discussions on the ethics of fieldwork and filmmaking. It would fit in well to use David Mayberry-Lewis's *Millennium* series, especially the first episode, "The Shock of the Other." You could also use *N!ai: Story of a !Kung Woman* because it includes segments showing the making of the commercial film *The Gods Must be Crazy* and the impact the filming had on interpersonal relations among the !Kung.

CHAPTER 3 PREP CARD

Globalization, Neoliberalism, and the Nation-State

What's Inside: money and the market economy; the necessity of perpetual growth; capital conversion; neoliberalism; market externalities; free trade; the role of the state; states' use of force; economic collapse in 17th-century Netherlands; the housing bubble of 2007

Problem 3

This central problem of this chapter is: What is globalization, and what does it have to do with me? In examining this problem, we will consider the following questions:

- How do we define happiness and well-being?
- Where does the wealth needed to sustain growth come from?
- What kind of economic system is necessary to sustain growth?
- What is the role of the nation-state in sustaining growth?
- Why do economies collapse?

Chapter Outline

Key Terms

Multimedia

Title: Tskigi Fish Market

Topic: Economic Systems

Run Time: 4:45

Ask Your Students: What role do face-to-face interactions have within the Tskigi fish market economy? What types of standards do New England fishermen need to internalize in order to serve the Japanese market? What role do women play within Tskigi and why is it important?

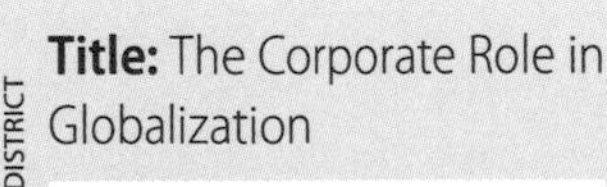

Title: The Corporate Role in Globalization

Topic: Globalization

Run Time: 5:24

Ask Your Students: What is structural power? How do multinational corporations exercise structural power? How do exploitative conditions arise in response to globalization? How do "hard" and "soft" power differ?

Internet Resources

- The Smithsonian Institution exhibit on sweatshops: http://americanhistory.si.edu/sweatshops/ffchain/game.htm
- Downsides to Economic Growth: http://www.youtube.com/watch?v=I5YVXnnfS28
- The Story of Stuff: http://www.storyofstuff.com/
- Wal-Mart: The High Cost of Low Prices: http://video.google.com/videoplay?docid=-3836296181471292925#
- Three short films on meat production:
  - The Meatrix: http://www.youtube.com/watch?v=IMOAaciER6o
  - The Official Meatrix II: http://www.youtube.com/watch?v=VAN6G8sBNIE&feature=related
  - The Meatrix II ½: http://www.youtube.com/watch?v=guDkddg95Ao&feature=related

Exercises

All Over the World

This exercise provides an excellent illustration of the extent to which the global economy is integrated. Begin by presenting a list of brands that are uniquely identified with one culture, such as the United States and the Big Three automakers (Ford, GM, Chrysler), Japan and Sony, or BMW and Germany. Next, demonstrate how the various activities of these firms reveals their global nature. Some examples might include:

- The U.S. auto manufacturer Chrysler, founded in 1925, merged with Daimler-Benz AG of Germany in 1998 to form DaimlerChrysler AG. In 2007, the Chrysler division was sold to Cerberus Capital Management, a private equity firm based in New York with holdings in a number of foreign countries. On April 30, 2009, after filing for Chapter 11 bankruptcy, Chrysler announced plans for the formation of Chrysler Group LLC, 51 percent of which will eventually be owned by the Italian firm Fiat S.p.A.
- The Sears Tower, which was the tallest building in the world until 1998, is now known as the Willis Tower, after the London-based insurance broker Willis Group Holdings, Ltd. Willis has headquarters in London but is incorporated in Bermuda, and operates offices in nearly 100 countries.
- Manchester United, one of the iconic teams of English soccer, is owned by the American businessman Malcolm Glazer. Since 1982, the club has had three primary sponsors: Sharp Electronics (1982–2000), based in Tokyo, Japan; Vodafone (2000–2006), a UK-based mobile communications firm with subsidiaries in five continents; and AIG (2006–2010), an American insurance corporation that was founded in Shanghai, China in 1919.

After this discussion, have students prepare similar briefs on the global extent of other brands or companies that have strong associations with a particular culture.

The Story of Stuff

Divide the class into groups of three or four students. Assign each group an object or commodity, such as shoes, coffee, laptop computers, or the like, that encompasses our cultural and everyday life. The students' task is to write a biography of the commodity by answering such questions as:

- What is the history of the item?
- How it is produced?
- What is its impact on the environment?
- What are the social functions it performs?
- What is the political impact of the item?
- What sort of meaning does it have in our lives?

There is no single "right" answer, so you should encourage students to be creative and wide ranging with their analysis.

CHAPTER 4 PREP CARD

The Social and Cultural Construction of Reality

What's Inside: the problem of belief; metaphors and the domains of experience; symbolic actions; key scenarios; interpretive drift; secondary elaboration; selective perception; suppressing evidence; using humor to express anxieties; revitalization movements

Problem 4

The central problem of this chapter is: Why do people believe different things, and why are they so certain that their view of the world is correct and other views are wrong? To examine this problem, we pose the following questions:

- How does language affect the meanings people assign to experience?
- How does symbolic action reinforce a particular view of the world?
- How do people come to believe what they do, and how do they continue to hold their beliefs even if they seem contradictory or ambiguous?
- Can humor be used to resolve the contradictions inherent in language and metaphor?
- How can people reorder their view of the world if it becomes unsatisfactory?

Chapter Outline

Key Terms

Multimedia

Title: Linguistic Research

Topic: Linguistics

Run Time: 5:27

Ask Your Students: What methods did linguists from outside the tribe aid the Serrano tribe to recapture their traditional language? What aspects make up grammar? How did linguists translate an oral language into a writing system?

Title: Religion & Spirituality

© COAST COMMUNITY COLLEGE DISTRICT

Topic: Religion

Run Time: 6:05

Ask Your Students: How do religion and spirituality differ? What is a worldview? How do anthropologists approach religions?

Internet Resources

- Resources for the study of religion:
  - Adherents.com http://www.adhernets.com/
  - BeliefNet http://www.beliefnet.com/
  - Comparative Religion—A Directory of Internet Resources for the Academic Study of Religion http://www.academicinfo.net
  - Finding God in Cyberspace: A Guide to Religious Studies Resources on the Internet http://www.fontbonne.edu/libserv/fgic/intro.htm
  - Virtual Religion Index http://religion.rutgers.edu

Exercises

Metaphors of Nature

Ask students to examine the photograph below. Have them describe what they think is happening in the photograph, and ask them to draw some conclusions about the nature of baboon society from their description.

I got the idea for this exercise from a segment of *The Nature of Things* with David Suzuki in which he shows a filmed sequence of baboon behavior looked at from two perspectives. The first interprets behavior as aggressive, competitive, and characterized by male dominance; then, with the same clip, Suzuki shows how the behavior can be equally viewed as harmonious, cooperative, and playful. A good illustration for students of how the preconceptions, theories, and metaphors that people bring to their observations can determine how they interpret them.

It's Better to Laugh than Cry

In the last three years, people have experienced financial losses of historical proportions. They've lost their jobs, their homes, and their life savings. In spite of all their best efforts, many people have been unable to find any kind of work. And though the federal government has spent hundreds of billions of dollars, any recovery that has taken place only seems to have made Wall Street richer while leaving those on Main Street worse off. As a group, your assignment is to create a short, humorous sketch that expresses and addresses these anxieties.

As described in the text, humor is used to give expression to the anxieties and uncertainties of life. This was illustrated by looking at an Apache skit that depicted a caricature of the white man, and in doing so, expressed Apaches' anxieties about how the white man affected their lives. This exercise will give students a similar opportunity to articulate the fears and worries that many now have because of the economic recession.

First divide the class into several small groups. Then review with the students how humor functions as an expression of anxieties. Next, explain to the students that their task is to use humor to articulate what people feel about current economic and social conditions. You can choose to do this assignment in one class period, or to give students a few days to prepare and create their skits. Afterwards, each group should present their work to the rest of the class.

© DWPHOTOS/ISTOCKPHOTO.COM

CHAPTER 5 PREP CARD

Patterns of Family Relations

What's Inside: family relations; family composition; family cycle; sexuality, love, and wealth; threats to family unity; polygamy; inheritance

Problem 5

The central problem of this chapter is: What do we need to know before we can understand the dynamics of family life in other societies? To examine this problem, we pose the following questions:

- What is the composition of the typical family group?
- How are families formed and ideal family types maintained?
- What are the roles of sexuality, love, and wealth?
- What threatens to disrupt the family unit?

Chapter Outline

Key Terms

Multimedia

Title: AIDS in Africa: Marriage and Gender Issues

© ELON UNIVERSITY

Topic: AIDS in Africa

Run Time: 2:10

Ask Your Students: "AIDS is not gender neutral." If this statement is true, how are genders impacted differently by this disease? Should different issues be prioritized for different genders? Namibian men have the power to choose when, where, and why they have sex. Has the concept of polygamy affected their society and more importantly contributed to HIV/AIDS pandemic?

Internet Resources

- Brian Schwimmer on Kinship and Social Organization: http://www.umanitoba.ca/faculties/arts/anthropology/kintitle.html
- *A Small Happiness: Women of A Chinese Village* (summary and short clips of a documentary on the role of women in Chinese families): http://tsquare.tv/longbow/sh.html
- N!ai: The Story of a !Kung Woman (excerpt from full length documentary): http://video.google.com/videoplay?docid=5539611461104638184#

Exercises

Comparing Family Organization

The American family is obviously different from the !Kung, Trobriand Islander, or traditional Chinese families, as you might expect. While our families are embedded in an urban-industrial society, the !Kung are hunters and gatherers, the Trobriand Islanders horticulturists and fishermen, and the Chinese peasant farmers. Yet there seem to be features of family life in all three that are similar to family life in the United States. Your problem is simply to list those features of family life among the !Kung, Trobriand Islanders, and Chinese that resemble those of American families. Put another way, what features of family life in the United States would be familiar to a !Kung, a Trobriand Islander, or someone from rural China?

One reason I use the contrast between the Chinese peasant family, the !Kung family, and the Trobriander family is the historical similarity between the Chinese and the traditional Euro-American family, and the common features of the !Kung and Trobriander family with the contemporary American family. The family has been undergoing considerable change in regards to a woman's control over her sexuality, rights over children, the frequency of divorce, and the relative importance of husbands and wives, and fathers and mothers, during a time of increasing numbers of nontraditional family forms such as single-parent households and gay family groups. I use this exercise to make students aware of these changes and contrasts.

Inheritance in a Peasant Family

You are a peasant family consisting of the following people: Old Mishkin, the family head; his wife Zelia; young Mishkin, the oldest son; Sasha, the middle son; Josef, the youngest son; Natasha, the oldest daughter (born just after young Mishkin); Katania, the youngest daughter; young Mishkin's wife Vera, and their son, Mishkin the tiny.

Approximately 50 miles away is a typical preindustrial city market (where you sell some of your produce), some specialists' shops (a shoemaker, a potmaker, a blacksmith, etc.), and government offices. There are also a monastery and a convent outside the city.

Your possessions consist of:

- rights to work 30 acres of land (for which Old Mishkin has agreed to pay to the landlord in rent 1/3 of what the family produces)
- a store of grain to use for planting next year
- a house (or hut)
- livestock (a plow horse, a cow, 20 chickens, six geese, and two pigs)
- assorted farm implements (a plow, two hoes, etc.)
- assorted household furnishings (three beds, a stove, some blankets, a couple of tables, dishes, etc.)
- a small store of savings equal to about $75

Six years ago, you experienced a crop failure; one child died and Old Mishkin assumed debts that he is still paying off. However, in each of the past five years you have managed to meet your various obligations. More specifically, last year, working the 30 acres (only 10 of which you farm each year, letting 10 acres lie fallow and using the other 10 acres for grazing your livestock), you produced the following:

- 3,000 pounds of wheat (1,000 pounds went to the landlord, 300 went as a donation to the church, 700 pounds was stored to plant next year's crop, 100 pounds went to pay off debts, and 900 pounds was used by the family to make bread)
- 300 bales of hay (100 bales went to the landlord and 200 was used to feed the livestock)
- 900 dozen eggs (300 dozen went to the landlord, 200 dozen were sold at the town market, and 400 dozen went to feed the family and for gifts to neighbors)
- 500 gallons of milk (175 gallons went to the landlord, 50 gallons to the local priest, and the rest was consumed by the family)

Old Mishkin has family scattered around the countryside: one brother is a priest, another works land in a district some 20 miles away, and another is in the army.

THE PROBLEM:

As a family, you need to provide for the future of your members; what happens when Old Mishkin dies, when children marry or want to marry, etc.? To solve this problem you should:

1. Assign each member of your group a family role, beginning with Old Mishkin, Zelia, Young Mishkin, Sasha, Josef, etc. Even if you don't have enough people to play all the roles, assume that the other people are still there.
2. As a family, decide what future you will plan for each of the family members (including Old Mishkin and Zelia). What do you expect them to be doing in ten years?
3. Discuss with Old Mishkin how he will pass on his property and possessions. Old Mishkin, however, has the last word and must agree with the arrangements!
4. Be able to give a reason for each of your decisions.

I have used this simulation to illustrate the dilemma of peasant inheritance. Students need to know a little about partible and impartible inheritance and the structure of peasant society. The exercise illustrates the economic dilemmas of peasants and the profound differences in family structure and economic life that result when either impartible or partible inheritance is emphasized.

CHAPTER 6 PREP CARD

The Cultural Construction of Identitfy

What's Inside: social identity; individualistic and holistic; egocentric and sociocentric; the identity toolbox; positive identity and negative identity; construction of gender; rites of passage; phallocentrism; the principle of reciprocity; commodities and possessions; Christmas in America; *moka* in Papua New Guinea

Problem 6

The central problem of this chapter is: How do people determine who they are, and how do they communicate who they think they are to others? To examine this problem, we pose the following questions:

- How does the concept of personhood vary from society to society?
- How do societies distinguish individuals from one another?
- How do individuals learn who they are?
- How do individuals communicate their identities to one another?
- How do individuals defend their identities when they are threatened?

Chapter Outline

Key Terms

Multimedia

Title: Personality

© COAST COMMUNITY COLLEGE DISTRICT

Topic: Personal Identity

Run Time: 4:19

Ask Your Students: How does the study of identical twins help us to understand personality? What are some of the aspects of enculturation that influence one's personality?

Internet Resources

- African Lives (a series of articles profiling life in Africa): http://www.washingtonpost.com/wp-srv/inatl/longterm/africanlives/

Exercises

Telling Others about Yourself

Suppose you were to travel to Gulliver's island of Laputa. You could only communicate to people with objects that you carried with you, and you could take *only* five things with you to "tell" people about yourself. What would they be?

This is good exercise to help students gain an understanding of the ways that they manipulate material objects to convey to others how they wish others to view them. If I'm in a particularly dramatic mood on the day I use the exercise, I may show up wearing a strange conglomeration of items (e.g., mechanic's overall, cowboy hat, white gloves, deck shoes) and carrying such objects as a golf club, blackboard pointer, etc. as an illustration of different material symbols of identity.

Men and Body Image

Men rarely talk about dieting, or at least not as much as women do. However, concerns about body image are certainly not restricted to women. How, then, do men address the gap between body image and the cultural ideals represented in advertisements and the media? Do men talk about this issue, and, if so, how is it articulated?

CHAPTER 7 PREP CARD

The Cultural Construction of Social Hierarchy

What's Inside: social and economic inequality; social classes; integrative and exploitative theories of social hierarchy; Marx and the origins of class; constructing "intelligence"; the subordination of women; culture of poverty; modern nonstratified communities

Problem 7

The central problem of this chapter is: Why are modern societies characterized by social, political, and economic inequalities? To examine this problem, we pose the following questions:

- How do societies rank people in social hierarchies?
- Why do societies construct social hierarchies?
- How do people come to accept social hierarchies as natural?
- How do people living in poverty adapt to their condition?
- Can a nonstratified community exist within a larger hierarchical society?

Chapter Outline

Exercises

Devising Measure of Sensitivity to Others (STO)

The National Space Settlement Agency (NSSA) has hired your research and consulting company, Testers, Inc., to develop a test to determine a person's sensitivity to others. The test will be used by NSSA as part of its national program for selecting candidates

Key Terms

Gini coefficient 154
social classes 155
castes 156
integrative theory of social stratification 159
exploitative theory of social stratification 159
means of production 160
surplus value of labor 161
political or social repression 161
ideology of class 161
violent revolution 162
culture of poverty 171
generalized reciprocity 171
balanced reciprocity 171
negative reciprocity 171

Multimedia

Title: Howard Taylor: Standardized Tests and Bias

© CENGAGE LEARNING

Topic: The Social Construction of Intelligence

Run Time: 5:25

Ask Your Students: In what ways do you think intelligence tests are biased? How do they contribute to social hierarchy?

Internet Resources

- Economic inequality:
  - National Poverty Center, University of Michigan http://www.npc.umich.edu/poverty/

  - Historical Income Inequality Tables http://www.census.gov/hhes/www/income/histinc/ineqtoc.html
  - Working Group on Extreme Inequality http://extremeinequality.org
- Image Archive on the American Eugenics Movement http://vector.cshl.org/eugenics/
- Fair Test: The National Center for Fair and Open Testing http://www.fairtest.org

to participate in a program of space settlement. Since space settlers will be required to spend many months and years together in close quarters, NSSA has determined that settlers' sensitivity to others is critical for the success of its mission.

This is a pioneering effort, so you are free to approach the task in any way that you see fit. There are, however, some guidelines.

1. You must carefully define what constitutes sensitivity to others. This involves not only a straightforward definition, but also a list of those behavioral or personality features that would characterize a person's degree of sensitivity to others (STO).
2. You must devise a test that would allow you to measure the behavioral or personality features that characterize sensitivity as you have defined it.
3. The test needs to be simple to enable it to be graded by machines (e.g. multiple choice or true false questions). Your test should contain no more than ten "questions."
4. The test that you devise must allow the tester to clearly discriminate differences among people in STO. That is, your questions must elicit a significant portion of "wrong" answers. Obviously if everyone gets a question right or wrong, nothing is determined. NSSA requires that each person tested be assigned an STO score.
5. You must suggest how to test the test. That is, how can you determine that it does effectively measure the degree of a person's sensitivity to others?

Use the above exercise to illustrate some of the fallacies of intelligence testing.

Have groups of 4–6 students devise the above test of sensitivity. Then ask one person in each group to give the test that they design to another group. By the end of the exercise, each student will be assigned a number purporting to assess the degree of his or her sensitivity to others.

It is one of the more elaborate exercises, but surprisingly effective. Initially, I was surprised at how easily students were able to actually devise a test, and how completely they accepted the basic premises of the exercise. I want them to appreciate the following problems with measures of so-called innate characteristics.

1. Any test that purports to measure some psychological construct requires that the testers define and know beforehand what they intend to measure and assume beforehand that significant differences exist between persons. In the case of intelligence (and sensitivity), it means that testers have to accept preconceptions of what it is (even if it doesn't exist), and design a test that does indeed make clear distinctions among individuals (even though significant differences may not exist).
2. The test must confirm the expectations of those who will use the test. In the case of intelligence testing, the test must rank people in the same way that the teacher would subjectively rank them; in the case of college entrance exams, the test results must match a student's academic performance. In effect, the tests must begin at some level with people who have already been judged intelligent or sensitive, and must then select people as much like the selected population as possible.
3. The test is situational. In the case of intelligence testing, the situation in which the person must perform is the school setting. (In the exercise, the situation is space travel.) There is only an assumption that school performance measures general intelligence that can be extended to other settings (an assumption not, I believe, borne out empirically).
4. The test is culturally biased. In the exercise, students clearly use their own experiences (roommate conflict, school situations) to devise test questions. When I asked them what a southern migrant labor would make of the questions they devised to measure sensitivity, they clearly saw the bias.
5. The exercise should illustrate that the concepts themselves (sensitivity to others and intelligence) are culturally specific. Only a culture in which insensitivity (along with all the psychodynamic paraphernalia that the idea generates) would find significance in the concept, as only a culture that requires justification for hierarchical ranking consistent with a belief in individuality and freedom of opportunity ("all people are created equal") would find the concept of intelligence necessary or intelligible.

CHAPTER 8 PREP CARD

The Cultural Construction of Violent Conflict

What's Inside: justifying violence and conflict; the Kiowa and the Yanomamö; revenge killings in Thull; militant religious groups; creating peaceful societies; the differences between peaceful and violent societies; war and population; war and the development of states; male solidarity; nuclear weapons

Problem 8

The central problem of this chapter is: How do societies give meaning to and justify collective violence? To examine this problem, we pose the following questions:

- How do societies create a bias in favor of collective violence?
- How do societies create a bias against violent conflict?
- What are the economic, political, or social differences between peaceful and violent societies?
- What are the effects of war on societies?
- How is it possible to justify the creation of weapons of mass destruction?

Chapter Outline

Key Terms

war 179
feud 179

Multimedia

Title: Female Islamic Educator Discusses Islam

© ABC

Topic: Constructing Religious Justifications for Violence

Run Time: 2:33

Ask Your Students: How has the Western media contributed to the image of Muslims as evil? Conversely, what do you think makes the United States a target of terrorism?

Internet Resources

- Ethnic Conflict Management in Africa: A Comparative Case Study of Nigeria and South Africa: http://www.beyondintractability.org/case_studies/nigeria_south-africa.jsp?nid=6720

Exercises

Collective Violence in the News

Examples of group-sanctioned violent conflict are readily available in reports in our newspapers. To examine the justifications for such conflict, ask students to follow a daily newspaper for a couple of days. Have them document the instances they find of group-sanctioned violence and the reasons attributed for it, and report their findings to the class.

The purpose of this exercise is to illustrate for students the different ways in which world societies, including American society, justify collective violence. The nature of the discussion will vary according to the news, but generally you will be able to use the student observations to discuss everything from civil war and revolution to gang war and domestic violence.

The People of Aipokit

For the following exercise, split the class into two groups. Each group, without knowing that the instructions are different, should be given either Version A or Version B.

VERSION A: THE SHARK CLAN

Background:

You are people of the island of Aipokit. You are members of the Shark Clan, the chief clan of the island. For as long as you can remember, your group has owned much of the land on the island. Clan members inherit rights to the land and can plant crops anywhere on clan land. You live by growing taro, yams, bananas, and a few other crops that you supplement with fish from the sea. You also get some food by gathering wild roots and berries that grow on your land. Each year you plant half of your land with crops and let the other half lie fallow. You believe that the height of a crop is proportional to the wild vegetation it replaced.

While your clan owns much of the land, you have traditionally allowed people of the non-landowning Dolphin Clan to use parcels of your land, as long as no one else is using it. You have also allowed people of the Dolphin Clan to gather wild roots and berries on your land.

The Situation:

The situation on Aipokit is changing. One hundred years ago, there were 750 people on the island; today there are over 1,500. Moreover, in the past few years, two hurricanes have severely damaged the crops and produced near-famine conditions. Years ago, theft was unknown; today some people are stealing crops. Even members of your own clan are arguing over land rights. Because the island is isolated and boats arrive only three or four times a year, it is difficult to get food from the outside to help alleviate the famine conditions.

The Problem:

What can you do about the increasing shortage of food on the island and the increasing conflict over crops and land?

VERSION B: THE DOLPHIN CLAN

Background:

You are people of the island of Aipokit. You are members of the Dolphin Clan. The chief and ruling clan of the island is the Shark Clan. They officially own all the land on the island. However, they have allowed you to use whatever land they are not using, except land that the Sharks designate as fallow land. Fallow land consists of land planted the previous year on which wild vegetation is allowed to grow to permit the land to regain some of its fertility. You also get some food by fishing and gathering wild roots and berries on Shark land. You grow taro, yams, bananas, and a few other crops.

The Situation:

The situation on Aipokit is changing. One hundred years ago, there were only 750 people on the island; today there are over 1,500. Moreover, in the past few years, two hurricanes have severely damaged the crops and produced near-famine conditions. The Sharks have prohibited you from using some of the land you previously used and have posted signs prohibiting you from gathering wild roots and berries on their land. Because the island is isolated and boats arrive only three or four times a year, it is difficult to get food from the outside to help alleviate famine conditions.

The Problem:

What can you do about the increasing shortage of food and your reduced access to farmland and wild crops?

This exercise is based on a situation faced by people on the Pacific island of Tikopia, and described in some detail by Raymond Firth. Half the students receive Version A and the other half Version B, but (and this is important) they do not know, until the discussion phase of the exercise, that they have received different instructions or that they represent different groups. The exercise encourages students to opt for either cooperative or competitive strategies dealing with the impact of declining resources. The Dolphins usually consider violent revolution, but students have also come up with some interesting cooperative strategies. Discussion between the two groups is often spirited and may give you the opportunity to examine American justifications for collective violence.